THE COMPLETE
FLY-FISHER'S
HANDBOOK

THE COMPLETE
FLY-FISHER'S
HANDBOOK

*The natural foods of trout and grayling
and their artificial imitations*

Malcolm Greenhalgh

Illustrated by

Denys Ovenden

DORLING KINDERSLEY
LONDON • NEW YORK • SYDNEY • MOSCOW

A DORLING KINDERSLEY BOOK

First published in Great Britain in 1998
by Dorling Kindersley Limited,
9 Henrietta Street, London WC2E 8PS

Visit us on the World Wide Web at http://www.dk.com

ISBN 0 7513 0499 9

A CIP catalogue record for this book is available from the British Library

Printed by Mladinska Knjiga, Ljubljana

CONTENTS

FOREWORD

THERE ARE books on the trout and its habits, books on freshwater biology, books on insects and other fish foods, books on fly-patterns and fly-tying – we have shelvesful. So it may seem reckless, if not positively anti-social, to be adding to them here.

But there seemed to be a gap. What was lacking, it seemed to us, was a sufficiently detailed and fully illustrated modern overview of the whole subject: the natural foods of trout and grayling in European freshwaters, with the periods and conditions in which each hatches; their identification; their accurate imitation in artificial tied flies so as to incorporate the same stimuli or "triggers"; and finally the correct presentation of the fly to the fish.

For this, as we shall try to show, is the essence of intelligent fly-fishing. Anticipate or identify what the trout is feeding on, then choose its correct imitation to stimulate the appropriate response. The result is the difference between knowledge and skill on one side, and mere luck on the other. Which gives the better catches, and the greater satisfaction, becomes very quickly clear. The combination of science and art makes the quiet sport of fly-fishing, often in the loveliest of natural surroundings, a lifelong joy, and an ever deepening lesson in natural history.

In writing the text and in the studies – since a schoolboy, too long ago – on which it is based, M.G. has been helped by more people than it would be possible to list here. But he is especially grateful to the following for particular help and often hospitality: Veli Autti, Mark Bowler, Frank Casson, Marjan Fratnik, David Goodchild, Andrew Graham-Stewart, John and Steve Gross of Lureflash, Ed Jaworowksi, Hans van Klinken, Chris Lee, Crawford Little, Klaus Maier, Mike Mee, Roman Moser, Hans Odegard, Marc Petitjean, Juha Pusa, the late Rita Rogan, Michel Rogo, Matti Seppala, Ellis Slater, John Todd, Thorbjorn Tufte, Juha Vainio, Runar Warhuus, Phil White, and to the European/American Conclave of the Federation of Fly Fishers who provided a wonderful opportunity to meet and talk to many of the world's greatest fly dressers in Holland; to all members of Pirkanmaan Perhokalastajat Ry, the Fly Dressers' Guild, and the Freshwater Biological Association; the Norwegian Federation of

Hunters and Fishers; Dr Dick Shelton and Ross Gardner of the Freshwater Fisheries Laboratory at Pitlochry; Roxton, Bailey & Robinson Co.; the Grayling Society, the Piscatorial Society (for happy visits to their choice streams) and the Bowland Game-Fishing Association; Alan Bramley and Partridge Hooks; and to Oliver Edwards, Jack Gartside, Darrel Martin, Marvin Nolte, Terry Ruane, Dave Whitlock and Davy Wootton for allowing him to watch them tie their superb flies. More generally, the personal encouragement and help of three people were crucial to his earlier learning, both as biologist and as angler: the late Dr T.T. Macan, the late Jack Norris, and the late Hugh Falkus.

In earlier years *Trout & Salmon* and *Trout Fisherman*, and in recent years *Salmon, Trout & Sea Trout* and *Fly-Fishing & Fly-Tying* magazines have published much of his work on natural trout flies and their imitations, and M.G. is grateful to their editors for having given him space there to air some of his views.

Illustrating this book was a problem from the beginning. Domino Books, who had suggested the book to M.G. in the first place, initially experimented with pictures from some of the best angling photographers. Abject failure. The trouble with the camera, even in the cleverest hands, is its annoying trick of recording only what it sees. Ask it to show you a dozen species of Mayfly all at exactly the same stage of size and development – presenting themselves of course all in exactly the same stance, detail and lighting for our easier comparison, with no rebellious quirks from individual insects – and it will respond with a glassy stare. And even with tied flies, the problems of varying perspective and depth of field between subjects of different types and sizes are all too obvious in many published photographs of them.

The solution lay in the introduction to the project of D.O. as artist and co-author. This led to the happiest and most fruitful collaboration imaginable. The preparation and painting in minute detail of every insect and every tied fly needed for the book, and the subsequent checking and control by a number of devoted fly-tyers – all seemed at first a task verging on the Herculean. But with the harmony of a shared passion for natural history – and, a *sine qua non*, the indulgent support of both our wives – it was from the start an extraordinary pleasure.

In both text and illustration, however, every book published falls short of perfection; all can be improved in later editions. Both authors would therefore be more than grateful for any criticisms, corrections, or suggestions for improvement. Please write to us c/o the publishers.

Malcolm Greenhalgh
Lowton
Cheshire

Denys Ovenden
Chalfont St. Peter
Buckinghamshire

INTRODUCTION

In the second century **Claudius Aelianus** in Macedonia recorded (in *De Animalium Natura*) that "between Beroea and Thessalonica runs a river called the Astraeus, and in it are fish with speckled fins [trout?]. The fish feed on a fly particular to that country.... [The anglers] do not use these flies at all for their bait for fish; for if a man's hand touches them they lose their natural colour, their wings wither, and they become unfit food for the fish... They fasten red wool round a hook and fix onto the wool two red feathers which grow under a cock's wattles, and which in colour are like wax."

This is the first record of fly dressing and fly fishing; it contains all the essential elements: the identification of the fly that the fish is feeding on, and the simulation of the natural fly with material on a hook. Aelianus also implies that if the natural fly were sufficiently large and robust it would be used as bait itself. In some regions of Europe 'natural flies' are still used today as an alternative to artificial imitations and usually fished on the same fly-fishing tackle: mayflies, daddy-long-legs, grasshoppers, stonefly creepers (nymphs) and caddis larvae.

A thousand years later, in 1496, **Wynkyn de Worde** published the first major work on angling – as an addition to the second edition of *The Boke of St. Albans*. 'Written' by the fictitious **Dame Juliana Berners**, this was called *A Treatyse of Fysshynge wyth an Angle*. Twelve artificial flies are described in the *Treatyse* and all can be matched with an appropriate natural insect: "Thyse ben the .xij flyes wyth whyche ye shall angle to the trout & grayllyng and dubbe lyke as ye shall now here me tell. Marche. The donne flye of the donne woll & the wyngis of the pertryche. Another donne flye, the body of blacke wool: the wyngis of the blackyst drake: and the Iay vnder the wynge and vnder the tayle. Apryll. The stone flye. The body of black wull: & yelowe vnder the wynge. and vnder the tayle & the wynges of the drake. In the begynnynge of May a good fly. The body of roddyd wull and the lappid abowte wyth blacke silk: the wynges of the drake & of the redde capons hakyll. May. The yelow flye. the body of yelow wull: the wynges of the redde cocke hackyll & the drake lyttyd yellow...." Here we have patterns that match hatches of the large dark olive, march brown, stonefly and mayfly, and the female red spinner.

What is remarkable is that Dame Juliana's list of flies continued in print about for 400 years, carefully copied out by a series of writers! But several of these plagiarists added a little extra to the development of fly dressing. One, **Gervase Markham**, recommended (in *Country Contentments*, 1656) that: "Now for the shapes and proportions of these flies, it is impossible to describe them without painting, therefore you shall take of these several flies alive, and laying them before you, try how neere your Art can come unto Nature by an equal shape and mixture of colours." In other words, the best flies are those tied with the natural fly as model.

The first edition of **Izaak Walton's** *Compleat Angler* (1653), though one of the most seductive books on the out-doors world ever written, gave the fly-fisher nothing new as regards imitative flies, for it simply copied earlier works. However, it became perhaps the starting point of modern fly fishing when in the 1676 edition **Charles Cotton** added his *Instructions How to Angle for a Trout or Grayling in a Clear Stream*. Cotton was a student of aquatic life as well as an angler. He produced 65 artificial flies, all of them imitations of natural trout and grayling foods. Today, over 300 years later, many of Cotton's patterns would still be effective:

Cotton's Mayfly: body yellow (dubbed fur); rib a gold twist (oval tinsel); wings grey mallard breast feathers dyed yellow; hackle red capon (cock).

Cotton's Hawthornfly: body black ostrich herl; rib silver twist (oval tinsel); hackle black cock.

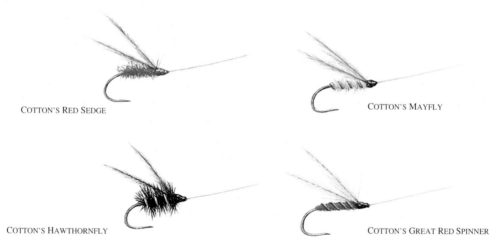

COTTON'S RED SEDGE

COTTON'S MAYFLY

COTTON'S HAWTHORNFLY

COTTON'S GREAT RED SPINNER

For over a thousand years the artificial fly was a simple affair: fur or herl body, perhaps ribbed with thread or silk, and a pair of hackles for wings.

Cotton also advised on how to choose the correct fly when one is not sure what the fish are eating: "When you do not certainly know what fly is taken, or cannot see any fish rise, you are to put on a small hackle, if the water be clear, or a bigger, if something dark, until you have taken one; and then thrusting your finger through his gills, to pull out his gorge, which being opened with your knife, you will then discover what fly is taken, and may fit yourself accordingly." In other words: catch a fish on a general pattern and then choose an appropriate imitative fly on the basis of autopsy. Today we would use a 'spoon' instead of Cotton's messy procedure (p. 25).

Robert Venables was a contemporary of Cotton and in 1662 he published *The Experienc'd Angler*. Much of Venables' work was a copy of earlier books, but he made one important point which fly-fishers today still overlook: "Observe principally the belly of the fly, for that colour the fish observe most, being most in their eye."

A few years later **James Chetham** recommended (in *Angler's Vade Mecum*, 1681) that the best artificial flies were tied at the waterside with the natural fly as model, and for this purpose he gave a huge list of silks, fur and feathers that had to be carried by the angler in an enormous bag. Chetham was the first to publish a magic formula, based on the idea that fish can smell or taste their potential prey, for increasing the effectiveness of the artificial fly: "Next folow Ointments and Receipts which I have read and been informed of, by several knowing Anglers...they'll not only allure, but even compell Fish to bite...Take Man's Fat and Cat's Fat, of each half an Ounce, Mummy finely powdred three drams, Cummin-seed finely powdred one Dram, dilstill'd Oyl of Annise and Camphor four Grains, make an Ointment according to Art; and when you Angle annoint 8 inches of the Line next to the Hook therewith...."

We mercifully do not need to go to this extreme. Though several anglers have attempted to increase the attraction of their flies by soaking them or anointing them in compounds containing amino-acids, meat extracts, fish oils, and commercially available flavourings used by bait anglers, doctoring flies in this way is frowned on and, on some waters, prohibited. It is also, in fact, unnecessary.

By this time fly-fishing had become established in mainland Europe, and once again it was considered essential to have artificial flies that copied natural flies. The first book was *El Manuscrito de Astorga* by **Juan de Bergara**, written in 1624, which was 'a book on how to tie and dress feathers in order to fish for trout' in the rivers around Leon in northern Spain. Despite its age, the *Manuscrito* is worthy of study, containing some fascinating flies dressed with some most obscure materials, including pin-tailed sandgrouse, little bustard and camelhair, together with coq de Leon hackles. These are the oldest form of bird bred specially for their fly-tying feathers: we still use them today (p. 219). Next came **Louis Liger**'s *Amusemens de Campagne* (1709), reprinted in Holland in 1714 as *Traité de toute sorte de Chasse et de Peche*. Among Liger's list of flies and fly patterns is one: "Dans le mois de May ils en font une, couverte aussi de soye, mais elle est de couleur rouge, et avec des filets tirans sur l'or: la tete en est noire, et on y joint les plumes rouge d'un capon." This is a perfect imitation of the red spinner of the late march brown.

Besides having an artificial fly that looks like the natural fly, it is important that the artificial *behaves* like the real thing. Presentation is very important. In this these earlier writers were greatly hindered by their crude tackle. The reel was not used in trout fishing until the latter half of the eighteenth century. Before then the line was attached directly to the rod tip. Rods were long, commonly 18 feet or more and the line possibly shorter but certainly not much longer than this. Rods were used as 'double-handers' so if the line was much longer it would have been unmanageable. Such a line could not be 'cast' as we know it today. Anglers were advised to use the wind so that as little line lay on the water as possible: the fly would flutter in or on the surface. This is similar to dapping, commonly practised on large lakes today. Alternatively the fly was lowered on to the water over a rising trout, rather as a modern bait fisher might handle a huge pole to drop the bait lightly on the water. This is neither wet nor dry fly fishing; it is dibbing or dibbling. Occasionally anglers were recommended to let the fly land on the water on a slack line and let it drift downstream until all the slack had been taken up or walk downstream with the fly. That is the nearest these early anglers could come to our modern style. It was not until the early nineteenth century that reels and rods were developed that could cast and be used to manipulate first a heavy fly line, and then the various forms of imitative flies that we have today – dry, wet, nymph and so on – and the various ways of presenting these flies to the fish in a realistic way.

At present, ideas about fly-fishing have been taken to some curious extremes. On the one hand we have people who go so far as to deny altogether the importance of identifying natural foods and matching them. This is foolish. The sport is not simply about catching fish but how one catches them. An understanding of entomology, knowledge of the fish's feeding behaviour, and the ability to deceive it with an artificial fly tied to match the natural all contribute to the art and pleasure of fly-fishing.

At the other extreme some purists consider that artificial flies should imitate only winged insects (dry flies are fine, perhaps lightly dressed wet flies and unweighted nymphs) and in extreme and often unnecessary detail. They condemn weighted flies that match natural shrimps, bugs and fish fry as 'fishing with an artificial bait'. Happily, between these two extremes are a host of fly fishers throughout Europe and indeed the world, who are simply interested in the fish, their behaviour and food, and in imitating those foods.

Occasionally the right imitative flies can be bought, but as often not. Where can you buy a size 24 Midge imitation, for instance? So learn to tie your own. For the price of a vice, hackle pliers, bobbin holder, fine scissors, dubbing needle and a range of silks, furs and feathers, some instruction on basic fly-dressing techniques and a little practice, the whole world of imitative fly dressing lies open.

SELECTIVE FEEDING

I have seene a younge flie swimme in the water too and fro, and in the end, come to the upper cruste of the river, and assay to flie up: howbeit, not being perfitely ripe or fledged, hath twice or thrice fallen downe again into the bottome: howbeit, in the ende receiving perfection by the heate of the sunne, and the pleasant fat water, hathe in the ende within some halfe houre after taken her flyte, and flied quite away into the ayre, and of such younge flies before they are able to flie away, do fish feed exceedingly.

JOHN TAVERNER, *Certaine Experiments Concerning Fish and Fruits*, 1600

One of the commonest terms used to describe trout and grayling is 'selective feeders'. It is a term that figures frequently in fly fishing magazines; it has been the central theme of more than one book. Yet what does it mean? Perhaps the best way to start answering this important question is with some real angling experiences.

February on a spate stream; grayling feeding. At 1 p.m. a hatch of large dark olives commenced; the fish took the hatching olives keenly but then, at 3 p.m. tiny grey midges also began to hatch at the water surface. Immediately the grayling completely ignored the olives and fed exclusively on the midges. They selected the midges.

Late May on a chalkstream; trout feeding. Through late morning and afternoon large numbers of hawthorn flies were blown onto the river and drifted downstream. During this time there was also a steady hatch of medium olive and mayfly duns. In one hour three trout, that were kept in constant view, took 132 hawthorn flies but no olives or mayflies. At the end of one hour a trout was caught, killed and its stomach spooned: its gut contained just hawthorn flies. The trout selected hawthorn flies.

Two days in late May on a limestone river; trout feeding. On both days there were large simultaneous hatches of iron blue duns and mayflies. On the first day the mayflies were ignored and only iron blues were eaten: two trout were killed; their stomachs were full of iron blues. On the second day they took iron blues before the mayfly hatch began, but thereafter the only food seen taken was mayflies. This was confirmed by three stomach analyses. The trout selected iron blues on the first day, but 24 hours later were selecting mayflies.

April on a limestone stream; trout and grayling feeding. A massive hatch of spring olives with a scattering of iron blues; the sort of hatch that would normally encourage the fish to feed at the surface, but not one fish rose. A leaded shrimp pattern was fished close to the river bed and a trout taken on the second cast. Its stomach was crammed with freshwater shrimps. Several other fish were caught on the same fly. The fish were selecting shrimps on the bottom and rejecting flies at the surface.

August on a limestone stream; trout and grayling feeding. A huge hatch of pale watery duns through the evening together with a smaller hatch of blue winged olives and a tiny fall of black gnats. The fish rose to eat only pale wateries, but were impossible to catch on a wide range of standard pale watery imitations. Close observation revealed that the fish did not take every insect that floated over them; further observation revealed that about 15% of the duns were having difficulty freeing themselves from their nymphal shuck (either the tails or one wing remained trapped in the shuck). Nine fish were caught on an emerger pattern; the stomach contents of three were examined. This confirmed that the fish were selecting those pale wateries that were having difficulty hatching and rejecting those that had hatched completely.

A lake in May; trout feeding. Large numbers of midge pupae were rising to the surface and adult midges hatching on the surface; the trout were feeding keenly at the surface. There were also a few lake olives and dark mayflies on the water but the fish ignored them. The fish refused dry midge imitations; they also refused pupal imitations fished below the surface film. 28 trout were then caught on a Suspender Buzzer that imitates the pupae hanging down from the surface film just before the adult hatches. The stomach contents of two were examined: they were crammed with buzzer pupae (some were still alive and three hatched into the adult midge in the examination dish). The trout were selecting midge pupae at the surface film just before they hatched; but they rejected those rising to hatch and the fully hatched adult midge.

Such examples illustrate the way that fish can feed: when given a choice of natural food they may select one – whether a species or a stage in the life-cycle – and reject others. And their selectivity may change rapidly as new food items appear on or in the water: in as short a space of time as 7 hours, I have known trout and grayling to change diet five times and feed selectively on six different food species. When they are feeding so selectively, the imitative fly fisher must be aware of what is being eaten, be on the look-out for a change of diet, and be ready to change fly as necessary.

What if there is only one food species on the water being taken by the fish: are they not being selective because they have no choice? This is frequently the case when the fish are feeding at the water surface during a hatch of one species of insect (of course, the fish may be selecting this surface food in preference to foods also available on the bottom which we cannot see). Consider the following instances:

July on a Lapland river; grayling and trout feeding at the surface on small black midges. Several grayling to 1.5 kg and two small trout were taken on a size 8 Great Red Sedge. There were no sedges (caddisflies) in evidence; the stomachs of two fish contained a mass of tiny midge pupae and adults.

May on a stream in SW Germany; trout and grayling feeding at the surface on medium olives. Fish were caught on imitations of sedges, black gnats as well as some very general dry flies and wet flies; also two medium olive imitations. Stomach analysis of three fish revealed just medium olives.

April on a stream in central Finland, trout feeding at the surface on February red stoneflies. The fish refused 21 different dry flies that did not have some resemblance to the natural insect; three February red imitations caught 140 trout, the stomach of one being crammed with February reds.

August evening on an English spate stream; trout feeding at the surface on spent female spinners of the 'autumn duns'. All fish refused standard dry and wet flies but then accepted one of three patterns that imitated the natural spinner. The stomach contents of two of the 28 fish caught consisted entirely of autumn duns.

In the first two cases the fish were feeding in a most unselective way and would probably have taken other natural foods (perhaps in preference to the food available) had they been present as well as a wide range of anglers' flies. In the second two cases the fish were clearly fixed on the one food item available: they were conditioned to that one food and the artificial fly had to match the natural closely.

Anyone can catch fish that are feeding in an unselective or an unconditioned way. Almost any fly will score. But when the fish are feeding in a selective way and are conditioned to taking one sort of natural food it is essential, for success, to identify that food and present a good imitation to the feeding fish. How good an imitation? Well, that depends on what the fish looks for in a natural food item when it is feeding selectively on or is conditioned to that one food. Imitative fly-tying and fishing are all about identifying the features of the natural food that act as triggers in the fish's tiny brain.

TRIGGERS

> But the angler having found the fly which the fish at present affect, let him make one as like it as possibly he can, in colour, shape, proportion; and for his better imitation let him lay the natural fly before him.
>
> COLONEL ROBERT VENABLES, *The Experienc'd Angler*, 1662

It is first of all necessary to stress that fish do not look at natural foods as a freshwater biologist studies similar animals in the laboratory. No trout ever looks up through the water at a blue winged olive dun that is floating on the surface, counts three tails protruding from the end of the abdomen and six legs terminating in six feet dimpling the water surface, and carefully checks that the fly has two pairs of wings. No trout looks at an olive dun and checks the eye colour to decide whether it is a male or a female or checks the arrangement of wing veins against a scientific key to the upwinged flies. But when the fish are selecting one particular kind of food from several available, then we know that they can identify (to some extent) what they are eating – that they can look at a potential food item and decide whether it is the same as the last one that they ate. So what do they look for?

It is important not to exaggerate the intellectual powers of fish. For too long anglers have referred to fish (especially trout) being 'intelligent', 'cunning' and 'wily'. When such a fish superbrain refuses the angler's fly (which to the angler seems to match the natural fly quite reasonably) then the angler often thinks that the fish was too clever to fall for the deception. Not so. Fish that are feeding keenly on one item of food identify that food by characteristics which act as *triggers*. When a feeding fish refuses the artificial fly then it simply means that the artificial did not have all the triggers that the trout brain was looking for.

Most river trout and grayling anglers will have noticed that fish feeding in fast turbulent water are easier to catch than fish feeding in a slow, even flow. Why? It is not, as some writers would have us believe, because fish living in the slower flatter pools are more intelligent than those living in rough water. It is because those in the fast water must decide whether an item being carried downstream is good to eat on the basis of fewer triggers than those fish in the slower flatter water. They must decide in a split second, before the item disappears downstream of their lies; those in the slower water have more time to accept or reject. Many anglers will have noticed that in slower river pools trout will often rise to the artificial fly but turn away at the last moment. Their brains initially accepted the triggers tied in the artificial, but some other trigger(s) were missing. This 'last moment rejection' rarely occurs in rough water because the fish have no time to evaluate certain triggers that operate for fish in slower water.

Similarly, smaller younger fish are easier to catch than larger older ones because they have not developed in their brain a full repertoire of the triggers of natural foods. In artificially stocked waters the fish recently released from the stewponds are much easier to catch than those that have been in the water for several months.

The same contrast occurs in lakes: during high winds and a big wave the fish are easier to deceive than in a flat calm because they use fewer triggers when the lake surface is rough. Similarly, bright days contrast with dull days, and daylight with dusk and night. In dull weather, or as the sun goes down the fish cannot see as much detail as they can in bright weather. They must use fewer triggers, and often crude triggers, to identify their natural food.

The following are likely to be the triggers used by selective or conditioned feeding trout to identify the natural food and can be incorporated into artificial fly patterns.

Size

Often size is a critical trigger, though many species of natural foods do vary in size and usually the fish will accept this variation. Trout will often take mayflies, in the one hatch, in a range of body length 16-25mm or blue winged olive 8-12mm. However when feeding selectively on, say, small midges with a body length of 3-5mm they will reject insects with a body length of 10+ mm, and vice versa.

General body shape

This too is often important; whatever the water and light conditions general shape and form is what fish will see and may respond to. Many insect larvae, pupae and nymphs have a curved body with a pronounced thorax; some adult insects have a slender abdomen and thicker thorax; freshwater shrimps have a curved body outline. There are times when it is essential to incorporate such features into the imitative artificial fly.

Presence and number of appendages (wings, legs, tails)

Sometimes these are important triggers; sometimes of no importance. Fish cannot count so the number of appendages is irrelevant: in an artificial fly it can pay to have more legs than in the natural (artificial Daddy-long-legs with 8 legs are often more

As a trout rises it is looking for triggers. The triggers by which it identifies the natural insect must be tied into the artificial fly

effective than those with the natural number of 6), perhaps because it strengthens the trigger. In subsurface foods legs seem to be less important as a trigger: artificial damselfly nymphs, lesser waterboatmen, stonefly and upwinged fly nymphs without legs are no less effective than those with legs. The pin-points of light where the feet of natural flies touch the water surface around the body can be an important trigger.

In fast, rough or murky water, or at night, the presence of wings on natural surface flies is often not a trigger. But in clear, slow, flat water when visibility is good the fish often react to the appearance of the wings in relation to the body. In such conditions fish can see the wings of upwinged flies, held vertically together above the body. They can see the veiling effect of wings over the body of sedges. When they are feeding on dead spent flies the presence of wings spread in the surface film is often a trigger. Spent upwinged flies often lie with one wing lying flat in the surface and one held upright at right angles from the surface; sometimes, in stillwater or a slow flat flow and good visibility, fish will select these instead of those flies with both wings flat in the surface. Tails are often not a trigger, especially in surface flies. Though they are used in dry flies, perhaps the fish see them (if they notice them) as legs: some effective small midge imitations have tails, though the natural insect lacks a tail. Perhaps the tail is effective because it helps hold the dry fly on the surface. There is no evidence that gills, breathing tubes, reproductive organs and fine detail of wings (venation and subtle shape) or legs (number of joints, hairs and spines, claws and feet) are considered as triggers by the fish.

BRIGHT DAY   DULL DAY OR EARLY EVENING

Fish-eye view of mayflies on surface. By day the fish can see far more of the insects and may use more triggers.

Colour

For years arguments have raged among fly-fishers as to the importance of colour in natural and artificial flies. Some argue that the fish cannot see colour but see in silhouette black, greys and white; others that colour is important to the feeding fish and painstakingly match the colour of the natural flies in their artificial flies.

In daylight the trout eye can see colours clearly; it is more sensitive to reds than our eye and can distinguish infra-red light. Some fish foods may appear black to us but to the trout they may seem deep red because they reflect infra-red light; which is perhaps why some black fly-tying materials are more effective under different conditions than others. At night (dusk to dawn) fish are colour-blind; like us they see in a rather blurred black-and-grey-and-white.

There are also the effects of water on colour vision. As sunlight passes through pure water the red end of the spectrum is absorbed first, then orange, yellow, green and finally blue. But no European fish lives in pure water; there are substances present in the water that completely alter this pattern (salts, chemicals called 'yellow substances' and microscopic green plants). In normal lake or river water yellow, orange and yellow-greens (olives) are absorbed first; green-blue and blue light penetrates further.

Thus a fish feeding on nymphs, larvae or lesser fish in 2 metres of water will not see the food in the colour that we see when we take that food from the water and examine it in the air. It may well appear black or some shade of grey. An effective imitation of the fly could equally well be tied with the colours of the natural food as we see them in the air or in shades of grey.

It is the same with a fish lying deep in the water, feeding on foods floating at the surface. As we look down through the air at that food item, it may appear olive-yellow to us; to the fish looking up through the water, it may appear grey. But as the fish rises to take it, the fly will gain colour and that colour will change as the fish draws nearer until, at the last moment, the fly may appear to some extent to the trout as we see it. The fish is looking at the underside of the fly that is shaded from the light thus much of the colour of the fly's underside will be far more subdued to the fish than the fly would appear to us, in the air and held against the light.

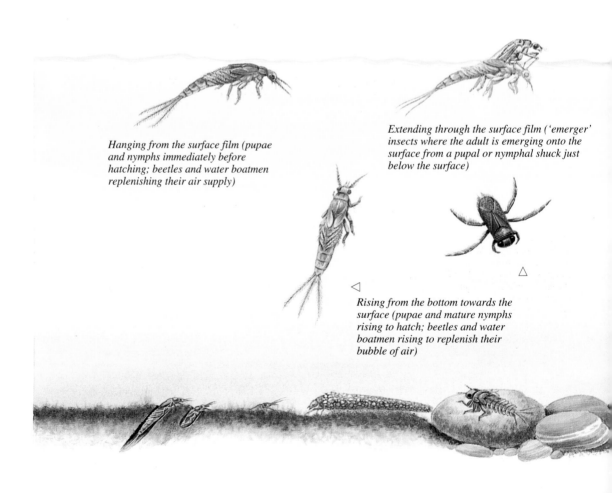

Extending through the surface film ('emerger' insects where the adult is emerging onto the surface from a pupal or nymphal shuck just below the surface)

Hanging from the surface film (pupae and nymphs immediately before hatching; beetles and water boatmen replenishing their air supply)

Rising from the bottom towards the surface (pupae and mature nymphs rising to hatch; beetles and water boatmen rising to replenish their bubble of air)

Position in the water

This can be an important trigger, and is often neglected by fly fishers. Natural fish foods may occur in one of several depth zones in the water, and when fish are feeding selectively on one stage of the life cycle of an insect species, the precise depth of the prey will often be a trigger.

For instance, when trout are feeding on spent upwinged fly spinners that are lying flat in the surface film, they will often ignore a wet imitation fished just below the surface or a dry fly standing on the surface. When they are taking midge pupae that are resting by hanging down from the surface film just before the adult emerges, trout will often ignore a perfect imitation if it is as little as 1cm below the surface film. When trout and grayling are grubbing on the bottom, they will often ignore the most splendid imitation if it is fished above their heads: it must be at the correct level.

Behaviour

Again, this is a trigger that is often overlooked. No matter how fine the imitative fly, if it does not behave like the real thing then the fish will often refuse to take it. For instance, a newly-hatched dun will drift passively downstream; so should the imitation (it should not drag across the flow). By contrast, an egg-laying female sedge or stonefly may scuttle across the surface: this movement may be an important trigger.

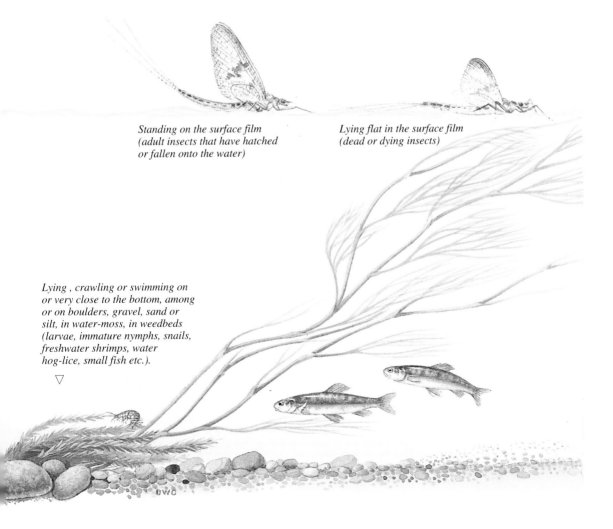

Standing on the surface film (adult insects that have hatched or fallen onto the water)

Lying flat in the surface film (dead or dying insects)

Lying , crawling or swimming on or very close to the bottom, among or on boulders, gravel, sand or silt, in water-moss, in weedbeds (larvae, immature nymphs, snails, freshwater shrimps, water hog-lice, small fish etc.).

It is the analysis of all these triggers in one particular food item, and the incorporation of these triggers – both in the artificial fly itself and in the presentation of it to the fish – that makes the difference between success and failure. This book is therefore concerned with identifying food items and the triggers they incorporate, and later with methods of incorporating these triggers in the artificial flies we tie, and in the fishing of these flies.

DESIGNING IMITATIVE FLIES

"The creatures that trout eat have not evolved over vast expanses of time to be attractive to trout; rather the reverse. It may therefore be possible, in designing artificials, so to exaggerate certain of the points by which trout recognise them, as to make the artificial more attractive than its natural prototype." RICHARD WALKER, *Fly Dressing Innovations*, 1974

The art of imitative fly-dressing has become split into separate factions during recent years. There are those who continue to tie the old established series of imitative flies or carry on the tradition of designing and tying new flies based on the old methods: their imitative wet flies, nymphs and dry flies are very similar to those invented 30 and more years ago. The flies are tied solely to deceive the fish. Then there is the new trend of 'super-imitation' where a species of natural food is taken and a model constructed, on a hook, that looks exactly like it: the number, shape and colour of the legs are perfect, with joints in just the right places; the wings precisely the right shape with veins drawn in to match exactly the veins on the real wings; the abdomen, thorax and head form a detailed replica of the body with the correct number of segments and with eyes and antennae. Most dressers who tie these super-imitations admit that they do so for pleasure and not to deceive fish; but there are some who deceive themselves, and would like to convince others, that these elaborate representations are essential when the fish are selecting a particular food species. It is just not true.

We, who are far more intelligent than the average fish, rarely use fine detail when we identify something. When we walk through the crowds of a city street our brain will pick out a close friend easily from among the throng at such a distance that it would be difficult to define how we identified them. And our brain assumes that some objects are what they are on the most trivial of evidence:

What is this? A tree. But are you sure? You cannot see the leaves, the branches, the texture of the bark, the colours. Your brain interprets the drawing as a tree using features or triggers that do not depend on fine detail.

So too the fish. Their brain responds in the same way by assuming, from trivial triggers, that something is a brown sedge, a mayfly, a stonefly nymph and so on. So all we need to do, when the fish are feeding selectively on one species of food, is to mimic these trivial triggers with our fly dressing. And as Richard Walker suggested, our imitations are likely to be more effective if we exaggerate, just slightly, these triggers. There is, perhaps, more skill in identifying the triggers and creating the simplest imitative fly using just these triggers than there is in blindly copying all the natural structures with a model of the fly on a hook.

Simplicity in fly design is therefore the key.

Fly dressing has long been dominated by named published patterns that readers of books and magazines are urged to use. The inference is that if readers do not use Schmidt's Stonefly, Amundsen's Ant, Maurice's Mayfly or the Killer Caddis then they will not catch as many fish. This too is false. By all means use established patterns as a starting point; but when you find the fish feeding selectively on one species of food, look at that food, try to decide what are the triggers, and tie these triggers to the hook. Then test your fly against the fish (many patterns are invented today and published in books and magazines without ever being seen by a feeding fish.). Reject. Modify. Alter. Keep testing your fly against the fish as you add or take away triggers. Eventually you will have a fly that works. You can name it after yourself if you like.

Similarly with the materials used to tie flies: it used to be thought essential to use wing slips from the starling for dry flies, then someone found that slips from quills of mallard and teal were easier to use and that the fish didn't mind. One famous dry fly, Kite's Imperial, had to be tied with a honey dun hackle; these are very difficult to obtain, but the commoner ginger, honey, or even blue dun hackle seems to work just as well. During the 1980s many inventors of flies extolled the virtue of two sorts of synthetic furs from the USA; the manufacture of these two furs ceased and the fly-tying materials company in the USA sold other furs (with a completely different texture) under the old name (without telling the fly-tying public). These newer furs are no better or worse than the older ones, but one is left wondering about the claims made on behalf of the older discontinued furs.

In spite of all claims that it is essential to use a particular material if we are to tie effectively a certain fly, I have never met a trout or grayling that can distinguish between real jungle cock and artificial jungle cock; or swan herl dyed dark olive and heron herl dyed in picric acid: or a rusty dun hackle and a blue dun hackle. When it comes to tying imitative flies all that matters is to choose a material which, tied in place, matches the trigger on the natural fly. Certainly some materials will be better than others when matching a particular trigger; but it is wrong to say that only one material will do the job and that all others are inferior.

When it comes to whether an artificial fly matches a natural fly, the sole judge is the fish. It is essential that when you have designed and dressed an artificial imitative fly you let the fish test it. Find some fish feeding on that particular insect and if they do not take your new design go back to the drawing board and modify it until they do.

While we are considering what makes a good, effective fly, do not worry (especially if you are new to the art) if experienced fly-dressers suggest your flies are not neat enough. The idea that beautifully neat flies are more effective than scruffy ones is simply not true. You will often find that an artificial fly improves with age – that a fly which has been chewed by a few fish is more effective than a new one. Except for competitive fly-dressing, where humans judge the fly using human criteria, the sole judge is the fish. Only it will decide whether or not you have successfully imitated the natural fly triggers.

This is what fly-fishing is all about – how it began on the River Astraeus 1,500 years ago and evolved to the present day. A fish is seen to take a fly. We identify that fly and look carefully for the triggers that the fish used in deciding that it was good to eat. We then imitate the triggers, go to the water and deceive the fish. Magic.

STUDYING FISH FOODS

Adult insects that have hatched onto the water surface (e.g. sedges, upwinged fly duns) or that have fallen onto the water (e.g. spent spinners, spent female sedges, landbred flies) can be collected from the water surface or caught when in flight.

Specimens are best captured on the water with the aid of a 'flat net' made from fine curtain net or muslin stretched tightly across a ring of wire which is attached to a handle. The net is held, half submerged, at an angle to the water surface and the insect allowed to drift onto the net. Avoid using bag-nets, for the wings, tails and legs of the insect will become trapped and crumpled in the wet mesh.

BAMBOO STICK FOR HANDLE

FLAT NET

For flying insects a fairly deep 'butterfly-style' or 'sweep-net' is ideal. Make your own from a loop of heavy-duty fence wire and fine curtain net: the bag should be about twice as deep as the diameter. This net can be used to catch individual insects, or can be used to sweep through waterside vegetation (beware of thorns and thistles) to see what insects are likely to be on the water during the next 24 hours.

BAMBOO STICK FOR HANDLE

SWEEP-NET

Another good way of collecting insects that have hatched from the water and are sheltering in cover is to spread a sheet (e.g. polythene bag) on the ground under tree branches, bushes etc. The vegetation is then shaken and the insects fall onto the sheet.

Specimens are easily collected from the water with another simple net. In streams the ideal net consists of a rectangular piece of net curtain, one metre long and about 70 centimetres deep with an open hem along the lower edge. Two canes are attached as handles along either side and some pebbles dropped in the open hem to weight the net when it is in use. The net is held almost vertically in the water so that the flow washes small animals into it.

One sharp blow with the handle of a landing net - or similar instrument - is enough to dislodge most small creatures. Further attacks are pointless, since the quarry is now forewarned and clings tight.

When nymphs or pupae are rising to the surface, or when spent spinners are being washed downstream, it is simply a matter of standing there with the net. But should specimens of immature nymphs, larvae and pupa, that live among weed and boulders of the river bed, be required then it is a matter of working quietly upstream, holding the net in one hand with the handles held apart in a 'V' and lifting boulders or disturbing weed with the other. Animals thus disturbed will be washed by the flow into the net. It does help if there are two of you, for one can hold the net while the other lifts boulders or disturbs the weed beds.

A simple net for sampling streams (note stones in hem for weighting net)

In stillwaters the traditional 'pond-net' is ideal. A simple one can be fashioned by making a rim of heavy-duty fencing wire and fixing the ends of the wire into a cane handle. To the rim is attached a cylindrical section cut from the leg of a pair of lady's tights. The bottom of such a net bag can be tied around a small glass specimen jar in which the captives can be examined.

Where the water is too deep to wade and a boat is not available then weedbeds can be sampled with a weed-drag. This is a sort of grappling hook made from two 60cm lengths of heavy-duty fence wire. The two lengths of wire are bent in half and their ends pushed through a 15cm length of lead pipe, which is then hammered to fix the wires in place. The four ends of wire are then bent back, and some heavy cord or rope is tied to the loops formed when the wire was bent. Hold onto the loose end of the rope (!) and throw in the drag. Slowly tow the drag back to shore and the four wire arms will have collected a mass of weed together with its inhabitants.

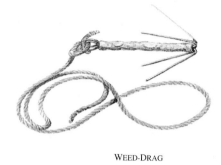

WEED-DRAG

POND NET

Many of the invertebrates of lakes and rivers that we are interested in live in the bottom mud, silt, sand or gravel. These are easily gathered within the mud, silt, sand or gravel with a gardening trowel. Gently scoop up a sample of substrate and put it in a white bowl or bucket of water. Slowly wash the scoopful apart to reveal the inhabitants.

Collecting specimens from deeper water is often difficult for the amateur. Planktonic organisms, such as planktonic crustaceans and the larvae of Phantom-flies, can be obtained by slowly towing a fine mesh pond net from a boat. But those animals living in, on or close to the bottom in deep water are out of range to the amateur collector.

Where possible examine and identify your specimens as soon as possible. If you wish to take them home, try to keep them alive, especially if the specimens are also going to be fly-tying models. Dead and preserved animals often lose their colours quickly, and some chemical preservatives result in distortion of the body.

Adult winged flies can be carried in any sort of container such as an empty match-box or a glass or plastic tube that has some crumpled blotting paper or absorbent kitchen-roll inside. The paper prevents condensation and subsequent injury to the specimens: in an empty glass jar the insects usually finish up stuck in condensation on the sides. Always examine living adult insects. Dead ones, or those preserved in alcohol, lose colour and shrivel up.

Collections of adult insects: do not forget absorbent paper

Taking aquatic specimens home so that they arrive safe and well can be very difficult. Most freshwater animals require high levels of oxygen; in a sealed bottle the oxygen level may fall too low. Also many aquatic animals will, if kept together in close proximity, attack each other. So always sort out the catch by emptying the net or weed-drag into a white plastic bowl or bucket that contains a little lake or river water. Examine the catch and then transfer the specimens that need to be taken home for further study individually into specimen bottles (small potted-meat jars are ideal). Half fill the jars with water and, if possible, add some aquatic weed or a piece of leaf or grass.

It ought to be stressed that only small numbers of specimens should be taken home and that the rest of the catch should be returned gently to the water. It might appear that most of the invertebrates that are of interest to the angler-entomologist are abundant; but there are many instances of lengths of rivers and lake shores being rendered temporarily quite impoverished after intensive sampling. In any case, besides wanting to learn more about the invertebrates of lakes and rivers, we anglers need to help conserve their populations so that the fish have natural foods to eat and we have something to imitate with our artificial flies.

A COLLECTING BOTTLE WITH WEED AND AIR SPACE

Many aquatic invertebrates will live quite happily in a small aquarium, provided that the water is kept cool and well-oxygenated. But beware: should the collection include a dragonfly nymph or a large beetle larva then within a few days only one very fat specimen will remain.

If you have a specimen that you want to preserve put it first into a tube of 60% industrial alcohol and then store permanently in a sealed tube of 3% formalin. Both chemicals are usually obtainable from local pharmacists; keep them locked away when not in use.

It is well worth trying to get specimens of upwinged flies to change from one stage of their life cycle to the next at home. This means that, by identifying a dun to its species the spinner that emerges from the dun is also identified. But it is essential that the animals concerned are handled very carefully, making sure that the wings are not

DUNS HATCHING INTO SPINNERS

held otherwise they may not be able to moult to the spinner, and kept in as ideal conditions as possible. Keep them in large well-ventilated jars with a few twigs on which the duns can perch and moult.

All trout and grayling anglers should keep a 'marrow spoon' (obtainable from tackle shops) in their fishing bag, together with a small white bowl. When a trout has been caught and dispatched the spoon is inserted through the mouth and down into the trout's stomach. The spoon is then twisted and withdrawn to reveal the trout's last meal. This can then be examined in a little water in the white bowl and the choice of imitative fly made in the knowledge that one is imitating what the fish are eating. But it

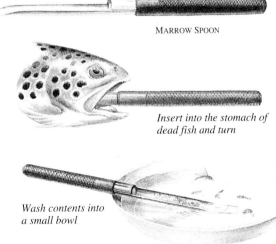

MARROW SPOON

Insert into the stomach of dead fish and turn

Wash contents into a small bowl

is also a good source of specimens for examination at home. It is worth pointing out that often nymphs and pupae obtained from such an autopsy will still be alive, and that sometimes they will metamorphose to adult stages in the white bowl. Thus there is the opportunity of observing and identifying more than one stage in an insect life cycle from the one sample.

Of course, an increasing proportion of fishermen have stopped killing and are releasing fish back into the water after disgorging the hook. (Note that in Germany it is illegal to catch fish and to release them after disgorging the hook). Such anglers must simply use observation as a guide to what the fish are eating at any one time. In clear streams and on the margins of clear lakes it is possible to creep up the bank, using boulders or vegetation as cover, and watch the fish feeding at close range. Polaroid glasses help to remove surface glare.

It should be possible to identify all the invertebrates described in this book with the naked eye or a hand lens with a magnification of between six and ten. Do not bother with microscopes, especially the cheap ones sold in High Street stores: optically they are generally very poor. A good microscope is expensive and needed only for more advanced study.

*Examine all spiders' webs: they will hold a sample of the
insects that might be on the water that day.*

NATURAL FOODS

There is no point trying to decide whether an insect is a blue winged olive or pale watery dun, or a black silverhorn or medium sedge without knowing whether it is an insect at all; or to what group it belongs. The following six pages therefore summarise the principal groups of animals on or in the water – or at least those of any interest to the fish. The major groups are then discussed in turn as follows:

THE MAIN GROUPS OF NATURAL FOODS

INSECTS p. 35

Look for a jointed external skeleton or tough skin covering the body; body divided into three sections: the head, thorax and abdomen; thorax has three pairs of jointed legs and, often, one or two pairs of wings (but note that in some larvae and pupae these body sections are not apparent and there are no true legs; see p. 71). Body segmented; thorax with three segments, abdomen with several segments (up to eleven, but often one or more not visible).

Insects together form probably the most important food-source for trout, grayling, whitefish and other small freshwater fish (such as roach, rudd, chub, dace). They fall into a large number of distinct and very varied groups, with the following as the most important fish foods.

UPWINGED FLIES (OR MAYFLIES, DAY-FLIES, AND EPHEMERIDS).
Order Ephemeroptera p. 38

Immature stages are aquatic nymphs. They have a pair of antennae, 3 pairs of legs, an abdomen with 10 visible segments, a pair of gills on some or all abdominal segments, and in most cases 3 long tails (Epeorus has just two). There are wing buds on the top of the thorax, which become more pronounced as the nymph grows. Body shape is usually long, slender and tapering to the tails, but does vary (in nymphs of the family Heptageniidae it is often flattened, squat and broad, especially at the front).

Upwinged fly Heptagenid nymph

There are 2 flying stages: the dun and the spinner (see p. 40). Both have 1 or 2 pairs of wings that are held upright over thorax at rest; there are either 2 or 3 long slender and tapering tail filaments. Duns are usually duller than spinners, with opaque rather than transparent wings.

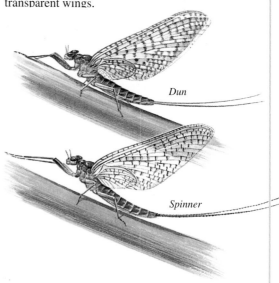

Dun

Spinner

STONEFLIES
Order Plecoptera p. 52

Immature stages are aquatic nymphs. They have a pair of antennae, 3 pairs of legs, an abdomen with 9 clearly visible segments, and in all cases a pair of long tails. There are no gills on the abdomen. There are wing buds on the top of the thorax, which become more pronounced as the nymph grows. Body shape often long, slender but stout in many species.

Adults usually have 2 pairs of often hard, shiny wings (in flight they are not synchronised, resulting in very weak flight) which are held low over the abdomen (often folded around the abdomen) at rest; some males have reduced wings and are flightless. Medium-to-large species usually have two stout tails; in smaller species tails absent or reduced to insignificant stumps.

Stonefly nymph

Adult stonefly

BUGS
Order Hemiptera p. 56

These include aquatic species (pond skater, water boatman) and some land insects that fall onto the water and feature regularly in the fishes' diet (e.g. aphids and froghoppers). Nymphs resemble miniature adults, except that they cannot fly. The main characteristic is the mouth: a piercing syringe used to pierce the skin of other animals and plants to extract juices. Some adults are wingless; others winged. In all aquatic forms and many land-bred forms the wings overlap and the front section of the forewings is hard and the rear section soft and membranous.

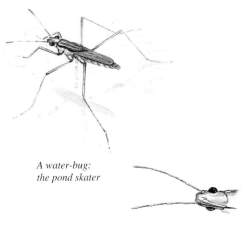

A water-bug: the pond skater

Syringe-like bug mouthparts

SEDGES (OR CADDIS-FLIES)
Order Trichoptera p. 60

Immature stages are larvae and pupae. Many larvae and all pupae occur in a case made of sand, tiny pebbles or bits of plant material. Some larvae lack a case; some live in silk nets or silk-and-mud tubes. Caseless forms and cased ones when case removed have 3 pairs of jointed legs attached to thorax and a pair of 'prolegs' (not true legs but a leg-like extension of body) at the end of abdomen. Body soft (cream or pale straw-coloured in cased caddis, green or brown in caseless), with hardened darker brown plates on head and thorax. Small simple gill filaments on body segments.

Cased and caseless sedge larvae

Adults have 2 long antennae on head, 3 pairs of sturdy legs, 2 pairs of wings (covered with fine hairs and at rest held tent-like over abdomen, cf Alders and Moths, p. 31); there are no tails.

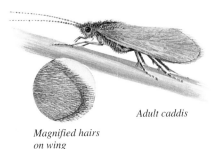

Adult caddis

Magnified hairs on wing

TWO-WINGED FLIES (OR FLAT-WINGED FLIES)
Order Diptera p. 70

Both water-bred and land-bred species are major fish foods. Immature stages are larvae and pupae. Unlike other insects the immature stages are legless. In aquatic species these vary tremendously in form. Some larvae are worm-like, lacking a clear thorax and abdomen, but with a distinct head and a pair of prolegs at end of body. Some resemble bait-fishers' maggots. Others have a head, and simple thoracic and abdominal regions. Many have long bristles either along the body or in tufts. Some pupae are immobile inside cocoons; others are more larval in appearance and can swim.

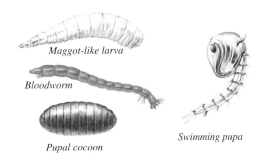

Maggot-like larva

Bloodworm

Pupal cocoon

Swimming pupa

Adults have very short antennae, and often large eyes. The thorax is usually well pronounced, and in some gives the appearance of being hunch-backed. There is just 1 pair of membranous wings that at rest are held flat over the abdomen. In some the three pairs of legs are extremely long. The abdomen has no tails.

Adult

BEETLES
Order Coleoptera p. 76

Both water-bred and land-bred species may be important fish foods. Immature stages are larvae and pupae. Aquatic larvae vary considerably, but two main types: one with head bearing jaws, thorax with 3 pairs of legs, and 8 visible abdominal segments ending with 0 or 2 tails or bristles; one as above but with body segments with spines or feathery gills. Aquatic larvae crawl to land to pupate in damp earth at the water's edge. Thus the pupae of aquatic beetles are of no significance to fish or angler.

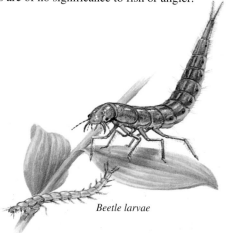

Beetle larvae

Adults with distinctive hard, horny external skeleton including forewings that form a 'shell' over membranous flying hindwings. Forewings meet at mid-line of body.

Aquatic adult beetle

The following are perhaps less important insect groups that are nonetheless taken by fish in large numbers on occasion:

DRAGONFLIES AND DAMSELFLIES
Order Odonata p. 59

Immature stages are aquatic nymphs. They have a pair of short antennae, 3 pairs of legs, an abdomen with 9 visible segments. There are no gills on the abdomen. At the end of the abdomen in damselflies there are three leaf-shaped tails; in dragonflies the abdomen ends in 3 very short pointed tails. The large jaws used to catch prey are hinged and held beneath the head when the nymph is not feeding.

Dragonfly nymph

Damselfly nymph

Damsel nymphs are usually very slender; dragonfly nymphs are usually short and squat. Adults are the well-known dragonflies and damselflies.

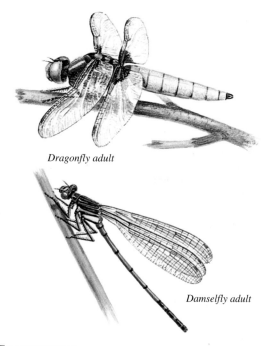

Dragonfly adult

Damselfly adult

GRASSHOPPERS
Order Orthoptera p. 78

Land-bred insects that fall, jump or are blown onto the water. Stout body and long jumping legs are characteristic.

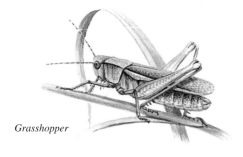

Grasshopper

THRIPS
Order Thysanoptera p. 78

Tiny land-bred insects. Slender cigar-shaped body, usually with 2 pairs of wings, and blackish in colour.

Adult thrips

LACEWINGS
Order Neuroptera p. 78

Fragile-looking land-bred insects with long membranous wings held tent-like over body when at rest; body soft, and either pale green or buff.

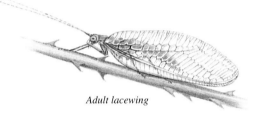

Adult lacewing

MOTHS AND BUTTERFLIES
Order Lepidoptera p. 79

Mostly land-bred insects (there are some species with aquatic larvae). Larvae are typical caterpillars, with a head that bears jaws used to devour plant material; a thorax with three very short pairs of jointed legs, and abdomen with five pairs of soft prolegs. Body overall soft.

Caterpillar

Adults are the well-known butterflies and moths (some can be confused with Sedges and Alders, but wings are covered with scales, not hairs, and wings held upright in butterflies and flat over the body in moths, not tent-like as in Sedges and Alders).

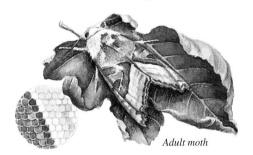

Magnified scales on wing

Adult moth

ALDERS
Order Megaloptera p. 76

Larvae are aquatic and resemble some beetle larvae. Large head bears strong jaws; thorax 3 pairs of legs; first 7 of 9 visible abdominal segments have a pair of long slender gills; tapering abdomen terminates in single slender tail.

Alder larva

The larva crawls from water before pupating in waterside soil, and adults lay eggs on vegetation overhanging the water. Whilst adult Alders are often seen flying over the water they rarely alight on the surface. The eggs hatch on overhanging vegetation and the larvae fall into the water. Alder-flies resemble sedges (see p. 29) with their longish antennae and tent-like wings. But wings are bare, lacking fine hairs and scales, and are strongly veined.

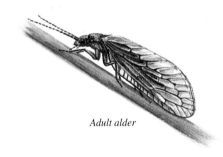

Adult alder

ANTS, WASPS AND BEES
Order Hymenoptera p. 78

Land-bred insects that often fall onto the water and are eaten by fish. Look for 2 pairs of wings (but ants are often wingless) and a very narrow waist between abdomen and thorax.

Flying ant

CRUSTACEANS P. 80

Crustaceans have a clearly segmented body (though some segments may be hidden beneath a shell-like carapace) divided into head, thorax and abdomen. The head usually bears 2 pairs of antennae; the thorax 5-8 pairs of walking and/or swimming legs, and each abdominal segment may have a pair of short limbs. Often the abdomen terminates in a pair of tails. The external skeleton is often very thick and hard. Crustaceans include well-known species such as crabs, crayfish and shrimps. Many species of freshwater crustaceans are tiny and live as plankton in lakes. In these the body structure is often much simpler and the number of limbs reduced.

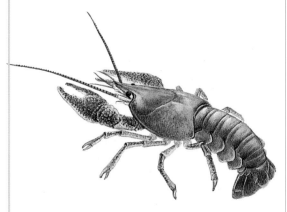

The crayfish: Europe's largest freshwater crustacean

MOLLUSCS p. 82

There are two main types of freshwater mollusc: snails and mussels (clams). Snails have a single, usually coiled shell; mussels have 2 shells. The body is soft; when not feeding, the animal retreats into the protection of the shell.

Clam

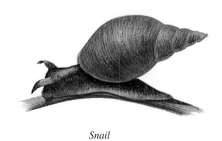

Snail

SPIDERS AND MITES

Spiders and mites have four pairs of legs. In spiders the body consists of a combined head and thorax which carries the legs, and a large rounded abdomen. In mites (very small animals up to 2mm long) the body is almost spherical and often brightly coloured. Because these are rarely eaten by trout, though autopsy occasionally reveals an odd specimen, they are not considered further in this book.

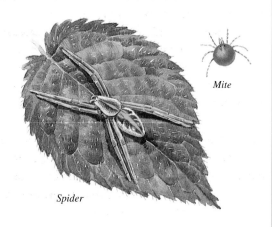

Mite

Spider

WORMS p. 84

Although there are many species of aquatic worm and fish eat them, they are not often imitated by fly fishers. They all have soft bodies. Some are segmented and can contract and extend the body (like earthworms); others have unsegmented bodies and may or may not (depending on the group of worm) be able to contract the body.

Earthworms include both land and aquatic species: both are eaten by fish

FISH
p. 84

Trout sometimes feed selectively on smaller fish – both smaller species and the fry of larger species.

Minnow: a common food of larger predatory fish

MAMMALS
p. 84

Large trout will sometimes feed on small mammals swimming on water such as lemmings and small voles.

Lemming: recorded in the diet of pike and larger trout in Finland and Scandinavia

AMPHIBIANS
p. 84

Frogs, toads, newts and their tadpoles often feature in the trout diet, especially tadpoles.

Tadpole

Frog

All the major food-groups have now been outlined, and more detailed treatments follow on pages 34-85. But first a word on the larger creatures shown on this page.

Many fly-fishers consider them almost irrelevant. Grayling, it is true, feed almost exclusively on invertebrates. But trout are opportunistic feeders, and will often take these larger food items. On most lakes with a population of other fish such as roach, perch and bream, they may ignore hatches of insects in summer and concentrate instead on fish fry. The loughs Owel and Allen in Ireland are typical. Here the trout will feed on invertebrates through to June or early July, but then comes a period when apparently every trout turns to roach and bream fry. And I have sometimes wondered why trout were not rising to a hatch or fall of flies on a river, but then discovered that they were preoccupied with tadpoles or tiny toads.

Furthermore, some big trout feed almost *only* on vertebrates. The ferox trout of deep glacial lakes in Scandinavia, Scotland and the Alps concentrate on smaller fish, and seem to prefer arctic charr and whitefish. The marbled trout of the river Soca in Slovenia feed mainly on the grayling that abound there. Similarly there are trout in the lake-river systems of Finland and Russia that feed mainly on small fish. The anglers there know this and use big imitations to catch them.

Lastly, even where we see trout rising to flies on a lake or river, there are usually also some big trout there which rarely bother with tiny insects. They are the predatory, vertebrate-eating trout that seek out crayfish and lesser fish, amphibians and small mammals. To catch these fish, it is essential to identify the likely vertebrate foods and imitate them. Few anglers do – which is why so few of these bigger fish are caught.

IDENTIFYING THE NATURAL FOODS

SCIENTIFIC GROUPING

Scientifically, the classification of insects and other animals depends on characters which are often tiny, sometimes microscopic, and irrelevant to anglers (and to fish). For instance, there are about 500 species of midges in the family Chironomidae in Europe. But the identification to species is slow, complex and needs considerable experience and familiarity with both the insect group in question and the scientific text books covering them. So anglers, in their amiably casual way, tend to call any midge in the family Chironomidae '*Chironomus*' (just one of many genera in the family) or perhaps '*Chironomus plumosus*' (one of about 20 species in the genus). Though scientifically nonsense, this is quite in order *provided* we realise that we are talking in loose terms. But just bear in mind: a small black midge with a wing length of 3.5-4mm may well be the common *Polyedilum nubeculosus*, but (although the fish does not notice the difference) it could equally be any one of 50 very similar species.

IDENTIFICATION

We describe simple characters, easily seen by either the naked eye or a × 6-10 lens, and also where the food item lives, how it behaves in the water, when it occurs most commonly, and geographical distribution.

If a creature occurs only in rivers we can discount similar species that live only in lakes. If it is on the wing only in spring, we can discount it if we see large numbers hatching in autumn. If a fly hatches only at night, we can discount it if we are trying to identify one hatching at lunchtime. If we catch a fly in France, we can discount species that live only in Fenno-Scandinavia. A few individuals refuse to obey rules and, instead of hatching in July-September, hatch in March or April. For the angler this is almost irrelevant: out-of-season hatches are usually insignificant in contrast to those in the main period. For instance, last March I identified 7 blue-winged olives (which are usually out in summer and autumn) amongst the expected hatch of thousands of large dark olives. The trout took the large dark and ignored the few blue-winged. Interesting for the entomologist, but unimportant for trout and angler. Be aware of this when you come across solitary specimens.

SELECTION

There are hundreds of freshwater animals which occur in relatively tiny numbers. What is included is based on our experience and that of many other anglers, on lakes and rivers throughout most of Europe.

One group of insect foods has been traditionally afforded a status that far exceeds its importance: the upwinged flies or Ephemeroptera. Most angling-entomologist writers have been based on the chalkstreams of southern England where the group is very important and where the rule of 'dry fly only' fishing has predominated: dry fly means imitating what is standing on the water and upwinged fly duns and spinners are conspicuous in this respect, especially on chalkstreams. In his *An Angler's Entomology*, J.R. Harris described only five species of caddisflies (sedges) but gave full treatment to almost every species of upwinged fly including the 'turkey dun' *Paraleptophlebia submarginata*. Yet he said this about the turkey dun: 'It is doubtful if this species is of much value for angling purposes, even though it is frequently mentioned in the literature.'

INSECTS

An insect's body consists of a head, thorax and abdomen (though this is indistinct in some, notably the larvae of two-winged flies Diptera). The thorax and abdomen are usually conspicuously segmented. In most adult insects the thorax bears one or two pairs of wings (some aphids and ants are exceptions); in all adult insects and many immature stages the thorax bears three pairs of jointed legs (larvae of many two-winged flies are exceptions, lacking legs). The head often has a pair of antennae; the abdomen sometimes has, at its tip, one, two or three 'tails' called cerci. Like the crustaceans, the body of insects is covered by an external skeleton (or exoskeleton) that may be either tough and flexible or hard and rigid. Joints in the body and along the legs allow for movement.

Insects do not grow in the same way that many other animals grow. They have what are known as 'life cycles', and each stage of the life cycle is usually quite different in appearance from other stages. This is important, because a fish will often be feeding not simply on one species but on one stage in the life cycle of that species. It is essential to understand these stages. There are two basic insect life cycles: those of incomplete and complete metamorphosis.

Incomplete metamorphosis

The **egg** hatches into a tiny nymph (sometimes called a larvula or larva, but the term can lead to confusion with true larvae of complete metamorphosis).

The **nymph** is the main feeding and growing stage. The nymph grows and as it does so it expands within its external skeleton. When there is no further room for expansion the nymph moults. The old skeleton splits, usually along the back of the thorax, and the new nymph emerges. This moulting of insects is called 'ecdysis'. After emerging from the old skeleton (now called a 'shuck') the nymph is a little paler in colour and has a very soft outer skin; as the new external skeleton hardens so the colour of the nymph darkens.

Upwinged fly nymph. Note 3 tails and gills

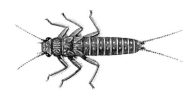

Stonefly nymph. Note 2 tails and no gills

The new external skeleton hardens in such a way that it allows for some increase in the amount of nymph tissues within it. So through its life as a nymph the insect will moult several times as it becomes larger. Aquatic nymphs are readily identifiable as insects: they have the distinct head, thorax and abdomen; they have jointed legs; some have tails; aquatic forms often have gills. In older nymphs some adult features may be noted, especially wing-buds on the back of the thorax.

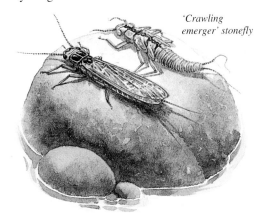

'Crawling emerger' stonefly

When the nymph is fully grown, it moults for the final time and the adult emerges from the nymphal shuck. In some aquatic species the fully-grown nymph crawls or climbs on to a rock or boulder or swims to the shore and the adult emerges on dry land. However, some nymphs swim to the water surface and the adult emerges from the nymphal shuck (that lies immediately below the surface film) onto the surface. The stage where the adult is struggling from the nymphal shuck is known as the 'emerger'. Emergers are very important to the angler for they are easy prey for fish.

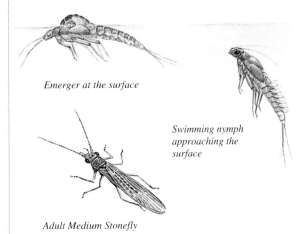

Emerger at the surface

Swimming nymph approaching the surface

Adult Medium Stonefly

The swimming nymph is active; the newly-hatched adult, standing on the water surface might fly off at any time; but the emerger is helpless and vulnerable. Sometimes the fish will ignore nymphs

Egg laying female stonefly

swimming to the surface, or adults standing on the surface, and instead will feed selectively on the emerger stage.

The **adult** flies from the water using its one or two pairs of wings (some male stoneflies have reduced wings and are flightless). In some species, such as the dragonflies, the adult can take in some food and water; in others, such as the mayflies, it can neither feed nor drink. This is the sexually mature stage. Mating occurs either in flight or on land. Often the males never return to the water. When they do they are invariably outnumbered by females, for the adult females must return to water to lay their fertilized eggs. Some females swim on or under the water; some crawl down boulders or reed stems beneath the water to lay their eggs. Others fly above the water and land momentarily on the surface to release their eggs or merely touch the water surface with the tip of the abdomen to deposit eggs. After egg laying is complete, the females of most species quickly die; often they fall on the water and are then called 'spent females'.

Complete metamorphosis

The **eggs** hatch into larvae (sometimes called maggots, caterpillars, bloodworms etc.), the main feeding and growing stage. As with nymphs, the larvae moult their external skeletons several times as they grow. It is sometimes difficult to pick out the features that classify larvae as insects for many have indistinct head, thorax and abdomen body regions, and often lack legs (e.g. maggots, bloodworm).

When fully grown the larvae enter a resting stage, the **pupa** (sometimes called chrysalis), within which the body tissues are reorganised into the adult form. In some species (beetles, alders) the aquatic larvae crawl from the water to pupate on land: these are of no interest to fly fishers because the fish rarely encounter them. In some aquatic species (mosquitoes, p. 72) the pupae are capable of swimming. In others (caddis-flies, p. 62) the larva spins a cocoon, enclosed in a case made from stones or bits of twig, in which it pupates.

The adult emerges from the pupa once body tissues have been reorganised into the adult form (some hibernate as pupae and wait for warm spring weather before emerging). Sometimes the pupa swims to the surface, where the adult emerges; in these cases there is an emerger stage where the adult is actively emerging from the pupal shuck at the surface film. In others the adult emerges from the pupal shuck underwater, and swims or crawls from the water.

The **adults** of aquatic species mate either in the air or on land. Males often die over land after mating, and rarely return to water. Females lay their eggs usually on or in the water (in some species the eggs are laid in overhanging vegetation and the newly-hatched larvae fall into the water). In most species the females die and fall on the water as 'spent females'.

Land-bred insects

Although aquatic insects in their different stages are important foods for most species of freshwater fish, fish feeding at the surface are often opportunistic feeders and will rise to anything that is edible. And that may be any of a wide variety of land-bred insects, often in huge numbers. While land-bred insects have either an incomplete or complete life cycle, only rarely will their larvae, pupae or nymphs reach the water (for example, when a spate washes them from the land into the river). In these species the adult is the important stage for fish and angler.

In certain waters (barren unproductive lakes and rivers) where the populations of aquatic forms are sparse, land-bred insects are virtually the only surface foods taken by fish. In all rivers and lakes a good fall of land-bred insects will encourage the fish to rise; sometimes fish will select land-bred insects that have fallen onto the water in preference to water-bred insects hatching at the surface. When the fish are feeding selectively on land-bred flies, the fly-fisher may need a reasonable imitation of them.

Altogether, insects in their great variety and numbers are the most important source of food for fish such as the trout and grayling, and are therefore of the greatest importance to the imitative fly-fisher. It is because of this – the domination by flying insects – that all imitation 'baits' (crustaceans, snails, small fish etc.) are referred to as 'flies', even when it is not insects at all that they are imitating.

INCOMPLETE METAMORPHOSIS: THE STONEFLY LIFE CYCLE

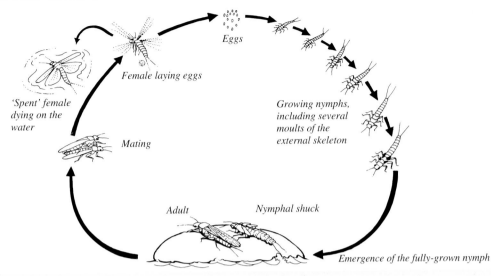

Eggs

Female laying eggs

'Spent' female dying on the water

Growing nymphs, including several moults of the external skeleton

Mating

Adult

Nymphal shuck

Emergence of the fully-grown nymph

Important stages for feeding fish and for imitation

Growing nymphs
Nymphs rising to the surface to hatch
Nymphs resting at the surface just before hatching
Emergers
Adults on water surface after hatch
Egg laying females
Spent females

Insect groups with incomplete metamorphosis life cycle

Upwinged flies (Ephemeroptera) A
Dragonflies and Damselflies (Odonata) A
Stoneflies (Plecoptera) A
Grasshoppers and Bush Crickets (Orthoptera) L
Bugs (Hemiptera) A/L
Thrips (Thysanoptera) L

Key: A = All species aquatic. A/L = Some aquatic, some land-bred. L = All land-bred.

COMPLETE METAMORPHOSIS: THE AQUATIC MIDGE LIFE CYCLE

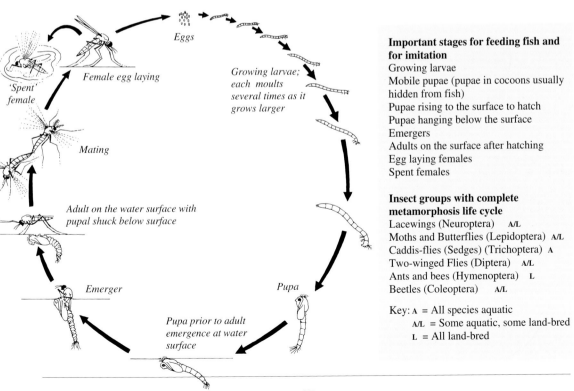

Eggs

Female egg laying

'Spent' female

Growing larvae; each moults several times as it grows larger

Mating

Adult on the water surface with pupal shuck below surface

Emerger

Pupa

Pupa prior to adult emergence at water surface

Important stages for feeding fish and for imitation

Growing larvae
Mobile pupae (pupae in cocoons usually hidden from fish)
Pupae rising to the surface to hatch
Pupae hanging below the surface
Emergers
Adults on the surface after hatching
Egg laying females
Spent females

Insect groups with complete metamorphosis life cycle

Lacewings (Neuroptera) A/L
Moths and Butterflies (Lepidoptera) A/L
Caddis-flies (Sedges) (Trichoptera) A
Two-winged Flies (Diptera) A/L
Ants and bees (Hymenoptera) L
Beetles (Coleoptera) A/L

Key: A = All species aquatic
A/L = Some aquatic, some land-bred
L = All land-bred

UPWINGED FLIES
Order Ephemeroptera

Life cycle — incomplete metamorphosis. Tiny nymphs hatch from eggs; nymphs feed and grow, moulting their shuck at regular intervals as they do so. When fully grown the nymphs either crawl to the shore or swim to the surface and the first winged stage, the dun, emerges from the nymphal shuck. In some species, (*Epeorus*, yellow dun, dark dun) the adults hatch from the nymphal shuck underwater, and the adult floats to the surface before flying away. Many anglers imitate the nymph and the dun stages. However, often the fish will take the natural insect from the surface as an 'emerger' — the nymph with the dun emerging from the nymphal shuck — and often fish will select these emergers and ignore nymphs and duns.

The dun flies from the water to thick vegetation or shelter among rocks. A further moult then takes place as the sexually mature spinner emerges from the dun shuck. The spinners mate (usually away from the water), and the males then fall dying to the ground. The females return to the water to lay their eggs; they too then die, usually falling onto the water surface. But note: in some species of *Baetis* olives, the female spinner crawls down vegetation, boulders, bridge masonry etc. to lay her eggs underwater and does not "fall" on the water surface.

Upwinged fly nymphs have 3, often long, slender tails (*Epeorus* is an exception, having 2 tails), a tapering abdomen (that in most species bears conspicuous gills), and a pronounced thorax which bears 3 pairs of legs and wing-buds (these are more conspicuous in older nymphs). The head bears simple often inconspicuous jaws.

Adult upwinged flies are unique: there are two flying stages — the sexually immature 'dun' emerges from the nymphal stage and flies from the water; the dun moults into the sexually mature 'spinner' (there are exceptions, e.g. *Palingenia*, *Ephoron*).

Duns are usually drabber than spinners. Both duns and spinners of the Ephemoptera are identified from other flying insects by 2 or 3 long fine tails (longer in spinner); usually 2 pairs of wings (sometimes hind wings greatly reduced or absent) which are held side by side in upright position over body when at rest (usually wings in duns opaque, gauzy and transparent in spinner); the forelegs are long, especially in males. Males are also identified from females by having short incurved claspers at the tip of the abdomen, which are used when mating. Antennae very short.

Claspers of male mayfly

Upwinged Fly Nymphs

There are six categories of upwinged fly nymphs. These categories are based on the niche in which the nymph lives during its aquatic life, and to some extent the way the nymph moves; also, in some cases, the mode of emergence of the adult from the fully-grown nymph. The identification of nymphs to scientific species is often very difficult and since the fish appear unable to distinguish between closely related species, irrelevant to the angler. Further, with some exceptions, it is impossible for the fly dresser to imitate individual nymph species.

For the tying of imitation nymphs: see pp. 124, 126, 140, 142-8, 162. Note also that many soft-hackled wet flies (pp. 127, 134) are effective deceivers of trout that are eating nymphs.

Behavioural Groups

Upwinged fly nymphs can be separated into six groups, based on the behaviour of the nymph and where the nymph lives in the lake or river.

BOTTOM BURROWERS

Mayfly *Ephemera* species, *Palingenia* and *Ephoron*
These very large (up to 25mm long) nymphs tunnel through silt, sand or gravel of the river or lake bed. In this position they are rarely encountered by fish. However as they rise to the water surface to hatch into duns large numbers of mature nymphs may be eaten.

The nymphs of the two commonest *Ephemera* species may be identified by their long (up to 25mm), cream-coloured bodies and dark gills held low over the abdomen. On each abdominal segment of the dark mayfly is a pair of triangular dark markings which become only slightly larger the further down the abdomen; in the mayfly nymph the markings are quite obscure at the base of the abdomen and are most conspicuous on the last three distinct segments.

SILT CRAWLERS

Angler's Curse *Caenis* and *Brachycerus* species
Tiny nymphs (the largest species, only 6.5mm long) that crawl over or just in the surface of silt or mud. Fish do feed on them when they are grubbing on the river or lake bed. Large numbers are also eaten as they rise to hatch into duns at the water surface. Their tiny size has dissuaded many anglers from attempting imitations; but in the early stages of a hatch of Caenis duns suitable imitations of the rising nymphs (e.g. Winter Ptarmigan, p. 134) are often more effective than dun imitations.

MOSS CREEPERS

Blue-winged Olive *Ephemerella ignita*
Yellow Evening Dun *E. notata*

Medium-sized nymphs (up to about 10mm), found only in rivers, that crawl or creep among water moss, dense weed (e.g. Ranunculus), on boulders or among dead plant material trapped by boulders, bridge supports etc. They have a slender though sturdy build, and powerful legs that hold them in place in often very fast water. Many of these nymphs are eaten by fish — grubbed from the riverbed, or after being washed into the flow by particularly violent spates. Large numbers are also eaten as they rise to hatch at the water surface, especially at the 'emerger stage' as the dun struggles from the nymphal shuck (p. 18).

STONE CLINGERS

March Brown *Rhithrogena*
False March Brown group *Ecdyonurus*
Epeorus *Epeorus*
Dark Dun *Heptagenia*
Southern Mayfly *Oligoneurella*

Large nymphs (up to 15mm) found in barren stony lakes and fast-flowing, turbulent, boulder-strewn streams. They can scuttle over boulders in fairly rough water, without being dislodged by the current, by using their strong legs, clawed feet and flattened streamlined profile. Huge numbers of these often abundant nymphs are eaten by fish grubbing on the bottom. During heavy spates (when riverbed boulders are dislodged by the force of water) many stone clinger nymphs are swept downstream; fish take large numbers as they are swept along the edge of the main flow. Many stoneclingers (especially of the genus *Ecdyonurus*) emerge by crawling ashore: the dun hatches from the nymph on a waterside boulder. Neither emerging dun nor hatched dun is encountered by fish. Some (e.g. march browns and dark duns) do hatch at the water surface, and many of the nymphs that are rising to hatch are eaten by fish.

LABOURED SWIMMERS

Family Leptophlebiidae, including the **Sepia** and **Claret Duns** *Leptophlebia marginata* and *L. vespertina* and *Chloroterpes*

These are slender, medium-sized (up to 12mm long) nymphs, with three extremely long tails and usually a distinct reddish coloration. They live mostly in lakes or very slow-flowing streams. They usually occur crawling in cover (claret dun among weeds or reeds in sheltered bays, sepia dun among boulders in deep water) where fish rarely encounter them. When disturbed they can swim very weakly. Many nymphs are taken by fish as they rise to the surface to hatch into duns.

AGILE DARTERS

Summer Mayfly *Siphlonurus* species, several species of **Olive, Iron Blue, Pale Watery** of the genera *Baetis, Cloeon, Centroptilum, Procloeon*, **Yellow Mayfly** *Potamanthus*

This is often the most important group of nymphs for anglers, as at least one species occurs in all types of rivers and in clean lakes from the lowlands of southern and central Europe to the highest of mountain tarns and streams, and to northernmost Lapland, Russia and Iceland. What makes members of this group so important is their ability to swim vigorously, whether as immature nymphs among weeds or boulders, or as mature nymphs rising to hatch at the water surface. They all have slender streamlined bodies and tails that are fringed with hairs (which, with the flexing of the abdomen, aid propulsion). Most are small-medium long (5-10mm), though the nymph of the widespread and abundant large dark olive *Baetis rhodani* may attain a length of 15mm and summer mayfly nymphs 19mm.

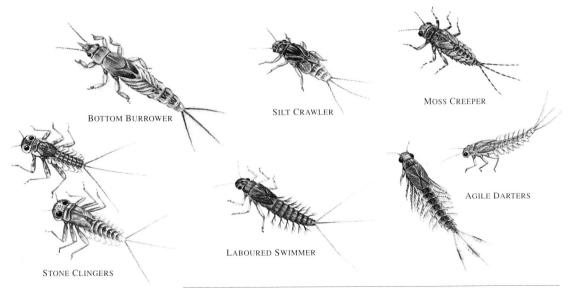

BOTTOM BURROWER

SILT CRAWLER

MOSS CREEPER

STONE CLINGERS

LABOURED SWIMMER

AGILE DARTERS

Duns and Spinners

Upwinged fly duns and spinners have been considered the major fish foods par excellence. Studies of this Order since around 1850 have traditionally divided it into over 200 European species. About 50 occur in Britain and may have been given different English names, which have been adopted by British anglers. Distinctions are often by very subtle differences in the veins and structure of wings, or eye-colour or details of reproductive organs, features that the fish will not notice, and will therefore not function as triggers when fish are feeding selectively.

Furthermore they are features that the fly dresser often cannot mimic in the artificial fly. For example, five species were once included under the name 'pale watery': *Baetis fuscatus, B. scambus, Centroptilum luteolum, C. pennulatum, Procloeon bifidum*. In recent years some angler-entomologists have split them: *B. fuscatus* retains the name of pale watery, *B. scambus* has become the 'small dark olive', *C. luteolum* the 'small spurwing', *C. pennulatum* the 'large spurwing' and *P. bifidum* the 'pale evening dun'. For the practical angler this proliferation of common names is irrelevant and often misleading. The features that the fish *do* notice and which act as triggers – size, shape and general coloration – are common to all five species: to the fish, and the angler, they are by and large all pale wateries.

To some extent the importance of upwinged fly duns and spinners is exaggerated: in many European rivers and lakes other groups are far more abundant and important as fish foods (e.g. caddis-flies or sedges *Trichoptera* and midges *Chironomus*); in many rivers and lakes where upwinged fly duns and spinners were once very abundant pollution has resulted in their decline and a corresponding increase of other insects (notably midges).

Finally, some of the upwinged fly species are quite scarce, very local in distribution, or occur on the water in such tiny numbers that they are of little importance. The Turkey Brown *Paraleptophlebia submarginata*, already mentioned on p. 34, is found through much of Europe, but rarely (if ever) occurs on the water in such numbers that the fish feed selectively on it (often one has to hunt around to find more than the odd specimen).

Here we consider those species or groups of species of upwinged flies that may occur, in Europe, on the water as duns or spinners, in sufficient numbers to encourage the fish to feed on them selectively.

Imitations of emergers: pp. 124, 140, 148-50, 164. Imitations of duns: pp. 124, 138, 151-9, 164. Imitations of spinners: pp. 126, 138, 160-2, 166. Several soft-hackled wet flies (pp. 127, 134) are excellent catchers of fish feeding on duns and spinners. The Stewart/Hamilton Wet Flies (p. 136) are good emerger dun imitations.

Identification of duns and spinners

Number of tails: the first thing to look for when examining an unknown dun or spinner. There will either be two or three. Sometimes one will be lost or malformed; this will be apparent when it is one of the tails in a 2-tailed insect or an outer tail in a 3-tailed insect, but less clear when the middle tail is missing or badly malformed in a 3-tailed individual (there will usually be a stump indicating the missing tail).

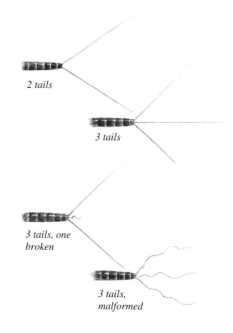

2 tails

3 tails

3 tails, one broken

3 tails, malformed

Variations in tail filaments

Size: especially length of body and tails. Note that during a hatch some individuals may be significantly smaller than others; some waters produce smaller flies of the same species; and size may vary through the season (on some waters the large dark olives *Baetis rhodani* that hatch in very early spring are often larger than those hatching later). Also note that tails in duns are usually shorter than in spinners of the same species (and that the bodies of males tend to be shorter then females, but tails are usually longer).

Are you looking at duns or spinners? Look at the wings: duns usually have opaque wings but spinners have gauzy, transparent wings (there are a few exceptions). Look at the position of the fly: duns float on the water with wings held high, and when they fly leave the water for cover on the bank and rarely take flight again; spinners are often seen flying in mating swarms (sometimes 100 metres or more from the water), the females then fly to the water to lay their eggs and later they die on the water with wings fluttering weakly, outstretched on the surface or with one wing held high and the other flat on the water.

Coloration: compare what you see on the natural insect with the illustrations and notes given here. Again, natural duns and spinners can vary in general coloration; the notes give the usual colour range.

Habitat: some upwinged flies occur almost exclusively on rivers, or almost always only on lakes (a river species may occasionally be seen on a lake, and vice versa, but this will be exceptional and usually involve very few individuals).

Timing of dun hatch and fall of spent female spinner: a useful clue to identification, though small numbers may appear 'out of season'. The tables (pp. 87-121) give the main months when the species might be encountered, together with major hatch and fall times during the day.

Dun hatching: the stage where the dun is in the process of emerging from the nymphal shuck is referred to as the 'emerger'.

Dead, spent ♀ spinner, lying flat in the surface film.

It is worth stressing again the differences between duns and spinners, for these differences are so important when it comes to identifying them.

◆ Duns will be seen floating high on the water.

◆ Spinners will be seen falling onto the water and, when dead on the water, are very difficult to see as they float flat in the surface film.

◆ Duns will be seen flying singly from the water to the land. When they reach dry land and find a suitable hiding place, duns do not fly.

◆ Spinners will be seen flying in groups, sometimes in vast swarms, over or close to the water, often in late afternoon or early evening. Then they will be seen flying *to* the water, not *away* from it.

Upwinged flies with three tails

Mayfly (Green Drake/Spent Gnat) *Ephemera danica*

Rivers and lakes (most abundant limestone or chalk). Duns hatch late morning-afternoon in May-early June (occasionally to early August). Spinner fall: mid afternoon-evening.

A very large upwinged fly (body 16-25mm, tails 20-45mm) with 3 tails. Dun: body cream or yellowish with dark markings (see Dark Mayfly, below); wings grey-green or yellow-green. Female spinner: body white with dark markings (see Dark Mayfly below); wings gauzy blue-black.

Dark Mayfly (Brown Mayfly/Brown Drake *Ephemera vulgata*

Slow rivers and lakes, often with mud, silt or sandy bottom. Duns hatch late morning-afternoon in May to early July. Spinner fall: mid afternoon-evening.

A very large upwinged fly (body 14-24mm, tails 18-30mm) with 3 tails. Dun: body dark yellow-buff with distinct triangular markings on each segment; wings yellow-buff. Female spinner: body cream-olive with distinctive dark markings; wings gauzy black-brown.

E. lineata is usually found in slow, small rivers and lakes (in the Alps it has been recorded from large lakes such as Neuchâtel) but is generally rare, occurring in small numbers. It has recently been reported from clean gravel pits (e.g. in the Colne Valley in SE England) and might increase in this habitat. E. glaucops (scarce in some lakes and rivers, not Britain) is much smaller than the other species.

Yellow Mayfly *Potamanthus luteus*

An insect of fast clean rivers, especially parts of Fenno-Scandinavia, NW Russia (extremely rare in British Isles). Duns hatch late evening in June-early August. Spinner fall: late evening and night. (often overlooked because of its nocturnal flying stages.)

A very large upwinged fly (body 10-16mm, tails 14-22mm) with 3 tails. Dun: body dull orange-yellow with conspicuous broad brown stripe running full length of upper side of abdomen and conspicuous black spots along side of abdomen; wings dull yellow; tails brown. Female spinner: similar but with brighter yellow body (still with brown band and black spots), transparent yellow wings and tails yellow-brown with blackish rings.

Southern Mayfly *Oligoneuriella rhenana*

Occurs in large clean rivers in parts of Iberia, Italy and eastern Europe. Duns hatch very late afternoon-evening in late June-end August. Spinner fall: late evening and into darkness. Frequently overlooked owing to its often nocturnal behaviour.

A large upwinged fly (body 12-17mm) with 3 relatively short (up to 5mm in females and 15mm in males) tails. Dun body dark grey, wings cloudy grey-white with noticeably few veins (*Oligoneuriella* = few nerves or veins), tails pale grey. Note legs, small and weak. Spinner similar to dun but coloration more translucent.

Note that, like *Caenis* and *Palingenia* the moult from dun to spinner takes place almost immediately after the dun has hatched from the nymph. And because the weak legs in this species do not allow the insect to perch while it moults, it moults from dun to spinner in flight.

Blue-winged Olive *Ephemerella ignita*

One of the most abundant and widespread upwinged flies that occurs in all types of clean river and stream. Duns hatch late May to late October (occasionally -end November) in late afternoon-evening early in season (but in cool cloudy weather through afternoon), becoming earlier as season progresses to early afternoon in October. Spinner fall: late afternoon-evening, often into dark; some around dawn.

Medium-sized (body 8-12mm, tails 10-16 but in duns sometimes twisted and malformed) with 3 tails (care! occasionally one breaks and only stump signifies a 3-tailed insect). Dun is highly variable in colour; body of female bright olive-green to olive-brown, male olive-brown to bright orange-brown (tends to be darker later in season). Wings uniform dark grey-blue, tails grey- or brown-olive barred dark brown. Spinner: body olive-brown to deep orange red (this gives name to spinner of 'sherry spinner'); wings transparent with light brown veins; tails olive-grey with dark brown rings.

There are two other species of blue-winged olive, *E. mucronata*, which occurs through eastern and central Europe from Fenno-Scandinavia south to the Balkans, and *E. major*, which occurs throughout the Alps and SE Europe.

Indistinguishable in the field from *E. ignita*. The duns of both species have bodies brown-olive above and yellow-olive below; wings uniform grey; tails with dark rings. The spinners of both species have bodies dark brown or red-brown; wings transparent with brown veins; tails with dark rings.

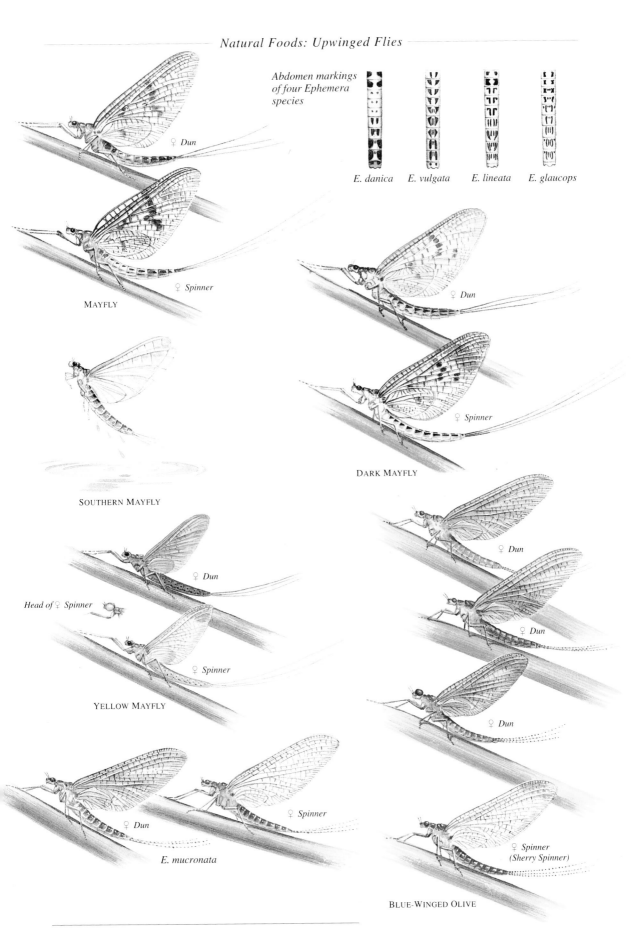

Abdomen markings
of four Ephemera
species

E. danica   E. vulgata   E. lineata   E. glaucops

♀ *Dun*

♀ *Spinner*

MAYFLY

♀ *Dun*

♀ *Spinner*

DARK MAYFLY

SOUTHERN MAYFLY

♀ *Dun*

Head of ♀ Spinner

♀ *Spinner*

YELLOW MAYFLY

♀ *Dun*

♀ *Dun*

♀ *Dun*

♀ *Dun*

♀ *Spinner*

E. mucronata

♀ *Spinner*
(Sherry Spinner)

BLUE-WINGED OLIVE

43

Yellow Evening Dun *Ephemerella notata.*

A fly of rivers, especially fast-flowing reaches of limestone streams. Duns hatch May-June and as name suggests in late afternoon-evening (often into dark). Spinner fall: late evening (often into dark). (Because of timings of dun hatch and spinner fall this species is often overlooked.)

A medium-sized fly (body 8-13mm, tails 10-17mm) with 3 tails. Dun has yellowish body; wings pale grey with yellow veins. Female spinner: body yellow-olive; wings transparent with yellow veins.

Purple Dun *Paraleptophlebia cincta* and *P. werneri*

A species of fast rivers, often most abundant in limestone and chalk upland areas. Duns hatch late morning-afternoon, May to early August. Spinner fall: late afternoon and evening.

A small-medium fly (body 6-9mm, tails 8-16mm) with 3 tails (which prevents confusion with similar 2-tailed iron blue dun, p. 46). Dun overall coloration very dark brown-olive with distinct purple tinge; wings pale grey in *P. werneri*, blackish-grey in *P. cincta*. Female spinner: dark purple-brown with transparent colourless wings and pale yellow tails.

Angler's Curse or **Caenis** *Caenis* or *Brachycerus* species

An abundant group of similar species that inhabit clean rivers and lakes. Dun hatches occur May-August, with peaks June-July. There are two sub-groups within the angler's curse species. In *C. luctuosa* the duns hatch *on rivers* in the early morning soon after dawn. These are a little larger than the species that hatch on lakes and rivers during the afternoon and evening. The angler's curse is remarkable because the moult from dun to spinner takes place immediately after the dun has left the water, mating then occurs followed by egg-laying and the fall of spent females. Often duns will land on the angler in huge numbers and use him/her as a moulting perch. The duration of hatching dun to spent spinner may last only 1-2 hours (in most upwinged flies 1-5 days).

Body 3-4mm in afternoon species, 4-6mm in morning species, tails 5-18mm, with 3 tails. Both dun and spinner have thorax conspicuously black (morning species) or brown (afternoon species); abdomen grey-cream, almost white in females of morning species. Wings broad and whitish. Difference between dun and spinner mainly longer tails and more transparent wings in spinner.

An important food species which many anglers ignore because they are not prepared to use tiny imitative fly patterns. It has been given the common name of angler's curse because long considered (erroneously) that fish feeding on it are uncatchable.

Claret Dun *Leptophlebia vespertina*

A common insect of lakes, especially acidic or peaty ones, found often in shallow bays and weedy margins. Duns hatch early May-early July during the late morning and afternoon. Spinner fall: evening.

A medium-sized upwinged fly (body 8-12mm, tails 10-16mm) with 3 tails. Dun has very dark brown body; dark grey forewings with noticeably paler hindwings. Spinner: glossy brown body (with distinct 'claret' tinge when examined closely); wings transparent with light brown veins. Tails pale brown ringed with black.

Sepia Dun *Leptophlebia marginata*

Common in lakes, especially acidic ones; often hatches from deeper water than claret dun so frequently found far from shore. Duns hatch April-mid-May in the early afternoon. Spinner fall: late afternoon and evening.

A medium sized fly (body 7-10mm, tails 8-15mm) with 3 tails. Dun has body dark brown; wings fawn-medium brown (cf Claret Dun). Spinner: body dark red-brown; wings transparent with distinctive sooty patch at front leading edge of forewings; tails uniform dark brown.

Habroleptoides *Habroleptoides* species

Several very similar species occur in central and southern Europe, in large streams and rivers, often in forested areas where the water receives large amounts of forest litter. Duns hatch in afternoon, late April-early June. Spinner fall: late afternoon and evening, also early morning.

Medium-small flies (bodies 6-9mm, tails 8-11mm) with 3 tails. Dun: body very dark grey-brown with light brown banding; wings grey with brown cast, dark veined; tails very dark brown. Female spinner: very similar to dun but with transparent brown-veined wings.

Chloroterpes *Chloroterpes picteti*

A fly of clean rivers (not British Isles). Duns hatch in August-October (occasionally to November) during late morning and afternoon. Spinner fall: late afternoon-evening.

A medium-sized fly (body 8-12mm, tails 8-14mm) with 3 tails. The dun has blackish-brown body; wings very dark purple-grey; tails blackish-brown. Female spinner yellow-brown abdomen and reddish thorax, wings transparent with dark veins, tails brown ringed darker brown-black.

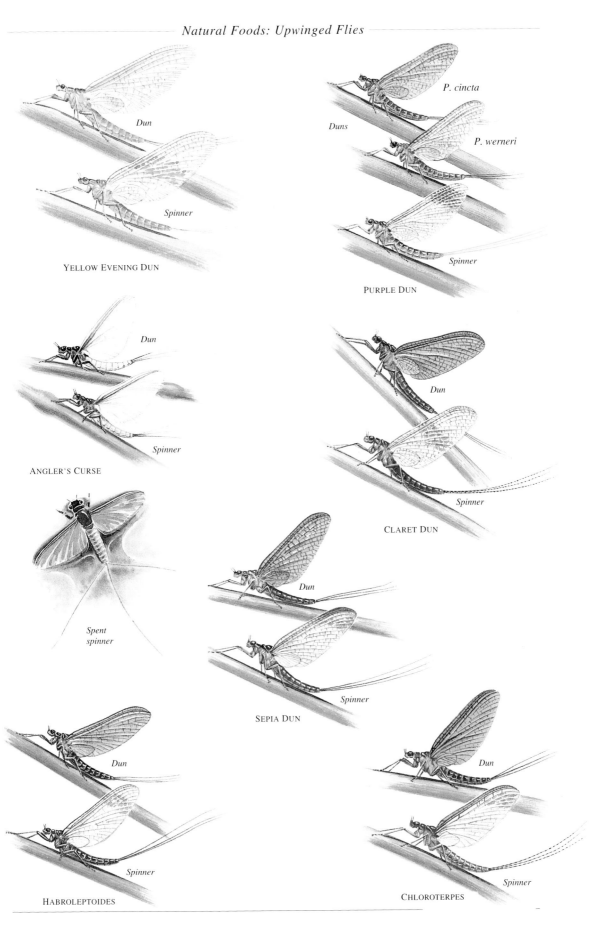

YELLOW EVENING DUN

Dun

Spinner

PURPLE DUN

Duns

P. cincta

P. werneri

Spinner

ANGLER'S CURSE

Dun

Spinner

CLARET DUN

Dun

Spinner

Spent spinner

SEPIA DUN

Dun

Spinner

HABROLEPTOIDES

Dun

Spinner

CHLOROTERPES

Dun

Spinner

Upwinged flies with two tails

Large Dark Olive (**Spring Olive**) *Baetis rhodani*

Perhaps one of the most widespread and abundant of Europe's upwinged flies; it occurs in rivers and streams other than the most grossly polluted. Duns hatch through afternoon in February-April; fewer September-October. The spinner fall is considered by most anglers to be of little significance as numbers of spent females falling onto the water at any one time are usually tiny. However note that in this species egg-laying occurs by the female crawling underwater and so the females may die there rather than fall onto the water.

Body 6-11mm, tails 16-18mm, with 2 tails. Dun body coloration variable, grey-olive, olive-green to brown-olive; wings uniform dull grey. Spinner body red-brown with olive banding; wings transparent with brown veins; tails grey-brown with red rings.

An almost identical species of dark olive dun *B. atrebatinus* occurs in some rivers in summer (outside the main flight periods of *B. rhodani*).

Alpine Olive *Baetis alpinus*

Very similar to the large dark olive, this species occurs in rough mountain streams of central Europe (not British Isles). Duns hatch in the afternoon in late May-June. Spinner fall: evening and early morning.

Body 8-10mm, tails 12-16mm, with 2 tails. Dun has body drab olive-green or grey-olive; wings medium grey. Female spinner: abdomen bright red-brown; wings transparent with brown veins.

Medium Olive *Baetis vernus*

Occurs in all clean rivers and streams. Duns hatch May-June, with stragglers to late August, in the afternoon and evening. Spinner fall: evening through into dark (female crawls underwater to lay eggs). A medium-small group (body 6-8mm, tails 11-16mm) with 2 tails. Dun body varies from pale olive, through medium olive to grey-brown; wings dull grey. Spinner body yellow- to red-brown; wings transparent; tails noticeably white. Other medium olives (*B. bucceratus*) are indistinguishable in the field from commoner *B. vernus*.

Iron Blue *Baetis muticus* and *B. niger*

A widespread and often abundant river insect, *niger* occurring in weedy rivers and muticus in rougher, stony rivers. Duns hatch during late morning and afternoon in late April-early June with a second (usually smaller hatch) September-October. Spinner fall: peaks early morning and late afternoon-evening.

Body 5-7mm, tails 8-12mm with 2 tails. Dun instantly recognisable by its overall, dark blackish-grey or very dark blue-grey coloration. Female spinner has a blackish thorax, dark ruddy-brown abdomen with lighter banding; tails pale grey; wings transparent.

Pale Watery   Several species

Primarily river insects though at least one species may be found hatching from lakes (especially lowland lakes set in chalk or limestone). Duns hatch from May-November (peak June-September), generally during late afternoon-evening earlier in season, and from midday through afternoon later in season; in cool summer weather also through afternoon. Spinner fall: evening, often into darkness.

Body 4-8mm, tails 7-14mm, with 2 tails. The dun body varies from off-white/pale cream, through the palest olive to light olive-brown; wings from pale to dark grey. Spinner body varies from translucent white (with last 3 segments orange), through gold, amber to bright red-brown; wings transparent.

In recent years some authorities have separated pale watery species as follows: *Baetis fuscatus*, Pale Watery; *B. scambus*, Small Dark Olive; *Centroptilum luteolum*, Small Spurwing; *C. (Pseudocentroptilum) pennulatum*, Large Spurwing; *Procloeon bifidum*, Pale Evening.

These five species exhibit a great overlap in size and coloration and may be separated as follows:

Pale Watery dun has oval hind wings, dull yellow eyes and pale-medium grey wings

Small Dark Olive dun has an oval hind wing, dull brown-red eyes, medium-dark blue-grey wings and is the smallest of the group (its overall body colour can be a quite pale olive or green-olive, despite the word 'dark' in its name!)

Pale Evening dun lacks hindwings, has yellow eyes, and the wings are very pale grey-white with a distinct green tinge at the base

Small Spurwing dun has a tiny, pointed spur-like hind wing, orange or red eyes, and pale grey-blue wings with a yellow tinge at the base

Large Spurwing dun has a larger spur-shaped hind wing than the small spurwing; it also has orange or red eyes; the wings are grey-blue.

You will need a lens to see these features properly; the fish are unlikely to notice them!

One noticeable feature of the spurwing duns is that they float downstream after hatching, holding their wings slightly apart, and not close together as most upwinged flies.

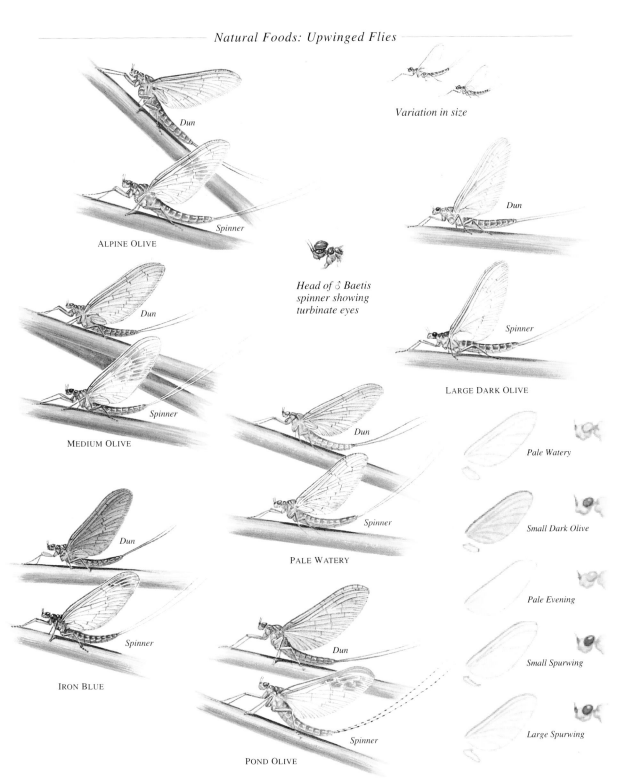

Variation in size

ALPINE OLIVE
Dun
Spinner

Head of ♂ *Baetis*
spinner showing
turbinate eyes

Dun
Spinner
LARGE DARK OLIVE

MEDIUM OLIVE
Dun
Spinner

Dun
Spinner
PALE WATERY

Pale Watery

Small Dark Olive

IRON BLUE
Dun
Spinner

Pale Evening

Small Spurwing

Dun
Spinner
POND OLIVE

Large Spurwing

Pond Olive *Cloeon dipterum*

A widespread and often abundant fly of stillwaters of all sizes; also reported from very slow, clean rivers. Duns hatch late morning to early evening, late May-September. Spinner fall: late evening through night to dawn (often overlooked). A medium sized upwinged fly (body 7-10mm, tails 11-18mm) with 2 tails. Dun: body grey-olive, wings uniform dark bluish-grey, tails dark grey. Spinner: body orange-pink ('apricot', giving the alternative name of this spinner as the 'apricot spinner'); wings transparent with red-brown veins and leading edge amber; tails very pale with dark banding. The pond olive spinner is unique in that the eggs hatch inside the female's body and are released at the water surface, a few at a time, as tiny nymphs or larvulae.

Lake Olive *Cloeon simile*

Generally in larger lakes; reported from slow, clean rivers. Duns hatch late morning to early evening, May-September, peaks May-June and late August-September. Spinner fall: late afternoon and evening. Medium sized (body 7-11mm, tails 12-18mm) with 2 tails. Dun similar to pond olive but drabber. Body varies from dull grey-olive, to grey-green to brown-olive; wings dark grey with green-olive veins and bright green roots or overall a dull ginger; tails medium grey. Spinner: body warm ruddy brown; wings transparent, olive-green patch at front edges; tails pale olive-grey, may have dark banding in females.

Olive Upright *Rhithrogena semicolorata*

A widespread fly of rough stony rivers, occasionally northern river-lakes. Duns hatch mid-May-July, through afternoon to dusk. Spinner fall: evening. Medium sized upwinged fly (body 9-15mm, tails 16-30mm) with 2 tails. Dun has body grey-green to brown-olive with pale olive banding; forewings medium to dark blue-grey, hind wings paler buff. Spinner: body red-brown (occasionally yellow-olive) with yellowish bands; wings transparent with brown veins.

Two very localised species of olive upright may be found, *R. braaschi* in the Balkans (dun hatch in April) and *R. loyolaea* to 2000m in the Alps, mountains of N. Spain and Balkans (dun hatch in August).

March Brown *Rhithrogena germanica*

A fly of rough, rocky rivers. A famous anglers' fly, but not as widespread as was once thought [up to 1940s scientists often confused these with the false march browns (see below); this confusion still exists among anglers]. Duns hatch at water surface between midday and mid afternoon, often in sporadic waves, traditionally during March-April though some other species of *Rhithrogena* march browns (see below) hatch to September. Spinner fall: late afternoon-evening. This is a large upwinged fly (body 11-15mm, tails 19-30mm) with 2 tails. The dun has body dark brown with pale yellow-straw banding; wings buff with dark mottling and veining but note clear patch in centre. Spinner: body medium to dark red-brown with buff banding; wings transparent with light brown veins. Note also dark, ovoid patch on femur of leg (found in most *Rhithrogena* species).

Alpine March Brown *Rhithrogena hybrida*

An insect of cool, rocky Alpine streams to 2000m. Duns hatch late August-September, afternoon. Spinner fall: late afternoon. Fairly local distribution, but abundant where it occurs. Body 9-11mm, tails 11-16mm, with 2 tails. Coloration overall dark. Dun: body dark grey-brown with lighter olive-brown banding; wings dull grey with blackish veins; tails dark brown-black. Spinner: similar but with transparent, black-veined wings sometimes with yellowish tinge. Note dark ovoid mark on femur of leg.

Two other species may be found, *Rhithrogena savoyensis* (rivers of central and eastern Europe) and

R. diaphana (Pyrenees). Superficially resemble *R. germanica* but smaller (body 5-8mm, tails 10-15mm). Dun has yellow brown body with dark banding, grey tails and more uniform grey-brown wings; spinner bright yellow-brown body with dark banding, grey tails, transparent wings. Duns hatch July-August.

False March Brown *Ecdyonurus* species

All on rough rocky rivers; some in barren stony lakes. Different species hatch mid-April to September. In most dun hatch is insignificant: most nymphs crawl from water to hatch, few occur on water (after a hatch many empty nymph shucks are found on waterside boulders). Spinner fall: evening into dark: extremely important. Body 11-16mm, tails 18-32mm, with 2 tails. Duns similar to march brown dun (often seen flying from waterside boulders to cover on the bank; some may be seen on the water). Spinner: body dark, rich red-brown (sometimes looks bright, glowing red in evening sun); wings transparent with darker veins. All ecdyonurids lack the oval patch on the femur of the leg, found in true march browns.

False March Browns can be separated as follows:

Late March Brown *E. venosus*: peak dun hatch late April to early June with stragglers to August; dun wings have dark mottling (similar to the march brown, but lacking the clear patch in the centre).

Brook Dun *E. torrentis*: peak dun hatch May-June on rough rocky rivers (large number of duns hatch at the water surface, unlike other species where most hatch out of water); dun wings have horizontal dark bands.

Autumn Dun *E. dispar*: peak hatch late July to September; dun wings uniform grey-buff with brown veins. The spinners are more difficult to separate in the field, especially during fading light.

Green Dun *Ecdyonurus insignis*

Another insect of rough stony rivers. The duns hatch May-October (peak late June-mid August) during mid-afternoon-evening; nymphs sometimes crawl ashore (as in false march browns) so dun may not appear on water. Spinner fall: evening into dark. A large fly (body 13-16mm, tails 24-30mm) with 2 tails. The dun has body of olive-green or grey-green with darker markings; wing membranes green or olive, veins brown-black. Spinner: body olive-green with brown banding; wings transparent with dark veins and a distinct sooty patch on outer forewing.

Brown Dun *Ecdyonurus helveticus*, *E. krueperi*, *E. picteti*

Found at 500-1600m in rough, rocky streams in the Pyrenees, Alps and (*krueperi*) Balkans. Duns hatch in afternoons in June-August (later at higher altitude) by crawling from water. Spinner fall: late afternoon and evening. Medium-large (body 10-15mm, tails 15-35mm) with 2 tails. Dun: body very dark brown (paler underneath); wings dusky brown, tails black. Spinner: body dark brown, yellow below; wings transparent with brown veins; tails black.

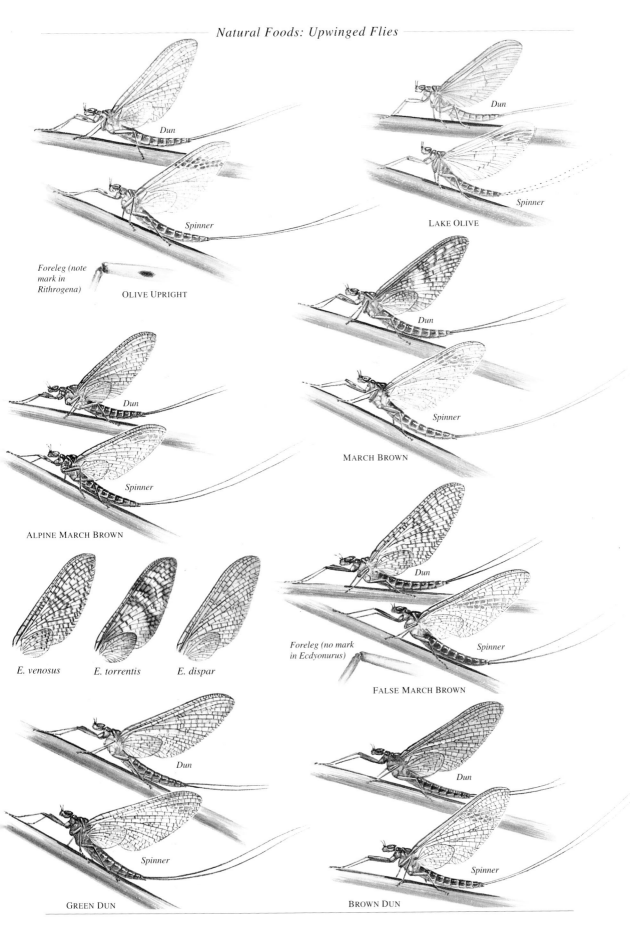

Dun

Spinner

Foreleg (note mark in Rithrogena)

OLIVE UPRIGHT

LAKE OLIVE

Dun

Spinner

Dun

Spinner

MARCH BROWN

Dun

Spinner

ALPINE MARCH BROWN

E. venosus   *E. torrentis*   *E. dispar*

Dun

Spinner

Foreleg (no mark in Ecdyonurus)

FALSE MARCH BROWN

Dun

Spinner

GREEN DUN

Dun

Spinner

BROWN DUN

Dark Dun (Dusky Yellowstreak) *Heptagenia (Electrogena) lateralis*

A fly mainly of small rocky upland streams and lakes where hatches can be quite prolific. Duns hatch mid-May to late August during late morning and afternoon. Spinner fall: late afternoon and evening. Large (body 12-15mm, tails 22-29mm) with 2 tails. Dun is overall dark brown-grey with grey wings; note the yellow streak on thorax just below wing base. Spinner has dark olive brown body with last three segments orange brown, brighter red rings at boundaries between segments; wings transparent with brown veins; tails brown.

Yellow Dun (Yellow May Dun) *Heptagenia sulphurea*

Widespread on rough, rocky rivers, occasionally rocky lakes; especially abundant in limestone streams. Duns hatch May-July, late morning and through afternoon. Spinner fall: evening. It has been said that fish do not like to eat this fly: this is not the case on some rivers where hatches are large. Superficially resembles the Yellow Mayfly (p. 42) and the Yellow Evening Dun (p. 44), but is a deeper, richer yellow; also look for 2 (not 3) tails. Body length 10-12mm and tails 12-16mm. The dun is bright sulphur yellow, including brown-veined wings; tails grey. Spinner bright golden-brown with pale lemon underside, with dark-veined transparent wings and brown-ringed pale yellow tails.

A very similar species, *H. flava*, occurs in rough, rocky rivers of central and southeastern Europe; dun hatches June-July. Overall coloration is a little duller orange-yellow than the former species.

Nixe *Nixe joernensis*

A species of small rivers and streams in Fenno-Scandinavia and NW Russia. Dun hatches late July-August, afternoon; spinner fall evening. Body 7-8mm, tails 8-12mm, with 2 tails. Dun: body olive-brown, darker above; wings mid-grey with olive tinge at base; tails dark brown. Spinner: body olive-green above, yellow-olive below; wings transparent with pale grey veins; tails brown.

Epeorus *Epeorus assimilis*

In clean, rough rocky streams through southern, central and eastern Europe (not Britain). Duns hatch underwater, late March to early June during afternoon. Spinner fall: evening. Large (body length 14-17mm, tails 35-45mm) with 2 tails. Dun: body dull yellow-straw to dark olive, dark angular markings on abdominal segments; wings yellow-brown with blackish veins; tails yellow brown with red ringing. Spinner body: pale yellow or green-olive with dark markings; wings transparent with black veins; tails dark brown.

Arctic Dun *Metropus norvegicus*

A fly of clean northern arctic and subarctic streams; also occurs on small 'river-lakes' in this region.

Duns hatch late morning and afternoon late June to August. Spinner fall: evening. Medium-sized (body 9-12mm, tails 12-22mm) with 2 tails. Dun overall a light olive-brown. Spinner translucent golden- or straw-brown with wings transparent with brown veins, except for a single opaque patch at front.

Summer Mayfly (or Large Summer Dun) *Siphlonurus* species

Five very similar European species occur in clean lakes and large slow-flowing rivers; and especially common in northern and upland regions. Duns hatch during afternoon-evening in June-August. Spinner fall: evening. A very large upwinged fly (body 14-21mm, tails 20-35mm) with 2 tails. Dun has body olive-brown with dark brown banding; wings grey, brown-grey or olive-grey. Spinner: body generally dark brown or red-brown with paler banding which may have distinct olive hue; wings transparent with dark veins.

Upland Dun *Ameletus inopinatus*

A species of arctic, subarctic or upland (about 450 metres or more) streams and rocky lakes in Fenno-Scandinavia, C. and SE Europe and N. Britain. Duns hatch June-July, afternoon and evening. Spinner fall: evening. A medium-sized fly (body 9-12mm, tails 11-16mm) with 2 tails. Dun: body brown-black with dark red-brown banding on abdomen; wings grey with dark veins; tails blackish. Spinner very similar to dun, but with clear transparent wings with dark veins.

Palingenia *Palingenia longicauda*

A species inhabiting large clean rivers in SE Europe. Duns hatch from late morning and through the afternoon in June-early August. Spinner fall: late afternoon-evening A huge upwinged fly (body 25-40mm, tails 50-120mm) with 2 tails. The dun has body warm yellow-brown or yellow-buff with dark grey-brown band down back, wings dark buffish-grey; tails yellow. Spinner: as dun (Palingenia is unusual in that female dun does not moult to spinner stage)

Ephoron *Ephoron (Polymitarcys) virgo*

Abundant on large slow rivers and lakes, S and C Europe. Duns hatch afternoon to evening, August-September. Spinner fall: late evening or dawn. Body 9-13mm, tails 15-30mm, with 2 tails in male and 3 in female (unique in Europe). Legs very weak, so male duns moult to spinner in the air and mate immediately with female, dun hatch to spinner fall usually taking 1-2 hours. Dun: body pale yellow with greenish tinge above and paler below; wings semi-opaque and milky white; tails pale grey or cream. Spinner: like Palingenia, female Ephoron does not moult so spinner is identical to the dun. Male spinner similar to dun except that the wings are more opaque.

DARK DUN

Dun

Spinner

YELLOW DUN

Dun

Spinner

NIXE

Dun

Spinner

ARCTIC DUN

Dun

Spnner

EPEORUS

Dun

Spinner

SUMMER MAYFLY

Dun

Spinner

UPLAND DUN

Dun

Spinner

PALINGENIA

EPHORON

STONEFLIES
Order Plecoptera

Life cycle — incomplete metamorphosis. Small nymphs hatch from eggs. These feed and grow, moulting their old exoskeleton and growing a new one at regular intervals. When fully grown — after one year in most species, but 2-3 years in the large stoneflies — the nymphs usually emerge from the water by crawling ashore or climbing up emerging vegetation or boulders. Here the adult moults from the nymphal shuck. Mating occurs on land or among vegetation (in many species the males have reduced wings and are flightless). The females then return to the water to lay their eggs.

Stonefly Nymphs

Stonefly nymphs are identified by two longish slender tails at the end of a tapering abdomen, a thorax with wing buds (more pronounced in older nymphs) attached to its upper surface, 3 pairs of legs, and a head bearing a pair of antennae and simple inconspicuous jaws. Gills are never visible on the abdomen (if present at all, then gills on underside of thorax).

For anglers and fish, stonefly nymphs are all fairly similar in structure and life-style: variation exists in size — large stoneflies (*Perla, Perlodes* and *Dinocras*) may reach 2.5cm, but in some species barely attain 5mm. The nymphs of most species have stoutish bodies, though some (e.g. Leuctra) are more slender. Identification to species is both difficult and pointless, requiring complex keys and microscopic examination (though Yellow Sally nymphs exhibit the yellow coloration of the adult). Stonefly nymphs occur only in the cleanest of water (both lakes and rivers) and are the first aquatic invertebrates to disappear when a water becomes polluted.

Stonefly nymphs are 'stonecrawlers'; they live by crawling on and among gravel and stones on the bottom; they cannot swim. In some regions the nymphs of the large stoneflies are known as 'creepers'; they are collected from among boulders in the shallows (usually in May-June when they are fully grown) and provide a very effective fish bait. Traditionally, natural stonefly 'creepers' were fished by casting them upstream on fly-fishing tackle; today artificial stonefly nymphs are fished in exactly the same way.

Fully-grown stonefly nymphs crawl from the water, usually at night, the adult emerging from the nymphal shuck in waterside vegetation or boulders. Thus fish will feed on stonefly nymphs only when they have been washed from the riverbed by a spate or when the fish are grubbing among stones on the bottom. For imitations of stonefly nymphs see pp. 167-9. Note also some soft-hackled flies are excellent stonefly nymphs, e.g. Orange Partridge, p. 128, Winter Brown, p. 130.

Adult Stoneflies

Adult stoneflies are identified by 2 stout tails at end of abdomen (or tails reduced to tiny stumps and may appear to be missing); 2 pairs of smooth wings lying either flat over body or folded tightly around body when at rest (in males wings sometimes reduced — these males sometimes confused with nymphs); antennae of moderate length. Flight very weak, with 2 pairs of wings fluttering separately in a seemingly uncoordinated manner.

Because adults emerge from nymphal shuck and mating occurs on dry land, the chief opportunity for fish to feed on adult stoneflies is when the females return to the water to lay their eggs (though occasionally some stoneflies that have hatched on emerging vegetation and boulders fall or are blown by the wind onto the water). Egg laying may occur in one of two ways: 1. female swims over water, creating much disturbance (and attracting fish as she does so), releasing eggs; 2. female flies over water and momentarily dips to the surface to release eggs from the tip of her abdomen (sometimes fish will leap from the water to take such females). In both cases many females die on the water, spent, after egg laying is complete.

Only a few of the 150 European species of stoneflies have received an anglers name; often that name applies to several scientific species (not always members of the same genus). As in the nymphs, identification to scientific species is often both pointless and difficult for anglers. Instead, identify to anglers' stoneflies using the following characters: size, general coloration, and, to a lesser extent, overall shape (e.g. how wings are held over body), and time of emergence of adult.

For imitations of adult stoneflies see pp. 138, 170. Several soft hasckled wet flies are also useful imitations: see pp. 128, 130, 134.

Large Stonefly *Perla, Perlodes, Dinocras*
The large stonefly occurs, often in large numbers, in clean rough rocky rivers and streams (also, especially Perlodes, occasionally shores of barren stony lakes). The adults hatch late April-July (occasionally from March and to late August). Egg laying is by the female swimming on water surface, afternoon-evening.

Length up to 3cm; wingspan 6cm. All adult females have 2 longish tails (as found in all stonefly nymphs), 2 fairly long antennae, and 2 pairs of long dark brown-veined wings. Overall colour dark brown, with some lighter brown markings. In some species body orange-brown; wings dark brown. Often the males have reduced wings and are flightless: frequently found in cover by water but rarely seen on the water.

Perlodes

STONEFLY NYMPHS

Leuctra (p. 54)

Dead, spent ♀ ♀ Stoneflies

Newly emerged adult

Nymphal shuck on stone

LARGE STONEFLY

MEDIUM STONEFLY

SMALL BROWN

Medium Stonefly *Diura*

Medium stoneflies occur commonly by rough rocky streams and the shores of barren stony lakes (often at high altitudes or in more northerly regions). Nymphs leave the water and adults hatch April-July (occasionally August). The females lay their eggs on the water both in flight and by swimming on water surface, afternoon-evening.

Length up to 1.8cm; wingspan 3cm. Tails absent or reduced to very short stumps and appear to be missing, 2 long antennae, 2 pairs dark glossy brown wings held folded around body when at rest. Overall body colour dark brown.

Small Brown *Nemoura, Nemurella, Amphinemura*

Small browns occur in all types of clean flowing water (different scientific species in different sorts of river — rough upland streams, subarctic waters, alpine streams, slow weedy lowland rivers, but species are difficult to separate). The adults hatch March-July (occasionally to November). Egg laying is predominantly carried out in flight (though occasionally large numbers of females may be seen swimming on the surface to deposit eggs), afternoon and evening.

Up to 1cm long (females; males smaller). Tails absent, 2 long antennae, 2 pairs of dark glossy brown wings held flat over body. Overall body colour very dark brown.

Black Stoneflies *Capnia, Capnopsis*

Black stoneflies are often abundant by stony lakes and fast rocky streams, throughout much of Europe. Adults hatch February-May in areas not frozen in winter, otherwise May-July. Egg laying carried out both in flight and by female swimming on water.

Usually small insects with a body length of 4-10mm. Two longish slender tails; 2 long antennae, 2 pairs of black-veined transparent grey wings. Body colour black.

Early Brown *Protonemura*

Early browns occur commonly usually in fast-flowing rocky rivers, often to high altitude in mountainous regions. The adults hatch March-May (occasionally June); or after ice-melt. Egg laying is predominantly carried out in flight, afternoon and evening.

Length up to 1cm (in females; males smaller). Tails absent, 2 long antennae, 2 pairs of pale grey-brown wings held flat over body. Overall body colour light-medium brown.

February Red *Brachyptera* and *Taeniopteryx*

February reds occur in slow-flowing lowland rivers that have areas of silt bottom, the prefered niche of their nymphs. The adults hatch February-April (in rivers that are frozen through the winter, soon after the thaw), occasionally to July (in *Brachyptera*). Egg laying is carried out both in flight and by the female swimming on water, afternoon.

Length up to 1.3cm (in females; males shorter). Tails absent; 2 long antennae; 2 pairs of dark red-brown wings with darker veining held fairly flat over body at rest. Overall body colour brown or reddish-brown, sometimes with undersurface of abdomen and/or terminal abdominal segments a warm dark orange or brown-orange (during a large hatch or fall of females some variation will be noticed).

Needle Fly/Willow Fly *Leuctra*

Probably the most widespread of stoneflies, occurring in upland stony fast-flowing rivers, chalk-streams and lowland silty rivers; also in clean stony lakes. Adults hatch July-November (peak August-September). Egg laying carried out predominantly in flight (but occasionally by females swimming).

Length up to 1cm (in females; males shorter) — smaller often referred to as needle flies, larger as willow flies (but many anglers use alternative names randomly). Tails absent, 2 long antennae, 2 pairs of dark brown or blackish-brown wings folded tightly around body at rest which makes them appear extremely slender (hence 'needle fly'). Overall body colour dark brown.

Yellow Sally *Isoperla*

All clean rivers, especially those flowing over limestone; less common at high altitudes. Adults hatch April-August. Egg laying often carried out by females swimming, but sometimes also in flight

Length up to 14mm (in females; males shorter). 2 tails; 2 long antennae; 2 pairs of wings held flat over body. Overall coloration lemon-yellow.

Small Yellow Sally *Chloroperla, Xanthoperla, Siphonoperla*

Widespread, especially in northern and upland districts, in rough stony rivers and rocky barren lakes. Adults hatch April-July (occasionally to August). Egg laying predominantly carried out in flight

Length up to 8mm (in females; males shorter). 2 tails; 2 long antennae; 2 pairs of wings held flat over body. Overall coloration pale yellow.

Despite their abundance in all clean European lakes and rivers, adult stoneflies can appear to be quite scarce. Remember that they emerge by crawling from the water, so you will find more adults *by* rather than *on* the water.

With the exception of large stoneflies, the females that have returned to the water can be inconspicuous because they sit low, rather than high, in the water surface (as do upwinged fly duns).

BLACK STONEFLY

EARLY BROWN

FEBRUARY RED

NEEDLE FLY

YELLOW SALLY

SMALL YELLOW SALLY

WATER-BUGS
Order Hemiptera

Life cycle — incomplete metamorphosis. The eggs hatch into nymphs; water-bug nymphs resemble adults, but are smaller and lack wings. Nymphs moult several times as they grow, the last moult resulting in the emergence of the adult stage. Adult water-bugs are small to medium sized with great variety of form. Some unmistakable species live on the water surface film; others live under the surface and are easily confused with water beetles. They have long pointed syringe-like mouthparts (blunt in lesser waterboatman), held under head when not feeding. Some species are wingless. In those where the adults are winged, only part of forewing is hard and thickened, the rest being soft and membranous, and the forewings overlap (in beetles the wings meet in a straight line along the back). For imitations see p. 174; also CDC Water-boatman p. 141.

Water-bugs that live on the water surface

Water Measurer *Hydrometra* species
Widespread and sometimes abundant on still or very slow-flowing waters. Very slender bugs 10-13mm long with extremely long legs, head and antennae. Most are wingless. Very dark brown overall.

Water Cricket *Velia* species
Widespread and often numerous, water crickets occur on canals, small pools and, on rivers, on slack water close to the main flow. These are sturdy bugs, up to 9mm long, with long legs. Usually brown.

Pond Skaters *Gerris* species
Occur on all sorts of waters, including slow-flowing rivers, canals, ponds and large lakes. They are slender bugs 15-17mm long, with long legs; the 2 rear pairs of legs conspicuously angled backwards and separated from the front forward-pointing pair. They are always winged. General coloration dark brown.

Fish will rise to take these surface-living water-bugs should they stray into open water; some fish cruise through margins and edges of weedbeds in lakes and slow rivers, in search of food including surface water-bugs. Despite this, few anglers have sought to imitate these.

Water-bugs that live below the surface

Lesser Water-boatman Family Corixidae
Widespread throughout Europe; often occurs in very high concentrations. Identifiction to species requires very detailed keys and a microscope.

The smaller species are up to 3-4mm long; the largest up to 12-14mm. Larger species are commoner in stillwaters or low-flowing canals and fenland drains, though several smaller species are abundant in clean rivers where the bottom is sand or gravel. All species have a characteristic flattened rowing-boat shape (see also water-boatman, below), with rear 2 pairs of legs very long, flattened and fringed with hairs (= oars) for swimming. Back flat and usually dark brown or blackish, underside whitish to pale buff. Swims back uppermost (cf water-boatman). Mouthparts are very blunt (they cannot pierce human skin).

Water-boatman *Notonecta* species
Especially abundant in stillwaters and canals, particularly among weedbeds. They are usually larger than lesser water-boatman (that they superficially resemble) with a maximum length 16mm. The back is dark brown or blackish, the underside pale buff or silvery-white. Shape as lesser water-boatman, but back has distinct keel. Swims back downwards (cf lesser water-boatman). Mouthparts are very long and sharp (can pierce human skin).

Water Scorpion *Nepa, Ranatra*
Both *Nepa* and *Ranatra* occur in still or slow-flowing weedy waters; often overlooked because of their slow movement and camouflage.

Ranatra occurs in southern and central Europe; *Nepa* is found through much of central and northern Europe. *Nepa* is up to 23mm long, with a broad and flattened body, a long 'tail' (breathing tube), and sturdy legs (front pair used to grasp prey — invertebrates, tadpoles, small fishes); coloration brown. *Ranatra* is up to 35mm long, with a very slender body, a long 'tail', and thin legs (front pair used to grasp prey); coloration brown.

Saucer Bugs *Ilyocoris, Aphelocheirus*
Broad, flattened bugs (some are almost circular, hence the name 'saucer') up to 16mm long. They have sturdy forelegs that are used to grab prey which are then pierced with long sharp mouthparts (this tubular mouth can inflict painful wound in human skin). Dark brown. Some live in weedbeds in stillwater; others among gravel of streams.

~

It was once argued that trout rarely eat water-bugs (despite the fact that lesser water-boatmen often feature in stomach analyses). But the fish do take these bugs and the scarcity of water-bugs in open water is due to the fish eating them quickly when they appear. Water scorpions and saucer bugs have never been considered worthy of imitation by anglers (only occasionally is one found in a fish's stomach). Lesser water-boatmen and, to a lesser extent, water-boatmen have been imitated, with greatest effect in smaller lakes, fished in the margins or close to weedbeds to imitate a real insect that has strayed from cover. They are especially effective in rivers for grayling fishing in late summer and autumn.

WATER MEASURER

WATER CRICKET

POND SKATER

LESSER WATER-BOATMAN

WATER-BOATMAN

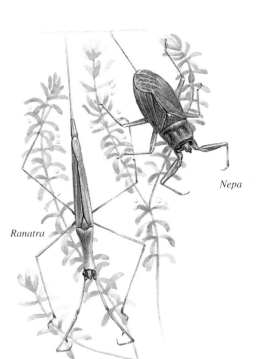

Ranatra

Nepa

SAUCER BUG

WATER SCORPION

LAND-BUGS

Many species of land-bug fall or are blown onto the water, sometimes in considerable numbers, and are eaten by fish. Of all the possible species that may be encountered, four are highlighted to indicate potential angling situations and suggest artificial flies that would cope adequately. For imitations see p. 174. Also Green Insect, p. 130.

Green Shield Bug *Palomena prasina*

An extremely abundant species, especially in late summer and autumn, in tree canopies and bushes; often falls onto the water. Trout and grayling, lying in heavily wooded streams, have been known to feed selectively on them and autopsies have revealed stomachs crammed with them.

Body characteristically 'shield-shaped', up to 10mm long and 7mm wide. Coloration emerald green, except for buff membranous tips to forewings.

Chinch-bug *Ischnodemus sabuleti*

Often very abundant in rank grasses and reeds close to the waterside. In breezy weather large numbers of the short-winged flightless form may fall onto the water. Trout, grayling and chub have been known to feed on chinch-bugs selectively; autopsies have revealed stomachs crammed with them.

Body about 4-5mm long and fairly slender. There are two varieties: a fully winged form and a short-winged flightless form. In the latter, the abdominal segmentation is quite distinct. Coloration black, with brown wings and legs.

Froghoppers (Aphrophoridae) and Leafhoppers (Cicadellidae)

Two large families of land bugs, several species of which occur in huge numbers in grasslands, on bushes and in trees. During the summer and early autumn many find themselves on the water surface, where they are eaten by trout and grayling; autopsies have revealed stomachs crammed with them.

Most species have a maximum body length of about 10mm; shape an elongate ovoid. Colour varies, but usually some shade of buff-brown or olive-green. They can jump a considerable distance.

Greenfly and Blackfly (Aphids)

These tiny insects, well-known as pests in gardens, occur in immense numbers on grasses and the leaves of trees and bushes (sycamore is often particularly badly infected). During 'plague years' huge swarms may be blown onto the water in summer and early autumn. During leaf-fall, huge numbers fall onto the water with the leaves; trout and grayling have often been seen nudging newly-fallen leaves to take aphids that are still clinging to them. Fish that are feeding on aphids can be obsessively selective; autopsy usually reveals a green, partly digested aphid sludge. Greenfly seem to be more important than black aphids as a fish food.

They are tiny, with a body length of only 2-3mm. They may be winged or wingless. Body pale green in greenfly, black in blackfly; other species are dark purple or darker green.

One clue to when fish are feeding on land-bugs is that they will be feeding at the surface but no food is visible on the surface: these tiny insects usually lie in the surface film. Thus they are often overlooked by anglers, who wrongly consider that the fish are 'nymphing' or 'smutting' (taking nymphs or reed-smutts from just below the surface). An artificial fly, with the correct size, general shape and colour, will often succeed, provided that it too is fished in the surface filmand not on the surface.

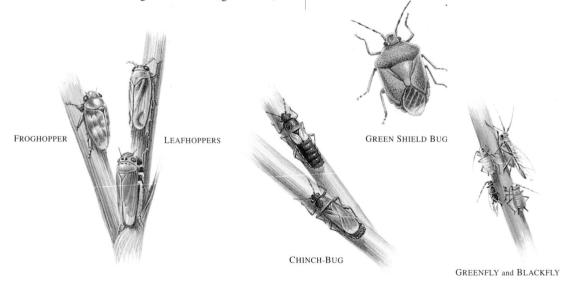

FROGHOPPER   LEAFHOPPERS   GREEN SHIELD BUG   CHINCH-BUG   GREENFLY and BLACKFLY

DRAGONFLIES AND DAMSELFLIES
Order Odonata

Life cycle — incomplete metamorphosis. The eggs hatch into tiny nymphs which feed initially on small invertebrates and later on larger invertebrates, tiny fish and amphibians. During the nymph stage growth is rapid; the growing nymph moults its exoskeleton several times. When fully-grown, nymphs move to emergent vegetation, up which they climb from the water before finally moulting into the adult.

Although well-known aquatic insects, dragonflies are of minimal importance as food for trout and grayling. The nymphs are inconspicuous as they hide away in the weediest water; they move slowly and are well camouflaged. Adult dragonflies are rarely seen on the water.

By contrast damselflies are eaten by fish, especially in lakes and weedy streams. Damselfly nymphs usually occur in much higher densities than dragonfly nymphs. They swim well, with an undulating wriggling motion, and are especially conspicuous when swimming through the margins to reed stems, which they will climb up before moulting into the adult. For this reason an imitative damsel nymph, cast and fished through the margins or in clear water between weedbeds, is very effective from late spring to autumn. Adult damselflies often fly low over the water: occasionally fish will rise to take them from the air. Most adult damselflies (females) are taken during or after egg-laying: they walk backwards down reed stems, until the abdomen is well below the waterline, to lay their eggs on or in the reed stem. Trout, cruising in the margins, will take these egg-laying damselflies from the reeds.

Dragonfly and Damselfly Nymphs

These are identified by three flattened plate-like tails at the end of the abdomen (in damselflies), or the abdomen ends in three triangular points (in dragonflies). Wing buds often very conspicuous, especially in older, larger nymphs. Mouthparts large, hinged, and kept folded under head unless feeding. 3 pairs of legs; fairly slender in damselflies, sturdier in dragonflies. Body shape varies: usually long and very slender in damsel-flies; shorter, stouter and sometimes quite rounded in dragon-flies.

Dragonfly and damselfly nymphs are found in most clean water: small and large lakes, weedy fenland drains, canals and weedy margins of rivers. Dragonfly nymphs occur in weedier areas than damselfly nymphs. For imitations see pp. 140, 172.

DAMSELFLY NYMPH

DRAGONFLY NYMPH

Adult Dragonflies and Damselflies

Often very large and gaudy, and well known. They have 2 pairs of long gauzy wings – at rest held folded back over body in damselflies, spread apart at either side in dragonflies. Abdomen long, slender in damselflies but often quite stout in dragonflies.

As stated above, dragonflies are of little practical importance to anglers; adult damselflies are sometimes eaten in large numbers by fish. Although many species of damselflies have been recorded in Europe, in practice only two matter to us:

Common Blue Damselfly *Enallagma cyathigerum*
This is the commonest of several species in which the abdomen is bright metallic blue (in males; in females often metallic green and black).

Large Red Damselfly *Pyrrhosoma nymphula*
A widespread species through much of Europe with metallic red and black markings on the abdomen.

Both of these species are widespread through most of Europe; many other species that may be encountered are superficially very similar in appearance to these two species. For imitations see p. 173.

COMMON BLUE DAMSELFLY

LARGE RED DAMSELFLY

BANDED DAMSEL

SEDGES (CADDIS-FLIES)
Order Trichoptera

Life cycle: complete metamorphosis. Larvae of most species live in caddis cases constructed from sand, small stones, bits of twig, leaves or pondweed. Larvae of several (usually river) species construct gallery-like tubes of silk, sometimes with covering of silt, on or among stones. One group of sedges has free-living larvae feeding on lesser invertebrates, fish eggs and tiny fish fry. All sedge larvae (including cased forms that have lost their case) can be identified by their elongate body; exoskeleton very hard and thickened on head and plates on thorax, otherwise body very soft; three pairs of legs. At end of abdomen is a pair of short, hooked extensions called 'prolegs'. In cased caddis larvae the first abdominal segment has extensions to which the case is attached. Pupae occur in caddis cases (where the larvae are caseless, a case of tiny stones or sand is constructed just before pupation). Under close examination pupal cases can be separated from larval cases by the two entrances being blocked.

Adults vary from about 5mm ('microcaddis') to 60+mm (great red sedge). They superficially resemble moths and alderflies, but the wings are held tent-like over body at rest (flat in moths) and are covered with fine hairs (loose scales in moths and bare membrane wings in alders). Antennae usually long (in some greater than body length). Colour often a shade of brown, though some black.

Sedge (Caddis) Larvae.

There are three important groups of sedge larvae, related to niche in river/lake:

Free-living larvae: Family Rhyacophilidae

These caseless larvae live among boulders, or among growths of aquatic mosses or weed, on the bed of clean, especially rocky rivers. They are the only caddis larvae that construct no protective covering at all; usually they belay themselves to the river bed by a length of silk to prevent them being washed away by the currents. They are identified by a green colour and large tufts of gills on each abdominal segment. Their relatively large size (up to 20mm long) and free-living habits contributes to them being a major component of the diet of river fish. Rhyacophila larvae are carnivores, devouring lesser invertebrates including upwinged-fly and stonefly nymphs, chironomid larvae and smaller sedge larvae. They have also been recorded preying on the large eggs of salmon, grayling and trout.

Net-spinning larvae: Families Hydropsychidae, Philopotamidae, Polycentropidae, Psychomyiidae

Most of these larvae occur in rivers, but some are found in lakes (especially near inflowing and out-flowing streams). They are caseless, though they construct nets of various forms from silk (in some species the net becomes covered with silt and appears as a muddy tube or gallery); the net shelters the larva and is often also used to trap food. Huge numbers of nets can sometimes be found, in late spring and summer, among beds of aquatic moss and gravel, and on boulders; the larvae are territorial so that, when densities are high, there is often a fairly regular spacing between them. During spring and summer, when the larvae are growing quickly, many larvae lose their territories (they are forced out by other larvae) and they drift downstream. Fish devour large numbers of these drifting larvae. While it is possible to identify these net-making caseless caddis larvae from the form of their net, in practice it is difficult because the nets collapse into a shapeless mush when removed from the water. Net-spinning larvae are usually a shade of brown or buff in colour with a darker head; they may reach up to 3cm long.

Cased caddis

It is possible to identify some cased caddis larvae to genus, and perhaps species, from the composition and arrangement of materials in the case. The larval case of the great red sedge *Phryganea grandis* is invariably composed of vegetable matter, laid longitudinally in the case but with a spiral arrangement. The case of the medium sedge *Goera pilosa* is invariably made of sand grains with a row of larger pebbles along each side. The case of the brown sedge *Anabolia nervosa* consists mainly of small stones or coarse sand grains, but with pieces of twig attached along the case that extend beyond the case at both ends. The larval cases of the grousewing *Mystacides*, Welshman's button *Sericostoma* and some of the silverhorns *Athripsodes* are curved, taper to a point at the 'tail end' and are composed of sand grains or very tiny pebbles.

In many species the composition and form of the case may vary according to the material available, the time of year and age of the larva. The larval case of the cinnamon sedge *Limnephilus lunatus*, though usually made from plant material, may also be constructed with tiny pieces of gravel or shell. The larval case of the caperer *Halesus* may consist of plant material, or sand, or small stones or resemble that of the brown sedge (see above) by having long twigs attached. In such cases identification of cased caddis must be confirmed by examination of the larva, something that requires a more detailed key and close examination with a hand lens.

While cased caddis larvae are a very important source of food for fish, there is no evidence that feeding fish select certain species and reject others. For imitations of caddis larvae see p. 176; also p. 141 for CDC Caseless Caddis imitations.

Rhyacophila free-living larvae

Hydropsyche net spinner

Disturbed and disposessed Hydropsyche larvae

Snare nets of Hydropsyche

NET SPINNING LARVAE

HALESUS

PHRYGANEA

LIMNEPHILUS

ANABOLIA

CASED CADDIS LARVAE

GOERA

Larva removed from its case

Sedge (Caddis) Pupae

All caddis, whether cased or uncased in the larval stage, have a cased pupa. In the cased caddis larvae, the larval case is attached to a stable substrate with silk threads and the front entrance and rear exit blocked. In uncased caddis, the fully-grown larvae construct a case from small pieces of sand or gravel which is firmly anchored, with silk threads, to a stone.

Three completely distinct stages of the sedge life cycle may occur within the pupal case (hence care should be exercised when opening up a case to identify what is inside):

1. the fully grown larva may rest for a period of between three or four days and three or four months (this is still a larva for it has not spun its pupal cocoon, within which the transformation to adult occurs);

2. the true pupa stage (the larva, within its stone case, spins a silk cocoon which hardens to a medium- to dark brown case within which the larval tissues are reorganised to produce the adult sedge. This stage may last from a few days to several weeks.);

3. the adult stage which may remain in the pupal case for several days before emergence. The adult, in this condition, is referred to as a 'pharate adult', from the Greek *pharos* meaning 'clothed': the adult is clothed loosely in a fine semi-transparent sheath within the pupal cocoon.

Emergence of the adult

The pharate adult sedge cuts through the brown pupal cocoon and stone/vegetation case and emerges into the water enclosed in its semi-transparent sheath. The adult may leave the water in one of three ways:

1. by crawling along the river or lake bed, enclosed in the pupal sheath;

2. by drifting for a short time deep in the water, as the pupal sheath is filled with air, before swimming close to the river or lake bed to the shore;

3. by a combination of swimming, assisted by the buoyant sheath, vertically to the water surface. In all 3 cases the sheath is shed just before adult leaves the water.

Large numbers of 'pharate adults' are eaten by fish in the period between them leaving the pupal case and emerging into the air. Pharate adults are often called 'pupae' by anglers. Because of this angling convention, we will use this latter term when considering imitations on pp. 140, 178-80.

Adult Sedges (or Caddis Flies)

About 400 species of sedge have been recorded in Europe; and although some of these are quite rare or local in distribution, nevertheless there are still more common scientific species than "anglers' sedges". Generally, anglers' names of sedges bear no relationship to scientific classification: they are based on size and coloration rather than fine anatomical detail. Where one scientific species has been given a name by anglers in one region, often the same name can be applied to other species. Also some 'anglers' sedges' often include several scientific species, often of different families or genera. So the identification of anglers' sedges is based on: size (this can vary within one species); coloration (this can also vary slightly; note that newly-hatched adult sedges tend to be paler than those that have hatched some time); length of antennae; the sort of water from which the adult emerges (river, lake etc.); the timing of the hatch (many adult sedges are most active at dusk and in the night; some are also active in the day).

Large numbers of adult sedges are taken by fish: newly-emerged sedges resting on or skittering across the water surface before leaving the water; females crawling on the water surface or swimming beneath the water surface during egg laying ('diving sedges'); females that have died 'spent' after egg laying. For adult sedge imitations see p. 180-7; also pp. 132, 136, 138.

Great Red Sedge (or **Murragh**) *Phryganea grandis* and *P. bipunctata*

A widespread and often abundant sedge of stillwaters and, to a lesser extent, the large slow pools of big rivers. Adults emerge in the evening and through the night at the water surface and scuttle across the surface film to the shore; peak hatch occurs from late May to mid-July. The largest common sedge with a forewing length of 25-30mm and overall length of 60mm including antennae. Body grey; forewing red-brown with blackish markings; antennae stout and as long as or slightly shorter than forewing.

[Green] Peter *Agrypnia (Phryganea) obsoleta*

A lake sedge. Adults emerge from late afternoon at the water surface and scuttle across the surface to the shore; peak hatch occurs from late June to August. A medium-sized sedge with a forewing length of about 12mm. Body olive-green or occasionally dark olive; forewing dark brown with indistinct paler areas; antennae stout, not quite as long as the forewing.

[Speckled] Peter *Agrypnia (Phryganea) varia*

A common lake species in some areas; also occurs in bigger slow clean lowland rivers. Adults usually emerge in the evening at the water surface from July to September. Resembles the green Peter but is slightly larger, with a wing length of up to 16mm. Forewing coloration slightly different in that it is has distinct white speckles that give the wing a mottled appearance.

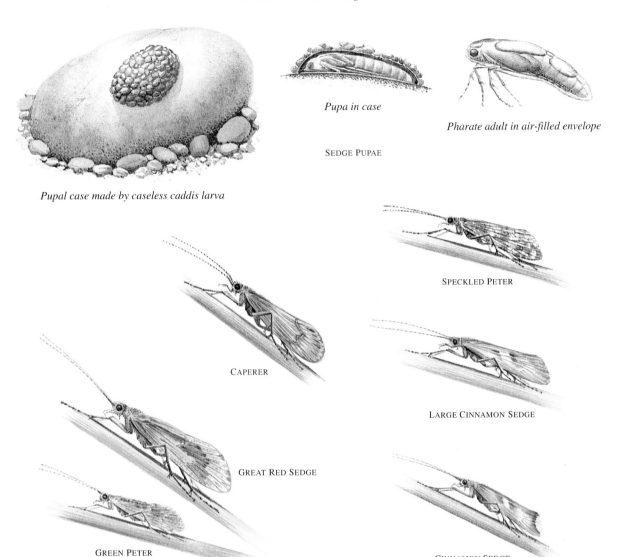

Pupa in case

Pharate adult in air-filled envelope

SEDGE PUPAE

Pupal case made by caseless caddis larva

SPECKLED PETER

CAPERER

LARGE CINNAMON SEDGE

GREAT RED SEDGE

GREEN PETER

CINNAMON SEDGE

Caperer *Halesus digitatus, H. radiatus*

A conspicuous river sedge hatching between August and early November in late afternoon and evening.

A large sedge with forewing length of about 20-23mm. Body colour varies from warm cinnamon to olive brown; wing colour yellow- or buff-brown with irregular oblique blackish bars or streaks towards the tips; antennae slightly longer than forewing, stout.

Large Cinnamon Sedge *Potamophyllax and Limnephilus*

Primarily a river sedge, also in some lakes close to feeder streams; hatches in peak numbers through the evenings during July and August.

A very common sedge that resembles the caperer. It is very slightly smaller with a wing length of up to 18mm; the yellow-brown (cinnamon) forewings often have a small but characteristic pale patch in the centre; and the body has a distinct olive tinge. The stout antennae are not quite as long as the wings.

Cinnamon Sedge *Limnephilus* species

This sedge occurs in both lakes and rivers (mainly fairly slow reaches); hatches, usually small, occur throughout the day and evening. Most emerge at the water surface close to reeds, rushes etc. in the margins where cruising trout often seek them. Though the name 'cinnamon' is often given to L. lunatus, many others have similar appearances.

A smaller version of the large cinnamon, with a wing length of 13-15mm. The forewings are rich deep buff-yellow with brown or blackish markings; some species have a pale moon-shaped patch on the forewing. The body varies from olive to bright green (in some males). The antennae are about the same length as the wings.

Sand-fly *Rhyacophila dorsalis*

A widespread river sedge that is especially abundant in faster, well-oxygenated streams. Large numbers hatch during the late afternoon and evening from early April to November.

Perhaps the most variable of all sedges, with a forewing length of 8-15mm, a green or olive body colour and a forewing colour that varies from pale sandy brown to dark brown; the antennae are shorter than the forewings and very fine.

Chestnut-winged Sedge *Triaenodes bicolor*

A sedge of the margins of small weedy upland or northern stillwaters, hatching through the afternoon and early evening from June to September.

A medium-sized sedge with a forewing length of up to 10mm. Body colour is light brown; forewing colour a rich chestnut brown; antennae almost twice as long as the forewing and very slender.

Medium Sedge *Goera pilosa*

One of the most widespread and abundant species of sedges, occurring in lakes and rivers. It is one of the few species to hatch through the day as well as in the evening, from late April to September.

Well named, this is a medium-sized species (forewing 10-12mm), with an overall medium buff-brown coloration. The almost uniform buff wings have a greyish cast; the antennae are very short and stout.

Brown Sedge *Anabolia nervosa, Plectrocnemia conspersa, P. geniculata, Hydropsyche angustipennis*

This is a good example of the way the angler's sedges bear little relationship with the scientific taxonomy of the Order Trichoptera! Here we have four species (more might be included) in three genera under the angler's umbrella of 'brown sedge'. Common and often abundant on both rivers and lakes, at least one species emerges throughout the period from late April to November during the evening.

They are all medium sized sedges, with a forewing length of up to 14-16mm, and their coloration – body and forewing – is a medium to dark brown.

Welshman's Button *Sericostoma personatum*

The Welshman's Button is, correctly, an artificial fly that was used in Wales to imitate cockchafers (Robert Lascelles, *A Series of Letters on Angling, Shooting & Coursing* in three parts, 1819), consisting of a peacock herl body, black hackle and red-brown wings from a partridge tail. The great Victorian angler-entomologist F.M. Halford took this name and gave it to an imitation of a very common sedge that he then called the Welshman's button (*Modern Development of the Dry Fly*, 1910). The name stuck.

Welshman's Button is of medium size, with a forewing length of up to 15mm. Body is a dark

olive-grey; forewing dark golden- or chestnut-brown; antennae are stout and as long as the forewings. A widespread, common and conspicuous species that often occurs in large swarms over the water. It is one of the few species to hatch throughout the day from late May to late August. Although chiefly a river insect, it occurs also where inflowing streams enter lakes.

Grannom *Brachycentrus subnubilis*

A river insect of fairly local distribution. Where it does occur then it is usually abundant, occurring in dense swarms and is a major trout food species. It is commonest on chalkstreams and limestone rivers. Hatches occur through the afternoon, during March and April in the south of its range and during April and May in the north.

A medium-sized sedge, with a forewing length of about 10mm. It has an overall sandy coloration: the body is fawn, often with an olive tinge; the wings are a sandy yellow with dark brown blotches; the antennae are stout and as long as the forewings. Artificial Grannoms are invariably tied with a green tip to the abdomen which imitates the green egg mass of the mated, pre-ovipositing female.

Marbled Sedge *Hydropsyche contubernalis, H. guttata*

A common species of rougher rocky streams; hatches in the late afternoon and evening from June to early September.

One of the most beautiful of sedges, the marbled sedge is medium-sized (forewing length up to 13mm). It has a dark olive-green body, and wings that have a streaked and blotched marble-like combination of dark brown and olive-grey on a green-brown background. The antennae are as long as the body and very stout.

Mottled Sedge *Glyphotaelius pellucidus*

Rivals the marbled sedge in its beautiful coloration. Though widespread in distribution, occurs only in small weedy ponds and lakes; hatches through the evening from May to mid-October

A large sedge, with a forewing up to 18mm long; the body is a dull olive-green and the forewings are a pale silvery grey with large prominent dark brown blotches. It has short stout antennae. The tips of the wings are a further aid to identification: in most sedges the tips of the wings are rounded, in this species they are angular and notched.

Grey Flag (or **Grey Sedge** or **Silver Sedge**)
Hydropsyche instabilis, H. pellucidula and Odontocerum albicorne

All grey flags inhabit fast boulder-strewn rivers, most commonly in upland regions, though *H. pellucidula* tends to occur further downstream than the other two species where the river is somewhat

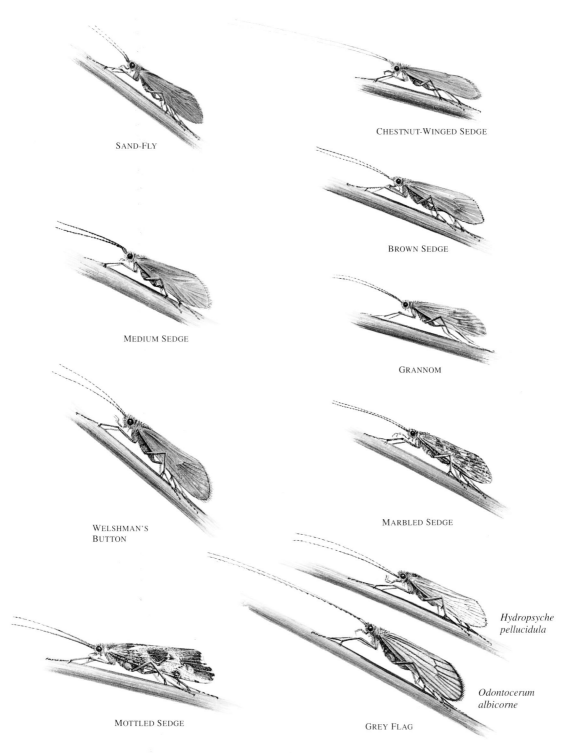

SAND-FLY

CHESTNUT-WINGED SEDGE

MEDIUM SEDGE

BROWN SEDGE

GRANNOM

WELSHMAN'S
BUTTON

MARBLED SEDGE

*Hydropsyche
pellucidula*

*Odontocerum
albicorne*

MOTTLED SEDGE

GREY FLAG

slower; it has also been recorded from lakes close to the inflowing and outflowing streams. Adults hatch throughout the day, from early June to early September; in mild weather *Odontocerum* may still be on the wing into November.

This group of species are characteristically grey in coloration, the body varying from olive-grey to brown-grey, and the wings from silvery-grey to a very dark grey with a brown cast. *Hydropsyche* species are smaller than *O. albicorne* (forewing length up to 12mm, compared with 13-18mm), but in the field this may not be apparent.

Small Red Sedge *Tinodes maclachlani,*
T. waeneri, T. assimilis

Widespread and very abundant species, occuring in a wide range of habitats from small ponds to large lakes, canals, chalkstreams and the slower reaches of spate rivers. Hatches occur from late April to early November during the late afternoon and evening.

A small sedge, with forewing length of 7-8mm and slim, conspicuously hairy, red-brown wings. Body colour dark grey- or red-brown; the antennae are much shorter than the wings and noticeably sturdy.

Yellow Sedge *Cyrnus flavidus*

A stillwater species, occurring especially in smaller weedy upland pools; hatches through the evening during late June, July and early August.

A conspicuous medium-sized sedge (forewing length up to 11mm), with olive body, yellow forewings and pale stout antennae that are about the length of the forewings. A more locally distributed river sedge, *Rhyacophila obliterata*, is also a 'yellow sedge'. It occurs only in rough, rocky rivers. It has a forewing length of 13mm, and wing length shorter than the forewing. A third 'yellow sedge' is Oecetis testacea, a species of lakes and slow rivers: this has antennae of length ´ 2 forewings.

Small Yellow Sedge *Psychomia pusilla*

Only in rivers and streams, hatching from early May through to October during the evening.

A small sedge with a forewing length of up to 6mm. General coloration yellow or yellow-buff: body varies from a rich cream to a dull yellow; the forewings a dull yellow-buff to a bright golden yellow, and the short antennae are noticeably yellow with fine brown rings.

Grousewing *Mystacides longicornis*

Occurs solely in still waters, from small ponds to larger lakes; widespread and abundant. Hatches occur from late afternoon and through the evening, from early June to late September.

Easily identified from the characteristic coloration of the forewings: they are up to 10mm long and a rich ruddy brown with three narrow conspicuous blackish bars running across them. This coloration resembles the colour of the red grouse wingcoverts, hence the name given to the insect. Body grey-brown; antennae almost three times the length of the forewing, slender and white with brown rings.

Black Silverhorns *Mystacides azurea, M. nigra,*
Arthripsodes aterrimus and *A. nigronervosus*

Occurs abundantly in both lakes and rivers; hatch through the afternoon and evening from June to late August.

Silverhorns are characterised by their extremely long slender antennae (at least twice as long as the forewings), that are grey or blackish with numerous fine white rings (*A. nigronervosus* being the exception as its antennae are uniformly black*). This combination of dark and white give the antennae a silvery grey appearance. Black silverhorns have blackish body, and slim black wings; small to medium-sized, with a forewing length of 7-10mm.

* Sometimes *A. nigronervosus* has been called the Black Sedge.

Brown Silverhorns *Arthripsodes cinereus,*
A. annulicornis, A. albifrons

Occurs abundantly in both lakes and rivers; hatch throughout the afternoon and evening from June to late August.

Similar to the black silverhorns save for general coloration: body varies from a medium olive to a dark green-brown; wings are a warm brown, uniform in *cinereus*, tipped with white in *annulicornis* and speckled with white in *albifrons*.

Longhorns *Oecetis* species

A widespread stillwater sedge, especially common in lowland areas; hatches through the afternoon and evening from late May to early October.

A most conspicuous medium-sized sedge (forewing up to 14mm) with huge antennae that are three times the length of the forewings. Overall coloration pale buff-grey: body a dull green, slim wings pale yellow or creamy grey.

Small Silver Sedge *Lepidostoma hirtum*

A widespread species, scarce in many areas but abundant in others. It occurs mostly in rivers or, in lakes, around outflowing streams. Peak hatches in the late evening through May and June with lesser numbers to mid-August.

Superficially a smaller version of the grey flag or silver sedges (see above) with a forewing length of about 9mm. Body colour varies from pale olive-brown to green and the forewings are usually grey though sometimes with a brownish cast. Antennae are slightly longer than the forewings.

Black Sedge *Silo nigricornis, S. pallipes* and
Tinodes rostocki

Silo occurs in rivers, *Tinodes* mostly in lakes and ponds. Main hatches occur in the evening during May and June.

Conspicuous black sedges that can be separated from the black silverhorns by their short stout antennae. *Tinodes* is small, with a wing length of up to 6mm; *Silo* is rather larger with a wing length of up to 10mm. They have dark grey or blackish bodies with black or blackish-brown wings.

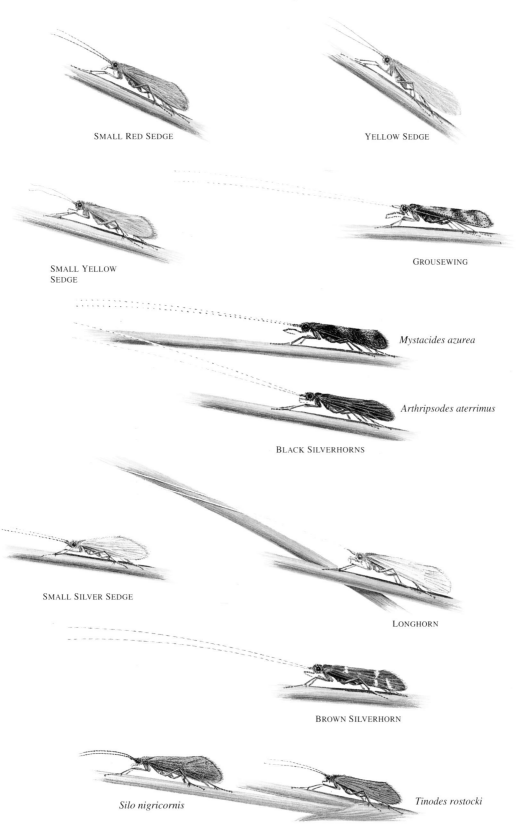

SMALL RED SEDGE

YELLOW SEDGE

SMALL YELLOW SEDGE

GROUSEWING

Mystacides azurea

Arthripsodes aterrimus

BLACK SILVERHORNS

SMALL SILVER SEDGE

LONGHORN

BROWN SILVERHORN

Silo nigricornis

Tinodes rostocki

BLACK SEDGE

Little Black Sedge *Agapetus fuscipes, Lype phaeopa, L. reducta*

An extremely abundant series of sedge species, especially common in northern stony barren lakes and rough rocky rivers; hatches through the late afternoon and evening from April to late October.

A small sedge (forewing about 5mm) with a general black coloration, though the wings have conspicuous light brown hairs on close examination. Antennae very short.

Yellow-spotted Sedge *Cyrnus trimaculatus, Diplectrona felix, Holocentropus picicornis, Polycentropus flavomaculatus* *

Occurs in both rivers and lakes; hatches from June to October during the evening.

This common name was first given to Cyrnus trimaculatus; but the same description equally applies to at least three other common sedges. Small-medium-sized sedges, with forewing length of up to 8-9mm (some female P. flavomaculatus attain a length of 12mm). Overall brown or reddish-brown, with fine yellow or buff spots on wings. Antennae stout and short.

P. flavomaculatus has also been called the Dark Spotted Sedge

Speckled Sedge *Philopotamus montanus*

Because this sedge occurs mainly in the rougher headwaters of upland river systems it has been often ignored by angler-entomologists. However in such waters fish take it keenly and anglers visiting such waters ought to be on the look out for it! It hatches from April to early October, during the evening.

Similar to the yellow-spotted sedge except that wings more conspicuously speckled with golden-yellow dots. A medium-sized sedge, with forewing length of of up to 13mm.

Microcaddis Family Hydroptilidae.

Microcaddis species are found in both lakes and rivers. Hatches occur throughout the evening, mostly from May to October.

These are tiny sedges, with a forewing length that rarely exceeds 3-4mm. They are frequently overlooked and, because of their small size, rarely imitated, despite the fact that they may occur in huge numbers and during a hatch or fall of egg-laying females the fish may take them selectively. Microcaddis are identified from other sedges mainly by their small size; they also have conspicuously hairy wings and short hairy antennae. Colour varies from pale sandy buff, through a range of browns, to black.

LITTLE BLACK SEDGE

SPECKLED SEDGE

YELLOW-SPOTTED SEDGE

MICROCADDIS

Further notes on the identification of anglers' sedges

Because anglers' sedges often have little relationship to scientific classification it is impossible to produce a definitive key. Their identification is based too heavily on characters that vary widely, such as colour and size. While several of those we have just described and illustrated can be identified readily, others are not easy to tell apart.

As a further aid, they are arranged below under a series of headings. By checking through the following tables you may be able by process of elimination to identify a specimen precisely, or to one of two or three possible species.

1. Habitat

Primarily lakes	Great Red Sedge, Green Peter, Speckled Peter, Chestnut-winged Sedge, Mottled Sedge, Yellow Sedge, Grousewing, Longhorns.
Primarily rivers	Caperer, Large Cinnamon Sedge, Sand-fly, Welshman's Button, Grannom, Marbled Sedge, Grey Flag, Small Yellow Sedge, Small Silver Sedge, Speckled Sedge.
Both lakes and rivers	Cinnamon Sedge, Medium Sedge, Brown Sedge, Small Red Sedge, Black Silverhorn, Brown Silverhorn, Black Sedge, Little Black Sedge, Yellow-spotted Sedge, Microcaddis.

2. Size

Most sedges have a medium forewing length of 10-20mm. The following are either distinctly large, or distinctly small or tiny. If you wish to identify anglers' sedges by the water, take a short length of ruler with you.

Large: forewing 20mm+	Great Red Sedge, Caperer; note that the Large Cinnamon Sedge, Mottled Sedge and one scientific species within the group anglers call Grey Flag may approach this measure (to 18mm).
Small: forewing 6-10mm	Chestnut-winged Sedge, Grannom, Small Red Sedge, Yellow Sedge, Grousewing, Black Silverhorn, Brown Silverhorn, Small Silver Sedge, Black Sedge (genus *Silo*), most Yellow-spotted Sedges.
Tiny: forewing up to 6mm	Small Yellow Sedge, Black Sedge (genus *Tinodes*), Little Black Sedge, Microcaddis.

3. Antennae

Length: most sedges have an antenna length that is about (range 90-120%) that of forewing. The following have distinctly short or distinctly long antennae.

Distinctly short (maximum antenna length is $\frac{3}{4}\times$ forewing length or less)	Medium Sedge, Small Red Sedge, Small Yellow Sedge, Black Sedge, Little Black Sedge, Yellow-spotted Sedge, Speckled Sedge, Microcaddis.
Distinctly long (minimum antenna length is greater than $1\times$ forewing length)	Chestnut-winged Sedge, Grousewing, Black Silverhorn, Brown Silverhorn, Longhorn, Yellow Sedge (genus *Oecetis*).

4. Wing colour

Colour in all species of sedges does vary from individual to individual and also within the life of one adult sedge. Thus it is both difficult to define precisely the colour of one group of anglers' sedges (that may include several scientific species) and to place one specimen into its correct group of anglers' sedges purely on grounds of colour (see, for instance, sand-fly and brown sedge on p 64). The following are useful colour characters, but they must be taken in conjunction with other features when making an identification.

Predominantly bright, light cinnamon (warm yellow-brown): Caperer, Large Cinnamon Sedge, Cinnamon Sedge, some Sand-flies.

Predominantly grey: Grey Flag, Longhorn, Small Silver Sedge.

Grey with bold darker markings: Mottled Sedge

Predominantly yellow: Yellow Sedge, Small Yellow Sedge.

Predominantly black: Black Silverhorn, Black Sedge, Little Black Sedge.

Predominantly rich chestnut- or golden- or red-brown: Chestnut-winged Sedge, Welshman's Button, Small Red Sedge.

Brown with bold black markings: Great Red Sedge, Grousewing.

Brown with conspicuous paler areas: Green Peter.

Brown with conspicuous white speckles: Speckled Peter, Brown Silverhorn (*A. albifrons*).

Brown with conspicuous yellow speckles: Yellow-spotted Sedge, Speckled Sedge.

TWO-WINGED FLIES
Order Diptera

Life cycle — complete metamorphosis. Eggs hatch into larvae. Dipteran larvae vary greatly in shape. Some are worm-like; others resemble grubs or maggots. In many larvae there is a distinct head, but thorax and abdomen not clearly identifiable being just a fairly uniform segmented body. True legs are always lacking in these larvae; in some species there are extensions to the body (known as 'prolegs' and occurring singly or as pair close to head and/or end of abdomen) that resemble simple legs. Often breathing tubes or gills are present in aquatic forms, usually on the head or at the end of the body. When the larva is fully grown it turns into a pupa. In some species the pupa is a simple segmented and static cocoon (chrysalis); in others the pupa is capable of swimming by making flicking motions with its body. The adult emerges from the pupal shuck. Adult dipterans are immediately recognised by a single pair of membranous wings (the second pair is reduced to a short drumstick-like 'haltere'). The head often appears large, with prominent compound eyes and mouthparts which are either a sucking proboscis or piercing and needle-like. The thorax is often pronounced, giving a hunch-backed appearance in some species. The abdomen is tailless.

There are several 1000 species of two-winged flies in Europe. Many species have aquatic larval and pupal stages which, with the emerging adults and egg-laying and spent females, are major fish foods. Many species are land-bred; but the adults of some of these are commonly found on the water where they have fallen or been blown by the wind. These too can be important fish foods.

Aquatic Two-winged Flies

Reed-smut *Simulium* species

Reed-smuts are abundant in rivers, especially fast-flowing clean rivers. All stages of the life cycle are important foods for trout and grayling. The larvae and pupae are grubbed from boulders or weed; abseiling larvae are taken from the flow (one reason why small dark wet flies are very effective in rivers). When fish are feeding on adult reed-smuts at the surface they are said to be 'smutting' and are then reputedly difficult to catch: the fish are usually taking the adult reed-smut in its tiny air bubble just beneath the surface. For imitations see pp. 138, 188, 194; or any small black soft-hackled wet fly, pp. 127-35.

Reed-smut larvae are up to 10mm long with a distinctive club-shaped body. There are 2 fans of bristles on head that are used to catch food particles from the stream. These larvae attach, by the end of their abdomens, to boulders and weeds in often immense numbers. They are able to move position without being swept away by the current by 'looping'; they can also move from one boulder or patch of weed to another by drifting (or abseiling) downstream on a silk thread that is attached to the first boulder or weedbed.

The pupae are enclosed in a cocoon that is attached to boulders, weed etc.

The adult reed-smut emerges from the pupal cocoon and rises to the surface in a bubble of air: as the bubble bursts at the surface the adult fly is launched into the air. Adult reed-smuts resemble small houseflies, 2-6mm long with blackish body (sometimes they are called 'blackfly'). The females are famous for inflicting a painful bite; one species, the birchfly *S. tuberosum*, is particularly vicious and inhabits rivers in northern European birch forests.

Phantom Fly *Chaoborus*

Phantom flies are lake insects. The larvae are a very important source of food for fish that feed in open water on planktonic organisms (e.g. trout, arctic charr); like the lesser planktonic organisms on which they feed, the larvae show a vertical migration during the day, being deeper during light hours and closer to the surface at night, and being closer to the surface on dull cloudy days than bright sunny days. Large numbers of pupae are taken from the surface film. Many adult female phantom flies are taken from the surface when they return to lay their eggs. For imitations see p. 188.

Phantom fly larvae are up to 10mm long, slender, pale and transparent except for 2 pairs of airsacs that appear black (1 pair in thorax and 1 pair rear end of abdomen). They have moustache-like antennae that are used to seize smaller planktonic organisms in the water. They can hang, motionless in a horizontal position, at various depths in the water by altering their body density with the air sacs.

The fully-grown larvae moult into a pupal stage but do not produce a cocoon. Instead the transparent pupae hang vertically from the surface film; when disturbed they can swim. Phantom fly pupae resemble mosquito pupae, with a large head/thorax and slender, tapering curved abdomen that hangs vertically in the water (not curved as in mosquitoes); the head has a breathing tube through which it draws air from the surface and a pair of large, flap-like extensions on either side.

Adult phantom flies resemble mosquitoes and Chironomid midges, but the wings are always at least slightly shorter than the abdomen (cf mosquitoes); at rest wings usually held slightly apart (cf chironomid midges). Also abdomen is uniform in colour (pale olive-green, or grey) without the paler banding at edges of segments (cf mosquitoes and chironomids). Imitation of adult phantom flies as for midges (see p. 71).

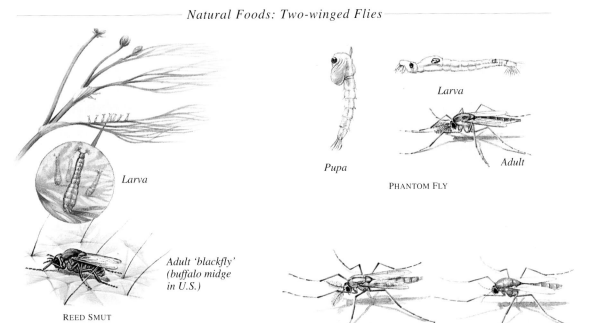

Larva

Pupa

Adult

PHANTOM FLY

Larva

Adult 'blackfly' (buffalo midge in U.S.)

REED SMUT

MALE MIDGE

FEMALE MIDGE

Larvae

Variation in colour and size of adult midges

Midge (Buzzer or **Chironomid** Family)
Chironomidae

Midges are among the most widespread and abundant invertebrate fish foods. They are found in all lakes and rivers. Fish devour huge numbers of larvae (two are used as baits: 'jokers' and 'bloodworm') from the bottom or among dense weed. Huge numbers of pupae are taken when they are rising to hatch at the water surface; sometimes the fish will ignore rising pupae and select only the pupae that are hanging from the surface at the point of hatch. Fish will also take adults that have just hatched or females that have returned to the water surface to lay their eggs.

Individual species are very difficult to identify with certainty: there are over 1500 European species. There seems little point in anglers trying to separate them, despite the fact that a few have been given anglers' names. Instead it seems a more practical proposition to be prepared with a series of sizes and colours of imitations that match all the main stages of the midge life-cycle.

A similar family (Thaumaleidae) occurs in northern and upland streams. Species are very small: larvae up to 15mm, adults up to 5mm. Identification from members of the Chironomidae, which they closely resemble in appearance and behaviour, is difficult and the angler should treat them with this family. Imitations: larval p. 188, pupal and emerger p. 190-2, adult pp. 138, 192-4. Several soft-hackled wet flies are effective midge imitations (pp. 128-35); also Spider Greenwell (p. 124). These series of imitations can also imitate adult phantom fly (p. 70), mosquito, biting midge, torrent midge and meniscus midge (pp. 72-3)

Larvae worm-like; up to 30mm. The presence of simple 'prolegs' at the end of the abdomen and just behind the distinct head, and in some species gills at end of abdomen, confirms identification. Colour varies from white, through yellow, olive and green to brown and red (red larvae, known as 'bloodworms', are especially common in mud that contains little oxygen at bottom of ponds). The larvae of many species swim with a flicking or looping motion of body.

Chironomid pupae have a distinctly bulging head and thorax (usually bearing feathery gills and wing-buds) and a tapering abdomen. Colour varies, usually black or some shade of olive or brown.

Adult midges hatch from pupae at the water surface: they are usually shorter than both larva and pupa (maximum 13mm but in many species they are much shorter, down to 2-3mm). Adults have a small head (with plumed antennae in males), large humped thorax, and slender abdomen that has pale bands at the edges of segments; wings held overlapping low over abdomen reaching only 2/3 to tip of abdomen; legs long. Colour varies, even within some species: usually red-brown, olive, green, gold, grey, black. These midges do not bite (see Biting Midges, below).

Mosquito *Anopheles, Culex, Aedes*

Mosquitoes are most abundant in small pools but wherever they occur — larvae, pupae and adults on the water surface as newly hatched or egg-laying females — they are eagerly devoured by fish. It has been suggested that the scarcity of mosquitoes in many fish-inhabited waters is because they have been eaten by the fish! Adult mosquito imitations are extremely effective, especially on small lakes and slow river pools on summer evenings when the adults are flying over the water surface. Imitations of adult mosquitos as for adult midges, see p. 71.

Mosquito larvae are identified by up to 8mm long, tapering body covered with bristles; bristles most concentrated at tail where, in some species, there is also a breathing tube. Colour grey or olive. Larvae hang horizontally below (those lacking breathing tube), or at an angle to (those with breathing tube) the surface film. These larvae feed by filtering tiny algae or organic matter from the water with brush-like mouthparts. When disturbed they swim to bottom with wriggling motion.

Mosquito pupae resemble a large grey comma, with a massive head/thorax and tapering abdomen curved below (cf phantom-fly). They also hang from surface film and swim away when disturbed.

Adult mosquitoes are very slender, up to 10mm, with long legs, pronounced thorax and wings that extend to or beyond the end of the abdomen (cf phantom-flies and midges). Body colour is usually blackish or dark grey with pale banding in most species; wings transparent with dark veins. Female mosquitoes are famous for their biting, blood-sucking habits (a meal of blood required to produce eggs). The malaria blood parasite *Plasmodium*, once endemic in Europe, is carried by the female *Anopheles* mosquito and passed to humans when she sucks her meal of blood.

Biting Midges *Culicoides* and *Probezzia* species

Adults that have hatched in boggy river or lake margins or boggy pools close to rivers and lakes, are often found on the open water; fish feed on them keenly. They closely resemble chironomid midges (p. 71), with slender abdomen, pronounced thorax and wings held flat over abdomen. They are much smaller than most species in that group, with body length of up to 5mm; the wings extend beyond the end of the abdomen. They can inflict a painful bite and are best known from northern regions (Scandinavia, Scotland) where huge numbers not only provide trout, grayling, charr and whitefish with abundant surface foods but can make an angler's life a misery! For imitations see adult midges, p. 71.

The larvae and pupae of biting midge occur mostly in marshy or boggy habitats, or very shallow water where fish are not usually present. Some biting midge larvae may be found in deeper water, usually living in algae on the bottoms of lakes. These larvae are segmented and worm-like, with a small bunch of fine hairs at the rear end; they are transparent, up to 10-13mm long; they can swim weakly by a flicking of the body.

Torrent Midges *Liponeura* species

A group of midges very common and often abundant in rough, rocky mountain streams (not British Isles).

Larvae unmistakable, with large head (in fact, head, thorax and 1st abdominal segment fused), 4 distinct abdominal segments and a squarish 'tail'. Upper surface often covered with spines or bristles; under surface has suckers to enable insect to remain attached to rocks. Colour dark brown or brown-black. Length up to 12mm. Pupa has cocoon, attached to rock.

Adult emerges from cocoon in bubble of air; it is carried to surface in this bubble and is propelled into air when bubble bursts at surface. Thus newly-hatched adults rarely seen on water. Adults resemble small daddy-long-legs, with slender abdomen, thicker thorax, long (x2 body) transparent wings, and extremely long jointed legs. Body length up to 8-9mm; colour dark brown or grey-brown.

Fish grub larvae and pupae from boulders; and also take them when washed downstream during spates (when rocks grind together in heavy water, larvae and pupae lose hold). Large numbers of adults rising to the surface are eaten: no food will be visible on the surface but fish will be feeding keenly close to the surface (cf Reed-smuts). Adults may be taken from the surface after laying their eggs and dying on the water. For imitations see adult midges, p. 71.

Meniscus Midges *Dixa* and *Dixella* species

This group of tiny midges has been overlooked by many anglers, but can be important, especially in very weedy pools and the margins of slow rivers.

The larvae live in the surface film. They are identified by their characteristic U-shaped body, bristles especially conspicuous on head and tip of abdomen, and 1-2 prolegs at end of abdomen. Colour grey, grey-buff or drab brown. Length up to 9mm.

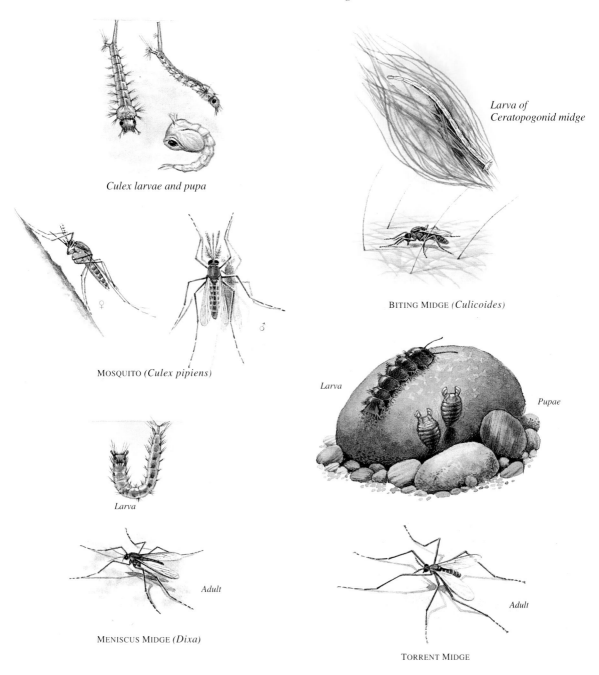

Culex larvae and pupa

*Larva of
Ceratopogonid midge*

MOSQUITO *(Culex pipiens)*

BITING MIDGE *(Culicoides)*

Larva

Larva

Pupae

Adult

MENISCUS MIDGE *(Dixa)*

Adult

TORRENT MIDGE

Pupation occurs just out of water on emergent vegetation where the fish do not encounter them.

Adults resemble mosquitoes, with long legs, slim abdomen and pronounced thorax; but the wings, that extend well beyond tip of abdomen, are more transparent and antennae fine and unfeathered. Body length up to 7mm. Body colour dark brown, grey-brown or blackish.

Tiny soft-hackled wet flies (pp. 128-35), fished in the surface film, are often effective where trout (and other species such as rudd and roach) are feeding in weedy water at the surface on larval and emerging adult meniscus midges. For imitations of adults see midges, p. 71.

Some other groups of aquatic or semi-aquatic two-winged flies may be encountered in freshwaters. Some are extremely small insects, identified only with great difficulty from the smaller species of those groups described above. Some occur in tiny pools or shallow water on marshy ground where fish (especially trout, grayling) are unlikely to occur. Some are in very stagnant water that is inhospitable to fish.

Land-bred Two-winged Flies

The adults of several species of land-bred two-winged flies commonly fall or are blown by the wind onto water, and are often major seasonal items in the diets of fish. In some very clean, relatively unproductive waters land-bred insects often compose a large proportion of fish food.

Hawthornfly *Bibio marci*, **Heatherfly** *Bibio pomonae* **Black Gnats** *Bibio, Dilophus, Hilara, Empis, Ocydromia* species

Every year hawthornflies, heatherflies and black gnats fall in some numbers on the water. In some years falls are huge: lake surfaces may be covered by them; rivers may resemble a conveyor belt carrying these black flies downstream. Often many of these insects sink into the surface film (in some lights they can be difficult for the angler to see in this position) and the fish will select them rather than those standing on the surface film. Often a proportion of the flies that fall onto the water will be mating pairs, attached together; sometimes the fish will select these pairs and ignore the unpaired flies. The black gnats *Hilara* and *Empis* are both predatory on other insects; both (but especially *Hilara*) can be seen catching aquatic insects that have just hatched at the water surface. In their struggles to secure and carry away their prey they sometimes land momentarily on the surface and are then taken by fish. These flies comprise one of the most important groups of natural flies for the fly-fisher. For imitations see CDC (category 3) pp. 138, 194. Also black thoraxed soft-hackled spiders, p. 134.

These flies are so closely related and similar that it is sensible to deal with them together.

Hawthornflies and heatherflies are quite large insects (up to 12mm long); the various species of black gnats are smaller (up to 9mm). All have a very slender (often curved) abdomen and pronounced thorax and head, black or very dark brown-black bodies and legs, and transparent or semi-transparent, pale grey or mid-grey wings. Hawthornflies and heatherflies have noticeably long trailing hind legs; in heatherfly the bases of the legs are red.

Hawthornfly are on the wing from the end April through May; heatherfly from late July-September; black gnats throughout period April-October (occasionally to early December) with peaks in spring and autumn. The heatherfly is especially abundant in moorland areas; hawthornfly and black gnat in farmland or wooded country.

Crane-fly (or **Daddy-long-legs** *Tipula* species)
Large numbers are drifted by the wind onto lakes and rivers, especially in the period June-October (some from mid-April). Fish often take them keenly. Sometimes fish that have been feeding fastidiously on one species of insect that happens to be numerous

on the water will quit being selective should a daddy-long-legs drift across the water. Artificial daddy-long-legs can have a similar effect; they will also sometimes attract a fish, that is feeding deep in the water, to the surface. In some regions naturaL daddy-long-legs are used instead of artificial patterns. For imitations see p. 196.

There are many species of crane-flies, and few parts of Europe do not have at least one. Some species have aquatic larvae ('leatherjackets') but they remain hidden in the river or lake bed and are rarely eaten by fish; some species have larvae that live in the soil on land where they are pests on grasslands.

Crane-flies are instantly recognisable by their slender abdomen, stout thorax, relatively small head, transparent or semi-transparent wings and (especially) extremely long, jointed legs. Body and leg colour is usually some shade of brown. Size varies, some having a body length of about 10mm and the largest reaching 35mm.

Dung-flies *Scathophaga*
Perhaps the commonest fly found on cow-pats, sheep and deer dung in large numbers. In cool windy weather these flies often shelter in stands of rank grasses, thistles etc. Grazing cattle or sheep (or anglers walking through vegetation at the water's edge) sometimes disturb clouds of these flies which are then carried by the wind onto the water. Fish are ever ready to receive such fare. Fly-fishers ought to be on the look-out for such events, for they can induce a rise of fish when there are no aquatic insects on the water. For imitation see p. 196.

~

Anglers ought to be prepared for falls of other species of land-bred flies on the water. Although these are not as common nor as predictable as those detailed above, they can cause fish to rise to feed at the surface and give the imitative fly-fisher a wonderful opportunity. In particular, watch out for:

Blow-flies Family Calliphoridae
These include such well-known and widespread species as the bluebottle, *Calliphora vomitoria*, greenbottle, *Lucilia caesar* and flesh-fly, *Sarcophaga carnia*. The larvae feed on dead animal matter; larvae are the bait anglers' maggots (or gentles), pupae are known as casters. Rarely do large numbers of these occur simultaneously on the water; but even one individual can cause a fish to rise to take it. They are often important where bait anglers use maggots and casters, and discard unused baits at the waterside (e.g. one February afternoon grayling were rising on one pool to bluebottles that had hatched from discarded casters and were falling from the bank into the water). For imitation see p. 196.

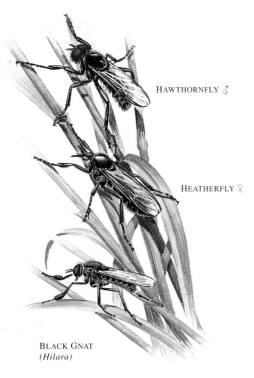

HAWTHORNFLY ♂

HEATHERFLY ♀

BLACK GNAT
(Hilara)

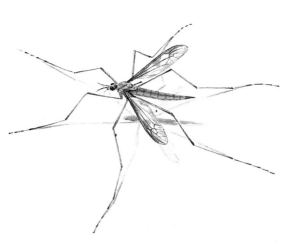

CRANE-FLY OR DADDY-LONG-LEGS

Hilara carrying Yellow May Dun

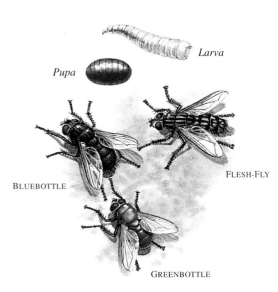

Larva

Pupa

FLESH-FLY

BLUEBOTTLE

GREENBOTTLE

BLOW-FLIES

YELLOW DUNG-FLY

Hover-flies Family Syrphidae

So named because of their ability to hover in one position with incredibly fast wing beats for many seconds. Most of them are quite brightly coloured, with black and yellow or orange banded abdomens that mimic wasps and bees (hover-flies cannot sting). Note: hover-flies have 2 wings; wasps and bees have 4 wings (p. 78). Individuals often fall onto the water; autopsies occasionally reveal hover-flies in a fish's stomach. The species concerned is often Helophilus pendulus which has a habit of flying low over the water surface. One species Eristalsis tenax has an aquatic larva known as the rat-tailed maggot. This larva usually occurs in large numbers in mud at the bottom of grossly polluted, fishless water; but has been reported from some rich lowland lakes. On such lakes an imitation of the adult is said to be extremely effective during the summer months. For imitation see CDC Wasp, p. 138.

Gravel Bed *Hexatoma* species

Many species of two-winged flies such as the Gravel Bed have their larval and pupal stages in damp marshy ground close to the water's edge; the adults are commonly seen flying low in swarms over the water and fish will eat them if they fall or land on the surface. It has been widely imitated by fly dressers. Up to 18mm long, with a slender abdomen, thicker thorax, fairly long jointed legs, and a pair of strongly veined wings. Overall colour dark brown-grey. It is most often found flying, in summer, by upland wooded rough streams that have a bed of coarse sand or gravel. For imitation see p. 196.

BEETLES
Order Coleoptera

Life cycle – complete metamorphosis. Eggs hatch into larvae which feed and grow; when fully grown the larvae become pupae, and from the pupal case emerges the adult beetle. Some beetles have an aquatic larval and adult stage; other beetles live entirely on land though sometimes large numbers of adult beetles are blown or fall onto the water.

Aquatic beetle larvae vary in shape, but are usually elongate with distinct head, thorax and abdomen. The head usually bears a pair of powerful jaws (most are predatory on lesser invertebrates, small fish fry and amphibian tadpoles); the thorax bears 3 pairs jointed legs. In some species the abdomen is soft and bare, in others it is tougher and bears numerous gills or spines. In some species the larvae have 1-3 tails at the end of the abdomen.

Beetle pupae occur only exceptionally in water: aquatic larvae crawl from the water and pupate in soft damp soil.

Adult beetles are identified by their extremely hard body, including the horny forewings that completely

cover the membranous second pair and upper surface of the abdomen – these forewings do not overlap but meet along the midline of the body (cf bugs, p. 56). In aquatic species the legs are often flattened and fringed with hairs to aid swimming. Most water beetles breathe by taking a bubble of air from the water surface at regular intervals: this silvery bubble is sometimes quite a conspicuous feature.

While there are many species of aquatic beetles, they rarely occur in such large concentrations to evoke a selective feeding response from fish. Only occasionally is an aquatic beetle larva or adult found in autopsies. However an aquatic beetle larva or adult imitation can be useful, fished deeply close to weedbeds in lake margins, on dour summer days.

More important are land-bred beetles which often fall or are blown onto the water in large numbers from surrounding vegetation. In lakes and rivers surrounded by heather moorland or forest it is not unusual (in spring-autumn) to find the stomachs of fish crammed with tiny land beetles. The fish may be rising to take food from the surface, but nothing is visible on the surface: often the food will be tiny black, brown or green land-beetles, 3-10mm long, that have sunk into the surface film. A suitably sized artificial fly that also sinks into the surface film will usually succeed in such situations. See p. 196; also Jassid, p. 174.

ALDERS
Order Megaloptera

Life cycle — complete metamorphosis. The larvae hatch from eggs laid on overhanging foliage and then fall into water. These larvae feed and grow in the water, crawling ashore to pupate in moist soil close to the water's edge. After emergence from the pupa adults are often seen in vegetation or flying over the water; laying their eggs on overhanging vegetation; only a small proportion die and fall onto the water. Adult alder flies are less important as fish foods than has traditionally been thought: imitation alders are among the oldest of artificial fly patterns.

Alder larvae have an elongated body that tapers to a single pointed tail. Both the head (which bears strong jaws used to catch and devour lesser invertebrates) and thorax have a tough hard exoskeleton; the abdomen is quite soft. The thorax bears 3 pairs of legs; the abdomen has 7 pairs of slender jointed gills (both gills and tail are covered with many fine hairs).

Adult alders superficially resemble adult sedges (p. 62). They are up to 15mm, hunch-backed, with 2 pairs of wings, held tent-like over the abdomen, which are bare with distinct veins (cf sedges, moths) and 1 pair antennae. Body usually blackish; wings a rich brown with distinct darkeR veins. For imitations see p. 197; also any small dark brown sedge pattern, p. 184.

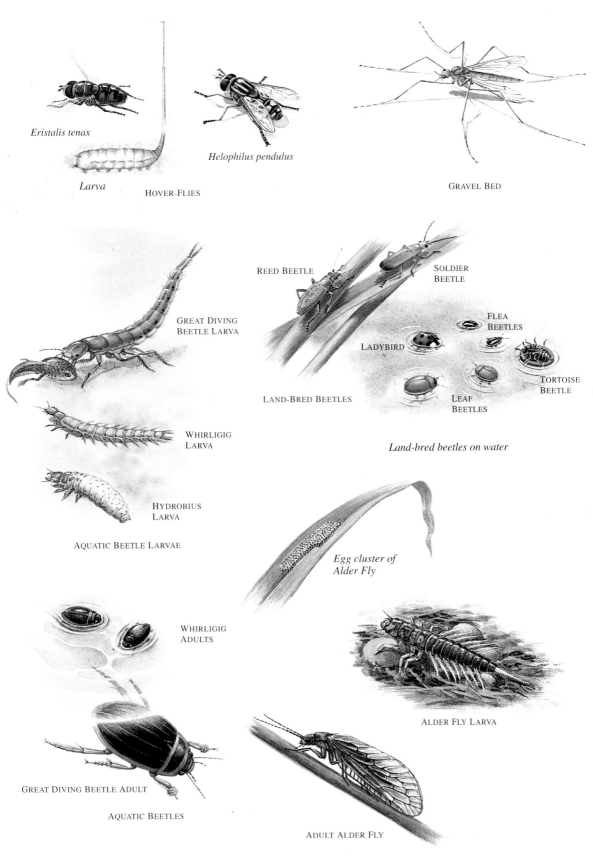

Eristalis tenax

Helophilus pendulus

Larva

HOVER-FLIES

GRAVEL BED

GREAT DIVING
BEETLE LARVA

REED BEETLE

SOLDIER
BEETLE

FLEA
BEETLES

LADYBIRD

TORTOISE
BEETLE

LAND-BRED BEETLES

LEAF
BEETLES

WHIRLIGIG
LARVA

Land-bred beetles on water

HYDROBIUS
LARVA

AQUATIC BEETLE LARVAE

*Egg cluster of
Alder Fly*

WHIRLIGIG
ADULTS

ALDER FLY LARVA

GREAT DIVING BEETLE ADULT

AQUATIC BEETLES

ADULT ALDER FLY

ANTS, BEES AND WASPS
Order Hymenoptera

Life cycle — complete metamorphosis. Few of this group are aquatic; however the adults of many land-bred species may fall or be blown onto the water from surrounding vegetation and provide an important food resource for fish.

Ants Family Formicidae

Ants are easily recognised by their distinct head (with a pair of long antennae), thorax (with 3 pairs of legs), and abdomen; the boundaries between these three body regions are very narrow. In summer large swarms may occur of winged flying ants. Colour usually either red- or yellow-brown, or black. Length varies from species to species: body up to 5mm in workers of smaller species such as black garden ant. *Lasius niger* and yellow meadow ant, *L. flavus*; 10+mm in wood ant, *Formica rufa*.

Ants1 are especially important fish foods in summer and early autumn when their populations peak and large numbers of swarming ants (winged or unwinged) may fall on the water from marginal or overhanging vegetation or may be blown onto the water by the wind. Often the fish will feed selectively when large numbers of ants do fall on the water, and a good imitative pattern is required to deceive them. For imitation see p. 198.

Wasps and Bees (many Families).

Wasps and bees are often discovered in fish stomach analyses, but usually just one or two specimens are found. Occasionally a wasp or bee will be seen landing on the water and being taken by a surface-feeding fish. However such fish are unlikely to be feeding selectively, and they are quite likely to fall for a general dry fly; but see CDC Wasp, p. 138.

GRASSHOPPERS AND BUSH CRICKETS
Order Orthoptera

These are land insects, especially abundant in grasslands. In summer and early autumn, when their populations peak, variable numbers may accidentally jump or fall onto the water and be eaten by trout.

Easily identified by their stout build and long hind legs. Size varies tremendously: tiny nymphs may be only 3-4mm long; the adults of some species may reach 50+ mm. Coloration varies: in grasshoppers (Acrididae) usually predominantly brown, buff, or green; in bush crickets (Tettigoniidae) green.

In Ireland natural grasshoppers are often collected and used as an alternative to artificial imitations. Some European anglers use commercially raised locusts (species of grasshopper) similarly as bait. Unlike the USA, where artificial grasshopper patterns are widely used, in Europe fishing with artificial grasshoppers is not often practised. Such artificials are, however, very effective on both rivers and lakes, in hot breezy weather; the fly should be twitched in the surface to mimic the struggling, kicking grasshopper. For imitations see p. 198.

LACEWINGS
Order Neuroptera

These are mostly land-bred insects (Sisyra fuscata has larvae that fed on aquatic sponges); occasionally numbers fall on the water and are taken by fish, especially in the evening. Fragile-looking flies, with soft bodies and two pairs of long membranous wings held, tent-like, over the abdomen (cf Alder p. 76; some authorities place the alders in the same Order Neuroptera). Wing venation is quite distinct: a bold vein runs parallel with the leading edge of the wing. Body light green with wings either colourless or very light green (Green Lacewings); or body buff-brown with wings colourless with brown veins or overall light buff-brown (Brown Lacewings). Length up to 25mm. For imitation see p. 196.

THRIPS (OR THUNDER-FLIES)
Order Thysanoptera

These are very small (up to 3 mm long), slender, blackish land-bred insects that often occur in vast numbers (e.g. in cereal fields or where there are large densities of pollen- and nectar-rich flowers). From May to September, in warm, humid, thundery weather, huge numbers take to the air; many land on the water — sometimes the water can be covered by them. And the fish usually respond by feeding selectively on them. Few anglers would overlook such a fall of thrips; they will land in huge numbers also on the angler and are quite unpleasant as they crawl in the hair, down the neck, in the eyes and, when the mouth is opened, there as well! For imitation see La Petite Merde, p. 194, or a tiny Jassid, p. 174.

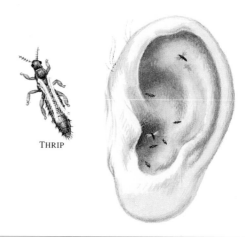

THRIP

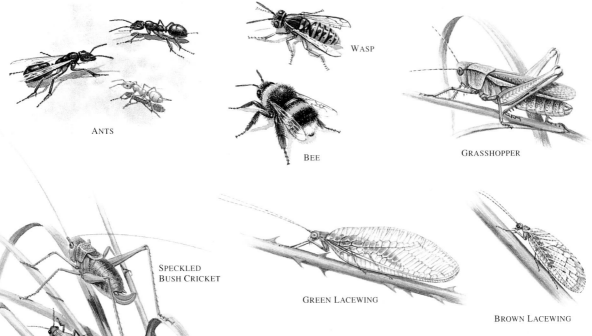

ANTS

WASP

BEE

GRASSHOPPER

SPECKLED
BUSH CRICKET

GREEN LACEWING

BROWN LACEWING

GROUND
HOPPER

*Orthopterans well adapted to
waterside life, competent swimmers
both on surface and under water*

MOTHS AND BUTTERFLIES
Order Lepidoptera

Life cycle — complete metamorphosis. Though some species have aquatic egg, larval and pupal stages they are rarely important as fish foods because they occur in niches where fish are unlikely to find them (e.g. in reed stems). Far more important are land-bred forms where larva or adult fall onto the water.

Larvae are typical butterfly-type caterpillars. Many caterpillars of land moths pupate by lowering themselves from the trees, in which they have fed and grown, to the ground on long silk threads. Where trees overhang rivers and lakes large numbers may descend onto the water and fish take them keenly. Many caterpillars are dislodged from overhanging vegetation by high winds and fall onto the water. An imitation caterpillar is often effective, from spring to autumn, on wooded streams or lake margins.

Adult moths (and in lesser numbers, butterflies) frequently fall onto the water in summer and autumn, and are often taken by fish. Sometimes the fall may be huge. Because most adult moths are nocturnal, their importance is often overlooked by anglers. Moths are easily confused with sedges (p. 62); but the wings are held flat over the body when at rest, and they are covered with fine scales that are easily dislodged.

For imitation of caterpillars: see p. 198. For imitation of adults moths: see Bustards, p. 136.

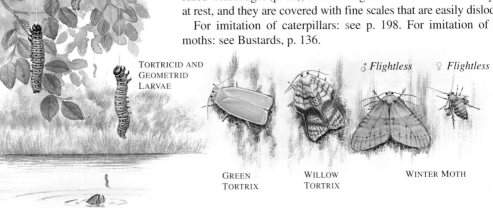

TORTRICID AND
GEOMETRID
LARVAE

♂ *Flightless*   ♀ *Flightless*

GREEN
TORTRIX

WILLOW
TORTRIX

WINTER MOTH

CRUSTACEANS

Crustaceans are superficially variable in appearance; but there are only a few large (10mm or more long) European freshwater species.

Crustaceans have a distinctly segmented body divided into a head, thorax and abdomen. In some species the head and thorax are hidden or partly hidden beneath a hood-like carapace (prawns, crayfish); in some the carapace hides the head and thorax and the abdomen is also hidden by being folded tightly beneath the thorax (crabs). In some tiny planktonic forms the body is enclosed in a cover or carapace that hides this segmentation. In most larger crustaceans the external skeleton is thick and very hard (and often misnamed a 'shell'). The head usually carries two pairs of antennae. The thorax usually has 5 or more pairs of legs. The abdomen may have one pair of legs per segment or none. The antennae and legs often two-branched; besides walking and swimming, some legs often adapted for other purposes (e.g. as pincers for grasping and cutting food, or as fans for wafting a fresh supply of water over gills).

Most species of freshwater crustaceans are very tiny planktonic animals (that occur in largest diversity and numbers in lakes); identification of these to species is very difficult without a microscope and detailed scientific key. They are important foods of fish, but are impossible to imitate by the fly-fisher. Neverthless they are included briefly here because they are so important in the diet of lake fish and are often discovered in autopsies. The few larger species are easy to identify: most are these are also major sources of food for fish.

Opossum Shrimp *Mysis relicta*

Most opossum shrimps are marine: this one found its way into European freshwaters 10,000 years ago when the last great Ice Age was nearing its end and is thus an 'Ice Age relict'; hence its species name. Now it is found mostly in cold clean lakes, less in northern rivers, in Ireland, Germany, Poland, northern Russia and Scandinavia and only one English lake (Ennerdale). They are eaten by a variety of fish, including brown trout, arctic charr and grayling. Similar species occur in brackish water in estuaries and coastal lagoons (an almost identical species, *Neomysis integer*, sometimes enters freshwater); also eaten by estuarine fish including those freshwater species that may enter brackish water out of their breeding season (e.g. trout and ide).

Opossum shrimps are slender, up to 20mm long, of a translucent very pale buff-grey or grey that makes them difficult to see in the water. The head bears a pair of large stalked eyes and a pair of long branched antennae. The thorax has 8 pairs of swimming legs; the females carry their eggs in a brood pouch on the underside of the thorax between the legs. Each abdominal segment has a pair of tiny limbs called swimmerets; at the end of the abdomen are three flat paddle-like tails used to aid swimming. For imitation see p. 198.

Mud Shrimp *Corophium* species

Most species of mud shrimp live in burrows in mud or silty-mud in brackish water; densities are often huge. One species, *C. curvispinum*, was recorded only in southeastern Europe in the Caspian Sea area up to the end of the 19th century; since then this species has colonised freshwaters and spread rapidly throughout Europe north to England. It lives in fine mud tubes on underwater plants, logs, rock, or in the surface of the silty bottom. Where it occurs (and it seems likely that it will spread, especially in still or slow-moving waters) it is taken by fish that are grubbing for food on the bottom.

Mud shrimps are slender, up to 8mm, with bodies that are slightly humped (most noticeably at the rear end) and rounded or only slightly flattened at the sides (cf water hog-louse and freshwater shrimp), conspicuously long, stout antennae and a pair of legs on each body segment. They are pale grey or sandy-grey. For imitation see Grey Shrimps, p. 198.

Freshwater Shrimp *Gammarus* species

This is the most abundant and widespread of the larger crustaceans, occurring in most clean rivers and streams, large lakes and small ponds, and estuaries down to the sea throughout northwest Europe. There are several species; and other similar species in different genera (one, *Niphargus* is colourless and lives in underground rivers). They occur most abundantly in weedbeds or among boulders and are a major source of food for fish.

Freshwater shrimps are easily identified by the way the body is flattened (laterally) along each side, the humped profile, and many appendages (antennae, legs) along the underside of the body. They are usually grey or olive-grey, though during the mating season (spring-summer) often assume a pink or orange mating coloration (fish will often select these brightly coloured shrimps as food). Many parasites invade freshwater shrimps, one of which produces a pink or orange spot on the side of the body. Size varies; some smaller species reach only 6mm; larger and commoner ones up to 25mm. Most swim on their sides. For imitation see p. 198-9.

Water Hog-louse (or **Water Slater**) *Asellus* species
Water Hog-lice cannot swim so they occur only in stillwater, canals and sluggish reaches or very sheltered niches in rivers. They are usually found on the lake or river bed, occasionally in very dense weedbeds, in highest concentrations where decaying plant material has accumulated (dead leaves, roots of water plants). The commonest species *A. aquati-*

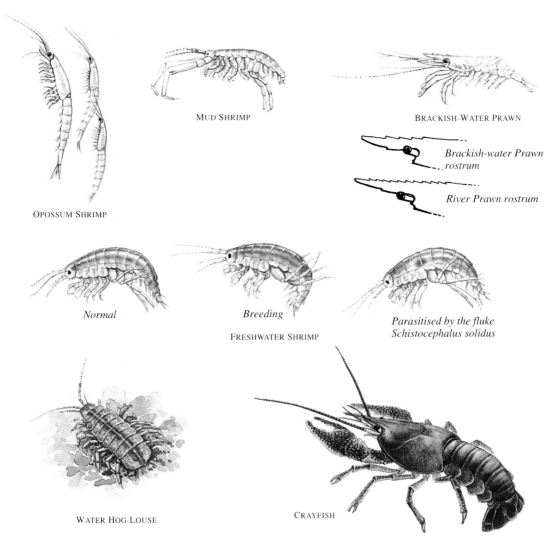

MUD SHRIMP

BRACKISH-WATER PRAWN

Brackish-water Prawn rostrum

River Prawn rostrum

OPOSSUM SHRIMP

Normal

Breeding

FRESHWATER SHRIMP

Parasitised by the fluke Schistocephalus solidus

WATER HOG-LOUSE

CRAYFISH

cus occurs throughout Britain and Europe. Water Hog-lice can be a major source of food for fish that feed on the bottom.

Water Hog-lice resemble wood-lice (to which they are related), with a body that is flattened along top and bottom (cf. freshwater shrimp and mud shrimps); the legs and antennae stick out to each side of body. They reach 15mm long. Usually olive-grey or grey-brown in colour. For imitation see p. 200.

Brackish-water Prawn *Palaemonetes varians*
River Prawn *Atyaephyra desmaresti*
The brackish-water prawn is primarily an estuarine species that extends upstream to the limits of the freshwater zone. It can be a major source of food for estuary fish including freshwater fish that have entered the brackish estuarine water. The river prawn is a freshwater species found in rivers draining into the Mediterranean, Biscay and the North Sea basin north to Holland and Germany.

Both are fairly slender prawns with a characteristic body shape (abdomen bent almost at right angles to the head-thorax), very long fine antennae, and long slender legs extending from under the 'shell' (carapace) that covers the head and thorax. Colour a very pale transparent sandy-grey with orange dots and lines. Body length up to 50mm (brackish-water prawn); 30mm (river prawn). To separate these two species count the number of teeth along the top of the rostrum (the pointed nose-like extension of the carapace): 4-6 teeth in the brackish-water prawn, 10+ teeth in the river prawn. For imitation see p. 200.

Crayfish Family Astacidae
Crayfish are small freshwater lobsters. They are the largest freshwater invertebrates, with a body length of up to 15cm. They have long antennae, a pair of broad powerful pincers, 4 pairs of walking legs, and an abdomen ending in a flat, broad fan-like 'telson' that is used with a flicking motion for rapid back-

ward swimming. Coloration is usually grey-brown or green-brown.

There are 4 species of crayfish native to Europe; in many areas populations have been lost due to pollution and populations in other areas are under threat. Two species have been introduced to Europe from North America; in some areas they have escaped and produced feral populations. The people who introduced these American crayfish also 'accidentally' introduced a virus that is currently decimating the native European crayfish in some regions.

Crayfish are usually found in clean limestone rivers or chalkstreams and occasionally in lakes. By day crayfish hide away under boulders or in holes and emerge at night to feed. The remains of crayfish are often found in the stomachs of large trout. For imitation see p. 200.

Mitten Crab *Eriocheir sinensis*

A species that was introduced to northern Europe from China at the beginning of the 20th century, this crab occurs in rivers draining into the sea from western France north to the Baltic (only one record from the British Isles). It is the only crab that can penetrate far upstream into freshwater; but it must return to saltwater to breed. It has been recorded in stomach analyses of fish, including trout.

Easily identified as a crab with a dense 'fur' (mittens) on the pincers.

Two other crabs may be recorded in brackish water close to the head of estuaries: the widespread European Shore Crab *Carcinus maenas* and the American Dwarf Crab *Pilumnopeus tridentatus* (that occurs from NW France to the Baltic). The former has been recorded in stomach analyses of trout. For imitation see p. 200.

Planktonic Crustaceans

Planktonic crustaceans are a major source of food for many fish, including trout, arctic charr and whitefish, especially in lakes. The fish feed on these tiny animals by filtering them from the water: often the stomachs of fish that have been feeding on planktonic crustaceans are packed with a bright orange-brown sludge of semi-digested tiny crustaceans.

If fish feeding on planktonic crustaceans were doing so selectively than they would be difficult (if not impossible) to catch: these tiny animals are mostly too small to imitate with artificial flies, and the densities of planktonic crustaceans during the summer 'bloom' can be so immense that an imitation (if it were possible) would be one in many millions of natural crustaceans. Fortunately trout and other fish that are feeding on planktonic crustaceans are not selective; often they will take a large orange streamer or wet fly fished through the clouds of plankton.

MOLLUSCS

Molluscs are animals with very soft bodies that are usually protected by hard shells into which they can retreat (land slugs are an exception). They include two common and important groups of freshwater animals, snails and mussels (clams).

Snails and Limpets *Gastropoda*

These have a single shell that is coiled in snails or conical in freshwater limpets. There are a large number of species of freshwater snails, but just two species of freshwater limpet (one in rivers and one in lakes). Species of snail are often separated by size (some are tiny when fully grown with a maximum height of 2-3mm, others reach 60mm or more) and shape of the shell (some have long pointed shells, some have squat pointed shells, some have flattened whorled shells). Most are dark brown or blackish. There is rarely, if ever, the need for a fly-fisher to identify snails to species.

Snails and limpets occur in all freshwater habitats, except those that are grossly polluted. They are most abundant in lakes and rivers with high levels of calcium (on chalk or limestone). Usually they are found among weeds or on the bottom, but in lakes in summer large numbers of snails may migrate to the surface, especially in hot weather to take air from above the water surface. They float upside down with their feet holding onto the underside of surface film.

There is no doubt that trout and grayling eat numbers of snails from weedbeds and the bottom; but stomach analyses suggest that they do not usually feed selectively on snails in these areas: snails appear to be part of a mixed diet. However when there is a migration of snails to the surface, the fish will often feed selectively on these floating snails. However selectivity is based on simple criteria (size, colour and position of the snails) rather than selection of a species of snail. For imitation see p. 200; also Williams's Favourite, p. 128.

Mussels (or Clams) *Bivalvia*

These are molluscs with two shells that are joined by a hinge which allows the animal to open when feeding or close up when it is not. There are many species, differences between which are based largely on shell size and shape. The smallest is only 2-6mm in diameter, the largest can reach 150+mm. Colour range yellow, olive, brown, black.

Mussels occur in all freshwater habitats, except those that are grossly polluted. Highest densities and the largest species are found in very slow-flowing rivers with silty bottoms or in large lakes. They mostly occur on the bottom, often partly buried in mud. They are less important as a food than snails, and because of their sedentary nature they are not imitated by fly-fishers.

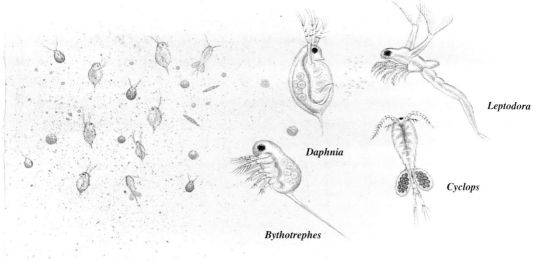

Daphnia

Leptodora

Cyclops

Bythotrephes

PLANKTON

MITTEN CRAB

SHORE CRAB

POND SNAIL

GREAT RAMSHORN

RIVER LIMPET

*Pond Snail travelling on
underside of surface film*

SWAN MUSSEL

PEA-SHELL COCKLE

WORMS

A great variety of worms live in freshwaters and are eaten by fish and found in stomach analysis. They are often very difficult to identify without the use of a microscope and scientific keys.

Annelida

These are segmented worms, well known to anglers from the earthworms and brandlings commonly used as bait. Many are aquatic, living in the bed of lakes and rivers other than the most polluted. They are mostly fairly large (up to 15cm), with elongated and distinctly segmented body which can be contracted and extended when the worm is moving.

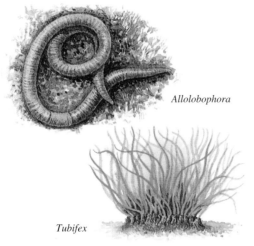

Allolobophora

Tubifex

This large group of worms includes freshwater relatives of the earthworms: they have tiny inconspicuous bristles on each body segment (the bristles can be felt if the finger is run down the side of body). Some have a 'saddle' or clitellum — a thickened part of body usually about 1/3 back from head.

The group includes the leeches which are worms lacking bristles, with a distinct sucker at either end of body. Some suck body fluids from fish and they are often found attached to the mouth or skin of fish.

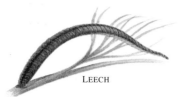

LEECH

Some anglers have attempted to imitate annelid worms with artificial flies (e.g. some have been called Leeches, but are fished rather like streamer patterns and not in a way that imitates the slow progress of the natural leech!); these imitations often bear little resemblance to the real thing. There are also on the market soft rubber worms which can be impaled on a hook. In either case, why not use the real thing and go worm fishing?

VERTEBRATES

Trout are opportunistic feeders. There are times when they will seek vertebrate foods and ignore smaller prey; and then the angler needs imitations of these larger foods.

Mammals

Small rodents and shrews occasionally feature in the diet of large trout; during years when their populations explode, large numbers of voles and lemmings have been observed swimming in lakes and rivers in Scandinavia and trout have been seen taking them selectively. See p. 208.

Amphibians

Small frogs, toads and newts, and especially their tadpoles, often figure in the trout diet: it was after finding a tiny toad in the stomach of a big sea trout that Hugh Falkus devised his famous Surface Lure, a floating fly that mimics a small frog or toad swimming against the current. In some stillwaters, trout feeding in the margins in summer are sometimes selective feeders on tadpoles. See pp. 200, 208

Fish

Trout (and to a lesser extent grayling) will eat small fish whenever the opportunity arises; evidence suggests that they prefer a diet of small fish to one of invertebrate foods. There are three circumstances when fish imitations are needed:

☐ in large lakes that have a head of big trout (e.g. the 'ferox trout') that feed almost exclusively on a diet of fish;

☐ in the shallows of lakes and rivers in late summer and autumn where there are large shoals of fish fry and smaller species such as minnows;

☐ in rivers that are in spate (water high in flood and coloured), where the smaller fish shelter in areas of slack water and the trout can approach easily due to the poor visibility.

The fry of all species are vulnerable: e.g. roach, *Rutilus rutilus*, bream, *Abramis brama*, dace, *Leuciscus leuciscus*.

Look also for smaller species: e.g. minnow, *Phoxinus phoxinus*, miller's thumb (also called sculpins and bullheads), *Cottus gobio*, loaches, *Cobitidae*.

In northern European lakes large-growing specialist fish-eating trout are often selective as to their quarry species. Some select whitefish, *Coregonus* species, some arctic charr, *Salvelinus alpinus*, others select smaller trout, and the parr and smolts of salmon, *Salmo salar*. For fish imitations see p. 200-7.

Air-encased water shrew, beetle and big brown trout

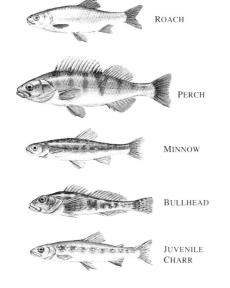

ROACH

PERCH

MINNOW

BULLHEAD

JUVENILE
CHARR

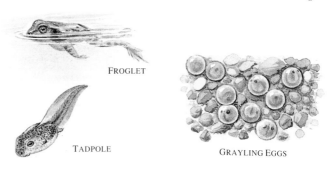

FROGLET

TADPOLE

GRAYLING EGGS

Fish Eggs

Many fish eggs are preyed on by other fish, notably the eggs of
trout, salmon, charr and grayling as they are shed into gravel redds.
It is not unusual, in late spring, to find large numbers of trout feeding in shallow water among spawning grayling: catch one and
spoon it. Almost certainly its stomach will be crammed with grayling eggs. For egg imitations, see p. 208.

Ferox trout preying on Charr

A MONTH-BY-MONTH HATCH GUIDE

Most anglers find it harder to identify insects – and particularly the hatched, adult insects – than the more substantial aquatic forms such as shrimps or fish-fry. It is also more important to do so, as the timing and circumstances of hatches can be short-lived, and they are so often the immediate stimulus to the fish. You arrive at a lake or river. The fish are feeding actively on something, or perhaps begin to do so at the approach of dusk. The urgent questions then are simply: what insect hatch are they feeding on? And having identified that, what dry or wet fly do I choose to imitate it? This section looks for the answers.

Monthly charts. Janus-like, the charts that follow on pages 90-121 therefore refer backwards to the accounts of natural foods in the earlier part of the book, and also forwards to what follows on their artificial imitations. They should also provide a general overview of how trout foods vary throughout the year, from the lean months of winter to the feasts of summer.

Only the commoner insect species are given in the monthly charts, including flies that hatch from the water, and flies that are landbred and fall onto the water. Very scarce species, or those that (as adults) are rarely eaten by fish (e.g. dragonflies) or those that might or might not land on the water at any time of the year (e.g. moths) are not included.

For each month, the first column has a page reference to the principal text treatment of the insect or other group concerned. Then follow the English name – sometimes of an individual species, sometimes of a whole group such as "Midges"; the Latin species or generic name; and the insect group. (If you need reminding as to the broad divisions of natural foods, see pages 27-85.)

Then come the types of water in or on which each insect is found – rivers fast or slow, mountain or lowland, ponds and lakes – and the times of day or weather in which each insect hatches. As a reminder, or for beginners as a comparative aid to identification, then follow the insect's body-length in millimetres, its general body-colour and its wing-colour.

So much for the natural creatures. At the right of each chart, against a green background rather than blue, are the artificial flies which imitate each insect or group: their names and page references to their main coloured illustration later in the book. The illustrations on either side of the tables themselves show in a reduced size the principal items covered on each page, but for fuller information the reader should refer forwards or backwards to the main sections of the book. The charts make it plain that there are often several different artificial patterns which can be tied to imitate a particular item of natural food, and conversely that one particular artificial fly may be effectively used to match several natural food species.

Where several imitations are suggested for matching one natural fly, choose one or more, your choice depending upon what fly-tying materials you have available and any preference you have for a particular style of fly (e.g. some anglers prefer wet flies to dry flies, or hackleless to hackled flies). Note that it is often worth carrying two or three different patterns that can be used to imitate one natural fly. Sometimes fish will take one and not the other, for reasons that are not clear to us. For instance, in a hatch of olive duns a wet Waterhen Bloa may outfish an olive Cul de Canard Dun; the next day the success may be reversed. Also, if a fish has seen your artifical fly twice and ignored it, a change of pattern (wet for dry, hackled dry for CDC, emerger for dry) will often evoke a response.

A grasp of these monthly possibilities can be a great help at the waterside in determining the insects attracting the fish. But some general warnings are necessary. The timings of insect hatches can vary considerably from year to year, and with latitude, altitude, and weather.

Annual variation. Exceptions to an insect species' normal hatch-timings may always be encountered in local populations, with small numbers occurring outside the main period. For example, in mild early winters hatches of autumn upwinged flies may occur well into December. I have noted Mayflies hatching in November and Yellow May Duns to December. As with many if not most insects the occasional individual may appear at almost any time in the year: I have recorded the common and widespread Blue Winged Olive in every month of the year and once, in March, counted a hatch of 27 specimens on one river pool. But these minor hatches are usually unimportant for both fish and fisher.

Latitude. The monthly lists given in these charts are roughly those for Denmark, southern Sweden, Britain, northern Germany, northern France and Ireland. The further north than this, the later an insect hatch may be expected, and the further south the earlier – often by several weeks. The Cinnamon Sedge, for example, generally begins to hatch in mid-May in central Britain and early June in Scandinavia, but can be as early as mid-April in southern France.

Altitude. Similarly, for those insects which occur both in lowland rivers and upland streams, the hatches on the latter will be later. The Mayfly that begins to hatch on the large limestone lakes of Ireland in early May will often postpone its hatches on higher lakes and rivers until later in the month, sometimes even June.

Weather. Lastly, the weather from year to year can also affect timings noticeably: the warmer it is for a particular month, the earlier will be the hatch, and the colder the later. From May through to the end of September variations in weather (and consequently, water conditions) often have a profound effect on the timing of hatches. It is impossible to take into account all possibilities; the dates in the tables give the 'normal' situation. But in extremes of weather the actual hatching times of day may be highly abnormal. During prolonged periods of hot, dry weather, when lake and river temperatures may reach 20°C or more, and spate rivers shrink to a mere trickle, species that would normally hatch through the afternoon may postpone emergence until well into the night. Two examples: during one prolonged May heatwave the hatch of Mayfly duns on several Irish lakes (which normally occurs between 11am and 4pm) occurred between 1am and 3am. During a similar heatwave, the hatch of Iron Blue duns (usually hatching through the afternoon) began on two rivers at 11.30pm and continued to 2.30am.

Should such a drought suddenly end with heavy rain and cooler air, then the timings of hatches will often also change quickly. During one August drought the hatches of Blue Winged Olives (normally through the two hours preceeding dusk) on seven rivers were postponed to between 2am and 3.30am. Within two days of the drought ending, the hatches were re-timed to the afternoon (12.30-7pm) and a week later, with a return to warm, dry weather, the hatches re-timed again to 7-8.30pm.

Of course, the various factors above can cancel each other out, and may effect one insect group more than another in a given locality or year. But acting together, their effect can be dramatic. A hatch we might expect in mid-May can be encountered in late June, or vice versa. So when using these charts bear in mind the circumstances of where you are fishing and of the weather, and it is usually worth looking at the charts for the following and preceding months as well as the current one.

Ice. The icing over of many northern lakes and rivers obviously has a radical effect on the situation – separating us from the fish and the fish from such few insects as may appear. The data given in the January-April tables on the timing of hatches therefore apply only to those lakes and rivers not iced over. In those that are frozen for all or part of this period (that includes mountain lakes in central and eastern Europe and most waters in Russia and Fenno-Scandinavia), hatches usually begin immediately after the thaw. In such waters the hatches that extend from January to April in milder regions may be compressed into just a few weeks after the ice has gone. For instance, the February Red hatch may extend over ten weeks in rivers that remain ice-free, but in Sweden and Finland the hatch may last for only two or three weeks in April. Most European lakes and rivers are ice-free from May to November.

One essential adage of imitative fly fishing is to fish when the fish are feeding! From May to September, in bright, hot and dry weather, be prepared to find flies hatching and fish

Insect Group	January	February	March	April	May
Upwinged Flies		Afternoon hatches.			During spring and autumn,
Stoneflies		Afternoon hatches.		Hatches mostly afternoon to well into	
Land-bugs					In windy
Dragonflies & Damselflies					Underwater
Sedges			In some rivers the grannom hatches in huge numbers.		Many species
Two-winged Flies (Aquatic)		Midges may hatch on the coldest of days.		In all waters these are the most abundant	
Two-winged Flies (Land-bred)			A fall can occur through year (in winter on mild days, black gnats).		
Beetles (Land-bred)					
Alders					Adults often fly but rarely land on
Ants, Bees & Wasps					
Grasshoppers & Crickets					
Lacewings					Small numbers
Thrips					Occasionally and cereal
Moths & Butterflies			Moths often fall on the water at night,		

White: hatches or falls of adult insects very uncommon.
Light colour: very few species (usually one or two) within the group hatching. In very early spring and late autumn there may be no hatch in cold weather, but huge hatches in mild weather.
Darker colour: the adults of several species within the groups hatching or falling onto the water.

feeding from dusk and through the night. In dull, cool and rainy periods, expect the hatches of most insects to be in the afternoon and (with the exception of nocturnal sedges) to tail off as night falls. It is constructive and well worthwhile to keep a record of hatching times observed (dates, times of day, weather conditions). Doing so progressively gives one an idea of what to expect in future years and on new waters.

One can assume that, if there are no flies hatching at or falling onto the water surface, the fish will be feeding deep. So it is essential to have a variety of weighted imitation larvae, pupae, freshwater shrimps etc as well as imitations of the adult flies listed below. It is also essential to have some unweighted nymph and pupae patterns that imitate the insects rising through the water to hatch, as sometimes the fish will take these in preference to the hatched adult fly on the water. Use a net (see p. 23) to investigate what nymphs and other aquatic insects and crustaceans the fish might be eating when are no adult insects at the surface.

With these caveats and provisos, therefore, below we offer an overview of the principal insect groups tabled on the following pages, with the months in which the adults are most active.

June	July	August	September	October	November	December
dun hatches peak in afternoon; during summer, in later afternoon to evening. Spinners fall on the water evening to dark.					Afternoon hatches.	
night; adult females often on water (egg-laying) at dawn.		Though few species, often a big hatch in afternoon or evening.				
conditions many may be blown onto water. Aug-Nov aphids can dominate the fish's diet in a 'plague' year or during leaf-fall.						
nymphs can be important fish foods but adults rarely land on the water and are never selectively eaten by fish.						
may be on the water, with peak hatches from afternoon and through the night.					Stragglers from autumn hatches.	
aquatic insects, hatches occurring through day but peak in late afternoon to evening.					Midges may hatch on the coldest of days.	
Species often seasonal, e.g. hawthorn fly in spring, daddy-long-legs in later summer to autumn.						
	Adults often fly over the water but rarely land on the water (p. 76).					
over the water, the water (p. 76).						
Specimens are often found in fish stomachs in hot, windy weather. Occasionally big falls of ants in late summer.						
These occasionally fall or leap onto water from overhanging vegetation, but rarely in large numbers.						
may fall on water, especially in the evening.						
big falls may occur from surrounding grasslands fields, especially on hot, windy days.						
especially in well-wooded areas.						

JANUARY

In northern and upland regions lakes, and often rivers, are frozen over. Lakes through much of Europe may be iced over in particularly cold weather. All foods are generally sparse (many creatures hibernate through the winter; many insects overwinter as eggs).

Midges

Common name	See page	Scientific name	Insect group	Water type	When on water
Midges	71	Chironomidae	Two-winged Flies	All	Mild afternoons

FEBRUARY

Many northern and upland rivers and lakes may be iced over through February. Many lowland lakes may also be frozen during particularly cold winter weather. Thus hatches and falls of winged insects are sparse, except during mild weather. Subsurface foods may still be hibernating.

Large Dark Olive

February Red

Common name	See page	Scientific name	Insect group	Water type	When on water
Large Dark Olive	46	*Baetis rhodani*	Upwinged Flies	Rivers	Afternoon
February Red	54	*Brachyptera* and *Taeniopteryx*	Stoneflies	Rivers	Afternoon
Midges	71	Chironomidae	Two-winged Flies	All	Afternoon

MARCH

Many northern and upland rivers and lakes may still be iced over through March. In some areas the thaw begins in this month, followed by the first hatches. In rivers and lakes that remained open through the winter water temperatures begin to rise and nymphs, larvae and species such as the freshwater shrimp, water hog-louse and lesser water-boatman are more active.

March Brown

Black Stonefly

Early Brown

Common name	See page	Scientific name	Insect group	Water type	When on water
Large Dark Olive	46	*Baetis rhodani*	Upwinged Flies	Rivers	Afternoon
March Brown	48	*Rhithrogena* sp.	Upwinged Flies	Rough rocky rivers	Afternoon
Epeorus	50	*Epeorus* sp.	Upwinged Flies	Rough rocky streams	Afternoon and evening
Black Stonefly	54	*Capnia* and *Capnopsis*	Stoneflies	Rough rivers and rocky lakes	Afternoon
February Red	54	*Brachyptera* and *Taeniopteryx*	Stoneflies	Rivers	Afternoon
Small Brown	53	*Nemoura* sp.	Stoneflies	Rivers	Afternoon and evening
Early Brown	54	*Protonemura* sp.	Stoneflies	Rivers, including fast mountain streams	Afternoon and evening
Midges	71	Chironomidae	Two-winged Flies	All	Afternoon and evening

Save for particularly warm, mild weather (when surface midge actively may encourage the trout to rise) weighted artificials that imitate freshwater shrimps, cased caddis larvae and other bottom-dwelling forms are most effective.

Body length in mm	General body colour	Wing colour	Imitation	See page
up to 5	Grey or black	Transparent	Wet Flies CDC Category 3 Emergers Adult Midges	124, 128-35 138 190-2 192-4

Black Magic, p. 135

Unless some of the species listed below are hatching and the fish rising to take them, use weighted artificial flies as suggested for January.

Body length in mm	General body colour	Wing colour	Imitation	See page
6-11	Dun: drab olive-grey or olive-brown; spinner: red-brown	Dun: dull grey; spinner: transparent with brown veins	Dun: Wet Flies CDC Category 1 Dry Olives Spinner: Red Spinner CDC Category 2	124, 128 138 150-9 130, 134, 160-1 138
up to 13	Brown or red-brown	Dark red brown	Wet Flies CDC Category 3 Adult Stoneflies	128, 130, 134 138 170-1
up to 5	Grey or black	Transparent	Wet Flies CDC Category 3 Emergers Adult Midges	124, 128-35 138 190-2 192-4

Waterhen Bloa, p. 129

Orange Partridge, p. 129

During a hatch or fall of flies the fish often rise to the surface to feed and then they will take an appropriate dry imitation. When there is no hatch the fish often seek food keenly on the bottom: weighted imitations of freshwater shrimp, water hog-louse, lesser water-boatman, cased and uncased caddis larvae, upwinged fly and stonefly nymphs may all be effective.

Body length in mm	General body colour	Wing colour	Imitation	See page
6-11	Dun: drab olive-grey or olive-brown; spinner: red-brown	Dun: dull grey; spinner: transparent with brown veins	Dun: Wet Flies CDC Category 1 Dry Olives Spinner: Red Spinner CDC Category 2	124, 128 138 150-9 130, 134, 160-1 138
11-15	Dun: dark brown with straw-yellow bands; spinner: dark red-brown with buff bands	Dun: buff with dark markings; spinner transparent with brown veins	Dun: Wet Flies Dry Flies CDC Category 1 Spinner: Dry Flies Wet Flies CDC Category 2	130-1 150-5, 157-8 138 126, 160-1 130, 132, 134 138
14-17	Dun: straw-yellow with black markings ; spinner: pale yellow	Dun: yellow brown with black veins; spinner: transparent with black veins	Dun: Dry Flies Comparadun CDC Category 1 Yellow Spinner	152 158 138 162
4-10	Black	Grey with black veins		
up to 13	Brown or red-brown	Dark red-brown	Wet Flies CDC Caegory 3 Adult Stoneflies	128, 130, 134 138 170-1
up to 10	Dark brown	Dark glossy brown		
up to 10	Light medium-brown	Pale grey-brown		
up to 12	Black; grey; grey-olive; silver-grey and orange	Transparent	Wet Flies CDC Category 3 Emergers Adult Midges	124, 128-35 138 190-2 192-4

March Brown 1, p. 131

Quill Stonefly, p. 171

Brown Stonefly, p. 171

APRIL

Ice may remain on northern and mountain lakes through much of the month, postponing hatches and falls of flies until after the thaw. During April most of those insects that have hibernated and been inaccessible to the fish emerge; those that have overwintered as eggs hatch. So there is an

Sepia Dun

Iron Blue

Pale March Brown

Large Stonefly

Yellow Sally

Sand-fly

Grannom

Hawthornfly

Common Name	See page	Scientific name	Insect group	Water type	When on water
Sepia Dun	44	*Leptophlebia marginata*	Upwinged Flies	Acid lakes, especially with boulder bed	Afternoon and early evening
Large Dark Olive	46	*Baetis rhodani*	Upwinged Flies	Rivers	Afternoon
Iron Blue	46	*Baetis*	Upwinged Flies	Rivers	Dun: late morning and afternoon; spinner: afternoon to dark
March Brown	48	*Rhithrogena*	Upwinged Flies	Rough rocky rivers	Afternoon
False March Brown	48	*Ecdyonurus*	Upwinged Flies	Rough rocky rivers and stony lakes	Dun: afternoon;spinner: evening
Epeorus	50	*Epeorus*	Upwinged Flies	Rough rocky streams	Afternoon and evening into darkness
Large Stonefly	52	*Perla; Perlodes* and *Dinocras*	Stoneflies	Rough rocky rivers and stony lakes	Afternoon and evening into darkness
Medium Stonefly	53	*Diura*	Stoneflies	Rough rocky streams and stony lakes	Afternoon and evening
February Red	54	*Brachyptera , Taeniopteryx*	Stoneflies	Rivers	Afternoon
Small Brown	53	*Nemoura*	Stoneflies	Rivers; one species stony lakes	Afternoon and evening into darkness
Black Stonefly	54	*Capnia, Capnoides*	Stoneflies	Rocky rivers, stony lakes	Afternoon
Early Brown	54	*Protonemura*	Stoneflies	Rivers, mountain streams	Afternoon and evening
Yellow Sally	54	*Isoperla*	Stoneflies	Rivers	Late morning to dusk
Small Yellow Sally	54	*Chloroperla*	Stoneflies	Rocky rivers,barren lakes	Late morning to dusk
Sand-fly	64	*Rhyacophila dorsalis*	Sedges	Rivers, especially upland regions	Late afternoon and evening into darkness
Medium Sedge	64	*Goera pilosa*	Sedges	Lakes and rivers	Late morning to dusk
Brown Sedge	64	Many species	Sedges	Lakes and rivers	Evening into darkness
Grannom	64	*Brachycentrus subnubilis*	Sedges	Rivers (especially chalk and limestone)	Afternoon
Small Red Sedge	66	*Tinodes* sp.	Sedges	Lakes and rivers	Late afternoon to dark
Little Black Sedge	68	*Agapetus fuscipes*	Sedges	Stony lakes	Late afternoon to dark
Midges	71	Chironomidae	Two-winged Flies	All	Mostly afternoon and evening into darkness
Hawthornfly	74	*Bibio marci*	Two-winged Flies	All	Through day
Black Gnat	74	Many species	Two-winged Flies	All	Through day

increasing variety and population of growing larvae and nymphs, aquatic bugs and beetles for the fish to take. April usually sees the first falls of landbred insects, notably hawthorn flies; but look out also for species such as dung-flies (p. 74) and chinch-bugs (p. 58) on warm days.

Body length in mm	General body colour	Wing colour	Imitation	See page
7-10	Dun: dark brown; spinner: dark red-brown	Dun: fawn-medium brown; spinner: transparent with sooty patch	Dun: CDC Category 1 Claret/Sepia Spinner: Pheasant Tail CDC Category 2 Brown	138 155 126 138 162
6-11	Dun: drab olive-grey or olive-brown; spinner: red-brown	Dun: dull grey; spinner: transparent with brown veins	Dun: Wet Flies CDC Category 1 Dry Olives Spinner: Red Spinner CDC Category 2	128 138 150-9 130, 134, 160-1 138
5-7	Dun: dark black-grey; spinner ruddy-brown with light bands	Dun: dark blue-grey; spinner transparent	Dun: Wet Flies CDC Category 1 Dry Duns Spinner: CDC Category 2 Dry Spinners	124, 128-9, 132 138 150, 152, 157 138 161-2
11-15	Dun: dark brown with straw-yellow bands; spinner: dark red-brown with buff bands	Dun: buff with dark markings; spinner: transparent with brown veins	Dun: Wet Flies Dry Flies CDC Category 1	130-1 151-5, 157-8 138
11-16	Dun: dark brown with pale straw bands; spinner rich red-brown	Dun: buff or grey-buff with variable dark markings; spinner: transparent with dark veins	Spinner: Dry Flies Wet Flies CDC Category 2	126, 160-1 130, 132, 134 138
14-17	Dun: straw-yellow with black markings; spinner: pale yellow	Dun yellow-brown with black veins; spinner: transparent with black veins	Dun: Dry Flies Comparadun CDC Category 1 Yellow Spinner	152 159 138 162
up to 25	Dark brown with lighter markings	Dark brown		
up to 18	Dark brown	Glossy dark brown		
up to 13	Brown or red-brown	Dark red brown	Wet Flies CDC Category 3 Adult Stoneflies	128, 130, 134 138 170-1
up to 10	Dark brown	Glossy dark brown		
4-10	Black	Grey with black veins		
up to 10	Light-medium brown	Pale grey-brown		
up to 14	Lemon-yellow	Yellow	CDC Category 3 Yellow Sally	138 170-1
up to 8	Pale yellow	Pale yellow		
11-15	Olive-green	Sandy to dark brown		
9-13	Buff-brown	Grey-buff	Wet Sedges Bustards CDC Category 3 Adult (Impressionistic) (Imitative)	132-3 136 138 180-1 182-6
12-16	Brown	Brown		
8-11	Olive-fawn	Sandy-yellow with darker markings		
6-8	Grey or red-brown	Red-brown		
5-6	Black	Black		
up to 13	Black; grey; olive; orange; ginger; green	Transparent	Wet Flies CDC Category 3 Emergers Adult Midges	124, 128-35 138 190-2 192-4
up to 12	Black	Semi-transparent pale grey	Wet Flies CDC Category 3, 4 Hawthorn/Gnats	128, 132 138-9 194-5
up to 12	Black or brown-black	Transparent or semi-transparent grey		

Claret/Sepia Dun, p. 155

Dark Watchett, p. 129

Adams, p. 153

Large Stonefly, p. 171

Spent Yellow Sally, p. 171

RM Sedge, p. 181

Dancing Caddis, p. 181

Hawthornfly, p. 195

MAY

Hatches of aquatic flies and falls of landbred flies are prolific in May. During the course of one day the fish may be feeding at the water surface, taking hatching insects from just below or hatched flies or landbred flies from off the surface, and changing diet as the hatch of one ceases and another commences. Change imitative surface flies as the fish change their preferred food species.

Mayfly

Yellow Dun

Angler's Curse

Claret Dun

Pond Olive

Olive Upright

Epeorus

Common name	See page	Scientific name	Insect group	Water type	When on water
Mayfly	42	*Ephemera danica*	Upwinged Flies	Rivers and lakes, especially alkaline	Dun: late morning-afternoon; spinner: afternoon-evening
Dark Mayfly	42	*Ephemera vulgata*	Upwinged Flies	Slow rivers and lakes, especially alkaline	Dun: late morning-afternoon; spinner: evening
Yellow Evening Dun	44	*Ephemerella notata*	Upwinged Flies	Rivers (especially fast; limestone)	Late evening, well into darkness
Yellow Dun	50	*Heptagenia* sp.	Upwinged Flies	Rough rocky streams	Dun: late morning and afternoon; spinner: dusk
Purple Dun	44	*Paraleptophlebia* sp.	Upwinged Flies	Fast rivers (especially limestone)	Dun: late morning-afternoon; spinner evening
Iron Blue	46	*Baetis* sp.	Upwinged Flies	Rivers	Dun: Late morning and afternoon; spinner: afternoon to dark
Angler's Curse	44	*Caenis* or *Brachycerus* sp.	Upwinged Flies	Rivers and lakes, especially with silty bed	Early morning or afternoon-evening
Claret Dun	44	*Leptophlebia vespertina*	Upwinged Flies	Acid or peaty lakes	Dun: late morning-afternoon; spinner: evening
Sepia Dun	44	*Leptophlebia marginata*	Upwinged Flies	Acid lakes, especially with boulder bed	Afternoon and early evening
Alpine Olive	46	*Baetis alpinus*	Upwinged Flies	Mountain streams	Dun: afternoon; spinner: evening and dawn
Medium Olive	46	*Baetis* sp.	Upwinged Flies	Rivers	Dun: late morning-afternoon; spinner: afternoon-evening
Pond Olive	47	*Cloeon dipterum*	Upwinged Flies	Lakes, especially small shallow bays and tiny pools	Dun: late morning-evening; spinner: evening and through night
Lake Olive	48	*Cloeon simile*	Upwinged Flies	Larger lakes	Late morning to dark
Olive Upright	48	*Rhithrogena* sp.	Upwinged Flies	Rough rock rivers	Dun: mid-day to dusk; spinner: dusk
Dark Dun	50	*Heptagenia* sp.	Upwinged Flies	Upland lakes and streams	Late morning to dark
Pale Watery	46	Many species	Upwinged Flies	Mostly rivers (1 species lakes)	Midday to dark
False March Brown	48	*Ecdyonurus* sp.	Upwinged Flies	Rough rocky rivers and stony lakes	Dun: afternoon; spinner in evening into darkness
Epeorus	50	*Epeorus* sp.	Upwinged Flies	Rough rocky streams	Afternoon and evening into darkness

On cool days, when surface activity is reduced, or in lulls between hatches, assume that the fish are feeding on or close to the bottom: leaded nymphs, pupae and larvae, freshwater shrimps, lesser water boatmen will be effective.

Body length in mm	General body colour	Wing colour	Imitation	See page
16-25	Dun: cream with dark markings; spinner: white with dark markings	Dun: grey- or yellow-green; spinner: gauzy blue-black	Dun: Dry Flies	164-5
14-24	Dun: yellow-buff with dark markings; spinner cream olive with dark markings	Dun: yellow-buff; spinner: gauzy black-brown	Spinner: CDC Category 2 / Dry Spinners	138 / 166
8-13	Dun: yellowish; spinner: yellow-olive	Dun: pale grey with yellow veins; spinner transparent with yellow veins	Dun: CDC Category 1 Yellow Dun Spinner	138 / 154-5, 157-9
10-12	Dun: bright yellow; spinner: bright golden-brown	Dun: yellow with brown veins; spinner: transparent with dark veins		162-3
6-9	Dun: dark brown-olive; spinner: dark purple-brown	Dun: pale to very dark grey; spinner: transparent	Dun: Wet Flies CDC Category 1 Dry Duns	128-9, 132 / 138 / 150, 152, 157
5-7	Dun: dark black-grey; spinner ruddy-brown with light bands	Dun: dark blue-grey; spinner transparent	Spinner: CDC Category 2 Dry Spinners	138 / 161-2
3-6	Dun and spinner: dark thorax; whitish abdomen	Dun and spinner: whitish	Wet Flies CDC Category 1 Dry Caenis	128-9, 134-5 / 138-9 / 154-5
8-12	Dun: dark brown; spinner: glossy claret-brown	Dun: forewings dark grey; hindwings pale; spinner: transparent with light brown veins	Dun: CDC Category 1 Claret/Sepia Spinner: Pheasant Tail	138 / 155 / 126
7-10	Dun: dark brown; spinner: dark red-brown	Dun: fawn-medium brown; spinner: transparent with sooty patch	CDC Category 2 Brown	138 / 162
8-10	Dun: drab olive; spinner red-brown	Dun: medium grey; spinner: transparent with brown veins		
6-8	Dun: olive; spinner: yellow- or red-brown	Dun: dull grey; spinner: transparent	Dun: Wet Flies CDC Category 1 DryOlives	124, 128 / 138 / 124, 150-9
7-10	Dun: grey-olive; spinner: apricot	Dun: dark blue-grey; spinner: transparent with red-brown veins	Spinner: Wet Flies Dry Flies CDC Category 2	130, 134 / 160-1 / 138
7-11	Dun: drab olive; spinner: red-brown	Dark grey with green markings; spinner: transparent with olive patch		
9-15	Dun: grey-green with olive bands; spinner red-brown	Dun: forewings dark grey; hindwings buff; spinner: transparent with brown veins		
12-15	Dun: brown-grey; spinner: dark olive-brown with red bands	Dun: grey; spinner: transparent with brown veins		
5-8	Dun: off-white to light brown-olive; spinner: white and orange to bright red-brown	Dun: pale to dark grey; spinner: transparent	Dun: Wet Flies CDC Category 1 Dry Duns Spinner: Wet Flies CDC Category 2 Dry Spinners	128-9 / 138 / 124, 150, 152, 156-9 / 128-9 / 138 / 161-2
11-16	Dun: dark brown with pale straw bands; spinner rich red-brown	Dun: buff or grey-buff with variable dark markings; spinner: transparent with dark veins	Dun: Wet Flies Dry Flies CDC Category 1 Spinner: Wet Flies Dry Flies CDC Category 2	130-1 / 151-5, 157-8 / 138 / 130-1 / 151-5, 157-8 / 138
14-17	Dun: straw-yellow with black markings; spinner: pale yellow	Dun yellow-brown with black veins; spinner: transparent with black veins	Dun: Dry Flies Comparadun CDC Category 1 Yellow Spinner	152 / 159 / 138 / 162

Mayfly Dun 1, p. 165

Yellow Dun 2, p. 155

Winter Ptarmigan, p. 135

Imperial, p. 153

Olive Dun 1, p. 155

Olive Dun 5, p. 155

CDC Category 1 MP10, p. 139

MAY continued

Medium Stonefly

Small Yellow Sally

Great Red Sedge

Welshman's Button

Mottled Sedge

Small Silver Sedge

Mosquito

Black Gnat

Common name	See page	Scientific name	Insect group	Water type	When on water
Large Stonefly	52	*Perla; Perlodes* and *Dinocras*	Stoneflies	Rough rocky rivers and stony lakes	Afternoon and evening, into darkness
Medium Stonefly	53	*Diura* species	Stoneflies	Rough rocky streams and stony lakes	Afternoon and evening
Small Brown	53	*Nemoura* species	Stoneflies	Rivers; one species stony lakes	Afternoon and evening, into darkness
Black Stonefly	54	*Capnia* and *Capnoides*	Stoneflies	Rough rocky rivers and stony lakes	Afternoon
Early Brown	54	*Protonemura* sp.	Stoneflies	Rivers, including fast mountain streams	Afternoon and evening
Yellow Sally	54	*Isoperla* sp.	Stoneflies	Rivers	Late morning to dusk
Small Yellow Sally	54	*Chloroperla*	Stoneflies	Rough rocky rivers and barren lakes	Late morning to dusk
Land-bug	58	Several species	Bugs	All	Through day (especially in wind)
Great Red Sedge	62	*Phryganea* sp.	Sedges	Lakes	Evening and dark
Cinnamon Sedge	63	*Limnephilus* sp.	Sedges	Lakes and rivers	Through day
Sand-Fly	64	*Rhyacophila dorsalis*	Sedges	Rivers, especially in upland regions	Late afternoon and evening into darkness
Medium Sedge	64	*Goera pilosa*	Sedges	Lakes and rivers	Late morning to dusk
Brown Sedge	64	Many species	Sedges	Lakes and rivers	Evening into darkness
Welshman's Button	64	*Sericostoma personatum*	Sedges	Rivers	Through day
Grannom	64	*Brachycentrus subnubilis*	Sedges	Rivers (especially chalk and limestone)	Afternoon
Mottled Sedge	64	*Glyphotaelius pellucidus*	Sedges	Weedy ponds and lakes	Evening into darkness
Small Red Sedge	66	*Tinodes* sp.	Sedges	Lakes and rivers	Late afternoon and evening into darkness
Small Yellow Sedge	66	*Psychomis pusilla*	Sedges	Rivers	Evening
Longhorns	66	*Oecetis* sp.	Sedges	Lakes	Afternoon-evening
Small Silver Sedge	66	*Lepidostoma hirtum*	Sedges	Rivers	Late evening and into darkness
Black Sedge	66	Several species	Sedges	Lakes and rivers	Evening and into darkness
Little Black Sedge	68	*Agapetus fuscipes*	Sedges	Stony lakes	Late afternoon and evening
Speckled Sedge	68	*Philopotamus montanus*	Sedges	Rough upland streams	Evening
Microcaddis	68	Hydroptilidae	Sedges	All	Evening
Midges	71	Chironomidae	Two-winged Flies	All	Mostly afternoon and evening into darkness
Mosquito	72	Several species	Two-winged Flies	Small pools and weedy bays	Evening
Biting Midges	72	Several species	Two-winged Flies	All	Through day; but especially evening
Hawthornfly	74	*Bibio marci*	Two-winged Flies	All	Through day
Black Gnat	74	Many species	Two-winged Fies	All	Through day
Land Beetles	76	Many species	Beetles	All	Through day
Alder	76	*Sialis* sp.	Alders	Rivers and lakes	Through day

Body length in mm	General body colour	Wing colour	Imitation	See page		
up to 25	Dark brown with lighter markings	Dark brown				Dark Needle, p. 131
up to 18	Dark brown	Glossy dark brown				
up to 10	Dark brown	Glossy dark brown	Wet Flies CDC Category 3 Adult Stoneflies	128, 130, 134 138 170-1		
4-10	Black	Grey with black veins				
up to 10	Light-medium brown	Pale grey-brown				
up to 14	Lemon-yellow	Yellow	CDC Category 3 Yellow Sally	138-9 170-1		Yellow Sally, p. 171
up to 8	Pale yellow	Pale yellow				
Varies	Varies	Varies	Land-bugs	174-5		
22-32	Grey	Red-brown with black markings				Great Red Sedge, p. 183
12-16	Olive-green	Buff-yellow with darker markings				
11-15	Olive-green	Sandy to dark brown				
9-13	Buff-brown	Grey-buff				
12-16	Brown	Brown				
12-15	Olive-grey	Dark golden- or chestnut-brown				G & H Deerhair Sedge, p. 181
8-11	Olive-fawn	Sandy-yellow with darker markings	Wet Sedges Bustards CDC Category 3 Adult (Impressionistic) (Imitative)	132-3 136 138 180-1 182-7		
16-18	Dull olive-green	Silver-grey with dark brown blotches				
6-8	Grey or red-brown	Red-brown				
5	Dull yellow	Yellow-buff to bright yellow				CDC Category 3 MP53, p. 139
12-15	Drab green	Pale yellow or cream-grey				
8-10	Olive-brown to green	Greyish				
up to 11	Blackish	Blackish				
5-6	Black	Black				Grey Sedge 1, p. 185
9-14	Olive-or reddish-brown	Brown with yellow dots				
up to 5	Buff to black-brown	Buff to black				
up to 13	Black; grey; olive; orange; ginger; green	Transparent	Wet Flies CDC Category 3 Emergers Adult Midges	124, 128-135 138 190-2 192-4		
up to 10	Dark grey or black with pale bands	Transparent with dark veins				Black Midge 4, p. 193
up to 5	Grey or black	Transparent with fine dark veins				
up to 12	Black	Semi-transparent pale grey	Wet Flies CDC Category 3, 4 Hawthorn/Gnats	128, 132 138-9 194-5		
up to 12	Black or brown-black	Transparent or semi-transparent grey				
most up to 10	Mostly black	Mostly black; dark green or brown	Beetles Jassid	196-7 174		Black Gnat, p. 195
up to 15	Blackish	Rich brown with dark veins	Alder Small dark Sedges	197 184		

JUNE

A month with superb fly hatches which encourage the fish to feed keenly and selectively at the water surface and often demand that the angler matches the hatch with suitable artificial flies. Beware: sometimes the fish will select pupae and nymphs just below the surface rather than the flies that have hatched and are standing on the water. Identify the species that is hatching. If the fish are feeding at the surface but not taking the hatched flies, try imitations of the nymphs or pupae or emergers

Dark Mayfly

Yellow Mayfly

Southern Mayfly

Summer Mayfly

Blue-winged Olive

Purple Dun

Angler's Curse

Iron Blue

Common name	See page	Scientific name	Insect group	Water type	When on water
Mayfly	42	*Ephemera danica*	Upwinged Flies	Rivers and lakes, especially alkaline	Dun: late morning-afternon; spinner: afternoon-evening
Dark Mayfly	42	*Ephemera vulgata*	Upwinged Flies	Slow rivers and lakes, especially alkaline	Dun: late morning-afternoon; spinner: evening
Yellow Mayfly	42	*Potamanthus luteus*	Upwinged Flies	Fast clean rivers	Late evening and dark
Yellow Evening Dun	44	*Ephemerella notata*	Upwinged Flies	Rivers (especially fast; limestone)	Late evening, well into darkness
Yellow Dun	50	*Heptagenia* sp.	Upwinged Flies	Rough rocky streams	Dun: late morning and afternoon; spinner: dusk
Southern Mayfly	42	*Oligoneuriella rhenana*	Upwinged Flies	Large rivers	Dun: late afternoon; spinner: evening and dark
False March Brown	48	*Ecdyonurus* sp.	Upwinged Flies	Rough rocky rivers and stony lakes	Dun: afternoon; spinner: evening
Summer Mayfly	50	*Siphlonurus* sp.	Upwinged Flies	Northern and upland lakes and slow rivers	Afternoon-evening
Palingenia	50	*Palingenia longicauda*	Upwinged Flies	Large rivers	Dun: late morning and afternoon; spinner: evening
Blue-winged Olive	42	*Ephemerella ignita*	Upwinged Flies	Rivers	Dun: afternoon-evening; spinner: evening and into darkness
Purple Dun	44	*Paraleptophlebia* sp.	Upwinged Flies	Fast rivers (especially limestone)	Dun: late morning-afternoon; spinner evening
Iron Blue	46	*Baetis* sp.	Upwinged Flies	Rivers	Dun: late morning and afternoon; spinner: afternoon to dark
Angler's Curse	44	*Caenis* or *Brachycerus* sp.	Upwinged Flies	Rivers and lakes, especially with silty beds	Early morning or afternoon-evening
Claret Dun	44	*Leptophlebia vespertina*	Upwinged Flies	Acid or peaty lakes	Dun: late morning-afternoon; spinner: evening

Look also for falls of landbred insects; these may dominate the fish's diet on some waters. During periods when the fish are not active at the surface, look to deep foods: they may be feeding on amphibian tadpoles (p. 84), damselfly nymphs (p. 59) or freshwater shrimps (p. 80), lesser water boatmen (p. 56) etc.

Body length in mm	General body colour	Wing colour	Imitation	See page
16-25	Dun: cream with dark markings; spinner: white with dark markings	Dun: grey- or yellow-green; spinner: gauzy blue-black	Dun: Dry Flies Spinner: CDC Category 2 Dry Spinners	164-5 138 166
14-24	Dun: yellow-buff with dark markings; spinner cream olive with dark markings	Dun: yellow-buff; spinner: gauzy black-brown		
14-16	Dun and spinner: yellow with brown stripe along body	Dun and spinner: yellow	Dun: CDC Category 1 Yellow Dun Spinner	138 154-5, 157-9 162-3
8-13	Dun: yellowish; spinner: yellow-olive	Dun: pale grey with yellow veins; spinner transparent with yellow veins		
10-12	Dun: bright yellow; spinner: bright golden-brown	Dun: yellow with brown veins; spinner: transparent with dark veins		
12-14	Dun: drab light brown with dark markings; spinner: bright orange brown	Look for reduced venation	Dun: Wet Flies Dry Flies CDC Category 1 Spinner: Wet Flies Dry Flies CDC Category 2	130-1 151-5, 157-8 138 130-1 151-5, 157-8 138
11-16	Dun: dark brown with pale straw bands; spinner rich red-brown	Dun: buff or grey-buff with variable dark markings; spinner: transparent with dark veins		
14-21	Dun: olive-brown with dark bands; spinner: dark brown with pale bands	Dun: a shade of grey; spinner: transparent with dark veins		
20-28;	Dun and spinner: yellow-brown	Dun and spinner: pale buff		
8-12	Dun: olives, olive-brown and orange-brown; spinner: olive-brown to deep red	Dun: dark blue-grey; spinner: transparent with light brown veins	Dun: Wet Flies CDC Category 1 Dry Duns Spinner: Pheasant Tail Wet CDC Category 2 Dry Spinners	128-30 138 150-3, 156, 158-9 126 128-9, 134 138-9 160-1
6-9	Dun: dark brown-olive; spinner: dark purple-brown	Dun: pale to very dark grey; spinner: transparent	Dun: Wet Flies CDC Category 1 Dry Duns Spinner: CDC Category 2 Dry Spinners	128-9, 132 138 150, 152, 157 138 161-2
5-7	Dun: dark black-grey; spinner ruddy-brown with light bands	Dun: dark blue-grey; spinner transparent		
3-6	Dun and spinner: dark thorax; whitish abdomen	Dun and spinner: whitish	Wet Flies CDC Category 1) Dry Caenis	128-9, 134-5 138 154-5
8-12	Dun: dark brown; spinner: glossy claret-brown	Dun: forewings dark grey; hindwings pale; spinner: transparent with light brown veins	Dun: CDC Category 1 Claret/Sepia Spinner: Pheasant Tail CDC Category 2 Brown	138 155 126 138 162

Elk Mayfly, p. 165

Yellow Dun 1, p. 155

No-hackle March Brown 2, p. 157

March Brown Comparadun, p. 159

Red Spinner 1, p. 131

Snipe & Purple, p. 129

Caenis 2, p. 155

Red Spinner 5, p. 161

JUNE continued

Medium Olive dun

Lake Olive

Green Dun

Arctic Dun

Large Stonefly

Small Brown

Green Shield Bug

Green Peter

Brown Sedge

Common name	See page	Scientific name	Insect group	Water type	When on water
Alpine Olive	46	*Baetis alpinus*	Upwinged Flies	Mountain streams	Dun: afternoon; spinner: evening and dawn
Medium Olive	46	*Baetis* sp.	Upwinged Flies	Rivers	Dun: late morning-afternoon; spinner: afternoon-evening
Pond Olive	47	*Cloeon dipterum*	Upwinged Flies	Lakes, especially small shallow bays and tiny pools	Dun: late morning-evening; spinner: evening and through night
Lake Olive	48	*Cloeon simile*	Upwinged Flies	Larger lakes	Late morning to dark
Olive Upright	48	*Rhithrogena* sp.	Upwinged Flies	Rough rocky rivers	Dun: mid-day to dusk; spinner: dusk
Green Dun	49	*Ecdyonurus* sp.	Upwinged Flies	Rough rocky rivers, especially limestone	Afternoon-late evening into darkness
Dark Dun	50	*Heptagenia* sp.	Upwinged Flies	Upland lakes and streams	Late morning to dark
Arctic Dun	50	*Metropus norvegicus*	Upwinged Flies	Arctic and subarctic streams and lakes	Dun: late morning and afternoon; spinner: evening
Pale Watery	46	Many species	Upwinged Flies	Mostly rivers (1 species lakes)	Midday to dark
Large Stonefly	52	*Perla; Perlodes* and *Dinocras*	Stoneflies	Rough rocky rivers and stony lakes	Afternoon and evening, into darkness
Medium Stonefly	53	*Diura* sp.	Stoneflies	Rough rocky streams and stony lakes	Afternoon and evening, into darkness
Small Brown	53	*Nemoura* sp.	Stoneflies	Rivers; one species stony lakes	Afternoon and evening, into darkness
Yellow Sally	54	*Isoperla* sp.	Stoneflies	Rivers	Late morning to dusk
Small Yellow Sally	54	*Chloroperla*	Stoneflies	Rough rocky rivers and barren lakes	Late morning to dusk
Land-bug	58	Several species	Bugs	All	Through day (especially wind)
Great Red Sedge	62	*Phryganea* sp.	Sedges	Lakes, especially large limestone	Evening and dark
Green Peter	62	*Phryganea obsoleta*	Sedges	Lakes, especially large limestone	Late afternoon-evening
Cinnamon Sedge	63	*Limnephilus* sp.	Sedges	Lakes and rivers	Through day
Sand-fly	64	*Rhyacophila dorsalis*	Sedges	Rivers, especially in upland regions	Late afternoon and evening into darkness
Chestnut-winged Sedge	64	*Triaenodes bicolor*	Sedges	Upland and northern weedy lakes	Afternoon and evening into darkness
Medium Sedge	64	*Goera pilosa*	Sedges	Lakes and rivers	Late morning to dusk
Brown Sedge	64	Many species	Sedges	Lakes and rivers	Evening into darkness

Body length in mm	General body colour	Wing colour	Imitation	See page
8-10	Dun: drab olive; spinner red-brown	Dun: medium grey; spinner: transparent with brown veins		
6-8	Dun: olive; spinner: yellow- or red-brown	Dun: dull grey; spinner: transparent		
7-10	Dun: grey-olive; spinner: apricot	Dun: dark blue-grey; spinner: transparent with red-brown veins		
7-11	Dun: drab olive; spinner: red-brown	Dark grey with green markings; spinner: transparent with olive patch		
9-15	Dun: grey-green with olive bands; spinner red-brown	Dun: forewings dark grey; hindwings buff; spinner: transparent with brown veins	Dun: Wet Flies 　CDC Category 1 　Dry Olives Spinner: Wet Flies 　Dry Flies 　CDC Category 2	124, 128 124, 138 150-9 130, 134, 160-1 138
13-16	Dun and spinner: green with darker markings	Dun: green-olive with dark veins; spinner: transparent with dark veins and sooty patch		
12-15	Dun: brown-grey; spinner: dark olive-brown with red bands	Dun: grey; spinner: transparent with brown veins		
9-12	Dun: olive-brown; spinner: golden-brown	Dun: buff- or olive-grey; spinner: transparent with brown veins and opaque patch		
5-8	Dun: off-white to light brown-olive; spinner: white and orange to bright red-brown	Dun: pale to dark grey; spinner: transparent	Dun: Wet Flies 　CDC Category 1 　Dry Duns Spinner: Wet Flies 　CDC Category 2 　Dry Spinners	128-9 138 124, 150, 152, 156-9 128-9 138 161-2
up to 25	Dark brown with lighter markings	Dark brown		
up to 18	Dark brown	Glossy dark brown	Wet Flies CDC Category 3 Adult Stoneflies	128, 130, 134 138 170-1
up to 10	Dark brown	Glossy dark brown		
up to 14	Lemon-yellow	Yellow	CDC Category 3 Yellow Sally	138 170-1
up to 8	Pale yellow	Pale yellow		
Varies	Varies	Varies	Land-bugs	174-5
22-32	Grey	Red-brown with black markings		
10-12	Olive-green	Dark brown with pale patches		
12-16	Olive-green	Buff-yellow with darker markings	Wet Sedges Bustards CDC Category 3 Adult (Impressionistic) 　(Imitative)	132-3 136 138 180-1 182-7
11-15	Olive-green	Sandy to dark brown		
8-11	Light brown	Chestnut-brown		
9-13	Buff-brown	Grey-buff		
12-16	Brown	Brown		

Dry Greenwell's Glory 1, p. 125

Pheasant Tail spinner, p. 126

CDC Category 2

Dark Cahill, p. 153

Dark Stonefly 2, p. 171

CDC Category 3
MP52, p. 139

Land-bug, p. 175

Green Peter, p. 183

Brown Sedge 2, p. 185

JUNE continued

Marbled Sedge

Grey Flag

Small Yellow Sedge

Black Sedge (*Tinodes*)

Speckled Sedge

Microcaddis

adult Reed-smut

Torrent Midge

Tortoise Beetle

Common name	See page	Scientific name	Insect group	Water type	When on water
Welshman's Button	64	*Sericostoma personatum*	Sedges	Rivers	Through day
Marbled Sedge	64	*Hydropsyche* sp.	Sedges	Rough rocky streams especially in upland areas	Late afternoon and evening into darkness
Mottled Sedge	64	*Glyphotaelius pellucidus*	Sedges	Weedy ponds and lakes	Evening into darkness
Grey Flag	64	Several species	Sedges	Fast rocky rivers	Through day
Small Red Sedge	66	*Tinodes* sp.	Sedges	Lakes and rivers	Late afternoon and evening
Small Yellow Sedge	66	*Psychomis pusilla*	Sedges	Rivers	Evening and into darkne
Grousewing	66	*Mystacides longicornis*	Sedges	Lakes	Late afternoon and evening and into darkne
Black Silverhorns	66	Several species	Sedges	Lakes and rivers	Afternoon and evening
Brown Silverhorns	66	*Arthripsodes* sp.	Sedges	Lakes and rivers	Afternoon and evening
Longhorns	66	*Oecetis* sp.	Sedges	Lakes	Afternoon and evening
Small Silver Sedge	66	*Lepidostoma hirtum*	Sedges	Rivers	Late evening and into darkness
Black Sedge	66	Several species	Sedges	Lakes and rivers	Evening and into darkne
Little Black Sedge	68	*Agapetus fuscipes*	Sedges	Stony lakes	Late afternoon and evening
Yellow-spotted Sedge	68	Several species	Sedges	Lakes and rivers	Evening into darkness
Speckled Sedge	68	*Philopotamus montanus*	Sedges	Rough upland streams	Evening into darkness
Microcaddis	68	Hydroptilidae	Sedges	All	Evening into darkness
Reed—smut	70	*Simulium* sp.	Two-winged Flies	Rivers	Through day but peak in the evening
Phantom Fly	70	*Chaoborus* sp.	Two-winged Flies	Lakes	Mostly evening and through night
Midges	71	Chironomidae	Two-winged Flies	All	Mostly afternoon and evening
Mosquito	72	Several species	Two-winged Flies	Small pools and weedy bays	Evening and through nig
Biting Midges	72	Several species	Two-winged Flies	All	Through day; but especially evening
Torrent Midges	72	*Liponeura* sp.	Two-winged Flies	Rough mountain streams	Mostly afternoon and evening
Black Gnat	74	Many species	Two-winged Flies	All	Through day
Daddy-long-legs	74	*Tipula* sp.	Two-winged Flies	All	Through day but mostly evening in windy weath
Land Beetles	76	Many species	Beetles	All	Through day, especially windy weather
Alder	76	*Sialis* sp.	Alders	Rivers and lakes	Through day

Body length in mm	General body colour	Wing colour	Imitation	See page
12-15	Olive-grey	Dark golden- or chestnut-brown		
10-15	Dark olive green	Green-brown with dark brown and olive-grey blotches		
16-18	Dull olive-green	Silver-grey with dark brown blotches		
11-20	Olive- or brown-grey	Silvery or dark grey		
6-8	Grey or red-brown	Red-brown		
5	Dull yellow	Yellow-buff to bright yellow		
about 10	Grey-brown	Red-brown with broad black bars		
6-11	Black	Blackish	Wet Sedges Bustards CDC Category 3 Adult (Impressionistic) (Imitative)	132-3 136 138 180-1 182-7
about 10	Olive to green-brown	Brown (some with white markings)		
12-15	Drab green	Pale yellow or cream-grey		
8-10	Olive-brown to green	Greyish		
up to 11	Blackish	Blackish		
5-6	Black	Blackish		
9-13	Brown	Brown or red-brown with fine yellow speckles		
9-14	Olive-or reddish-brown	Brown with yellow dots		
up to 5	Buff to black-brown	Buff to black		
see text	Black or grey	Transparent	Wet Flies CDC Category 3 La Petite Merde Smuts	128, 134 138 194 188
up to 8	Grey or olive	Transparent with fine dark veins		
up to 13	Black; grey; olive; orange; ginger; green	Transparent		
up to 10	Dark grey or black with pale bands	Transparent with dark veins	Wet Flies CDC Category 3 Emergers Adult Midges	124, 128-135 138, 190-2 192-4
up to 5	Grey or black	Transparent with fine dark veins		
see text	Grey or black	Transparent		
up to 12	Black or brown-black	Transparent or semi-transparent grey	Wet Flies CDC Category 3, 4 Hawthorn/Gnats	128, 132 138-9 194-5
up to 35	Brown	Grey, buff; semi-transparent	Daddy-long-legs	196
most up to 10	Mostly black	Mostly black; dark green or brown	Beetles Jassid	196-7 174
up to 15	Blackish	Rich brown with dark veins	Alder Small dark Sedges	197 184

Elk Hair Caddis, p. 185

Grey Sedge 2, p. 185

CDC Category 3
MP66, p. 139

Black Sedge 1, p. 185

Medium Sedge 3, p. 185

CDC Category 3
MP65, p. 139

Williams's Favourite, p. 129

La Petite Merde, p. 195

Deer Hair Beetle, p. 197

JULY

The timings of fly hatches in summer vary depending on weather conditions. In hot weather when water temperatures are high hatches are often concentrated in the late afternoon and evening, with a particularly special period from dusk and into the darkness known as 'the evening rise'. In cooler unsettled weather hatches of the same species may begin in late morning, continue to late afternoon, then stop abruptly as air temperatures fall rapidly at sunset. In very hot conditions the fish may completely stop feeding save at dusk, through the night, to dawn. Weighted imitative flies, so effective when the fish are not feeding at the surface, are also most efficient late in the day or at dawn.

Mayfly

Yellow Mayfly

False March Brown

Palingenia

Blue-winged Olive

Purple Dun

Claret Dun

Pale Watery

Common name	See page	Scientific name	Insect group	Water type	When on water
Mayfly	42	*Ephemera danica*	Upwinged Flies	Rivers and lakes, especially alkaline	Dun: late morning-afternoon; spinner: afternoon-evening
Dark Mayfly	42	*Ephemera vulgata*	Upwinged Flies	Slow rivers and lakes, especially alkaline	Dun: late morning-afternoon; spinner: evening
Yellow Mayfly	42	*Potamanthus luteus*	Upwinged Flies	Fast clean rivers	Late evening and dark
Yellow Dun	50	*Heptagenia* sp.	Upwinged Flies	Rough rocky streams	Dun: late morning and afternoon; spinner: dusk
Southern Mayfly	42	*Oligoneuriella rhenana*	Upwinged Flies	Large rivers	Dun: late afternoon; spinner: evening and dark
False March Brown	48	*Ecdyonurus* sp.	Upwinged Flies	Rough rocky rivers and stony lakes	Dun: afternoon and evening; spinner evening into darkness
Summer Mayfly	50	*Siphlonurus* sp.	Upwinged Flies	Northern and upland lakes and slow rivers	Afternoon-evening
Palingenia	50	*Palingenia longicauda*	Upwinged Flies	Large rivers	Dun: late morning and afternoon; spinner: evening
Blue-winged Olive	42	*Ephemerella ignita*	Upwinged Flies	Rivers	Dun: afternoon-evening; spinner: evening and into darkness
Purple Dun	44	*Paraleptophlebia* sp.	Upwinged Flies	Fast rivers (especially limestone)	Dun: late morning-afternoon; spinner evening
Angler's Curse	44	*Caenis* or *Brachycerus* sp.	Upwinged Flies	Rivers and lakes, especially with silty beds	Early morning or afternoon-evening
Claret Dun	44	*Leptophlebia vespertina*	Upwinged Flies	Acid or peaty lakes	Dun: late morning-afternoon; spinner: evening
Pale Watery	46	Many species	Upwinged Flies	Mostly rivers (1 species lakes)	Midday to dark

Look also for falls of landbred flies for these can dominate the fish's diet in summer. When fish are not feeding on a hatch or fall of flies at the surface it is worth investigating the possibility that they are feeding on fish fry, especially when fishing a lake that has a large head of species such as bream and roach (p. 84). The fry shoals will be in the shallow bays and margins; the feeding trout may occasionally make raiding sorties from adjacent deeper water. A good imitation fry may be the answer.

Body length in mm	General body colour	Wing colour	Imitation	See page
16-25	Dun: cream with dark markings; spinner: white with dark markings	Dun: grey- or yellow-green; spinner: gauzy blue-black	Dun: Dry Flies Spinner: CDC Category 2 Dry Spinners	164-5 138 166
14-24	Dun: yellow-buff with dark markings; spinner cream olive with dark markings	Dun: yellow-buff; spinner: gauzy black-brown		
14-16	Dun and spinner: yellow with brown stripe along body	Dun and spinner: yellow	Dun: CDC Category 1 Yellow Dun Spinner	138 154, 157-9 162-3
10-12	Dun: bright yellow; spinner: bright golden-brown	Dun: yellow with brown veins; spinner: transparent with dark veins		
12-14	Dun: drab light brown with dark markings; spinner: bright orange brown	Look for reduced venation	Dun: Wet Flies Dry Flies CDC Category 1 Spinner: Wet Flies Dry Flies CDC Category 2	130-1 151-5, 157-8 138 130-1 151-5, 157-8 138
11-16	Dun: dark brown with pale straw bands; spinner rich red-brown	Dun: buff or grey-buff with variable dark markings; spinner: transparent with dark veins		
14-21	Dun: olive-brown with dark bands; spinner: dark brown with pale bands	Dun: a shade of grey; spinner: transparent with dark veins		
20-28	Dun and spinner : yellow-brown	Dun and spinner :pale buff		
8-12	Dun: olives; olive-brown and orange-brown; spinner: olive-brown to deep red	Dun: dark blue-grey; spinner: transparent with light brown veins	Dun: Wet Flies CDC Category 1 Dry Duns Spinner: Pheasant Tail Wet CDC Category 2 Dry Spinners	128-30 138 150-3, 156, 158-9 126 128-9, 134 138 160-1
6-9	Dun: dark brown-olive; spinner: dark purple-brown	Dun: pale to very dark grey; spinner: transparent	Dun: Wet Flies CDC Category 1 Dry Duns Spinner: CDC Category 2 Dry Spinners	128-9, 132 138 150, 152, 157 138 161-2
3-6	Dun and spinner: dark thorax; whitish abdomen	Dun and spinner: whitish	Wet Flies CDC (1) Dry Caenis	128-9, 134-5 138 154-5
8-12	Dun: dark brown; spinner: glossy claret-brown	Dun: forewings dark grey; hindwings pale; spinner: transparent with light brown veins	Dun: CDC Category 1 Claret/Sepia Spinner: Pheasant Tail CDC Category 2 Brown	138 155 126 138 162
5-8	Dun: off-white to light brown-olive; spinner: white and orange to bright red-brown	Dun: pale to dark grey; spinner: transparent	Dun: Wet Flies CDC Category 1 Dry Duns Spinner: Wet Flies CDC Category 2 Dry Spinners	128-9 138 124, 150, 152, 156-9 128-9 138 161-2

Mayfly Spinner 5, p. 166

Yellow Spinner, p. 163

Large Red Spinner 1, p. 161

CDC Category 1 MP10, p. 139

CDC Category 1 MP13, p. 139

Iron Blue Dun 1, p. 153

Upside Down Imperial, p. 159

One-feather Pale Watery, p. 159

JULY continued

Dark Dun

Lake Olive

Olive Upright

Small Brown

Yellow Sally

Speckled Peter

Cinnamon Sedge

Brown Sedge

Common name	See page	Scientific name	Insect group	Water type	When on water
Green Dun	49	*Ecdyonurus* sp.	Upwinged Flies	Rough rocky rivers, especially limestone	Afternoon-late evening into darkness
Dark Dun	50	*Heptagenia* sp.	Upwinged Flies	Upland lakes and streams	Late morning to dark
Medium Olive	46	*Baetis* sp.	Upwinged Flies	Rivers	Dun: late morning-afternoon; spinner: afternoon-evening
Pond Olive	47	*Cloeon dipterum*	Upwinged Flies	Lakes, especially small shallow bays and tiny pools	Dun: late morning-evening; spinner evening and through night
Lake Olive	48	*Cloeon simile*	Upwinged Flies	Larger lakes	Late morning to dark
Olive Upright	48	*Rhithrogena* sp.	Upwinged Flies	Rough rocky rivers	Dun: mid-day to dusk; spinner: dusk
Arctic Dun	50	*Metropus norvegicus*	Upwinged Flies	Arctic and subarctic streams and lakes	Dun: late morning and afternoon; spinner: evening
Large Stonefly	52	*Perla; Perlodes* and *Dinocras*	Stoneflies	Rough rocky rivers and stony lakes	Afternoon and evening into darkness
Medium Stonefly	53	*Diura* sp.	Stoneflies	Rough rocky streams and stony lakes	Afternoon and evening into darkness
Small Brown	53	*Nemoura* sp.	Stoneflies	Rivers	Afternoon and evening into darkness
Needle/Willow Fly	54	*Leuctra* sp.	Stoneflies	Rivers and lakes	Through day
Yellow Sally	54	*Isoperla* sp.	Stoneflies	Rivers	Late morning to dusk
Small Yellow Sally	54	*Chloroperla*	Stoneflies	Rough rocky rivers and barren lakes	Late morning to dusk
Land-bug	58	Several species	Bugs	All	Through day (especially in wind)
Great Red Sedge	62	*Phryganea* sp.	Sedges	Lakes, especially large limestone	Evening and dark
Green Peter	62	*Phryganea obsoleta*	Sedges	Lakes, especially large limestone	Late afternoon-evening
Speckled Peter	62	*Phryganea varia*	Sedges	Lakes and big slow rivers, especially alkaline	Evening and into darkness
Large Cinnamon Sedge	63	*Potamophyllax* and *Limnephilus* sp.	Sedges	Rivers	Evening
Cinnamon Sedge	63	*Limnephilus* sp.	Sedges	Lakes and rivers	Through day
Sand-fly	64	*Rhyacophila dorsalis*	Sedges	Rivers, especially in upland regions	Late afternoon and evening into darkness
Chestnut-winged Sedge	64	*Triaenodes bicolor*	Sedges	Upland and northern weedy lakes	Afternoon and evening into darkness
Medium Sedge	64	*Goera pilosa*	Sedges	Lakes and rivers	Late morning to dusk
Brown Sedge	64	Many species	Sedges	Lakes and rivers	Evening into darkness

Body length in mm	General body colour	Wing colour	Imitation	See page	
13-16	Dun and spinner: green with darker markings	Dun: green-olive with dark veins; spinner: transparent with dark veins and sooty patch	Dun: Wet Flies — CDC Category 1 — Dry Olives — Spinner: Wet Flies — Dry Flies — CDC Category 2	124, 128 — 138 — 124, 150-9 — 130, 134 — 160-1 — 138	Dark Thorax Dun, p. 159
12-15	Dun: brown-grey; spinner: dark olive-brown with red bands	Dun: grey; spinner: transparent with brown veins			One-feather Olive, p. 159
6-8	Dun: olive; spinner: yellow- or red-brown	Dun: dull grey; spinner: transparent			
7-10	Dun: grey-olive; spinner: apricot	Dun: dark blue-grey; spinner: transparent with red-brown veins			Brown Spinner 1, p. 163
7-11	Dun: drab olive; spinner: red-brown	Dark grey with green markings; spinner: transparent with olive patch			
9-15	Dun: grey-green with olive bands; spinner red-brown	Dun: forewings dark grey; hindwings buff; spinner: transparent with brown veins			Quill Stonefly, p. 171
9-12	Dun: olive-brown; spinner: golden-brown	Dun: buff- or olive-grey; spinner: transparent with brown veins and opaque patch			
up to 25	Dark brown with lighter markings	Dark brown	Wet Flies — CDC Category 3 — Adult Stoneflies	128, 130, 134 — 138 — 170-1	
up to 18	Dark brown	Glossy dark brown			CDC Category 3 MP66, p. 139
up to 10	Dark brown	Glossy dark brown			
up to 10	Dark brown	Very dark brown			
up to 14	Lemon-yellow	Yellow	CDC Category 3 — Yellow Sally	138 — 170-1	
up to 8	Pale yellow	Pale yellow			
Varies	Varies	Varies	Land-bugs	174-5	Speckled Peter, p. 183
22-32	Grey	Red-brown with black markings	Wet Sedges — Bustards — CDC Category 3 — Adult (Impressionistic) (Imitative)	132-3 — 136 — 138 — 180-1 — 182-7	
10-12	Olive-green	Dark brown with pale patches			
15-17	Dark olive	Dark brown with white speckles			Cinnamon Sedge, p. 183
15-20	Brown-olive	Cinnamon with pale patch in centre			
12-16	Olive-green	Buff-yellow with darker markings			Deer Hair Sedge, p. 181
11-15	Olive-green	Sandy to dark brown			
8-11	Light brown	Chestnut-brown			
9-13	Buff-brown	Grey-buff			Dark Sedge, p. 133
12-16	Brown	Brown			

JULY continued

Small Yellow Sedge

Grousewing

Brown Silverhorn

Yellow-spotted Sedge

Phantom Fly

Midges

Biting Midge

Black Gnat

Ladybird

Common name	See page	Scientific name	Insect group	Water type	When on water
Welshman's Button	64	*Sericostoma personatum*	Sedges	Rivers	Through Day
Marbled Sedge	64	*Hydropsyche* sp.	Sedges	Rough rocky streams, especially in upland areas	Late afternoon and evening into darkness
Mottled Sedge	64	*Glyphotaelius pellucidus*	Sedges	Weedy ponds and lakes	Evening into darkness
Grey Flag	64	Several species	Sedges	Fast rocky rivers	Through day
Small Red Sedge	66	*Tinodes* sp.	Sedges	Lakes and rivers	Late afternoon and evening
Yellow Sedge	66	*Cyrnus flavidus*	Sedges	Lakes; especially weedy northern or upland	Evening
Small Yellow Sedge	66	*Psychomis pusilla*	Sedges	Rivers	Evening and into darkne
Grousewing	66	*Mystacides longicornis*	Sedges	Lakes	Late afternoon and evening and into darknesss
Black Silverhorns	66	several species	Sedges	Lakes and rivers	Afternoon and evening
Longhorns	66	*Oecetis* sp.	Sedges	Lakes	Afternoon and evening
Brown Silverhorns	66	*Arthripsodes* sp.	Sedges	Lakes and rivers	Afternoon and evening
Little Black Sedge	68	*Agapetus fuscipes*	Sedges	Stony lakes	Late afternoon and evening
Yellow-spotted Sedge	68	Several species	Sedges	Lakes and rivers	Evening into darkness
Speckled Sedge	68	*Philopotamus montanus*	Sedges	Rough upland streams	Evening into dasrkness
Microcaddis	68	Hydroptilidae	Sedges	All	Evening into darkness
Reed-smut	70	*Simulium* sp.	Two-winged Flies	Rivers	Through day but peak in the evening
Phantom Fly	70	*Chaoborus* sp.	Two-winged Flies	Lakes	Mostly evening and through night
Midges	71	Chironomidae	Two-winged Flies	All	Mostly afternoon and evening
Mosquito	72	Several species	Two-winged Flies	Small pools and weedy bays	Evening and through nigl
Biting Midges	72	Several species	Two-winged Flies	All	Through day; but especially evening
Torrent Midges	72	*Liponeura* sp.	Two-winged Flies	Rough mountain streams	Mostly afternoon and evening
Black Gnat	74	Many species	Two-winged Fies	All	Through day
Daddy-long-legs	74	*Tipula* sp.	Two-winged Flies	All	Through day but mostly evening in windy weather
Land Beetle	76	Many species	Beetles	All	Through day especially ir windy weather
Ants	78	Formicidae	Ants	All	Through day

Body length in mm	General body colour	Wing colour	Imitation	See page	
12-15	Olive-grey	Dark golden- or chestnut-brown			Balloon Caddis, p. 181
10-15	Dark olive green	Green-brown with dark brown and olive-grey blotches			Brown Sedge 3, p. 185
16-18	Dull olive-green	Silver-grey with dark brown blotches			
11-20	Olive- or brown-grey	Silvery or dark grey			
6-8	Grey or red-brown	Red-brown			Light Silverhorn Sedge, p. 133
up to 12	Olive	Yellow			
5	Dull yellow	Yellow-buff to bright yellow	Wet Sedges Bustards CDC Category 3 Adult (Impressionistic) (Imitative)	132-3 136 138 180-1 182-7	
about 10	Grey-brown	Red-brown with broad black bars			Brown Sedge 4, p. 185
6-11	Black	Black			
12-15	Drab green	Pale yellow or cream-grey			
about 10	Olive to green-brown	Brown (some with white markings)			Legged Midge 1, p. 195
5-6	Black	Black			
9-13	Brown	Brown or red-brown with fine yellow speckles			
9-14	Olive-or reddish-brown	Brown with yellow dots			
up to 5	Buff to black-brown	Buff to black			
see text	Black or grey	Transparent	Wet Flies CDC Category 3 La Petite Merde Smuits	128, 134 138 194 188	Grey Midge, p. 195
up to 8	Grey or olive	Transparent with fine dark veins			
up to 13	Black; grey; olive; orange; ginger; green	Transparent			Herl Midge, p. 195
up to 10	Dark grey or black with pale bands	Transparent with dark veins	Wet Flies CDC Category 3 Emergers Adult Midges	124, 128-135 138 190-2 192-4	
up to 5	Grey or black	Transparent with fine dark veins			
see text	Grey or black	Transparent			
up to 12	Black or brown-black	Transparent or semi-transparent grey	Wet Flies CDC Category 3, 4 Hawthorn/Gnats	128, 132 138-9 194-5	Valasesiana 1, p. 133
up to 35	Brown	Grey	Daddy-long-legs	196	
most up to 10	Mostly black	Mostly black; dark green or brown	Beetles Jassid	196-7 174	Ladybird, p. 197
up to 10	Red; yellow-brown or black	Transparent or none	Ants	130-1, 198-9	

AUGUST

See notes for July as regards effects of hot weather on fly hatches etc. Two features of upwinged fly hatches to look for in August are:

1. Fish feeding on duns that are having difficulty emerging at the water surface from the nymphal shuck – the fish will sometimes select these instead of the nymphs rising to hatch and the fully emerged duns on the water surface (especially common in blue-winged olive and pale watery, see p. 39).

Yellow Mayfly

Blue-winged Olive

Chloroterpes

Angler's Curse dun

Pale Watery

Pond Olive

False March Brown

Summer Mayfly

Ephoron

Common name	See page	Scientific name	Insect group	Water type	When on water
Yellow Mayfly	42	*Potamanthus luteus*	Upwinged Flies	Fast clean rivers	Late evening and dark
Blue-winged Olive	42	*Ephemerella ignita*	Upwinged Flies	Rivers	Dun: afternoon-evening; spinner: evening and into darkness
Angler's Curse	44	*Caenis* or *Brachycerus* sp.	Upwinged Flies	Rivers and lakes, especially with silty beds	Early morning or afternoon-evening
Purple Dun	44	*Paraleptophlebia* sp.	Upwinged Flies	Fast rivers (especially limestone)	Dun: late morning-afternoon; spinner evening
Chloroterpes	44	*Chloroterpes picteti*	Upwinged Flies	Rivers	Dun: late morning and afternoon; spinner: evening
Pale Watery	46	Many species	Upwinged Flies	Mostly rivers (1 species lakes)	Midday to dark
Pond Olive	47	*Cloeon dipterum*	Upwinged Flies	Lakes, especially small shallow bays and tiny pools	Dun: late morning-evening spinner: evening and through night
Lake Olive	48	*Cloeon simile*	Upwinged Flies	Larger lakes	Late morning to dark
Green Dun	49	*Ecdyonurus* sp.	Upwinged Flies	Rough rocky rivers, especially limestone	Afternoon-late evening into darkness
Dark Dun	50	*Heptagenia* sp.	Upwinged Flies	Upland lakes and streams	Late morning to dark
Arctic Dun	50	*Metropus norvegicus*	Upwinged Flies	Arctic and subarctic streams and lakes	Dun: late morning and afternoon; spinner: evening
False March Brown	48	*Ecdyonurus* sp.	Upwinged Flies	Rough rocky rivers and stony lakes	Dun: afternoon and evening; spinner evening into darkness
Southern Mayfly	42	*Oligneuriella rhenana*	Upwinged Flies	Large rivers	Dun: late afternoon; spinner: evening and dark
Summer Mayfly	50	*Siphlonurus* sp.	Upwinged Flies	Northern and upland lakes and slow rivers	Afternoon-evening
Palingenia	50	*Palingenia longicauda*	Upwinged Flies	Large rivers	Dun: late morning and afternoon; spinner: evening
Ephoron	50	*Ephoron virgo*	Upwinged Flies	Large slow rivers and lakes	Afternoon and evening

2. Fish feeding at dusk on spent spinners – nothing is visible on the water but the fish are feeding keenly. Wade in and look. The spinners will be flat in the surface film and the fish will accept an imitation only when it too lies in the surface film (see p. 18). Fish fry and falls of landbred flies may be so abundant that they preoccupy the fish. Be prepared with imitative patterns.

Body length in mm	General body colour	Wing colour	Imitation	See page
14-16	Dun and spinner: yellow with brown stripe along body	Dun and spinner: yellow	Dun: CDC Category 1 Yellow Dun Spinner	138 154-5, 157-9 162-3
8-12	Dun: olive or olive-brown and orange-brown; spinner: olive-brown to deep red	Dun: dark blue-grey; spinner: transparent with light brown veins	Dun: Wet Flies CDC Category 1 Dry Duns Spinner: Pheasant Tail Wet CDC Category 2 Dry Spinners	128-30 138 150-3, 156, 158-9 126 128-9, 134 138 160-1
3-6	Dun and spinner: dark thorax; whitish abdomen	Dun and spinner: whitish	Wet Flies CDC Category 1 Dry Caenis	128-9, 134-5 138 154-155
6-9	Dun: dark brown-olive; spinner: dark purple-brown	Dun: pale to very dark grey; spinner: transparent	Dun: Wet Flies CDC Category 1 Dry Duns Spinner: CDC Category 2 Dry Spinners	128-9, 132 138 150, 152, 157 138 161-2
6-10	Dun: yellow-brown; spinner: yellow to dark brown	Dun: dark grey with red caste and dark veins; spinner: transparent		
5-8	Dun: off-white to light brown-olive; spinner: white and orange to bright red-brown	Dun: pale to dark grey; spinner: transparent	Dun: Wet Flies CDC Category 1 Dry Duns Spinner: Wet Flies CDC Category 2 Dry Spinners	128-9 138 124, 150, 152, 156-9 128-9 138 161-2
7-10	Dun: grey-olive; spinner: apricot	Dun: dark blue-grey; spinner: transparent with red-brown veins	Dun: Wet Flies CDC Category 1 Dry Olives Spinner: Wet Flies Dry Flies CDC Category 2	124, 128 138 124, 150-9 130, 134 160-1 138
7-11	Dun: drab olive; spinner: red-brown	Dark grey with green markings; spinner: transparent with olive patch		
13-16	Dun and spinner: green with darker markings	Dun: green-olive with dark veins; spinner: transparent with dark veins and sooty patch		
12-15	Dun: brown-grey; spinner: dark olive-brown with red bands	Dun: grey; spinner: transparent with brown veins		
9-12	Dun: olive-brown; spinner: golden-brown	Dun: buff- or olive-grey; spinner: transparent with brown veins and opaque patch		
11-16	Dun: dark brown with pale straw bands; spinner rich red-brown	Dun: buff or grey-buff with variable dark markings; spinner: transparent with dark veins		
12-14	Dun: drab light brown with dark markings; spinner: bright orange brown	Look for reduced venation	Dun: Wet Flies Dry Flies CDC Category 1 Spinner: Wet Flies Dry Flies CDC Category 2	130-1 151-5, 157-8 138 130-1 151-5, 157-8 138
14-21	Dun: olive-brown with dark bands; spinner: dark brown with pale bands	Dun: a shade of grey; spinner: transparent with dark veins		
20-28;	Dun and spinner: yellow-brown	Dun and spinner: pale buff		
9-13	Dun and spinner: yellow-brown	Dun and spinner: milky-white		

CDC Category 1
MP16, p. 139

Red Spinner 3, p. 161

Valasesiana 4, p. 133

Caenis 3, p. 155

Pale Watery Dun 2, p. 153

Apricot Spinner, p. 163

Red Spinner 2, p. 131

Brown Spinner 1, p. 163

August Dun, p. 131

AUGUST continued

Needle Fly

Landbugs

Caperer

Chestnut-winged Sedge

Small Red Sedge

Black Silverhorn

Microcaddis

Midges

Common name	See page	Scientific name	Insect group	Water type	When on water
Needle/Willow Fly	54	*Leuctra* sp.	Stoneflies	Rivers and lakes	Through day
Yellow Sally	54	*Isoperla* sp.	Stoneflies	Rivers	Late morning to dusk
Land-bug	58	Several species	Bugs	All	Through day (especially wind)
Grasshopper	78	Several species	Grasshoppers	All	Through day (especially hot windy weather)
Green Peter	62	*Phryganea obsoleta*	Sedges	Lakes, especially large limestone	Late afternoon and evening
Speckled Peter	62	*Phryganea varia*	Sedges	Lakes and big slow rivers especially alkaline	Evening and into darkne
Caperer	63	*Halesus* sp.	Sedges	Rivers	Late afternoon and evening
Large Cinnamon Sedge	63	*Potamophyllax* and *Limnephilus* sp.	Sedges	Rivers	Evening
Cinnamon Sedge	63	*Limnephilus* sp.	Sedges	Lakes and rivers	Through day
Sand-fly	64	*Rhyacophila dorsalis*	Sedges	Rivers, especially in upland regions	Late afternoon and evening into darkness
Chestnut-winged Sedge	64	*Triaenodes bicolor*	Sedges	Upland and northern weedy lakes	Afternoon and evening into darkness
Medium Sedge	64	*Goera pilosa*	Sedges	Lakes and rivers	Late morning to dusk
Brown Sedge	64	Many species	Sedges	Lakes and rivers	Evening into darkness
Welshman's Button	64	*Sericostoma personatum*	Sedges	Rivers	Through day
Marbled Sedge	64	*Hydropsyche* sp.	Sedges	Rough rocky streams especially in upland areas	Late afternoon and evening into darkness
Mottled Sedge	64	*Glyphotaelius pellucidus*	Sedges	Weedy ponds and lakes	Evening into darkness
Grey Flag	64	Several species	Sedges	Fast rocky rivers	Through day
Small Red Sedge	66	*Tinodes* sp.	Sedges	Lakes and rivers	Late a'noon and evening
Yellow Sedge	66	*Cyrnus flavidus*	Sedges	Lakes; especially weedy northern or upland	Evening
Small Yellow Sedge	66	*Psychomis pusilla*	Sedges	Rivers	Evening and into darkne
Grousewing	66	*Mystacides longicornis*	Sedges	Lakes	Late afternoon and evening into darkness
Black Silverhorns	66	Several species	Sedges	Lakes and rivers	Afternoon and evening
Brown Silverhorns	66	*Arthripsodes* sp.	Sedges	Lakes and rivers	Afternoon and evening
Longhorns	66	*Oecetis* sp.	Sedges	Lakes	Afternoon and evening
Little Black Sedge	68	*Agapetus fuscipes*	Sedges	Stony lakes	Late a'noon and evening
Yellow-spotted Sedge	68	Several species	Sedges	Lakes and rivers	Evening into darkness
Speckled Sedge	68	*Philopotamus montanus*	Sedges	Rough upland streams	Evening into darkness
Microcaddis	68	Hydroptilidae	Sedges	All	Evening into darkness
Reed-smut	70	*Simulium* sp.	Two-winged Flies	Rivers	Through day but peak in the evening
Phantom Fly	70	*Chaoborus* sp.	Two-winged Flies	Lakes	Mostly evening and through night
Midges	71	Chironomidae	Two-winged Flies	All	Mostly afternoon and evening
Mosquito	72	Several species	Two-winged Flies	Small pools and weedy bays	Evening and through nig
Biting Midges	72	Several species	Two-winged Flies	All	Through day; but especially evening
Torrent Midges	72	*Liponeura* sp.	Two-winged Flies	Rough mountain streams	Mostly afternoon and evening

Body length in mm	General body colour	Wing colour	Imitation	See page
to 10	Dark brown	Very dark brown	Wet Flies CDC Category 3 Adult Stoneflies	128, 130, 134 138 170-1
to 14	Lemon-yellow	Yellow	CDC Category 3 Yellow Sally	138 170-1
Varies	Varies	Varies	Land-bugs	174-5
st up to 20	Buff, brown, olive or green	Buff, brown, olive or green	Grasshoppers	198-9
0-12	Olive-green	Dark brown with pale patches		
15-17	Dark olive	Dark brown with white speckles		
out 20	Cinnamon to olive-brown	Yellow-brown with blackish streaks at tip		
15-20	Brown-olive	Cinnamon with pale patch in centre		
12-16	Olive-green	Buff-yellow with darker markings		
11-15	Olive-green	Sandy to dark brown		
8-11	Light brown	Chestnut-brown		
9-13	Buff-brown	Grey-buff		
12-16	Brown	Brown		
12-15	Olive-grey	Dark golden- or chestnut-brown		
10-15	Dark olive green	Green-brown with dark brown and olive-grey blotches		
16-18	Dull olive-green	Silver-grey with dark brown blotches		
11-20	Olive- or brown-grey	Silvery or dark grey		
6-8	Grey or red-brown	Red-brown		
p to 12	Olive	Yellow		
5	Dull yellow	Yellow-buff to bright yellow	Wet Sedges Bustards CDC Category 3 Adult (Impressionistic) (Imitative)	132-3 136 138 180-1 182-7
out 10	Grey-brown	Red-brown with broad black bars		
6-11	Black	Black		
out 10	Olive to green-brown	Brown (some with white markings)		
12-15	Drab green	Pale yellow or cream-grey		
5-6	Black	Black		
9-13	Brown	Brown or red-brown with fine yellow speckles		
9-14	Olive-or reddish-brown	Brown with yellow dots		
up to 5	Buff to black-brown	Buff to black		
ee text	Black or grey	Transparent	Wet Flies CDC Category 3 La Petite Merde Smuts	128, 134 138 194 188
p to 8	Grey or olive	Transparent with fine dark veins		
p to 13	Black; grey; olive; orange; ginger; green	Transparent	Wet Flies CDC Category 3 Emergers Adult Midges	124, 128-135 138 190-2 192-4
p to 10	Dark grey or black with pale bands	Transparent with dark veins		
up to 5	Grey or black	Transparent with fine dark veins		
ee text	Grey or black	Transparent		

Dark Needle, p. 131

Landbug, p. 175

Peter, p. 183

Chestnut-winged Sedge, p. 183

Spent Sedge, p. 187

Dark Silverhorn Sedge, p. 133

Microcaddis, p. 187

Olive Midge, p. 193

AUGUST continued

Heatherfly

Daddy-long-legs

Common name	See page	Scientific name	Insect group	Water type	When on water
Black Gnat	75	Many species	Two-winged Flies	All	Through day
Heatherfly	75	*Bibio pomonae*	Two-winged Flies	Upland and northern lakes and rivers	Through day
Daddy-long-legs	75	*Tipula* sp.	Two-winged Flies	All	Through day but mostly evening in windy weath
Land Beetles	77	Many species	Beetles	All	Through day especially windy weather
Ants	79	Formicidae	Ants	All	Through day

SEPTEMBER

Although the number of species of insect that might fall on or hatch from the water surface is less in September than in the preceding four months, the hatches and falls may be very large and result in intense surface feeding by the fish. Trout are preparing for the oncoming breeding season and grayling may not be fully recovered from theirs, so both species are feeding keenly.

Blue-winged Olive

Chloroterpes

Iron Blue

Pale Watery

False March Brown

Common name	See page	Scientific name	Insect group	Water type	When on water
Blue-winged Olive	42	*Ephemerella ignita*	Upwinged Flies	Rivers	Dun: afternoon-evening spinner: evening and in darkness
Chloroterpes	44	*Chloroterpes picteti*	Upwinged Flies	Rivers	Dun: late morning and afternoon; spinner: evening
Iron Blue	46	*Baetis* sp.	Upwinged Flies	Rivers	Late morning and afternoon
Pale Watery	46	Many species	Upwinged Flies	Most rivers (1 species lakes)	Midday to dark
Large Dark Olive	46	*Baetis rhodani*	Upwinged Flies	Rivers	Afternoon
Pond Olive	47	*Cloeon dipterum*	Upwinged Flies	Lakes, especially small shallow bays and tiny pools	Dun: late morning-evening; spinn evening and through nig
Lake Olive	48	*Cloeon simile*	Upwinged Flies	Larger lakes	Late morning to dark
False March Brown	48	*Ecdyonurus* sp.	Upwinged Flies	Rough rocky rivers and stony lakes	Dun: afternoon; spinner evening into darkness
Ephoron	51	*Ephoron virgo*	Upwinged Flies	Large slow rivers and lakes	Afternoon and evening
Needle/Willow Fly	54	*Leuctra* sp.	Stoneflies	Rivers and lakes	Through day

Body length in mm	General body colour	Wing colour	Imitation	See page
up to 12	Black or brown-black	Transparent or semi-transparent grey	Wet Flies CDC Category 3, 4 Hawthorn/Gnats	128, 132 138-9 194-5
up to 12	Blackish	Pale grey		
up to 35	Brown	Grey	Daddy-long-legs	196
most up to 10	Mostly black	Mostly black; dark green or brown	Beetles Jassid	196-7 174
up to 10	Red; yellow-brown or black	Transparent or none	Ants	130-1, 198-9

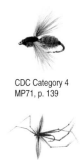

CDC Category 4
MP71, p. 139

Daddy-long-legs 1, p. 197

If there are no insects on the surface or fish feeding at the surface assume that they are taking nymphs, pupae, larvae and crustaceans etc from close to the bottom: choose heavily-weighted imitations of those.

Body length in mm	General body colour	Wing colour	Imitation	See page
8-12	Dun: olive, olive-brown and orange-brown; spinner: olive-brown to deep red	Dun: dark blue-grey; spinner: transparent with light brown veins	Dun: Wet Flies CDC Category 1 Dry Duns Spinner: Pheasant Tail Wet CDC Category 2 Dry Spinners	128-30 138 150-3, 156, 158-9 126 128-9, 134 138 160-1
6-10	Dun: yellow-brown; spinner: yellow to dark brown	Dun: dark grey with red caste and dark veins; spinner: transparent	Dun: Wet Flies CDC Category 1 Dry Duns Spinner: CDC Category 1 Dry Spinners	128-9, 132 138 150, 152, 157 138 161-2
5-7	Dun: dark black-grey; spinner ruddy-brown with light bands	Dun: dark blue-grey; spinner transparent		
5-8	Dun: off-white to light brown-olive; spinner: white and orange to bright red-brown	Dun: pale to dark grey; spinner: transparent	Dun: Wet Flies CDC Category 1 Dry Duns Spinner: Wet Flies CDC Category 2 Dry Spinners	128-9 138 124, 150, 152, 156-9 128-9 138 161-2
6-11	Dun: drab olive-grey or olive-brown; spinner: red-brown	Dun: dull grey; spinner: transparent with brown veins	Dun: Wet Flies CDC Category 1 Olives Spinner: Wet Flies Dry Flies CDC Category 2	124, 128 138 124, 150-9 130, 134 160-1 138
7-10	Dun: grey-olive; spinner: apricot	Dun: dark blue-grey; spinner: transparent with red-brown veins		
7-11	Dun: drab olive; spinner: red-brown	Dark grey with green markings; spinner: transparent with olive patch		
11-16	Dun: dark brown with pale straw bands; spinner rich red-brown	Dun: buff or grey-buff with variable dark markings; spinner: transparent with dark veins	Dun: Wet Flies Dry Flies CDC Category 1 Spinner: Wet Flies Dry Flies CDC Category 2	130-1 151-5, 157-8 138 130-1 151-5, 157-8 138
9-13	Dun and spinner: yellow-brown	Dun and spinner: milky-white		
up to 10	Dark brown	Very dark brown	Wet Flies CDC Category 3 Adult Stoneflies	128, 130, 134 138 170-1

CDC Category 2
MP81, p. 139

CDC Category 1
MP19, p. 139

Iron Blue Dun 2, p. 153

Yellow Partridge, p. 129

March Brown 2, p. 131

SEPTEMBER continued

Chinch-bug

Grasshopper

Medium Sedge

Longhorn

Torrent Midge

Daddy-long-legs

Land Beetles

Ants

Common name	See page	Scientific name	Insect group	Water type	When on water
Land-bug	58	Several species	Bugs	All	Through day (especially wind)
Grasshopper	78	Several species	Grasshoppers	All	Through day (especially hot windy weather)
Speckled Peter	62	*Phryganea varia*	Sedges	Lakes and big slow rivers, especially alkaline	Evening and into darkness
Caperer	63	*Halesus* sp.	Sedges	Rivers	Late afternoon and evening
Cinnamon Sedge	63	*Limnephilus* sp.	Sedges	Lakes and rivers	Through day
Sand-fly	64	*Rhyacophila dorsalis*	Sedges	Rivers, especially in upland regions	Late afternoon and evening into darkness
Chestnut-winged Sedge	64	*Triaenodes bicolor*	Sedges	Upland and northern weedy lakes	Afternoon and evening into darkness
Medium Sedge	64	*Goera pilosa*	Sedges	Lakes and rivers	Late morning to dusk
Brown Sedge	64	Many species	Sedges	Lakes and rivers	Evening into darkness
Marbled Sedge	64	*Hydropsyche* sp.	Sedges	Rough rocky streams especially in upland areas	Late afternoon and evening into darkness
Mottled Sedge	64	*Glyphotaelius pellucidus*	Sedges	Weedy ponds and lakes	Evening into darkness
Grey Flag	64	Several species	Sedges	Fast rocky rivers	Through day
Small Red Sedge	66	*Tinodes* sp.	Sedges	Lakes and rivers	Late afternoon and evening
Small Yellow Sedge	66	*Psychomis pusilla*	Sedges	Rivers	Evening and into darkness
Grousewing	66	*Mystacides longicornis*	Sedges	Lakes	Late afternoon and evening into darkness
Longhorns	66	*Oecetis* sp.	Sedges	Lakes	Afternoon and -evening
Little Black Sedge	68	*Agapetus fuscipes*	Sedges	Stony lakes	Late afternoon and evening
Yellow-spotted Sedge	68	Several species	Sedges	Lakes and rivers	Evening into darkness
Speckled Sedge	68	*Philopotamus montanus*	Sedges	Rough upland streams	Evening into darkness
Microcaddis	68	Hydroptilidae	Sedges	All	Evening into darkness
Reed Smut	70	*Simulium* sp.	Two-winged Flies	Rivers	Through day but peak in the evening
Phantom Fly	70	*Chaoborus* sp.	Two-winged Flies	Lakes	Mostly evening and through night
Midges	71	Chironomidae	Two-winged Flies	All	Mostly afternoon and evening
Mosquito	72	Several species	Two-winged Flies	Small pools and weedy bays	Evening and through night
Biting Midges	72	Several species	Two-winged Flies	All	Through day; but especially evening
Torrent Midges	72	*Liponeura* sp.	Two-winged Flies	Rough mountain streams	Most afternoon and evening
Black Gnat	74	Many species	Two-winged Fies	All	Through day
Heatherfly	74	*Bibio pomonae*	Two-winged Flies	Upland and northern lakes and rivers	Through day
Daddy-long-legs	74	*Tipula* sp.	Two-winged Flies	All	Through day but mostly in evening in windy weather
Land Beetles	76	Many species	Beetles	All	Through day especially in windy weather
Ants	78	Formicidae	Ants	All	Through day

Body length in mm	General body colour	Wing colour	Imitation	See page
Varies	Varies	Varies	Land-bugs	174-5
most up to 20	Buff, brown, olive or green	Buff, brown, olive or green	Grasshoppers	198-9
15-17	Dark olive	Dark brown with white speckles		
about 20	Cinnamon to olive-brown	Yellow-brown with blackish streaks at tip		
12-16	Olive-green	Buff-yellow with darker markings		
11-15	Olive-green	Sandy to dark brown		
8-11	Light brown	Chestnut-brown		
9-13	Buff-brown	Grey-buff		
12-16	Brown	Brown		
10-15	Dark olive-green	Green-brown with dark brown and olive-grey blotches	Wet Sedges	132-3
16-18	Dull olive-green	Silver-grey with dark brown blotches	Bustards CDC Category 3	136 138-9
11-20	Olive- or brown-grey	Silvery or dark grey	Adult (Impressionistic) (Imitative)	180-1 182-6
6-8	Grey or red-brown	Red-brown		
5	Dull yellow	Yellow-buff to bright yellow		
about 10	Grey-brown	Red-brown with broad black bars		
12-15	Drab green	Pale yellow or cream-grey		
5-6	Black	Black		
9-13	Brown	Brown or red-brown with fine yellow speckles		
9-14	Olive-or reddish-brown	Brown with yellow dots		
up to 5	Buff to black-brown	Buff to black		
see text	Black or grey	Transparent	Wet Flies CDC Category 3 La petite Merde Smuts	128, 134 138 194 188
up to 8	Grey or olive	Transparent with fine dark veins		
up to 13	Black; grey; olive; orange; ginger; green	Transparent	Wet Flies	124, 128-135
up to 10	Dark grey or black with pale bands	Transparent with dark veins	CDC Category 3 Emergers	138 190-2
up to 5	Grey or black	Transparent with fine dark veins	Adult Midges	192-4
see text	Grey or black	Transparent		
up to 12	Black or brown-black	Transparent or semi-transparent grey	Wet Flies	128, 132
up to 12	Blackish	Pale grey	CDC Category 3, 4 Hawthorn/Gnats	138-9 194-5
up to 35	Brown	Grey	Daddy-long-legs	196
Most up to 10	Most black	Most black; dark green or brown	Beetles Jassid	196-7 174
up to 10	Red; yellow-brown or black	Transparent or none	Ants	130-1, 198-9

Winter Brown, p. 131

Jassid, p. 175

Quill Hopper, p. 199

Light Sedge 2, p. 133

Fantastic Caddis, p. 187

Grey Midge, p. 195

Daddy-long-legs 2, p. 197

Deer Hair Beetle, p. 197

Black Ant, p. 199

OCTOBER

Hatches decline in both the number of species and quantity of flies, though during warm late mornings to sunset the fish may feed keenly at the surface; and when they do, imitations of hatching insects or insects falling onto the water will work well. Look out especially for greenfly (p. 58), for they can be the dominant insect, especially on heavily wooded lakes and rivers.

Blue-winged Olive

Large Dark Olive

Needle Fly

Caperer

Mottled Sedge

Little Black Sedge

Mosquito

Daddy-long-legs

Common name	See page	Scientific name	Insect group	Water type	When on water
Blue-winged Olive	42	*Ephemerella ignita*	Upwinged Flies	Rivers	Dun: afternoon; spinner: late afternoon
Chloroterpes	44	*Chloroterpes picteti*	Upwinged Flies	Rivers	Dun: late morning and afternoon; spinner: late afternoon
Iron Blue	46	*Baetis* sp.	Upwinged Flies	Rivers	Late morning and afternoon
Large Dark Olive	46	*Baetis rhodani*	Upwinged Flies	Rivers	Afternoon
Pale Watery	46	Many species	Upwinged Flies	Most rivers (1 species lakes)	Midday to dark
Needle/Willow Fly	54	*Leuctra* sp.	Stoneflies	Rivers and lakes	Through day
Greenfly	58	Aphids	Bugs	All	Through day (especially wind)
Caperer	63	*Halesus* sp.	Sedges	Rivers	Late a'noon and evening
Cinnamon Sedge	63	*Limnephilus* sp.	Sedges	Lakes and rivers	Through day
Sand-fly	64	*Rhyacophila dorsalis*	Sedges	Rivers, especially upland	Late a'noon and evening
Brown Sedge	64	Many species	Sedges	Lakes and rivers	Evening
Mottled Sedge	64	*Glyphotaelius pellucidus*	Sedges	Weedy ponds and lakes	Evening
Small Red Sedge	66	*Tinodes* sp.	Sedges	Lakes and rivers	Late afternoon and evening
Small Yellow Sedge	66	*Psychomis pusilla*	Sedges	Rivers	Evening
Longhorns	66	*Oecetis* sp.	Sedges	Lakes	Afternoon and evening
Little Black Sedge	68	*Agapetus fuscipes*	Sedges	Stony lakes	Late a'noon and evening
Yellow-spotted Sedge	68	Several species	Sedges	Lakes and rivers	Evening
Speckled Sedge	68	*Philopotamus montanus*	Sedges	Rough upland streams	Evening
Microcaddis	68	Hydroptilidae	Sedges	All	Evening
Reed-smut	70	*Simulium* sp.	Two-winged Flies	Rivers	Afternoon
Phantom Fly	70	*Chaoborus* sp.	Two-winged Flies	Lakes	Mostly evening
Midges	71	Chironomidae	Two-winged Flies	All	Mostly afternoon and evening
Mosquito	72	Several species	Two-winged Flies	Small pools and weedy bays	Evening
Biting Midges	72	Several species	Two-winged Flies	All	Through day; but especially evening
Black Gnat	74	Many species	Two-winged Fies	All	Through day
Daddy-long-legs	74	*Tipula* sp.	Two-winged Flies	All	Through day, most evening
Land Beetles	76	Many species	Beetles	All	Through day

During very cold weather, especially at the month end, hatches may be of very short duration and usually in mid-afternoon. On warm days hatches may last from late morning to beyond nightfall. If there is no hatch, use heavily weighted imitations of species such as freshwater shrimps, water hog-louse and large nymphs. Both grayling and trout will seek food throughout the shortening days.

Body length in mm	General body colour	Wing colour	Imitation	See page
8-12	Dun: olive, olive-brown and orange-brown; spinner: olive-brown to deep red	Dun: dark blue-grey; spinner: transparent with light brown veins	Dun: Wet Flies CDC Category 1 Dry Duns Spinner: Pheasant Tail Wet CDC Category 2 Dry Spinners	128-30 138-9 150-3, 156, 158-9 126 128-9, 134 138-9 160-1
6-10	Dun: yellow-brown; spinner: yellow to dark brown	Dun: dark grey with red caste and dark veins; spinner: transparent	Dun: Wet Flies CDC Category 1 Dry Duns Spinner: CDC Category 2 Dry Spinners	128-9, 132 138 150, 152, 157 138 161-2
5-7	Dun: dark black-grey; spinner ruddy-brown with light bands	Dun: dark blue-grey; spinner transparent		
6-11	Dun: drab olive-grey or olive-brown; spinner: red-brown	Dun: dull grey; spinner: transparent with brown veins	Dun: Wet Flies CDC Category 1 Dry Olives Spinner: Red Spinner CDC Category 2	124, 128 138 124, 150-9 130, 134, 160-1 138
5-8	Dun: off-white to light brown-olive; spinner: white and orange to bright red-brown	Dun: pale to dark grey; spinner: transparent	Dun: Wet Flies CDC Category 1 Dry Duns Spinner: Wet Flies CDC Category 2 Dry Spinners	128-9 138 124, 150, 152, 156-9 128-9 138 161-2
up to 10	Dark brown	Very dark brown	Wet Flies CDC Category 3 Adult Stoneflies	128, 130, 134 138 170-1
3	Pale green	Transparent or none	Green Insect Greenfly	130-1 174-5
about 20	Cinnamon to olive-brown	Yellow-brown, blackish streaks at tip		
12-16	Olive-green	Buff-yellow with darker markings		
11-15	Olive-green	Sandy to dark brown		
12-16	Brown	Brown		
16-18	Dull olive-green	Silver-grey with dark brown blotches		
6-8	Grey or red-brown	Red-brown	Wet Sedges Bustards CDC Category 3 Adult (Impressionistic) (Imitative)	132-3 136 138-9 180-1 182-6
5	Dull yellow	Yellow-buff to bright yellow		
12-15	Drab green	Pale yellow or cream-grey		
5-6	Black	Black		
9-13	Brown	Brown or red-brown with fine yellow speckles		
9-14	Olive-or reddish-brown	Brown with yellow dots		
up to 5	Buff to black-brown	Buff to black		
see text	Black or grey	Transparent	Wet Flies CDC Category 3 La Petite Merde Smuts	128, 134 138 194 188
up to 8	Grey or olive	Transparent with fine dark veins		
up to 13	Black; grey; olive; orange; ginger; green	Transparent	Wet Flies CDC Category 3 Emergers Adult Midges	124, 128-35 138 190-2 192-4
up to 10	Dark grey or black with pale bands	Transparent with dark veins		
up to 5	Grey or black	Transparent with fine dark veins		
up to 12	Black or brown-black	Transparent or semi-transparent grey	Wet Flies CDC Category 3, 4 Hawthorn/Gnats	128, 132 138-9 194-5
up to 35	Brown	Grey	Daddy-long-legs	196
up to 10	Most black	Most black; dark green or brown	Beetles Jassid	196-7 174

Olive Bloa, p. 129

Dry Greenwell's Glory 2, p. 125

Dark Stonefly 2, p. 171

Nocturnal Sedge, p. 181

Fluttering Sedge, p. 187

Black Sedge 3, p. 185

Ruz-Du, p. 133

Daddy-long-legs 3, p. 197

NOVEMBER

For most European anglers the trout season (except for some stillwater rainbow trout fisheries that remain open throughout the year) is over, as the native brown trout spawn from early November onwards. However grayling are still in their prime and readily take the fly. Because hatches and falls of flies at the water surface diminish rapidly during the month, many anglers turn entirely to flies that imitate bottom-foods.

Blue-winged Olive

Chloroterpes

Pale Watery

Greenfly & Blackfly

Sand-fly

Black Gnat

Common name	see page	Scientific name	Insect group	Water type	When on water
Blue-winged Olive	42	*Ephemerella ignita*	Upwinged Flies	Rivers	Dun: afternoon; spinner late afternoon
Chloroterpes	44	*Chloroterpes picteti*	Upwinged Flies	Rivers	Dun: late morning and afternoon; spinner: late afternoon
Pale Watery	46	Many species	Upwinged Flies	Most rivers (1 species lakes)	Late morning and afternoon
Needle/Willow Fly	54	*Leuctra* sp.	Stoneflies	Rivers and lakes	Afternoon
Greenfly	58	Aphids	Bugs	All	Through day (especially wind)
Caperer	63	*Halesus* sp.	Sedges	Rivers	Late afternoon
Cinnamon Sedge	63	*Limnephilus* sp.	Sedges	Lakes and rivers	Afternoon
Sand-fly	64	Rhyacophila dorsalis	Sedges	Rivers especially in upland regions	Afternoon
Brown Sedge	64	Many species	Sedges	Lakes and rivers	Afternoon
Small Red Sedge	66	*Tinodes* sp.	Sedges	Lakes and rivers	Afternoon
Reed Smut	70	*Simulium* sp.	Two-winged Flies	Rivers	Afternoon
Midges	71	Chironomidae	Two-winged Flies	All	Mostly afternoon and evening
Black Gnat	74	Many species	Two-winged Fies	All	Afternoon
Land Beetles	76	Many species	Beetles	All	Through day

DECEMBER

Many northern and upland waters are frozen over during December and the short day and low air temperatures often result in only a few sparse hatches on lakes and rivers that remain ice-free. However in particularly mild Decembers it is possible to find those species that were hatching or

Midges

Common name	See page	Scientific name	Insect group	Water type	When on water
Midges	71	Chironomidae	Two-winged Flies	All	Mostly afternoon
Black Gnat	74	Many species	Two-winged Fies	All	Afternoon

However, on mild days hatches may continue to result in a rise of grayling during the afternoons through to the month end. In upland and northern waters low temperatures in November cause the water to freeze over and bring conventional fly fishing (as distinct from 'ice-fishing') to an end for the year.

Body length in mm	General body colour	Wing colour	Imitation	See page
8-12	Dun: olive, olive-brown and orange-brown; spinner: olive-brown to deep red	Dun: dark blue-grey; spinner: transparent with light brown veins	Dun: Wet Flies CDC Category 1 Dry Duns Spinner: Pheasant Tail Wet CDC Category 2 Dry Spinners	128-30 138-9 150-3, 156, 158-9 126 128-9, 134 138-9 160-1
6-10	Dun: yellow-brown; spinner: yellow to dark brown	Dun: dark grey with red cast and dark veins; spinner: transparent	Dun: Wet Flies CDC Category 1 Dry Duns Spinner: CDC Category 2 Dry Spinners	128-9, 132 138 150, 152, 157 138 161-2
5-8	Dun: off-white to light brown-olive; spinner: white and orange to bright red-brown	Dun: pale to dark grey; spinner: transparent	Dun: Wet Flies CDC Category 1 Dry Duns Spinner: Wet Flies CDC Category 2 Dry Spinners	128-9 138 124, 150, 152, 156-9 128-9 138 161-2
up to 10	Dark brown	Very dark brown	Wet Flies CDC Category 3 Adult Stoneflies	128, 130, 134 138 170-1
3	Pale green	Transparent or none	Green Insect Greenfly	130-1 174-5
about 20	Cinnamon to olive-brown	Yellow-brown with blackish streaks at tip		
12-16	Olive-green	Buff-yellow with darker markings	Wet Sedges Bustards CDC Category 3 Adult (Impressionistic) (Imitative)	132-3 136 138 180-1 182-7
11-15	Olive-green	Sandy to dark brown		
12-16	Brown	Brown		
6-8	Grey or red-brown	Red-brown		
see text	Black or grey	Transparent	Wet Flies CDC Category 3 La Petite Merde Smuts	128, 134 138 194 188
up to 6	Black; grey; olive	Transparent	Wet Flies CDC Category 3 Adult Midges	128-134 138;194 192-4
up to 12	Black or brown-black	Transparent or semi-transparent grey	Wet Flies CDC Category 3, 4 Hawthorn/Gnats	128, 132 138-9 194-5
most up to 10	Most black	Most black; dark green or brown	Beetles	196-7

Red Spinner 4, p. 161

Iron Blue Paradun, p. 150

CDC Category 1
*MP21, p. 139

Green Insect, p. 131

Light Sedge 1, p. 133

CDC Category 3
MP65, p. 139

falling on the water in November continuing to do so well into this month. So be prepared with imitations of those.

Body length in mm	General body colour	Wing colour	Imitation	See page
up to 5	Black; grey; olive	Transparent	Wet Flies CDC Category 3 Emergers Adult Midges	124, 128-135 138 190-2 192-4
up to 12	Black or brown-black	Transparent or semi-transparent grey	Wet Flies CDC Category 3, 4 Hawthorn/Gnats	128, 132 138-9 194-5

CDC Category 3
MP63, p. 139

In the following section, fly patterns – or the bits and pieces to be tied onto the hook – are described by recipes, in which the various parts are listed as follows:

Hook – the size and type of hook on which to dress the fly.

Silk – the colour of thread to be used to tie in the various materials.

Underbody – some patterns (especially nymphs and pupae to be fished deeply) have an underbody of lead foil or wire.

Tails – the materials to be used for tails, if the pattern has tails.

Body – the colour and ideal materials to be used to form the body of the fly. In some imitations (notably nymphs and pupae) the body is divided up into:
    Abdomen – the rear portion of the body.
    Thorax – the portion of the body in front of the abdomen and behind the head.

Overbody – some patterns have an overbody (often of polythene, cut as a narrow strip from a polythene bag) to suggest translucence in the artificial fly (e.g. some larvae and pupae, fish fry imitations).

Rib – bodies are often ribbed (e.g. with wire, tinsel) to suggest the segmented nature of an insect body and to make the fly more durable so that it does not fall apart after catching one fish.

Back – some flies (especially nymphs and pupae) are given a separate 'back' on top of the body (this is tied in at the rear of the fly, brought forwards on top of the body (or just abdomen), and is secured in place by turns of rib material.

Wing cases – many nymphal and some pupal imitations have wing cases or wing buds tied over the top of the thorax.

Hackle – many artificial flies have a hackle (usually a small feather wound around the hook) that suggests legs, wings, antennae. Often used in dry flies to support the fly on the water surface. In most flies the hackle is at the front of the fly, just behind the head (in winged dry flies wound on either side of the wings). Some (e.g. many sedges) have a hackle that is wound in close turns down the body and secured by the rib: these are 'palmered hackles' and indicated by the use of the term 'palmered' in the recipes.

Wings – many artificial flies (especially dry flies) have wings that imitate the wings of the natural insect. Note also that wings on dry flies help the angler to see the fly on the water surface in rough or dull conditions.

Antennae – some artificial flies (e.g. some stonefly nymphs and adult sedges) have antennae tied in at the head to enhance the imitation.

Head – where this is not stated in the recipe, the head will be a few turns of tying silk, followed by the knot (a whip finish or at least three half-hitches) that completes the fly. Most tyers give the head a coat of thin, clear varnish to secure the head. Occasionally a recipe may stipulate that a material other than tying silk be used for the head.

Flosses and threads

Hackle-point wings

Light furnace hen

Antron

Goose quill

Furnace cock

ARTIFICIAL FLIES

Just as the fish's living food falls into natural groups, so to some degree do the artificial flies with which we imitate them. This section takes the artificial groups in turn, but there are three points to stress:

First, certain groups, such as Marc Petitjean's Cul de Canard patterns, do not so much represent exact imitations of a specific insect group as a series of fly patterns, each tied in a wide range of colours and sizes. From these the angler can choose a Cul de Canard fly that matches the insect the fish are eating. Similarly the soft-hackled wet flies. These old, well-proven patterns can be used to represent nymphs and pupae, spent spinners, and adult stoneflies and duns that have become waterlogged. Choose the one that most closely resembles the natural. Second, some traditional fly patterns can be modified easily to match a range of natural foods by altering size, hackle, wing, tail and body colour. For the novice, this is a good way to begin fly-tying.

Adapting Fly Patterns

It is possible to modify an older fly pattern so that it meets its original function better or serves a new purpose. In fact many so-called newer fly patterns are no more than such modifications.

For newcomers to fly dressing such adaptations are very useful: it enables them to learn to handle one set of materials really well, and it means that several flies can be produced with just one set of materials. Three examples are given: The Greenwell's Glory, GRHE and Pheasant Tails. But most traditional flies can be modified in this way.

Greenwell's Glory

Perhaps the world's most famous trout fly, invented in May 1854 by James Wright after the description, by Canon Greenwell, of an insect that he had never seen before.

Original Greenwell's Glory

Hook – size 14 wet fly
Silk – yellow, waxed with cobbler's wax
Rib – fine gold wire
Hackle – coch-y-bondu
Wing – hen blackbird secondary quill slip, bunched and split
This is a wet fly to imitate olive duns (p. 154).

Spider Greenwell's Glory

As above but lacking the wing. Very effective during a hatch of olive midges (p. 190), perhaps resembling a rising buzzer pupa or an emerger dun (p. 148).

Later 'Traditional' Greenwell's Glory

As the Original, but with a wing (usually of starling or mallard quill slips) tied back low over the body, and with a tail of coch-y-bondu (=furnace) hackle fibres. Perhaps the most widely used form of the Greenwell's Glory, especially on stillwaters where it matches the lake and pond olive.

Greenwell Nymph 1

As above, but with a tail of a few fibres of coch-y-bondu (=furnace) cock.

Greenwell Nymph 2

As Greenwell Nymph 1, but with a thorax of hare's ear to give better nymphal impression. Very effective during hatches of olive upwinged flies.

Dry Greenwell's Glory 1

As the 'Traditional', but with cock hackle fibre tail, cock hackle and starling, teal or mallard primary quill slips tied upright; dry fly hooks size 14-18.

Dry Greenwell's Glory 2

As Dry 1 but with blue hackle point wings Excellent imitators of a wide range of upwinged flies.

Dark Greenwell's Glory

As Dry 1 & 2, but with a dark olive silk body and excellent during hatches of darker upwinged flies (e.g. iron blue, chloroterpes).

Light Greenwell's Glory

As the Dry 1 & 2 but with a primrose silk body. Excellent during hatches of pale-bodied flies (e.g. pale wateries).

Para Greenwell's Glory

As Dry 1 & 2 but with a grey Antron wing and parachute hackle. With a few exceptions, it is well worth having a few examples of all dry flies tied in 'Para' fashion, where the body sits in (not above, as in conventionally hackled flies) the surface film, supported by the parachute hackle.

Gold-Ribbed Hare's Ear

Popularly abbreviated to GRHE, this is a very simple and old pattern

Basic GRHE

Hook – 14-16 dry fly
Silk – yellow or primrose
Tail – a few fibres from base of hare's ear
Body – hare's ear, thickened at thorax
Rib – fine flat gold tinsel
Hackle – fibres of fur picked out of thorax
Cast upstream to a fish feeding at the surface; the fly fishes in the surface film and is an excellent general emerger pattern (p. 148).

GRHE Nymph

As the Basic GRHE, but with fewer tail and hackle hairs, and wing cases of cock pheasant tail herls. A fine general nymph (also buzzer pupa) imitation for when the fish are feeding below the surface on nymphs (and pupae) (p. 144).

Dry GRHE

As the Basic GRHE, but with a hackle (dun, blue dun, ginger); wings may also be added (teal quill slips, hackle point etc.) A fine general dun imitation fish taking duns from off the surface (p. 154).

GRHE Goldhead

As the basic GRHE but with no tails, a rib of fine gold oval tinsel and a 'goldhead' in front of the body. In very deep or fast water, a few turns of lead wire may be added as ballast. This heavy fly is excellent during a hatch of sedges: perhaps it imitates a sedge pupa swimming to the surface or shore (p. 178).

ORIGINAL GREENWELL'S GLORY

SPIDER GREENWELL'S GLORY

LATER 'TRADITIONAL' GREENWELL'S GLORY

GREENWELL NYMPH 1

GREENWELL NYMPH 2

DRY GREENWELL'S GLORY 1

DARK GREENWELL'S GLORY

LIGHT GREENWELL'S GLORY

DRY GREENWELL'S GLORY 2

PARA GREENWELL'S GLORY

BASIC GRHE

GRHE NYMPH

DRY GRHE

GRHE GOLDHEAD

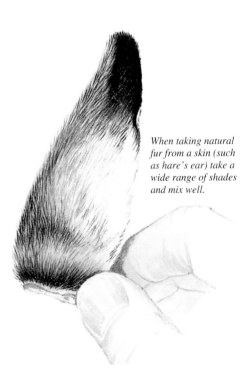

When taking natural fur from a skin (such as hare's ear) take a wide range of shades and mix well.

Peacock herl

Rabbit fur

Synthetic fur

Fluorescent lime wool

Cock pheasant tail

PHEASANT TAILS

Here the common feature is a body made from fibres of cock pheasant tail. Other similar 'series' could be constructed by using olive-, grey-, black- or cream-dyed herls.

Pheasant Tail Nymphs

Hook – size 12-16 wet fly
Silk – brown
Tails – tip of cock pheasant tail herls
Abdomen – cock pheasant tail herl
Rib – fine gold wire
Thorax – fur or wool (e.g. hare, rabbit, synthetic olive or brown) or fluorescent pink, green or red wool, or peacock herl
Wing cases – cock pheasant herl butts

These are very effective when fish are feeding on upwing fly and stonefly nymphs (and sometimes midge pupae) just beneath the surface (pp. 142, 167).

Hare's ear thorax

Peacock herl thorax

Brown synthetic fur

Fluorescent lime green wool thorax

PHEASANT TAIL NYMPHS

Sawyer's Pheasant Tail Nymph

Hook – size 14-16 wet fly
Silk – fine copper wire
Underbody – fine copper wire
Tails, abdomen, thorax and wing cases – 4-6 strands cock pheasant tail fibres

A heavily weighted nymph imitation that will take fish grubbing close to the lake/river bed for immature nymphs.

SAWYER'S PHEASANT TAIL NYMPH

Dry Pheasant Tail

Hook – size 14-18 dry fly
Silk – brown
Tails – cock hackle fibres (red, ginger, blue dun)
Body – cock pheasant tail
Rib – fine gold wire
Hackle – cock hackle (as tail)

An excellent dry fly, especially during a fall of spent upwinged fly spinners (that have a red-brown body): sometimes it is called the **Pheasant Tail Spinner.** When the fish are selecting spinners lying flat in the surface, trim away the hackle fibres below the hook shank so that the body of the fly is also flat in the surface film (p. 160).

DRY PHEASANT TAIL

Brown Partridge
Juvenile Starling
Snipe
Woodcock lower wing
Poly-yarn
Peacock herl
Badger cock
Dyed mallard
Cock pheasant
Woodcock upper wing
Water vole fur
Dark blue dun
Tup's fur
Light brown herl
Dark brown herl
Green peacock

SOFT-HACKLED WET FLIES

These are sometimes called 'spider wet flies', though the term 'spider' is somewhat misleading for it suggests that the flies imitate spiders. They don't.

Soft-hackled wet flies are among the oldest of all trout flies with a history of at least 300 years. They are extremely simple flies, both in the materials that are used in their construction, and also in their tying techniques. They are the ideal flies to start with for the person who has never tied flies before.

Because they are so simple, many modern fly dressers have tended to ignore them in favour of more complex patterns that look (to the angler) more like a real insect. This is a great pity, for those ancient anglers who devised this series of flies discovered the effectiveness of including just three or perhaps four triggers on the natural insect (p. 15) in their artificials: size, shape (a slender body), colour and, if these flies are used carefully, the correct position in the water in relation to the surface film.

The essential ingredients of these flies are:

The body. Use a round, not flat or floss, fairly coarse silk (traditionally Pearsall's Naples or Gossamer) that gives some semblance of segmentation; where the body has a dubbing of fur the dubbing should be so sparse that the underlying turns of silk are clearly visible; a few soft-hackled wet flies have a ribbed body.

The hackle. Small hackles are usually taken from the underwing coverts, upperwing coverts or neck of gamebirds (grouse, grey partridge, capercaillie, pheasant, snipe, woodcock, golden plover, waterhen = moorhen) and species such as starling and farmyard hen. These are all still available from tackle dealers. Some other species of birds, that were formerly exploited by fly dressers, are (rightly) protected by law throughout Europe: dotterel, land rail (=corncrake), swift, sea swallow (=terns). Some tackle dealers offer splendid substitutes for these (usually dyed hen or duck feathers).

There should be no more than two full turns of hackle: most shop-bought flies are grossly over-hackled.

Some soft-hackled wet flies have tails (add only 2-3 fibres if the recipe stipulates a tail), wings (usually a sparse bunch of hackle fibres or a slip from a tail or wing quill), or a head (usually a couple of turns of herl e.g. pheasant tail, peacock).

Soft-hackled wet flies are traditionally fished as a 'team' of two or three on the one leader, one on the point of the leader and the other(s) tied to 10cm droppers spaced up the leader (p. 274). But when fishing to keenly feeding fish a single fly is far preferable. By having the leader greased to within a couple of centimetres of the fly, the fly will fish in the surface film (and suggest either a dead adult insect or a pupa or nymph on the point of hatch – an emerger); by degreasing the leader the flies will sink a little more deeply and suggest a nymph or pupa that is rising to the surface to hatch, or a dun or spinner that has become waterlogged and fallen beneath the surface. Note that some Baetis olive spinners and sedges lay their eggs underwater: they will often die underwater. These simple wet flies will imitate the underwater spinners and sedges far better than the modern dry fly. And some patterns, such as Orange Partridge, Waterhen Bloa, Snipe and Purple, Winter Brown, Dark Needle and March Brown No. 2, are effective deep Nymph patterns fished either with a weighted leader or with a weighted fly (e.g. a GRHE Goldhead, p. 124) on the leader point.

When fishing choose pattern(s) according to the insects that you can see (or expect to find) on and in the water, concentrating especially on size and colour. Although many of these flies are regarded as imitating one particular species of insect, most of them have triggers that will deceive fish feeding on quite a range of species.

Orange Partridge

Hook – size 12-16 wet fly
Silk – orange (not hot orange)
Body – tying silk
Rib – fine gold wire
Hackle – brown speckled partridge

A great all-round pattern, imitating small brown stoneflies, upwinged-fly spinners, orange midges etc. Great during blue-winged olive hatches.

~

Yellow Partridge

Hook – size 14-18 wet fly
Silk – yellow
Body – tying silk
Hackle – grey partridge

A good summer fly, during hatches of pale wateries, caenis, and smaller yellow-grey midges.

~

Dotterel Dun

Hook – size 14-16 wet fly
Silk – either orange or yellow [both flies tied in plate]
Body – tying silk
Hackle – dotterel (substitute)

The yellow version imitates many smaller summer upwinged fly emergers and duns, the orange version smaller spinners. Useful during hatches of small midges.

~

Waterhen & Red

Hook – size 14-18 wet fly
Silk – crimson
Body – tying silk
Hackle – underwing covert of waterhen

Waterhen & Yellow, as above but with yellow silk
Waterhen & Orange, as Red but with orange silk.
All three of these are superb during a hatch of small pale midges, or in evening when adult female midges are dying on the water. Waterhen & Yellow effective during emergence of pale wateries and caenis; orange and red versions during falls of small upwinged fly spinners.

Waterhen Bloa

Hook – size 12-14 (spring), 14-16 (summer)
Silk – yellow
Body – tying silk dubbed sparsely water rat (vole)
Hackle – underwing covert of waterhen

One of the most effective olive upwinged fly nymph/emerger patterns. Note: instead of water vole, mole often used in body.

~

Dark Watchett

Hook – size 16-18 wet fly
Silk – orange
Body – tying silk and purple silk twisted, dubbed mole
Hackle – jackdaw throat

Almost essential during a hatch of dark-coloured upwinged fly duns (e.g. purple dun, iron blue). Also effective as a dark midge pupa imitation.

~

Snipe & Purple

Hook – size 16-18 wet fly
Silk – purple
Body – tying silk
Hackle – upper wing covert of snipe

An excellent alternative to Dark Watchett.

Snipe & Yellow

Hook – size 16-18 wet fly
Silk – yellow
Body – tying silk
Hackle – underwing covert of snipe

A summer pattern for pale watery emergers and pale midges.
Snipe Bloa, as Snipe & Yellow but with body dubbed mole. A summer pattern for smaller olive emergers.

~

Sea Swallow

Hook – size 16-20 wet fly
Silk – white
Body – tying silk
Hackle – sea swallow (substitute)

Superb during emergence of duns and fall of caenis spinners.

~

Olive Bloa

Hook – size 14 (spring), 16-18 (summer) wet fly
Silk – yellow
Body – tying silk
Hackle – lapwing back (dark olive hen)
Head – orange silk

Will imitate any olive-bodied upwinged fly; also small stoneflies.

~

Williams's Favourite

Hook – size 12-20 wet fly
Silk – black
Body – tying silk
Rib – fine silver wire
Hackle – black hen

Indispensable during hatch of black midges, reed-smuts. Trout feeding on tiny snails will take this pattern (p. 82).

~

Spring Black

Hook – size 14-20 wet fly
Silk – purple
Body – tying silk, dubbed magpie tail herls*
Hackle – starling neck or black cock

*Twist 1-2 herls round silk and wind body so that silk shows through herls.

Use as an alternative to Williams's Favourite.

ORANGE PARTRIDGE

YELLOW PARTRIDGE

Orange

Yellow

DOTTEREL DUN

WATERHEN & RED

WATERHEN & YELLOW

WATERHEN & ORANGE

WATERHEN BLOA

DARK WATCHETT

SNIPE & PURPLE

SNIPE & YELLOW

SNIPE BLOA

SEA SWALLOW

OLIVE BLOA

WILLIAMS'S FAVOURITE

SPRING BLACK

Knotted Midge

Hook – size 16 wet fly
Silk – ash coloured
Body – tying silk, dubbed heron (substitute) herl
Hackle – black cock, palmered
Head – magpie herl

The palmered hackle tend to make this fish in the surface, where it imitates dark emerger midges.

Stone Midge

Hook – size 14-18 wet fly
Silk – grey
Body – tying silk dubbed heron herl (substitute)
Hackle – lapwing neck (very dark olive hen)
Head – magpie herl

Matches grey midge emergers in the surface film.

~

Winter Brown

Hook – size 12-14
Silk – orange (not 'hot')
Body – tying silk dubbed red-brown wool, except at tip
Hackle – woodcock upper wing covert
Head – bronze peacock herl

Excellent river fly in late winter/after ice thaw, where there is an early hatch of stoneflies (e.g. February red).

~

Dark Needle

Hook – size 14-16 wet fly
Silk – brown-orange
Body – tying silk
Hackle – brown starling
Head – magpie herl

A most effective pattern when smaller stoneflies (needle/willow flies are on the water). In May-June tie in size 8-10 to match large and medium stoneflies.

Light Needle

Hook – size 14-16 wet fly
Silk – orange (not 'hot')
Body – tying silk
Hackle – light starling

Traditionally a small stonefly imitation; excellent during a fall of small/medium sized upwinged fly spinners.

~

Ant

Hook – size 16 wet fly
Silk – orange
Body – 3 sections: peacock herl, silk waist, peacock herl
Hackle – light blue hen

If, in high summer, ants fall onto the water, such a pattern is essential.

~

Green Insect 1

Hook – size 18-20 wet fly
Silk – yellow
Body – green wool or fur
Hackle – light blue cock

Green Insect 2

Hook – size 16-20 wet fly
Silk – black
Tail (=tag) – red floss
Body – green peacock herl
Hackle – white hen

These two flies are very effective when fish are feeding on a fall of greenfly (aphids), though exactly what triggers the fish use when selecting the second pattern are not known, but it is one of the best greenfly patterns, especially for grayling in autumn.

~

Woodcock & Green

Hook – size 16-20 wet fly
Silk – green
Body – tying silk
Hackle – woodcock underwing covert

Effective when fish are feeding on small greenfly and green-bodied upwinged flies (e.g. green dun, blue-winged olive dun).

~

Red Spinner 1

Hook – size 14-16 wet fly
Silk – red
Tail – 2 strands red cock
Body – tying silk
Rib – fine gold wire
Hackle – red cock
Wings – fibres from blue dun cock hackle

Red Spinner 2

Hook – size 12-16 wet fly
Silk – brown
Body – cock pheasant tail herls
Hackle – brown speckled partridge

Both are very effective during a fall of red or red-brown spinners. Modern Pheasant Tail Spinners (p. 126) are variants of No 2.

~

July Dun

Hook – size 14-16
Silk – yellow
Tail – 2 strands medium olive cock hackle
Body – tying silk dubbed mole
Hackle – medium olive hen
Wings – coot quill slip

An old, but still very effective, imitation of the blue-winged olive dun.

August Dun

Hook – size 12-14 wet fly
Silk – yellow
Tail – 2 strands olive cock hackle
Body – tying silk dubbed yellow wool
Rib – orange silk dubbed ginger fur
Hackle – medium olive hen
Wing – brown mallard

This fly is effective when the duns of a wide range of ecdyonurids and march browns are on the water.

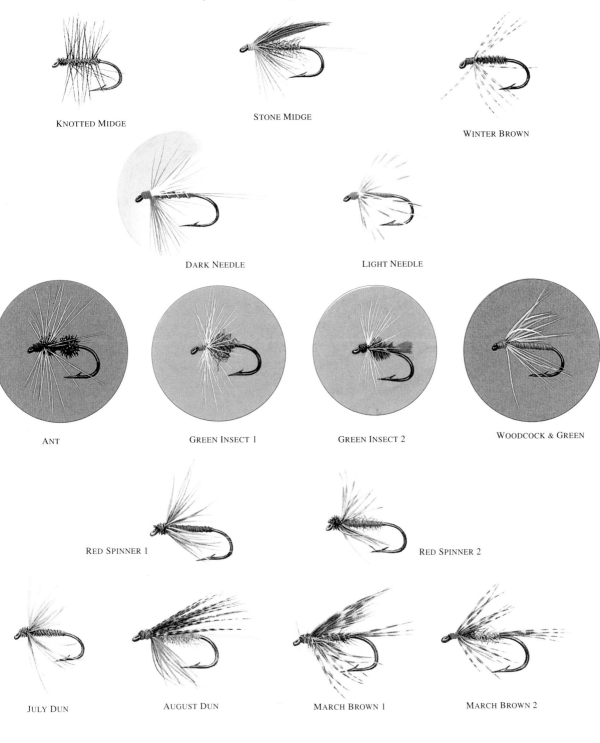

KNOTTED MIDGE

STONE MIDGE

WINTER BROWN

DARK NEEDLE

LIGHT NEEDLE

ANT

GREEN INSECT 1

GREEN INSECT 2

WOODCOCK & GREEN

RED SPINNER 1

RED SPINNER 2

JULY DUN

AUGUST DUN

MARCH BROWN 1

MARCH BROWN 2

March Brown 1

Hook – size 12-14 wet fly
Silk – orange (not 'hot')
Tail – 2 strands speckled partridge tail
Body – tying silk dubbed hare's ear
Rib – yellow silk
Hackle – brown speckled partridge
Wing – slip from speckled partridge tail

March Brown 2 as pattern 1, but lacking wing

Though very ancient patterns, these are still very effective during a hatch of the march browns and false march browns.

131

Poil de Lièvre

Hook – size 12-14 wet fly
Silk – orange
Body – Tying silk dubbed hare's fur; tip of silk showing to rear
Hackle – grey hen

A fly from Brittany; excellent in march brown or ecdyonurid hatch

~

Ruz-Du

Hook – size 14-18 wet fly
Silk – black
Body – Rear orange silk, front tying silk
Hackle – black hen

A superb Breton hatching-midge pattern

~

Touyllon

Hook – size 12-16
Silk – yellow
Body – tip of red silk, then 2-3 turns bronze peacock, rest tying silk
Hackle – natural red hen

The rear of the body represents a midge pupa shuck, the front a hatching adult midge

~

Valasesiana 1

Hook – size 14-16
Silk – black
Body – tying silk
Hackle – black hen

A splendid 'Black Gnat' wet fly; note that the fly is tied off behind the hackle to hold the hackle forward

Valasesiana 2

Hook – size 14-16 wet fly
Thread – olive
Body – tying silk
Hackle – starling neck

A splendid 'Dark Olive' wet fly; note that the fly is tied off behind the hackle to hold the hackle forward

Valasesiana 3

Hook – size 12-16 wet fly
Thread – red
Body – tying silk
Hackle – blue dun hen

A splendid 'Red Spinner' wet fly; note that the fly is tied off behind the hackle to hold the hackle forwards

Valasesiana 4

Hook – size 14-18 wet fly
Silk – purple
Body – tying silk
Hackle – black hen

A splendid wet fly that is the Italian version of the Snipe & Purple (p. 128.

Viroise

Hook – size 12-16 wet fly
Silk – black
Body – orange-yellow silk at rear, tying silk at front
Hackle – badger hen

An excellent representation of a hatching midge.

~

Dark Sedge

Hook – size 12-14 wet fly
Silk – yellow
Body – tying silk dubbed brown seal's fur (sub)
Hackle – upper wing covert tawny owl (sub)
Head – cock pheasant tail herl

~

Light Sedge 1

Hook – size 14-14 wet fly
Silk – yellow
Body – tying silk dubbed red squirrel fur
Hackle – red landrail (corncrake) substitute
Wing – landrail (substitute) quill slip

Light Sedge 2

As pattern 1, but lacking wing

~

Light Silverhorn Sedge

Hook – size 14 wet fly
Silk – ash
Body – tying silk dubbed red squirrel fur
Hackle – young starling flank
Wing – song thrush (substitute) secondary quill
Antennae – 2 fibres light mallard

Dark Silverhorn Sedge

Hook – size 14 wet fly
Silk – black
Body – tying silk dubbed mole
Rib – olive silk
Hackle – black cock
Wing – waterhen quill
Antennae – 2 fibres light mallard

These are five very effective sedge patterns.

Pheasant neck

Cock Capercaillie hackle

Red hen

Dyed Peacock herl

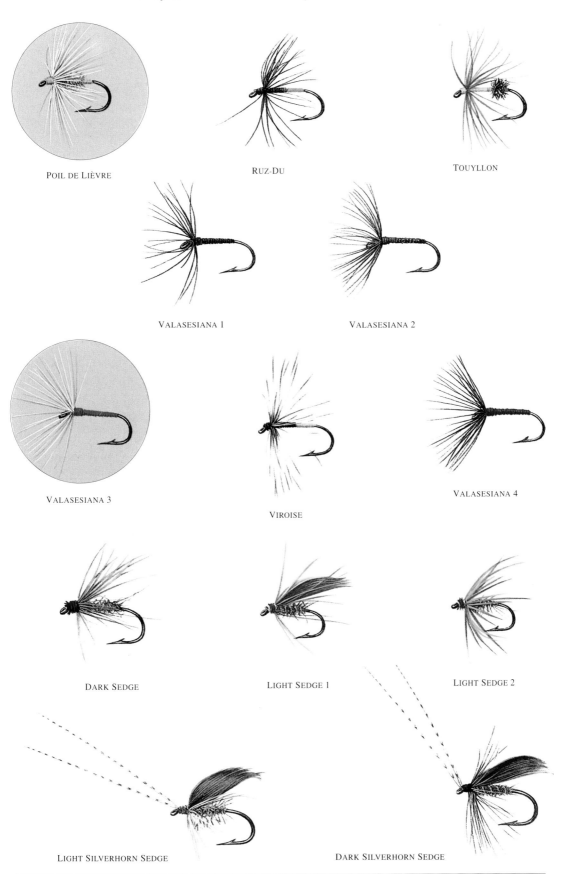

POIL DE LIÈVRE

RUZ-DU

TOUYLLON

VALASESIANA 1

VALASESIANA 2

VALASESIANA 3

VIROISE

VALASESIANA 4

DARK SEDGE

LIGHT SEDGE 1

LIGHT SEDGE 2

LIGHT SILVERHORN SEDGE

DARK SILVERHORN SEDGE

THORAXED SOFT-HACKLED SPIDERS

Anglers have tried to improve one trigger on the soft-hackled spiders by adding a thorax of either a few turns of herl or a little dubbed fur immediately behind the hackle. All the spiders on p. 127-33 can be modified (choose herl or fur of the same colour or a shade darker than the silk body). Below are some other patterns that have always had a thorax.

Large Dark Olive Nymph

Hook – size 14 wet fly
Silk – yellow
Tails – fibres dyed olive gallina
Body – dark olive-green seal's fur substitute, with thickening at thorax
Rib – fine gold wire
Hackle – short-fibred dark blue hen

Medium Olive Nymph

Hook – size 16 wet fly
Silk – primrose
Tails – 3 fibres soft blue dun hen
Abdomen – heron herl (or substitute) dyed olive
Rib – fine gold wire
Thorax – fine blue-grey fur
Hackle – short blue dun hen, 1 turn

Blue-winged Olive Nymph

Hook – size 14 wet fly
Silk – orange
Tails – 3 fibres brown partridge
Body – a fine, rich olive-green fur, thicker at thorax
Hackle – dark blue hen

~

Blackcock

Hook – size 12-16 wet fly
Silk – black
Abdomen – tying silk
Rib – fine silver wire
Thorax – black fur
Hackle – blackcock upper wing covert (substitute, any soft glossy black hackle)
A most effective midge/blackfly pattern in the rivers and lakes of Scotland and Fenno-Scandinavia.

~

Black Magic

Hook – size 14-18 wet fly
Silk – black
Abdomen – tying silk
Thorax – bronze peacock herl
Hackle – black hen
Outstanding river and lake midge pattern throughout Europe, better in stocked rainbow trout lakes than more precise buzzer imitations. The original tying was slightly weighted by a copper wire under-thorax.

~

Capercaillie & Red

Hook – size 12-18 wet fly
Silk – crimson
Abdomen – tying silk
Thorax – bronze peacock herl
Hackle – cock capercaillie neck feather
This is a new Scandinavian midge/blackfly imitation. The crimson body is usually very effective, but try **Capercaillie & Black** (use black thread), and **Capercaillie & Purple** (use purple thread).

Capercaillie Hen & Orange

Hook – size 10-14 wet fly
Silk – orange
Abdomen – tying silk
Rib – fine gold wire (optional)
Thorax – ginger-brown fur
Hackle – orange feather from neck of hen capercaillie
An early spring fly on northern rivers during the first hatches of stoneflies; or on rivers and lakes all season.

~

Henthorn Purple

Hook – size 12-16 wet fly
Silk – purple
Abdomen – tying silk
Thorax – bronze peacock herl
Hackle – upper wing covert of teal or mallard
By using a duck feather as hackle, this pattern tends to fish in the surface film. It is a splendid midge emerger.

~

Olive Dun

Hook – size 14-18 wet fly
Silk – olive or yellow waxed with cobblers wax
Abdomen – tying silk lightly dubbed fine olive fur (e.f. mole dyed olive)
Thorax – olive fur
Hackle – white hen hackle dyed medium olive
When fished in or just below the surface film, this is a good emerger pattern during a hatch of olive duns.

~

Red Spinner

Hook – size 12-16 wet fly
Silk – red
Abdomen – tying silk
Rib – fine gold wire
Thorax – fine brown fur
Hackle – natural red hen
Very effective during an evening fall of spinners.

~

Winter Ptarmigan

Hook – size 16-18 wet fly
Silk – white
Abdomen – tying silk
Thorax – cream fur
Hackle – a white neck feather from a winter plumaged ptarmigan (or a very soft fibred white hackle).
For a Caenis imitation give a peacock herl thorax, and tie on size 20-22 hooks.

~

LARGE DARK OLIVE NYMPH

MEDIUM OLIVE NYMPH

BLUE-WINGED OLIVE NYMPH

BLACKCOCK

BLACK MAGIC

CAPERCAILLIE & RED

CAPERCAILLIE & BLACK

CAPERCAILLIE & PURPLE

CAPERCAILLIE HEN & ORANGE

HENTHORN PURPLE

OLIVE DUN

RED SPINNER

WINTER PTARMIGAN

WINTER PTARMIGAN
with peacock herl thorax

BUSTARDS

A series of very old wet flies that were initially (in the late 18th century) devised to imitate night-flying moths, but that were later (by the early 1900s) used to imitate adult female sedges skittering on the water as they laid their eggs. They are still very effective, especially on warm summer evenings, from dusk to the early hours of the morning. Use a strong leader with a single Bustard on the point; cast down-and-across the stream (or straight out on lakes); retrieve in short jerks. For these flies, hook size is 8-12 wet fly; silk black.

White Bustard

Body – white chenille, wool or fur
Hackle – ginger cock
Wing – barn owl (use a pale quill as substitute)

Red Bustard

Body – red chenille, wool or fur
Hackle – furnace cock
Wing – barn owl dyed in red (use cinnamon quill as substitute)

Brown Bustard

Body – brown chenille, wool or fur
Hackle – dark red cock
Wing – tawny owl (use a brown quill as substitute)

WHITE BUSTARD

RED BUSTARD

BROWN BUSTARD

Landrail hackle

Cock starling hackle

Dotterel hackle

W.C. STEWART/CAPTAIN HAMILTON WET FLIES

Though the inventors of these flies restricted themselves mainly to just three patterns, their style could be profitably adopted in other soft-hackled wet flies. The difference is that the hackles are not wound tightly together at the head of the fly, but palmered around the front one third of the body. This tends to keep the fly close to the surface film, and makes it behave as an emerger: an adult fly emerging from its nymphal or pupal shuck. This style has proved effective throughout the world where trout are found.

Black Spider

Hook – size 14-16 wet fly.
Silk – brown
Hackle – cock starling neck

Red Spider

Hook – size 14-16 wet fly
Silk – yellow
Hackle – landrail (substitute)

Dun Spider

Hook – size 14-16 wet fly
Silk – yellow
Hackle – dotterel (substitute)

When Captain Hamilton took these to New Zealand in the 19th century, he tied them on much larger hooks (to size 8).

BLACK SPIDER

RED SPIDER

DUN SPIDER

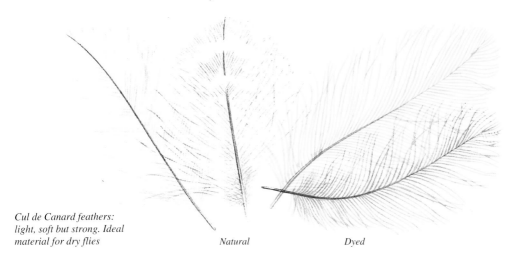

Cul de Canard feathers:
light, soft but strong. Ideal
material for dry flies

Natural

Dyed

CUL DE CANARD DRYFLIES

Usually shortened by fly-tiers to CDC. But since this means duck's bottom in French, the term is a misnomer and the less widely used Croupion de Canard (duck's rump) is anatomically more accurate. The feathers concerned are up around its preen gland, which is on the back just forward from the start of the tail.The preen gland, a little pimple secreting the water-proofing oils with which birds preen their outer feathers, is found in all birds except – interestingly enough – all members of the pigeon family, some parrots and a few others such as cormorants. Pigeons have none and instead secrete, with all their feathers, a fine powder which has the same effect.You can often see pigeons or parrots vigorously shaking themselves to disperse the powder, and when they are bathing it can be seen as a white film over the water surface.

But back to our ducks, the only good source of CDC feathers for the angler. Plucking a few 2 or 3 times a year causes neither pain nor inconvenience to the donors, though most come from ducks that have been killed for the market. Particularly light and strong, the CDC feathers are not only impregnated with water-repellent oil but have fibres fringed with tiny, twisted barbules which trap air. Dry flies made primarily from CDC will float almost indefinitely, without the need for regular oiling. Indeed, if a CDC fly is oiled at all, it is immediately ruined. After a fish has been caught, all that is needed to restore the fly to pristine condition is to wash it to remove dirt or slime, squeeze out surplus moisture, and blow it dry for a few seconds. CDC flies are so tough that if looked after properly they are capable of each catching many fish. In contrast, many traditional flies are ruined after catching one or two.

One problem confronting dry fly anglers is preventing the leader point floating and producing a 'negative-trigger' that puts the fish off: the floating leader looks, to the fish, like a long black line attached to the fly. This can make dry fly fishing especially difficult on slow river pools and calm lakes. With a CDC fly, after casting, pull the fly underwater (thus sinking the leader point): the fly will then resurface, leaving all the leader submerged.

Marc Petitjean, of Fribourg in Switzerland, has developed a series of CDC flies that can be used to imitate all the commonest European natural surface flies. Many anglers, throughout Europe, now fish his patterns almost exclusively. They are that good!

They are, however, expensive, and finding a source of CDC feathers to tie one's own can be both difficult and expensive too. If you can only afford a few, it is worth keeping them for particularly selective or difficult trout or grayling that have refused more conventional flies. An appropriate CDC pattern will often take these fastidious fish.

The preen
gland of a duck

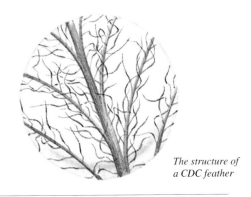

The structure of
a CDC feather

CDC PATTERNS

M. Petitjean gives each pattern a number; several have been rejected and the numbers now available and illustrated are those that have been proved most effective. There are four styles:

Category 1: Upwinged fly duns

These have two wings set upright in a 'semi-spent' arrangement and a bunch of hackle fibres for tails.

MP 10: buff and beige bodied duns (Epeorus, March Brown, False March Browns, Summer Mayfly).

MP 11: duns with light-olive bodies (Ephoron, Olive Upright).

MP 13, MP 14: duns with medium- or dark-olive bodies (the 'Olives', Blue-winged Olive, Pond and Lake Olives).

MP 16: duns with yellow bodies (Yellow Dun, Yellow Evening Dun, Yellow Mayfly).

MP 19: dark-bodied duns (Iron Blue, Chloroterpes, Dark Dun, Purple Dun, Claret and Sepia).

MP 21, MP 22: pale-bodied duns (Pale Wateries, Angler's Curse).

~

Category 2: Upwinged fly spent female spinners

These have long Pardo tails set wide apart, flat, spent wings, and (to aid visibility) a small tuft of CDC on top of the thorax.

MP 81: red or amber coloured spinners (Olives, Blue Winged Olive, March Brown).

MP 82: brown spinners (Summer Mayfly, Palingenia).

MP 85: Mayfly spinners

~

Category 3: Flies with a single wing tied low over the abdomen and lacking tails

These can be used to imitate adult stoneflies, adult sedges, midges, black gnats etc.

MP 52: dark brown sedges, stoneflies, midges, land-bugs.

MP 53: light brown sedges, stoneflies, midges, land-bugs.

MP 54: beige/tan sedges, stoneflies, midges.

MP 64: tiny brown midges, sedges and gnats.

MP 65: tiny black reed-smuts, midges, sedges, stoneflies and gnats.

MP 66: Yellow Sallys and Yellow Sedges.

Category 4: Specials

These imitate larger dark land-bred flies, wasps, bees and hover-flies.

MP 71: Hawthorn Fly, Black Gnats, also Beetles.

MP 72: Wasps

Each of these patterns is tied in a range of sizes, usually from hook size 14 – 18 or 20.
Note: M. Petitjean's imitations of mayflies are described separately on p. 164.

~

Choosing the right CDC dry fly

Look carefully at the natural fly that is hatching or floating on the water. Choose the fly of the style that matches the natural most closely in body length, shape and colour.

Example 1

Hatch of yellow may duns (p. 50): use **MP 16**, in size 16.

Example 2

Fall of autumn dun spinners (p. 48): use **MP 81**, in size 12.

Example 3

Hatch of pale watery duns (p. 46): use **MP 21** or **MP 22**, in size 16 or 18 depending on the species of pale watery that is hatching.

Example 4

Fall of small black gnats (p. 74): use either **MP 63, 64, 65** of appropriate size. In dull light 63 will be more visible with its white wing; in bright conditions the dark-winged 65 may be preferable.

Example 5

Fish feeding late in the evening, presumably on sedges (it is too dark to see clearly): use **MP 52, 53,** or **54** in either size 10 or 12.

Note: Other patterns using CDC feathers can be found on:
p. 148 (Fur-bodied Emergers)
p. 162-4 (Mayfly)
p. 172 (Damsel)
p. 180 (Emerging Sedge)
p. 186 (Be-Ge Sedge)
p. 188 (Emerger Smut)
p. 194 (La Petite Merde)
p. 195 (Hawthorn Fly)
p. 199 (Shrimps).

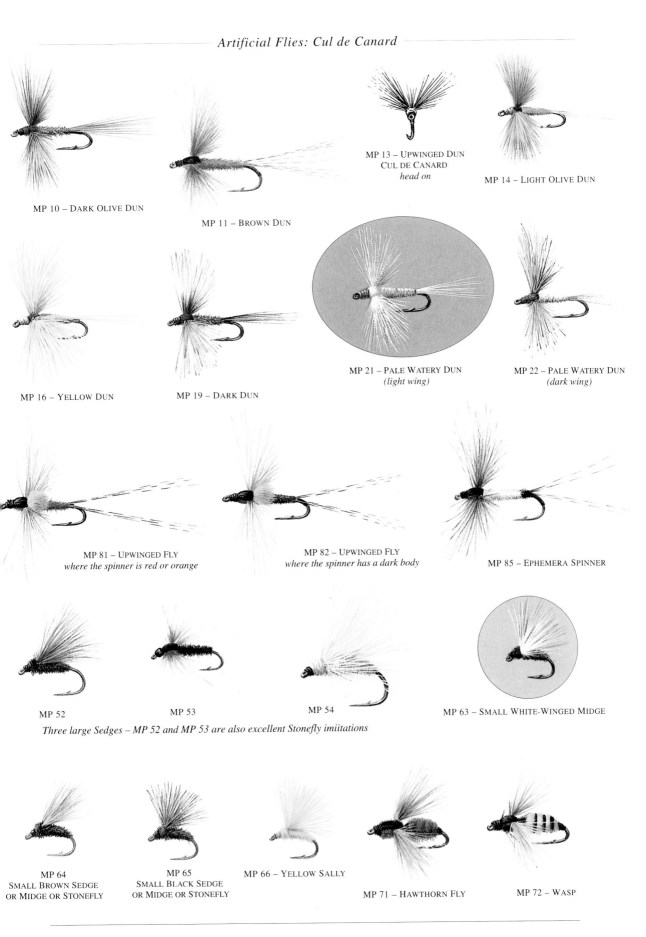

MP 10 – DARK OLIVE DUN

MP 11 – BROWN DUN

MP 13 – UPWINGED DUN
CUL DE CANARD
head on

MP 14 – LIGHT OLIVE DUN

MP 16 – YELLOW DUN

MP 19 – DARK DUN

MP 21 – PALE WATERY DUN
(light wing)

MP 22 – PALE WATERY DUN
(dark wing)

MP 81 – UPWINGED FLY
where the spinner is red or orange

MP 82 – UPWINGED FLY
where the spinner has a dark body

MP 85 – EPHEMERA SPINNER

MP 52

MP 53

MP 54

MP 63 – SMALL WHITE-WINGED MIDGE

Three large Sedges – MP 52 and MP 53 are also excellent Stonefly imiitations

MP 64
SMALL BROWN SEDGE
OR MIDGE OR STONEFLY

MP 65
SMALL BLACK SEDGE
OR MIDGE OR STONEFLY

MP 66 – YELLOW SALLY

MP 71 – HAWTHORN FLY

MP 72 – WASP

CUL DE CANARD EMERGERS, NYMPHS AND PUPAE

Although traditionally used for surface (dry) flies, the air bubbles held by CDC feathers can make most life-like subsurface flies – though of course these must be weighted to make them sink.

Nymphs

Hook – size 12-18 fine wire nymph
Silk: – as body colour
Tails – Pardo fibres, splayed
Abdomen – CDC feather (grey, beige-pink, olive, brown)
Rib – fine silver, gold or copper wire
Thorax – as abdomen, but pronounced
Wing Cases – black CDC
Legs – Fibres from thorax

These are fished beneath the surface to imitate nymphs rising to hatch at the surface.

This basic nymph tying can be greatly modified to match more closely specific nymphs; also other subsurface insects and crustaceans. By changing colour, shape (altering the shape of the lead underbody) and hook size and shape, you can imitate damselfly nymphs, heptagenid (stonecrawler) nymphs, large mayfly nymphs. Even water-boatmen and freshwater shrimps. A most versatile system!

Emerger Nymphs

Hook – size 12-18 fine wire nymph
Silk – as body colour
Tip – fine silver wire wound around bend of hook
Tails – Pardo fibres, one bunch either side of hook
Abdomen – CDC feather (grey, beige-pink, olive, brown)
Rib – fine silver wire
Thorax – as abdomen, but pronounced
Opening Wing Buds – two CDC feathers, colour as body, tied as 'loops' over thorax, with tips forming a feathery suggestion of legs

These fish in the surface film: the wire tip sinks the abdomen of the fly below the surface film, but the two loop wings trap bubbles of air and hold into the surface film. Incredibly effective when fish are taking emergers, and not nymphs or fully-hatched flies.

Front view   *Attitude in water*

Emerger Sedge Pupa

Hook – size 12-16 fine wire caddis hook
Silk – black
Abdomen – yellow CDC feather
Rib – fine gold wire
Thorax – as abdomen, but more pronounced
Opening Wing Buds – two beige-pink CDC feathers, with tips forming a feathery suggestion of legs.

MP 33 – OLIVE NYMPH

MP 34 – BROWN NYMPH

CUL DE CANARD NYMPHS

MP 31 – GREY NYMPH

MP 32 – GREY-PINK NYMPH

Olive-brown

Olive

MP SPECIAL DAMSELFLY NYMPH

Grey

HEPTAGENID NYMPHS

Grey

MAYFLY NYMPHS

MP 91 – RHYACOPHILA

MP 92 – HYDROPSYCHE

MP SPECIAL SEDGE PUPA
almost fully emerged

FREE-LIVING CADDIS LARVAE

MP WATER-BOATMAN

FRESHWATER SHRIMP

MAYFLY EMERGER

MP 41 – GREY EMERGER

MP 42 – PINK EMERGER

MP 44 – DARK BROWN EMERGER

MP 43 – RED-BROWN EMERGER

MP SPECIAL EMERGER (BUZZER)

The colour and size of these emergers is chosen to match the natural emerger

MP 74 – EMERGER SEDGE PUPA

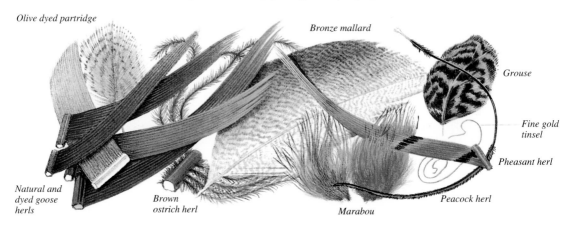

Olive dyed partridge

Bronze mallard

Grouse

Fine gold tinsel

Pheasant herl

Natural and dyed goose herls

Brown ostrich herl

Marabou

Peacock herl

UPWINGED FLY NYMPHS

(Natural Nymphs p. 38)

Of the several styles of upwinged fly nymph imitations the following are effective and easy to tie. The choice of size and colour is a matter of experience (initially trial-and-error), and what is likely to be present in that particular water. When fish are feeding deep in a lake or river (and not close to the surface on emergers, see p. 18) they are not selective in terms of the artificial closely matching the real nymph. Many experienced anglers carry only a few general nymphal patterns which they know will work in the majority of situations.

Tie a range of sizes (12-18), with various amounts of lead or copper wire underbody (so the nymphs can be fished close to the bottom in deep and very fast water, and in shallow and slow-flowing water), and in a series of shades to give some choice at the waterside. (Note: for Mayfly nymphs see p. 162).

Several soft-hackle spiders also imitate upwinged fly nymphs (pp. 127-135). See also CDC Nymphs (p. 140)

Bare Hook Nymph

Hook – size 12-18 wet fly
Silk – fine copper wire
Thorax – a few turns of copper wire, finished with 2 half-hitches
The easiest of all flies to tie, but very effective.

Pheasantless Pheasant Tail Nymph

The Pheasant Tail Nymph (see p. 126) remains effective even after all the herls have been chewed to pieces and only the wire underbody remains. Ed Zern came to the same conclusion and devised this very similar pattern:
Hook – size 14-18 wet fly
Body – finest copper wire wound in two layers on the rear two-thirds of the hook shank to simulate narrow abdomen; many overlapping turns on the front third to simulate the natural nymph's proud thorax
These are also excellent during a hatch of small midges, the fish taking them as pupae rising to the surface.

PIAM LEAD NYMPHS

The great French angler Jean-Pierre Guillemaud identified the same triggers used by Kite (in his Bare Hook Nymph) and Zern (in his Pheasantless Pheasant Tail Nymph) but uses lead to make his simple patterns. Finest lead wire is wound around the hook shank to form a neat segmented abdomen with a drop of molten lead added in front to create the thorax. M. Guillemaud goldplates his nymphs (as in Goldheads, p. 148) or paints them in 'natural' colours including creamy-yellow and olive. His Piam Nymphs are popular on rivers of southeastern France, such as La Loue. Samples provided have proved effective in trout rivers in Fenno-Scandinavia, the Alps and Britain; rainbow trout in small stillwaters have also been fooled by their simplicity.

HERL AND WIRE NYMPHS

These very simple nymphs are tied on size 12-18 wet fly or nymph hooks; instead of silk, fine copper wire is used to form an underbody. Variation is based on the types and colours of herl used.

Pheasant Tail Nymph

Underbody – fine red copper wire
Tail, Abdomen, Thorax and Wing cases – cock pheasant tail fibres
Ideally used to match Baetis nymphs.

Grey Herl Nymph

Underbody – fine gold copper wire
Tail, Abdomen, Thorax and Wing cases – grey herl (e.g. heron, goose secondary)
Used to match pale watery nymphs. Evolved in France in 1873 as les Nymphes Jeannot, and later in England as Sawyer's Pheasant Tail and Grey Goose nymphs.

On a visit to Sweden, Sawyer produced another:

SS Nymph

Underbody – fine dark red copper wire
Tail, Abdomen, Thorax and Wing cases – dark grey herl (goose primary)
Ideally used to match claret, sepia, heptagenid and summer mayfly nymphs.

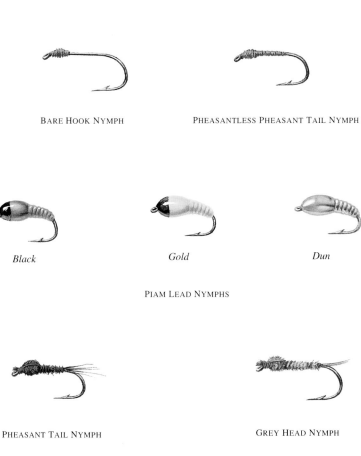

BARE HOOK NYMPH

PHEASANTLESS PHEASANT TAIL NYMPH

Black

Gold

Dun

PIAM LEAD NYMPHS

PHEASANT TAIL NYMPH

GREY HEAD NYMPH

SS NYMPH

DARK OLIVE HERL NYMPH

LIGHT OLIVE HERL NYMPH

Dark Olive Herl Nymph
Underbody – fine copper wire
Tail, Abdomen, Thorax and Wing cases – goose or
  swan herl dyed dark olive
Ideally used to match Baetis nymphs.

Light Olive Herl Nymph
Underbody – fine copper wire
Tail, Abdomen, Thorax and Wing cases – goose or
  swan herl dyed light olive
Matches pale watery nymphs.

FUR-BODIED NYMPHS

Fur has a degree of translucence and movement that imitates the flickering abdominal gills of upwinged fly nymphs better than harder, solider materials. Tie these on either wet fly or nymph hooks, sizes 12-18. Tie some unweighted (to fish close to the surface), others to fish deeply by adding fine lead or copper wire as underbody by (i) whipping 1-4 strands of wire along the hook shank, or (ii) wrapping wire around the hook under the thorax. Thread – use same colour as body unless otherwise stated.

Brown Rabbit Nymph

Tail – bronze mallard fibre tips
Abdomen – rabbit fur dyed brown
Rib – fine copper wire
Thorax – as abdomen, more pronounced
Wing cases – bronze mallard fibres
Legs – tips of bronze mallard from wing cases, clipped
A good general brown nymph, representing a range of Ephemerids; also stoneflies (p. 167).

~

Olive Rabbit Nymph

Tail – grey partridge hackle fibres dyed olive
Abdomen – rabbit fur dyed olive
Rib – fine gold wire
Thorax – as abdomen, more pronounced
Wing cases – cock pheasant tail fibres
Legs – grey partridge hackle dyed olive
A good general olive nymph. In large sizes a reasonable damselfly nymph imitator, p. 172.

~

Hare Nymph

Tail – 3 tips cock pheasant tail fibres
Abdomen – hare's fur (from mask)
Rib – fine copper wire
Thorax – as abdomen, more pronounced
Wing cases – cock pheasant tail fibres
Legs – brown speckled partridge hackle
This is best fished in or close to the surface film during a hatch of olives, march browns etc. Do not weight this pattern.
   The GRHE Nymph (p. 124) is a simpler version of the Hare Nymph

~

Beaver Nymph 1

Tail – tips of bronze mallard
Abdomen – beaver fur
Rib – fine gold wire
Thorax – as abdomen, more pronounced
Wing cases – bronze mallard fibres
Legs – bronze mallard from wing cases, clipped

Beaver Nymph 2

Tail – few fibres or brown speckled partridge hackle
Abdomen – beaver fur
Rib – fine copper wire
Thorax – as abdomen, more pronounced
Wing cases – grey herl (e.g. heron sub.)
Legs – brown speckled partridge hackle

Beaver Nymph 3

Tail – few fibres grey deer hair
Abdomen – beaver fur
Rib – fine copper wire
Thorax – as abdomen, more pronounced
Wing cases – grey deer hairs
Legs – grey deer hairs from wing cases, clipped
Many nymphs have a grey or grey-olive tone: these match such a colour. Beaver is a much under-used natural fur; it is especially super for nymph patterns (including stoneflies, p. 167).

~

Opossum and Hare Nymph

Silk – brown
Tail – 3 tips cock pheasant tail fibres
Body – cream-buff opossum fur
Rib – tying silk
Thorax – hare's ear, pronounced
Wing cases – cock pheasant tail fibres
Legs – a few hairs picked out from thorax
Excellent during a hatch of pale wateries when fished in the surface film.

~

Mole Fur (Iron Blue) Nymph

Silk – crimson
Tip – 2 turns tying silk
Tail – 3 fibres white cock hackle
Body – silk dubbed mole fur
Hackle – jackdaw throat hackle
One of the oldest imitative nymphs.

Mole Fur (Olive) Nymph

Silk – yellow
Tail – 3-4 fibres capercaillie (or other dark, speckled) hackle
Abdomen – tying silk, lightly dubbed mole (or water vole or beaver) fur
Thorax – heavily dubbed mole fur
Wing cases – black crow quill slip
Legs – capercaillie neck hackle
A very effective pattern when trout are eating Baetis nymphs. The yellow silk and light mole dubbing give a lifelike olive hue.

~

March Brown Nymph

Silk – orange
Tail – 3 cock pheasant tail fibres
Abdomen – mix of furs (75% brown, 15% olive, 10% amber)
Thorax – as abdomen
Wing cases – cock pheasant tail fibres
Legs – speckled grouse hackle
Tied on hook sizes 12-16, this matches most heptagenid nymphs provided that the outline is correct – aim for a triangular body outline, with a broad thorax and head at the front. The best way of achieving this is by building up a lead underbody.

*By adding a lead under-thorax a nymph pattern
is weighted and the thicker thorax is produced*

BROWN RABBIT NYMPH

OLIVE RABBIT NYMPH

HARE NYMPH

BEAVER NYMPH 1

BEAVER NYMPH 2

BEAVER NYMPH 3

Beaver fur: take the underfur for nymphs

OPOSSUM AND HARE NYMPH

MOLE FUR (IRON BLUE) NYMPH

MOLE FUR (OLIVE) NYMPH

MARCH BROWN NYMPH

Potomanthus Nymph

Silk – brown
Tail – 3-4 fibres bronze mallard
Abdomen – fawn fur
Rib – brown thread
Thorax – fawn fur
Wing cases – bronze mallard slip
Legs – grey partridge dyed golden olive

For Potamanthus nymphs, tie on sizes 10-12 hooks; this is a good pattern whenever the trout are feeding on light coloured nymphs.

~

Fox Squirrel Nymph

Silk – brown
Tail – bunch of guard hairs from the back of fox
  squirrel
Abdomen – 60% orange fur taken from the belly of the
  fox squirrel, mixed with 40% Antron or seal's fur (or
  substitute)
Rib – fine oval gold tinsel or wire
Thorax – fox squirrel back fur
Wing cases – dark brown feather slip or raffine
Legs – brown partridge

A variant of an excellent pattern by Dave Whitlock from the USA. As an alternative, dye some fox squirrel skin olive to produce an olive nymph.

~

Simple Fur Nymph

Silk – as fur colour
Tail – 3-5 fibres of bronze mallard, capercaillie,
  brown partridge or similar (to match fur colour)
Abdomen – brown, or olive, or grey fur (natural, with
  a mix of guard and under fur)
Thorax – as abdomen but more pronounced
Legs – guard hairs from thorax picked out

It does not matter what fur is used. Give some a lead under-thorax; have some unweighted. Tie in a range of sizes and colours. A simple but effective nymph (that might imitate any nymph species, including stoneflies, p. 167) for the novice fly-dresser.

HERL AND FUR NYMPHS

A wide range of excellent nymphs can be produced using the following formula:

Olive Nymph

Hook – size 12-18 wet fly or nymph
Silk – olive
Tail – brown speckled partridge
Abdomen – olive herl
Rib – fine gold wire
Thorax – olive fur
Wing cases – olive herl (from abdomen)
Legs – brown speckled partridge hackle

For other colours just alter colour/shade of silk, herl and fur to match the nymph you wish to imitate. Weight some of these with close turns of lead wire under the thorax.

QUILL AND FUR NYMPHS

Stripped peacock quill is a neglected material in nymph design, but it does produce a realistic, slender, segmented abdomen for small upwinged fly nymph imitations. For the thorax fur is essential to give the necessary bulk. Weight some with an under-thorax of fine lead wire or foil.

Quill and Fur Nymph

Hook – size 14-18 nymph
Silk – as thorax
Tail – 3 fibres dark elk hair or 3-5 brown partridge,
  bronze mallard or capercaillie hackle fibres
Abdomen – stripped peacock quill
Thorax – dark olive, grey or brown fine fur
Wing cases – dark brown or black feather slip
Legs – brown partridge or capercaillie hackle

Originally designed to match the nymphs of the sepia and claret duns in stillwaters, this pattern is effective when trout are feeding on a wide variety of tiny nymphs.

SYNTHETIC STRIP (FLEXIBODY) NYMPHS

These are synthetic quill and fur body nymphs: instead of stripped quill as abdomen, narrow strips of thin, flexible, synthetic film of appropriate colour are cut and wound. 'Flexibody' is currently available throughout Europe, and comes in super green-olive, brown-olive, brown and other colours. If unobtainable, thin strips can be cut from coloured polythene sheet. The following two patterns are modifications of Oliver Edwards's Baetis Nymph and Heptagenid Nymph. The former is effective where trout are feeding on small olive swimming nymphs, the latter in rough rivers and stony lakes where stone-clinging nymphs are abundant.

Baetis Nymph

Hook – size 16-18 nymph
Underbody – slender, lead foil strip from wine bottle
Silk – finest, olive
Tail – 3 dark brown hair tips (e.g. elk, skunk) or
  partridge, bronze mallard or grouse hackle fibres
Abdomen – olive 'Flexibody'
Thorax – olive fur, fine
Wing cases – crow quill slip
Legs – brown partridge hackle dyed olive

Heptagenid Nymph

Hook – size 12-16 nymph
Underbody – fine lead wire or foil, built up to a
  triangular shape (broader at front) and flattened
Silk – brown
Tail – 3 dark brown hair tips (e.g. elk, skunk)
Abdomen – brown or olive-brown 'Flexibody'
Thorax – brown or olive-brown fur, fine
Wing cases and Head – dark brown feather slip or raffine
Legs – brown partridge.

POTOMANTHUS NYMPH

FOX SQUIRREL NYMPH

Fox squirrel fur: a piece of skin from most mammals gives a wide range of fur colours

SIMPLE FUR NYMPH

OLIVE HERL AND FUR NYMPH

QUILL AND FUR NYMPH

Flexibody wound as an abdomen

BAETIS NYMPH

HEPTAGENID NYMPH

OSTRICH HERL NYMPHS

A wide range of excellent nymphs can be produced using the following formula:

Brown Ostrich Nymph

Hook – size 12-18 wet fly or nymph
Silk – brown
Tail – few cock pheasant tail fibres
Under Thorax – close turns lead wire
Abdomen – brown ostrich herls
Rib – fine silver wire
Thorax – as abdomen
Wing cases – cock pheasant tail fibres
Other colours of nymph can be made by varying the colour of the ostrich herl.

GOLDHEAD NYMPHS

The gold bead at the front of the fly gives weight and an attractive sparkle of light. In theory any nymph can be tied with a gold bead at the front: they are very effective. Just three are described here:

Goldhead Pheasant Tail Nymph

Hook – wet fly or nymph that can accommodate the goldhead (p. 222)
Head – gold-plated bead
Silk – brown
Tail – cock pheasant tail fibres
Abdomen – cock pheasant tail fibres
Rib – fine gold wire
Thorax – rabbit fur dyed brown
Wing cases – cock pheasant tail fibres

Dark Brown Goldhead Nymph

As Goldhead Pheasant Tail Nymph, but with herl dyed dark brown for tail, abdomen and wing cases, and hare's ear thorax

Goldhead Fox Squirrel Nymph

Hook – size 10-14 wet fly or nymph that can accomodate the goldhead (p. 222)
Silk – brown
Tail – bunch of guard hairs from the back of fox squirrel
Abdomen – 60% orange fur taken from the belly of the fox squirrel, mixed with 40% Antron or seal's fur (or substitute)
Rib – fine oval gold tinsel or wire
Thorax – fox squirrel back fur
Wing cases – dark brown feather slip or raffine
Legs – guard hairs from thorax

UPWINGED FLY EMERGERS

These are often overlooked, despite the fact that fish often select nymphs that are in the process of hatching rather than the nymph rising to hatch or the dun on the surface (see p. 41). The aim is to produce a nymphal pattern hanging from the surface film, with some semblance of the dun emerging from the nymphal shuck.

Fur-bodied Emerger

Dress an unweighted Fur-bodied Nymph (p. 144) but instead of tying in the wing cases tie in a Cul de Canard feather as follows: when the abdomen is completed tie in a Cul de Canard feather by its butt immediately behind the thorax; wind on the dubbed fur thorax in front of this feather; bring the Cul de Canard feather forwards and tie in at the head, leaving a gap between thorax and feather fibres, so that the feather provides a veil over the thorax (p. 249).

When this fly is fished, the nymphal body lies just below the surface supported by the Cul de Canard which passes through the surface film, simulating the dun struggling from the nymphal shuck.

Four examples are illustrated:

Olive Rabbit Nymph Emerger, Hare Nymph Emerger, Beaver Nymph Emerger, Mole Fur (Olive) Nymph Emerger

These are preceisely the same tyings as on p. 144, but the veil of Cul de Canard over the thorax will hold them just below the surface film in the attitude of an emerger.

~

Suspender Emerger

Hook – size 12-18 dry fly
Silk – as herl colour
Tail – 3-5 herls (cock pheasant tail, heron, grey goose, swan or goose dyed olive or cream-buff)
Abdomen – herls as Tail
Rib – finest gold wire or monofilament (0.5-1 kg test)
Float – polystyrene bead or ball cut from piece of Plastazote enclosed in nylon tights material (p. 222)
Thorax – dubbed fur slightly darker in shade than herls
The 'Float', tied in close to the eye of the hook, holds the fly in the surface film, in the attitude of a nymph when the dun is starting to emerge.

Four examples of this modified nymph are illustrated:

Pheasant Tail, Olive, Grey Goose, Cream
These are the same tyings as on p. 126, but the suspender ball will hold them just below the surface film, making them into emergers.

See also Spider Greenwell's Glory and GRHE (p. 124), CDC Emergers (p. 141).

BROWN OSTRICH NYMPH

1. Gold bead and hook

2. Slide bead onto hook over a foundation of thread

3. Gold head in place

GOLDHEAD NYMPH

GOLDHEAD PHEASANT TAIL NYMPH

DARK BROWN GOLDHEAD NYMPH

GOLDHEAD FOX SQUIRREL NYMPH

OLIVE RABBIT NYMPH EMERGER

HARE NYMPH EMERGER

BEAVER NYMPH EMERGER

MOLE FUR (OLIVE) NYMPH EMERGER

FUR-BODIED EMERGERS

1. Polystyrene bead in a piece of tights material

2. Bead being tied in place

3. Bead tied in place – the nymph can now be tied

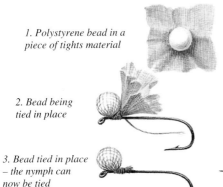

attitude in water

SUSPENDER EMERGER

Cul de Canard feather

PHEASANT TAIL NYMPH
SUSPENDER EMERGER

OLIVE NYMPH
SUSPENDER EMERGER

GREY GOOSE NYMPH
SUSPENDER EMERGER

CREAM NYMPH
SUSPENDER EMERGER

Hatching Nymph (sometimes called **Paradun**)

Hook – size 12-18 dry fly hook

Silk – as body colour

Abdomen – herl or dubbed fur, dyed or natural in brown, cream-buff, iron blue, grey, yellow or olive

Rib – fine gold wire

Thorax – herl or fur of slightly darker shade than abdomen

Wing – tuft of hair (deer, calf tail, synthetic e.g. Antron or Poly-yarn) or bunch of cock hackle fibres; white, cream or grey

Hackle – 3-4 turns cock hackle (cream, blue dun, ginger or olive) wound parachute style around base of wing

The wing is tied in before the thorax is wound, so the wing is supported in a vertical position, and the hackle is then wound around the base of the wing. When fishing these patterns, treat the wing and hackle with flotant: the hackle holds on the surface film and represents the legs of the hatching dun; the wing is clearly visible above the water; the abdomen and thorax lie in the surface film and mimic the nymph shuck. Choose size and colour of emerger according to species of natural upwinged fly.

Antron wing tied in place: the rest of the fly is now tied and the hackle wound around the base of the wing

Chopped and dyed red deer fur will hold the fly in the surface: ideal for emerger patterns

Four examples are illustrated that imitate emerging pale watery, iron blue and olive duns (p. 46) and yellow dun (p. 50).

PALE WATERY PARADUN

YELLOW PARADUN

IRON BLUE/PURPLE DUN/PARADUN

OLIVE/GREEN/DARK PARADUN

Deerhair Emerger

Hook – size 12-16 dry fly

Silk – orange or brown

Tail – few deer hair tips

Abdomen – dubbed chopped deer fur

Wing – tuft of Antron or Poly-yarn

Thorax – as abdomen, but thicker

A quite scruffy but effective general emerger that exploits the buoyancy of deer fur. This will take trout feeding on a wide range of natural flies.

DEERHAIR EMERGER

Loop-wing Emerger

Hook – size 12-18 dry fly

Silk – orange or brown

Tail – tips of grey mallard breast

Abdomen – olive seal's fur (or sub.)

Rib – fine silver wire

Thorax – as abdomen, but thicker

Wings – two lengths of Antron or Poly-yarn, tied in at base and then front of thorax

Grease the wings with 'Gink'. Very effective during a hatch of March Browns and ecdyonurids (p. 48).

LOOP-WING EMERGER

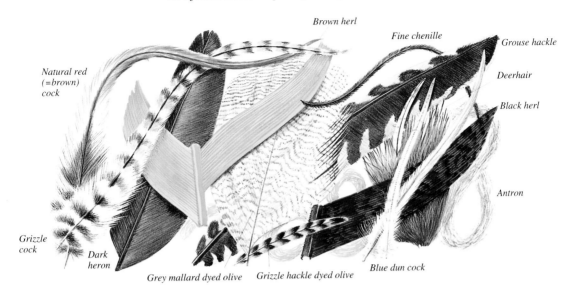

Brown herl

Fine chenille

Grouse hackle

Natural red
(=brown)
cock

Deerhair

Black herl

Antron

Grizzle
cock

Dark
heron

Grey mallard dyed olive   Grizzle hackle dyed olive   Blue dun cock

UPWINGED FLY DUNS

(Natural Duns pp. 40-51)

Upwinged fly duns are perhaps the group of natural flies with the greatest number of imitative patterns (this, despite the fact that on many European lakes and rivers other groups are equally if not more important as foods for trout, grayling, charr, whitefish etc.). It is not our intention to list a vast number of proven published patterns, though some of the best are described here. Instead we start with a basic recipe that can be adapted to match the natural duns. Adapt these recipes by choosing the appropriate hook size, and colour of tail, body, wing and hackle according to the species being imitated. Pages 42-51 provide a summary of the natural European duns; wherever possible catch specimens and compare them with your tying.

Basic Dun

Hook – size 12-18 dry fly, choosing a shank length equal to or slightly less than the body length of the natural fly (with few exceptions, evidence suggests that the fish are more likely to take an artificial dun that is a fraction smaller than the body of the real fly)

Silk – as body colour or neutral (e.g. grey, mid-brown)

Tail – a bunch of cock hackle fibres, deer hairs, synthetic tails (microfibbets), or cock pheasant tail fibres

Body – waxed tying silk, or herl (pheasant tail, swan or goose dyed, or heron or grey goose), or fine textured fur (natural, e.g. rabbit, hare, seal, dog or cat combings dyed as appropriate, or synthetic), or stripped quill (e.g. white cock dyed as appropriate), or raffine. Increase the 'body shape trigger' of the artificial by giving it a slender abdomen and then making extra turns of the body material at the front to simulate a thorax.

Rib – fine gold, copper or silver wire, or fine monofilament, or silk thread or stripped quill (quill bodies are not ribbed)

Overbody – (optional) thin strip cut from polythene bag to give a natural translucence to the body

Hackle – good quality cock hackle; colour is relatively unimportant, cream, ginger, dun, sandy dun, light blue dun, iron blue dun and natural red (brown) with some dyed golden-olive and medium olive are most useful.

The hackle may be wound conventionally around the hook shank behind the head or in parachute style (e.g. around the base of the wings): p. 243. How many turns of hackle? There is no one right answer. In a wingless (hackle) dry fly tie some with just 3-4 turns (for flat slow water) and others with 6+ turns for faster, rougher water. In a winged dry fly wind 3-4 turns in front of the wing and 2-3 behind the wing.

Wing – wing slips from mallard, teal, coot quills, or wings cut or burnt from whole feathers, or synthetic wings, or a tuft of hair (e.g. Poly-yarn, Antron, deer), or hackle points, full feathers, a bunch of cul de canard feather fibres, or a bunch of feather fibres.

Sometimes the wings are not a trigger so need not be tied on the artificial; sometimes the fish look at wings as a trigger (they can see an image of the upright dun wings in their 'window') and they are then essential in the artificial. One of the great advantages of tying winged dry flies as distinct from wingless is that they are more visible on the water. This is especially important: if you cannot see the fly on the water how do you know that a fish has taken it and that it is time to set the hook?

A typical traditional dun pattern

We will begin with five old but still effective patterns and then look at more precise imitations.

Adams

Hook – size 10-20 dry fly
Silk – grey or black
Tail – bunch mixed natural red and grizzle cock hackle fibres
Body – grey muskrat or fine substitute fur
Hackle – natural red and grizzle cock
Wing – 2 grizzle cock hackle points, tied upright and split

A dry fly that can be used to match several European upwinged flies, from the big mayfly, summer mayfly, Epeorus, Palingenia, Ephoron, several ecdyonurids, to the tiny pale wateries, by varying hook size.

~

Dark Cahill

Hook – size 12-20 dry fly
Silk – brown or grey
Tail – dark ginger cock hackle fibres
Body – grey muskrat or fine substitute fur
Hackle – dark ginger cock
Wing – fibres from wood-duck flank feather, tied upright and split (bronze mallard is a good substitute)

Light Cahill

Hook – size 12-20 dry fly
Silk – cream
Tail – cream cock hackle fibres
Body – fine fibred cream-yellow fur
Hackle – cream cock
Wing – fibres from wood-duck flank feather, tied upright and split (bronze mallard is a good substitute)

The two Cahills can be used to match most upwinged flies, the darker to be used when trout are eating mayfly, summer mayfly, Epeorus, several of the march brown – ecdyonurid – heptagenid species, Epeorus, Palingenia, Ephoron, and some of the drabber olives (e.g. lake and pond olive, green dun, dark dun). The Light version is successful during hatches of pale wateries and, if a yellower fur is used, yellow mayfly, yellow dun and yellow evening dun.

~

Imperial

Hook – size 12-18 dry fly
Silk – purple
Tail – honey dun, ginger, or sandy dun cock hackle fibres
Body – heron herl (or light grey substitute)
Rib – fine gold wire
Hackle – honey dun, ginger, or sandy dun cock

Olive Kite, the inventor of this pattern, insisted that the 'silhouette trigger' be strengthened by creating a distinct thorax on the fly (by 'doubling and redoubling' the heron herls just behind the wing). This is a great pattern: trout will fall for its deceptive powers when they are feeding on a wide range of duns, from march brown and olives, to blue-winged olive and pale wateries, Epeorus, Palingenia, Ephoron, the tiny iron blue and Chloroterpes. Because it lacks wings, it is a good dry fly for the beginner to start with.

Beacon Beige

Hook – size 12-16 dry fly
Silk – brown or black
Tail – bunch grizzle cock hackle fibres
Body – stripped peacock quill
Hackles – grizzle cock and natural red cock, well mixed

Another old, simple pattern that will deceive trout feeding on a wide variety of duns.

~

Pale Watery Dun 1

Hook – size 16-18 dry fly
Silk – cream
Tails – 2 bunches cream cock hackle
Body – opossum fur
Hackle – cream cock
Wing – single bunch grey mallard fibres

Pale Watery Dun 2

Hook – size 16-18 dry fly
Silk – white
Tail – 1 bunch cream cock hackle
Body – stripped cream cock hackle stalk
Hackle – cream cock
Wing – pale teal primary quill slips

Pale Watery Dun 3

Hook – size 16-18 dry fly
Silk – cream
Tail – bunch cream cock hackle fibres
Body – silk lightly dubbed cream fur
Hackle – cream cock
Wings – 2 bunches grey mallard fibres

Pale Watery Dun 4

Hook – size 16-18 dry fly
Silk – yellow
Tail – blue dun cock
Body – tip of yellow silk rest dubbed mixture of tup fur+cream seal fur+lemon spaniel+crimson seal's fur
Hackle – blue dun cock

This is the famous **Tup's Indispensable,** a traditional Pale Watery imitation. Tup fur is taken from the scrotal sac of the ram.

~

Iron Blue Dun 1

Hook – size 16-18 dry fly
Silk – crimson
Tail – dark (iron) blue cock hackle fibres
Body – tip of crimson silk; rest dark grey (heron) herl
Rib – fine gold wire
Hackle – dark (iron) blue cock

Iron Blue Dun 2

Hook – size 16-18 dry fly
Silk – grey
Tail – dark (iron) blue cock
Body – dubbed mole fur
Hackle – dark (iron) blue cock
Wings – coot quill slips

Both these patterns match the hatches of all dark, small duns (purple dun, chloroterpes, iron blue).

ADAMS

DARK CAHILL

LIGHT CAHILL

IMPERIAL

BEACON BEIGE

PALE WATERY DUN 1

PALE WATERY DUN 2

PALE WATERY DUN 3

PALE WATERY DUN 4

IRON BLUE DUN 1

IRON BLUE DUN 2

March Brown 1

Hook – size 12-14 dry fly
Silk – orange
Tail – bunch bronze mallard fibres
Body – synthetic fur 'march brown' shade
Hackle – blue dun cock parachuted round wing base
Wing – bunch bronze mallard fibres

March Brown 2

Hook – size 12-14 dry fly
Silk – brown
Tail – sandy-dun cock hackle fibres
Body – synthetic fur 'march brown' shade
Hackle – sandy-dun cock
Wing – woodcock wing quill slips

March Brown 3

Hook – size 12-14 dry fly
Silk – orange
Tail – dun cock hackle fibres
Body – hare's ear
Rib – orange silk
Hackle – few fibres pulled from front of body
Wing – bunch cream Antron fibres

March Brown 4

Hook – size 12-14 dry fly
Silk – orange
Tail – sandy-dun cock hackle fibres
Body – hare's ear
Rib – fine gold wire
Hackle – sandy-dun cock

These four will also match hatches of false march brown duns (e.g. brook dun) southern mayfly, Ephoron, Palingenia and summer mayfly.

~

Olive Dun 1

Hook – size 14-18 dry fly
Silk – olive
Tail – dun cock
Body – olive herl
Rib – fine gold wire
Hackle – dun or olive cock

Olive Dun 2 as pattern 1, but with ginger tail and hackle, and with wings of mallard primary quill slip
Olive Dun 3 as pattern 2, but with sandy-dun tail and hackle, and with wings of teal primary quill slips
Olive Dun 4 as pattern 3, but with bronze mallard tail, and a single bunch snipe primary quill fibres as wing.

Olive Dun 5

Hook – size 14-18 dry fly
Silk – olive
Tails – 2 bunches sandy-dun cock hackle fibres
Body – olive rabbit fur
Hackle – sandy-dun cock parachute base
Wing – bunch blue Antron fibres

Have several olive dun patterns in the fly box, so that whichever natural olive dun is on the water, the hatch can be matched. Also useful Olive Duns: Greenwell's Glory and Dry GRHE, p. 124.

Yellow Dun 1

Hook – size 12-16 dry fly
Silk – yellow
Tail – golden-olive cock hackle fibres
Body – goose herl or fine fur dyed yellow
Rib – fine gold wire
Hackle – golden-olive cock (parachute)
Wing – bunch Poly-yarn dyed yellow

Matches yellow mayfly, yellow evening dun, yellow (may) dun

Yellow Dun 2

Hook – size 12-14 dry fly
Silk – yellow
Tail – yellow cock hackle fibres
Body – mix of 80% yellow and 20% orange fine fibred fur
Hackle – golden olive cock
Wing – yellow hackle points, tied upright and split

Use this during hatches of yellow mayflies, yellow duns and yellow evening duns.

~

Caenis 1

Hook – size 18-24* dry fly
Silk – brown
Tail – white cock hackle fibres
Body – tying silk
Hackle – white cock

Caenis 2

Hook – size 18-24* dry fly
Silk – black
Tail – cream cock hackle fibres or microfibetts
Abdomen – stripped cream cock hackle stalk
Thorax – peacock herl
*Hackle*** – cream cock
*Wing**** – cream cock hackle points

Caenis 3

Hook – size 18-24* dry fly
Silk – black
Tail – cream cock hackle points or microfibetts
Abdomen – white floss silk
Rib – fine silver wire
Thorax – brown fur
*Hackle*** – pale blue dun cock
*Wing**** – white Poly-yarn

* have some in size 18-20 for the morning hatches, others size 22-24 for the afternoon/evening..
** caenis duns hatch, moult into spinners, mate and fall spent in a matter of 1-2 hours. Sometimes the spinner fall is more important than the dun hatch to the angler. These patterns adequately match both dun and spinner but tie some hackleless because often the fish will select only spent spinners lying flat in the surface film.
*** tie some with upright wings (as duns) and others with flat wings (as spinners).

MARCH BROWN 1

MARCH BROWN 2

MARCH BROWN 3

MARCH BROWN 4

OLIVE DUN 1

OLIVE DUN 2

OLIVE DUN 3

OLIVE DUN 4

OLIVE DUN 5

YELLOW DUN 1

YELLOW DUN 2

CAENIS 1

CAENIS 2

actual size

CAENIS 3

actual size

Claret/Sepia Dun

Hook – size 14-16 dry fly
Silk – brown
Tail – natural red or dark blue cock hackle fibres
Abdomen – dark brown herl or fine textured fur
Rib – fine gold wire or narrow lurex
Thorax – black herl or fur
Hackle – natural dark red or furnace
Wing – teal primary quill slips or dark blue cock
  hackle points

A splendid pattern during a hatch of claret or sepia
duns.

CLARET/SEPIA DUN

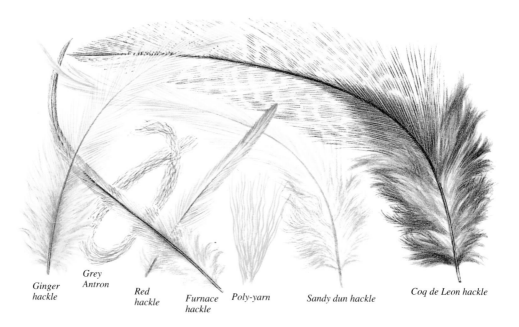

Ginger hackle | Grey Antron | Red hackle | Furnace hackle | Poly-yarn | Sandy dun hackle | Coq de Leon hackle

HACKLELESS DUNS

A proportion of duns have great difficulty emerging from the nymphal shuck and they often end up with bodies and tails trapped in the surface film. Frequently the fish will select these rather than duns standing high on the surface film. The hackleless dun imitates those duns that are having difficulty leaving the water.

It has been argued that the natural upwinged fly dun is badly matched by the basic dun pattern with a conventional hackle: in the natural the body (at least the body close to the thorax) lies on the water and the tip of the abdomen and tails are held off the water, whereas in the basic dun imitation the entire body is held off the water by the hackle and tail. The parachute hackle was devised to produce a better pattern on the water (see examples above). That basic, conventionally hackled duns do deceive the fish on perhaps the majority of occasions shows just how carelessly trout inspect what they are eating! Nevertheless, when the fish are inspecting duns closely and want the correct dun impression on the water surface, the hackleless dun is super. What is more, it is easier to tie than the conventional basic dun. (See also the hackleless CDC Category 1 patterns on p. 138).

The general tying is as follows:

Hook – size 12-18 dry fly
Silk – as body colour
Tails – 2 bunches of cock hackle fibres or synthetic tail fibres (blue dun, light ginger, cream) tied as outriggers
Body – soft, fine textured fur (opossum, rabbit, synthetic, either natural or dyed
Wing – wing slips, cut or burnt wings, or synthetic wings, or tuft of hair (e.g. Poly-yarn, Antron, deer, calf, mink), or cul de canard
Choose shade of fur and wings to match the appropriate natural fly. For the outriggers, take the tying silk down the hook shank, dub on a tiny amount – a mere wisp – of fur and wind it to produce a very, very small ball at the end of the hook shank. Take one bunch of tail material and tie it to one side so that it sticks out at a sharp angle supported by the little ball of dubbing; tie in another bunch of tail fibres on the other side in the same way (see also p. 237). Add more fur dubbing and wind, completing the body, to about 2-3 hook eye diameters behind the eye. Tie in the wings. Add a little more dubbing and wind this behind and in front of the wing bases so that it supports the wings and forms a thorax. Tie off and the fly is complete. Fish these flies, treated with flotant, as with a dry fly.

Any basic dun pattern (see above) can be tied as a hackleless dun, following the recipe and method given, provided it has a fur body. That is all there is to it! However some examples are given:

No-hackle Pale Watery

Hook – size 16-20 dry fly
Silk – cream
Tails – 2 bunches cream cock hackle fibres
Body – pale cream fur (e.g. opossum)
Wing – bunch white cul de canard feather

No-hackle Olive Dun 1

Hook – size 14-18 dry fly
Silk – olive
Tails – 2 bunches Pardo fibres
Body – olive-brown fur (e.g. rabbit)
Wing – bunch grey cul de canard feather

No-hackle Olive Dun 2

as 1, but with ginger cock hackle fibre tail, green-olive fur body, and blue Antron wing.

These match all duns with olive, olive-green or brown-olive bodies.

NO-HACKLE PALE WATERY

NO-HACKLE OLIVE DUN 1

NO-HACKLE OLIVE DUN 2

NO-HACKLE MARCH BROWN 1

NO-HACKLE MARCH BROWN 2

NO-HACKLE YELLOW DUN

NO-HACKLE IRON BLUE/PURPLE/CHLOROTERPES DUN

No-hackle March Brown 1

Hook – size 12-14 dry fly
Silk – brown
Tails – 2 bunches sandy-dun cock hackle fibres
Body – hare's ear
Wing – grey cul de canard feather

No-hackle March Brown 2

Hook – size 12-14 dry fly
Silk – orange
Tails – 2 bunches bronze mallard
Body – synthetic fur (Fly-Rite) march brown
Wing – deer hair

~

No-hackle Yellow Dun

Hook – size 12-14 dry fly
Silk – yellow
Tails – 2 bunches cream or light yellow cock kackle fibres
Body – fine textured yellow, or orange-yellow fur
Wing – bunch yellow hairs or feather fibres

~

No-hackle Iron Blue/Purple/Chloroterpes Dun

Hook – size 16-18 dry fly
Silk – purple
Tails – 2 bunches dark blue dun cock hackle fibres
Body – mole fur
Wing – bunch dark blue dun hairs of feather fibres

These match a wide range of buff/grey/straw bodied duns: Epeorus, Palingenia, Ephoron, southern mayfly and summer mayfly, as well as march browns and false march browns.

COMPARADUN

This is not one pattern, but a series of patterns of no-hackle dry dun imitations. Vary the colour of the tail, body fur and deerhair wing, and especially the size to match the natural fly. The important feature is the deerhair wing, tied in so that it stands vertically upright and extends through the upper 180° of the hook shank. The aim is a good pattern (the hackleless one) of the body and tails on the surface, with a strong wing image.

Hook – size 10-18 dry fly
Silk – as body colour
Tails – 2 bunches of cock hackle fibres or stiff hairs
Body – fine textured fur
Wing – deer hair

Five examples, to match most European duns, are illustrated:
Olive Comparadun: tail and body are olive; wing natural grey deerhair
Pale Watery Comparadun: tail and body are cream; wing natural grey deer hair
March Brown (also **Epeorus, Ephoron, Summer Mayfly, Southern Mayfly, Palingenia**) **Comparadun:** tails brown; body a mix of 40% yellow, 40% medium olive, 20% orange fur; wing dyed brown deerhair
Yellow Comparadun: tail, body and wing dyed yellow
Iron Blue (also **Purple Dun/Chloroterpes**) **Comparadun:** tail, body and wing are dyed blue-black.
In the section on special mayfly imitations (p. 164) a Mayfly Comparadun is also illustrated.

THORAX DUNS

The hackleless dry fly is just one attempt to improve on the conventional wound hackle dry fly. Another attempt was made by V.C. Marinaro when he devised the thorax duns (A Dry-Fly Code). Marinaro argued that a very selective trout (in crystal clear water) would see the upright wings of the natural through its mirror, and just the thorax and feet that were resting on the surface. The abdomen and tails of the natural, Marinaro argued, are held up in the air and are much less significant. Marinaro concentrated on these three features – feet and thorax touching the water and wings held high.
The basic tying is as follows:

Hook – dry fly; because the hook shank carries just an
  imitation of the thorax (and perhaps base of
  abdomen) a smaller hook is used for a thorax dun than
  for a conventional dun so reduce hook size by 2.
Silk – as body
Tail – few fibres cock hackle fibres, tied sloping
  upwards
Body – fine fibred fur to match colour of natural fly
Hackle – two short fibred cock
Wing – Marinaro recommended cut (or burnt) wings
Tie the wings in first in the middle of the hook shank. Take the silk to the end of the hook shank, tie in tails then dub the body to the wings. Tie in and wind one hackle to the rear of the wings and the second hackle in front of the wings. Dub more fur onto the tying silk and wind to the head before whip-finishing the fly.

Because one is not imitating the whole fly, Marinaro argued that just two patterns would suffice: one with dark grey wings and one with yellow-buff wings (in a range of sizes). Tests suggest that this is the case. The examples shown are:
Light Thorax Dun: Tails golden olive cock hackle fibres; body cream-buff fur; wings burnt or cut from light ginger cock hackles
Dark Thorax Dun: Tails dark blue dun cock hackle fibres; body dark grey fur; wings cut or burnt from dark blue dun cock hackles
Use the Light Thorax Dun when pale-bodied duns are on the water, Dark Thorax Dun for dark-bodied duns.

UPSIDE DOWN DUNS

One major defect of all imitative flies is the presence of the hook bend, point and barb, for no natural fly has these. Fortunately most trout seem not to notice them! But it is possible that the occasional trout might be put off by these features in the artificial fly. The upside down dry fly (and any dry fly can be tied upside down) lies on the surface of the water with the bend and point of the hook facing skywards so that the fish cannot see them. Special hooks have been made for tying special upside down flies (for instance, the Swedish Dry Fly Hook). But provided that the fly is tied with wings and a parachute hackle, any pattern can be tied upside down on a conventional dry fly hook. It is worth having some in the fly box just in case one comes across a particularly recalcitrant trout.

Modify basic dun patterns as follows: Tie the wings (a bunch of Poly-yarn or Antron, or bunch of feather fibres, or bunch of hair, or pair of cut (or burnt) feather wings) upright, on the underside of the hook shank. Tie in tails, then the body. Tie in a cock hackle and wind this around the base of the wing. Complete the fly. Test the fly by dropping it onto the ground : no matter how you hold it before dropping, it will always land wing and hook point uppermost.

Two basic patterns illustrate this tying:
Imperial (see p. 152): modified with the adddition of a grey Antron wing
Yellow Dun (see p. 154): modified with a wing of yellow squirrel tail hairs.

ONE-FEATHER DUNS

This is a simple but very effective way of imitating duns, producing a very light pattern that floats well.
Hook – size 14-16 dry fly
Silk – as hackle colour
Tail and Body – one feather (e.g. grey mallard),
  undyed or dyed to body colour of the natural dun
  (see below)
Hackle – cream, ginger, blue dun or natural red cock
Wings – tips of feather from tail/body tied upright as
  single bunch or split to give two wings
Take the dyed or undyed feather and hold the tip in a pair of hackle pliers. Now stroke back most of the fibres towards the stalk butt. Tie in the stalk and

Comparadun head-on

OLIVE COMPARADUN

PALE WATERY COMPARADUN

MARCH BROWN COMPARADUN

YELLOW COMPARADUN

IRON BLUE COMPARADUN

LIGHT THORAX DUN

IMPERIAL (UPSIDE DOWN)

ONE-FEATHER PALE WATERY

DARK THORAX DUN

YELLOW DUN (UPSIDE DOWN)

ONE-FEATHER OLIVE

stroked-backed fibres at the front of the hook, convex side down, with the tip as tail to rear; cut away the stalk. Lift the fibres and either tie them in as an upright single wing or split and tie in (with figure-of-eight turns with the silk around the bases) as a double upright wing. Cut out the centre of the tail, leaving 2-3 fibres on either side to mimic the 2 dun tails. Add the hackle and finish the fly. See also Emerger Mayfly, p. 164. To match any dun, simply use a grey mallard feather dyed to match the dun body colour.

One-feather Pale Watery

Silk – cream
Feather – undyed grey mallard
Hackle – cream cock

One-feather Olive

Silk – olive
Feather – grey mallard dyed olive
Hackle – ginger cock

Other upwinged fly dun imitations: several soft-hackled wet flies, pp. 127-35, CDC Category 1, p. 138.

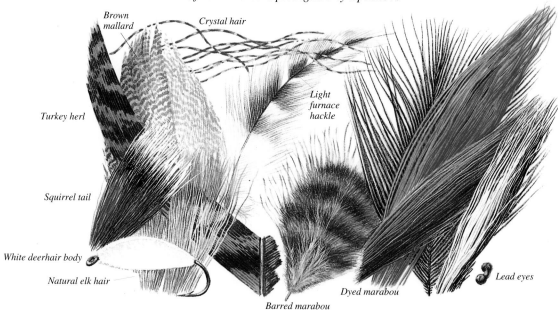

Brown mallard

Crystal hair

Turkey herl

Light furnace hackle

Squirrel tail

White deerhair body

Natural elk hair

Lead eyes

Dyed marabou

Barred marabou

UPWINGED FLY SPINNERS

(Natural Spinners p. 40-51)

The fish take spinners that have laid their eggs and then fallen, dying, onto the water. Some spinners, notably of the Baetis olive group, lay their eggs by crawling under the water; in these species many of the dead spent spinners will appear not on the water but under. To imitate these an underwater pattern is essential. These patterns will also imitate spinners that have fallen onto the water but have later sunk or been washed below the surface.

Underwater Spinners. Recommended especially are the following soft-hackled wet flies (p. 128): Orange Partridge, Red Spinner, Waterhen & Red, tied in sizes 16-18. They fit the bill perfectly.

Surface Spinners. Most dead spinners fall, fluttering weakly, onto the surface. When they have died, they sink into the surface film, usually with both wings flat in the water; some, however, die with one wing in the surface and the other held at right angles above the water. Sometimes the fish will select only those that are still alive and struggling (especially early in the fall); sometimes they will select only those with one wing held up in the air; often they will select only those lying completely flat in the surface film. It is worth carrying imitations that match all three postures.

When fishing spinner patterns it is worth remembering that most spinner falls occur late in the day, around dusk, when light levels are low and the fish can see only in black-and-white. Since colour, very fine detail or precise shades are of no importance the choice of spinner pattern is much easier than for duns: with the exception of species such as the big mayfly (p. 166) and tiny caenis, just one or two patterns can be carried. These patterns must have the following triggers: tails, a slender body (preferably with a slightly thicker thorax), wings, and the correct size.

Note: Caenis spinners are described on p. 154 and CDC Category 2 spinners on p. 138. The Pheasant Tail Spinner (p. 126), is also a great spinner pattern.

A general tying recipe:

Spent Spinner

Hook – size 12-18 dry fly

Silk – as body colour (red or brown)

Tail – bunch of cock hackle fibres (white, blue dun, natural red) deer hair or synthetic tails (e.g. microfibbets)

Abdomen – stripped cock hackle quill or herl (swan or goose dyed) or fine fur of colour of natural spinner

Rib – fine gold wire (no ribbing if quill body)

Thorax – fine fur dub or herl, same colour or a little darker than abdomen

Wings – hackle points or full feather wings, natural or synthetic hair (e.g. Poly-yarn, Antron), or raffine tied in a flat 'spent' position, some tied with one wing upright.

Hackle – (optional) choose a cock hackle that blends in with the overall coloration of the fly (natural red, blue dun are most used)

Tie in the wings before the thorax; the thorax herl or dubbing is wound behind and in front of the wings (figure-of-eight fashion) to add support to the wings. If a hackle is used, tie this after the wings and thorax, at the head of the fly. The fly is treated with flotant so that when it is being fished it floats in the surface film.

Any upwinged fly spinner can be matched using the above general recipe. Match size of natural with hook (shank length). Match general coloration details given in the section on upwinged flies (pp. 42-51).

A basic spent spinner

LARGE RED SPINNER 1   LARGE RED SPINNER 2

RED SPINNER 1   RED SPINNER 2   RED SPINNER 3

RED SPINNER 4   RED SPINNER 5

Large Red Spinner 1

Hook – size 12-14 dry fly
Silk – brown
Tail – natural red cock hackle fibres
Body – red fur (e.g. seal, synthetic)
Rib – fine gold wire
Wings – blue dun cock hackle points
Hackle – natural red cock

Large Red Spinner 2

Hook – size 12-14 dry fly
Silk – brown
Tails – 2 bunches fine grey deer hair
Body – rusty-red synthetic fur
Wings – bunches fine grey deer hair
Both are superb during a fall of march brown and false march brown spinners.

~

Red Spinner 1

Hook – size 14-18 dry fly
Silk – brown
Tails – 2 bunches dark blue dun cock hackle fibres
Body – orange fur (dyed samoyed dog in example)
Wings – white raffine

Red Spinner 2

Hook – size 14-18 dry fly
Silk – orange
Tail – bunch natural red cock hackle fibres
Abdomen – white cock hackle stalk dyed hot orange
Thorax – goose herl dyed hot orange
Wings – grey Antron

Red Spinner 3 as pattern 2 but with blue dun cock hackle point wings

Red Spinner 4 as pattern 2 but with white Poly-yarn wings

Red Spinner 5

Hook – size 18-20 dry fly
Silk – orange
Tails – 2 white microfibbets
Body – white cock hackle stalk dyed hot orange
Wings – cream cock hackle points
These five patterns will match the falls of most red or red-brown bodied spinners. Pattern 5 is for the smaller species (e.g. pale watery).

~

Brown Spinner 1

Hook – size 14-16 dry fly
Silk – brown
Tail – bunch brown cock hackle fibres
Body – brown herl (a fine fur dub as alternative)
Rib – fine gold wire
Wings – fibres stripped from dark blue dun cock hackle

Brown Spinner 2 (Lunn's Particular)

Hook – size 14-16 dry fly
Silk – red
Tail – natural red (brown) cock hackle fibres
Body – stripped natural red cock hackle stalk
Hackle – natural red cock
Wings – blue dun cock hackle points
These two match darker spinners; also effective in the evening for a wide range of species.

~

Yellow Spinner

Hook – size 12-16 dry fly
Silk – orange
Tail – bunch golden-olive cock hackle fibres
Body – yellow fur
Rib – fine gold wire
Wings – yellow Poly-yarn
Effective in fall of any yellow spinner (e.g. yellow mayfly, yellow may dun).

~

Apricot Spinner

Hook – size 14-16 dry fly
Silk – orange
Tails – 2 bunches dark blue dun cock hackle fibres
Body – apricot-coloured fur
Wing – white Poly-yarn
Effective in fall of pond olive spinner.

MAYFLIES

Artificial flies that match the large mayflies are treated here separately from other upwinged fly imitations. Most anglers carry a special box of the large mayfly patterns during the mayfly season. On a good mayfly water often nothing else need be carried during the short season because the fish gorge themselves on this huge food item. Mayfly imitations are so large compared with other artificial upwinged flies that they need a separate box.

MAYFLY NYMPHS

(Natural Nymphs – Bottom Burrower – pp. 38-9)

These must be weighted so that they sink quickly: whip lengths of fine lead wire along back of hook shank; or wind close turns of lead wire around all or front (under thorax) of hook shank.
Hooks – sizes 8-12 nymph or streamer/lure hooks.

Latex-bodied Mayfly Nymph

Silk – brown
Tail – tips of cock pheasant tail fibres
Underbody – yellow fur

Abdomen – thin strip of cream latex (cut from surgical glove) wound over underbody
Rib – thick brown thread
Thorax – yellow fur
Wing cases – cock pheasant tail fibres
Legs – bunch of tips of cock pheasant tail fibres

Fur Mayfly Nymph

Silk – brown
Tail – tips of cock pheasant tail fibres
Body – cream-yellow, fine fur
Rib – brown silk
Wing cases – cock pheasant tail fibres
Legs – bunch of tips of cock pheasant tail fibres

Angora-wool (RW) Mayfly Nymph

Silk – brown
Tails – tips of cock pheasant tail fibres
Abdomen – cream-yellow angora wool
Rib – thick brown thread
Thorax – as abdomen
Wing cases – cock pheasant tail fibres
Legs – 2 bunches cock pheasant tail fibres

Balloon Mayfly Nymph

Silk – black
Tail – 3 cock pheasant tail fibre tips
Abdomen – strip from deep yellow balloon rubber wound over underbody
Rib – fine gold wire
Thorax – hare's fur
Wing cases – cock pheasant tail fibres
Hackle – (legs) brown speckled partridge

Cul de Canard Mayfly Nymph

Silk – black
Tip – medium gold wire round hook bend
Tail – bunch olive cock hackle fibres separated into 3
Abdomen – CDC feather dyed yellow-olive
Rib – gold wire
Thorax – as abdomen
Wing cases – buff-pink CDC feather at side and black on back

Raffia Mayfly Nymph

Silk – black
Tail – short bunch brown deer hair
Abdomen – natural raffia
Rib – black thread
Thorax – brown fur
Wing cases – brown raffine
Legs – grey partridge hackle dyed brown olive

Wiggle Mayfly Nymph

Hook – two size 10 wet fly hooks tied in tandem, with rear having bend removed
Silk – brown
Tail – 3 tips brown ostrich herl
Abdomen – pale cream fur, marked on back with dark brown permanent felt tip pen
Rib – brown thread
Thorax – as abdomen
Wing cases – brown raffine

BROWN SPINNER 1

BROWN SPINNER 2 (LUNN'S PARTICULAR)

YELLOW SPINNER

APRICOT SPINNER

LATEX-BODIED MAYFLY NYMPH

Mayfly nymphs should be well weighted

FUR MAYFLY NYMPH

ANGORA-WOOL (RW) MAYFLY NYMPH

BALLOON MAYFLY NYMPH

CUL DE CANARD MAYFLY NYMPH

RAFFIA MAYFLY NYMPH

WIGGLE MAYFLY NYMPH

MAYFLY EMERGERS

Suspender Mayfly

As the Fur or Angora-wool Mayfly Nymphs, but with no lead underbody and with a polystyrene or Plastazote ball, enclosed in nylon tights material, tied in at the rear of the thorax/wing cases.

Cul de Canard Emerger Mayfly

As the CDC Mayfly Nymph, but with no heavy underbody, a fine silver wire tip and rib instead of medium gold, and the buff-pink CDC feathers at side of wing cases enlarged to simulate opening wings (these trap air and hold the fly at the surface film).

Emerger Mayfly

Silk – black
Nymph Shuck – rabbit-fur dyed golden-olive
Rib – oval gold tinsel
Dun Body, Tail and Wing – large grey mallard feather dyed medium-olive as in One-feather Duns (p. 159)
Hackle – medium olive cock wound parachute style around wing-base

MAYFLY DUNS   (Natural Duns p. 42)

Hooks: traditionally longshank, size 8-10, fine wire. If the hook hold is not good in the fish's jaw, these easily lever out and are prone to sinking because of the weight at the hook bend, unless the fly is heavily dressed. It has been found that dry flies tied on standard shank hooks, size 10-12, are as effective, even though the artificial is shorter than the natural fly. Dry patterns are also tied on shorter and lighter hooks, using flexible 'extended bodies'.

Mayfly Dun 1

Silk – black
Tail – 3 cock pheasant tail fibres
Body – primrose or olive floss
Rib – stripped peacock quill
Sheath – clear polythene
Hackles – medium olive cock and blue dun cock, wound separately
Wings – 2 pairs medium olive cock hackle points

Mayfly Dun 2

Silk – black
Tail – 3 cock pheasant tail fibres
Body – natural raffia or buff raffine
Rib – black and crimson silk, wound together
Hackle – natural red (rear), hot orange, grey mallard dyed olive or olive cock (front)

Mayfly Dun 3

Silk – brown
Tail – bunch deer hair
Body – natural rabbit (blue-grey)
Rib – black silk
Wing – deer hair, upright and split
Hackle – blue dun or sandy dun cock

Mayfly Dun 4

Silk – black
Tail – bunch cock pheasant tail fibres
Body – cream herl with 2 bands brown herl
Hackle – grizzle dyed olive (rear), hot orange (front)

Mayfly Dun 5: Elk Mayfly

Silk – black.
Extended body – length of 15 lb or 5 kg test monofilament whipped to hook, onto which tails and rear of body are tied
Tails – bunch fine grey elk hair
Body – elk dyed golden olive
Rib – black tying silk
Wing – bunch fine grey elk hair, upright
Hackle – sandy dun cock, parachute round base of wing

Mayfly Dun 6: Nescofilm Mayfly

Silk – black
Extended Body – Nescofilm or latex
Tail – 3 fibres cock pheasant tail
Thorax – olive fur
Wing – white Poly-yarn upright
Hackle – natural red cock, palmered round wing base

Mayfly Dun 7: French Partridge Mayfly

Silk – black
Tail – 3-5 cock pheasant tail fibres
Body – natural raffia (buff raffine)
Rib – fine gold wire
Body hackle – palmered olive cock
Hackle – French partridge

Mayfly Dun 8: Cul de Canard Mayfly

Silk – black
Tails – white microfibbets, marked with black pen
Body – cul de canard dyed yellow
Rib – olive thread
Wing – olive and grey-brown cul de canard feathers

Mayfly Dun 9: Compara Mayfly

Silk – black
Tails – sparse bunch moose hair
Body – fine textured light olive fur (opossum or beaver)
Wing – olive deer hair
(see p. 158 for Comparaduns)

Mayfly Dun 10: Grey Wulff

Silk – black
Tails – brown calf tail
Body – grey muskrat (or substitute)
Hackle – medium blue dun
Wing – brown calf tail tied upright and split

Mayfly Dun 11: Moose Mayfly

Silk – black
Tails – 4-5 black moose hairs
Body – light olive fur (synthetic or dyed natural)
Rib – black thread
Hackle – 0 or cream
Wing – bunch brown moose hair

Mayfly Dun 12: Calftail Mayfly Dun

Silk – black
Tail – bunch black calf tail
Body – primrose floss, tipped fore and aft with 2 turns peacock herl
Rib – black thread
Hackle – olive and red cock wound together
Wing – light yellow calf tail

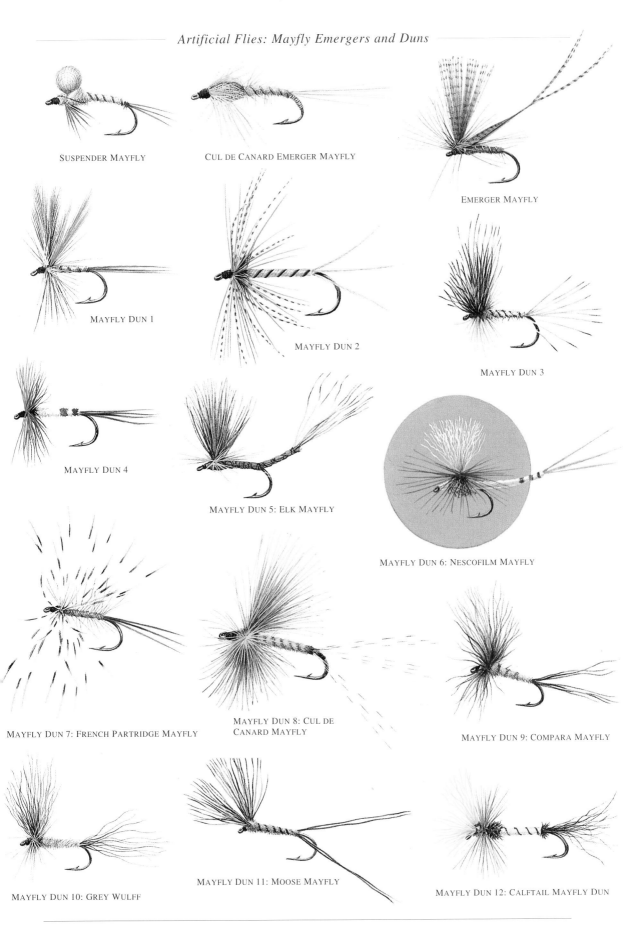

SUSPENDER MAYFLY

CUL DE CANARD EMERGER MAYFLY

EMERGER MAYFLY

MAYFLY DUN 1

MAYFLY DUN 2

MAYFLY DUN 3

MAYFLY DUN 4

MAYFLY DUN 5: ELK MAYFLY

MAYFLY DUN 6: NESCOFILM MAYFLY

MAYFLY DUN 7: FRENCH PARTRIDGE MAYFLY

MAYFLY DUN 8: CUL DE CANARD MAYFLY

MAYFLY DUN 9: COMPARA MAYFLY

MAYFLY DUN 10: GREY WULFF

MAYFLY DUN 11: MOOSE MAYFLY

MAYFLY DUN 12: CALFTAIL MAYFLY DUN

MAYFLY SPINNERS *(Natural Spinners p. 42)*

Tie Mayfly Spinners in three styles: 1. well-hackled, to imitate a female spinner fallen on the water and struggling to stay alive; 2. non-hackled and full spent, to imitate those females dead and lying flat in the surface film (or, trim away the hackle on the underside of the hackled spinner pattern); 3. some of batch 2 with wings at right angles to each other (so that one wing is flat in the surface film and the other sticks up in the air).

Hooks – as for duns (above).

Silk – black for all spinner patterns.

Mayfly Spinner 1

Tails – 3 cock pheasant tail fibres
Body – white floss
Hackle – badger cock
Wing – 2 pairs white cock hackle points

Mayfly Spinner 2

Tails – 3 cock pheasant tail fibres
Body – white raffine or floss
Rib – black thread
Sheath – clear polythene
Hackle – pale blue cock
Wings – 2 pairs black or dark blue dun cock hackle points

Mayfly Spinner 3

Tails – 3 fibres cock pheasant tail
Body – white floss
Rib – thick black thread
Wing – 2 bunches badger cock hackle fibres

Mayfly Spinner 4

Tails – 3 fibres cock pheasant tail
Body – white goose herl
Rib – black silk
Hackle – long fibred badger cock
Wing – 1 pair dark blue dun cock hackle points

Mayfly Spinner 5

Tails – 2 bunches long fibres dark blue cock hackle
Body – white fur (fine fibre, natural or synthetic)
Rib – black nylon thread
Wing – blue Antron fibres

Mayfly Spinner 6 as Mayfly Dun 3, but with wings spent or one-up-and-one-down

Mayfly Spinner 7

Silk – black
Tails – 3-4 black moose body hairs
Body – white fur
Rib – black thread
Wing – 2 bunches black moose body hair tied flat or 'one-up and one-down'

Mayfly Spinner 8

Silk – black
Tail – black calf tail
Body – white floss, tipped fore and aft with 2 turns peacock herl
Rib – black thread
Hackle – dark blue dun (optional)
Wing – black calf tail

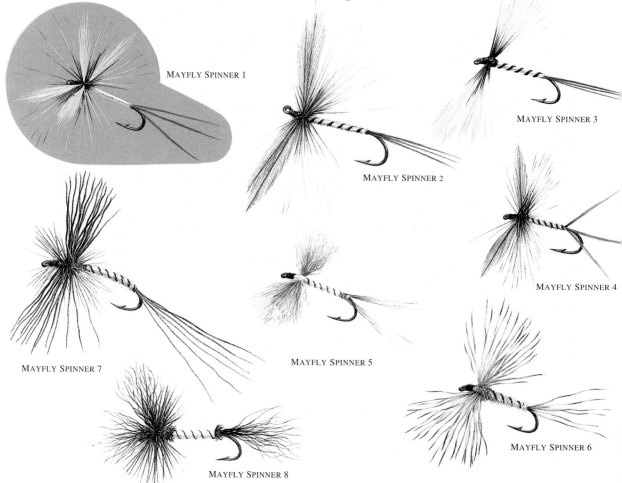

MAYFLY SPINNER 1

MAYFLY SPINNER 2

MAYFLY SPINNER 3

MAYFLY SPINNER 4

MAYFLY SPINNER 5

MAYFLY SPINNER 6

MAYFLY SPINNER 7

MAYFLY SPINNER 8

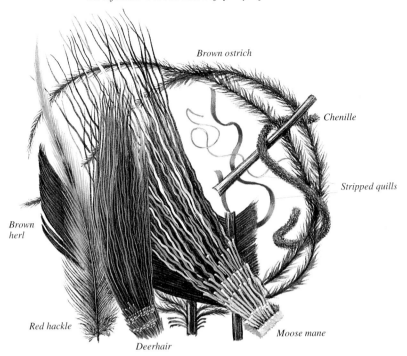

Brown ostrich

Chenille

Stripped quills

Brown herl

Red hackle

Deerhair

Moose mane

STONEFLIES

There are two stages in the stonefly life cycle that the angler might imitate: the nymph and the adult.

STONEFLY NYMPHS

(Natural Stonefly Nymphs p. 52)

Some stonefly nymph imitations should be weighted so that they fish deep in the water where the fish will normally encounter the natural nymphs. Weight the hook by tying strips of lead foil or wire along the top and sides of the hook shank; this also helps in producing the desired tapered shape of the imitative nymph. Keep some unweighted however; these can be used in very shallow rough boulder-strewn water where weighted patterns may constantly snag the bottom.

Many artificial stonefly nymph patterns that evolved in the USA are now tied by European fly dressers; some of these are quite beautiful creations with the anatomy of the natural nymph precisely copied on the hook. However these patterns usually imitate very large stoneflies, of which the USA has several important species, whereas Europe has just the one group of Large Stoneflies and many far more important smaller species. The following simpler basic stonefly nymph recipe, can be used to match all European stonefly nymphs provided that size and shade are varied.

Basic Stonefly Nymph

Hook – size 10-18 longshank wet fly, nymph or grub hook

Silk – as body colour

Underbody – leaded (see above)

Tails – 2 goose or swan biots, or 2 short lengths of very stout dark monofilament, or 2 stout synthetic tails, or 2 stripped dark hackle stalks, or 2 coarse hairs (e.g. elk)

Abdomen – short tip of fluorescent floss (optional), then dubbed fine textured fur (natural or synthetic) dyed dark olive, brown or black

Rib – fine gold wire, narrow flat copper or gold lurex, or orange or yellow silk, or dark peeled quill

Thorax – dubbed fur as abdomen

Wing cases – strip of dark quill or herl tied front and back over thorax (dark speckled turkey, peacock herl, dark speckled hen etc.), or burnt wing cases, or wing cases cut from dark brown latex

Legs – soft hackle fibres (either tied in false or as full hackle but sparsely); dark brown partridge, grouse, waterhen etc.

Head and Antennae – tie the wing cases down and cut square over the hook eye but leave 2 fibres longer as antennae

Keep the body slim, especially in smaller sizes. Before tying in the tails, first tie in a small ball of body material at the end of the abdomen; this will support the two tails (for tying method, see p.237)

Note: Several soft-hackled and thorax spider wet flies also imitate stoneflies (pp. 128-34). Also very effective are the Pheasant Tail Nymph (p. 126) and the darker fur-bodied nymphs on pp. 144-6.

A basic Stonefly Nymph

Peacock Stonefly Nymph

Hook – size 12-18 wet fly or nymph
Silk – black
Tail – 2 fibres brown mallard
Abdomen – stripped peacock quill
Thorax – bronze peacock quill
Legs – waterhen hackle
Antennae – 2 fibres bronze mallard clipped to length

~

Rabbit Stonefly Nymph 1

Hook – size 10-14 wet fly or nymph
Silk – brown
Underbody – lead wire
Tail – 2 brown goose biots
Abdomen – rabbit fur dyed olive-brown
Rib – fine copper wire
Thorax – as abdomen
Wing cases – cock pheasant tail fibres
Legs – partridge hackle dyed olive-brown

Rabbit Stonefly Nymph 2

Hook – size 10-14 wet fly or nymph
Silk – brown
Underbody – lead wire
Tail – 2 brown goose biots
Abdomen – rabbit fur dyed brown-olive
Rib – fine copper wire
Thorax – as abdomen
Wing cases – burnt wing cases, lacquered black
Legs – woodcock upper wing covert

~

Beaver Stonefly Nymph

Hook – size 10-14 wet fly or nymph
Silk – black
Underbody – lead wire
Tail – 2 black goose biots
Abdomen – beaver fur (or any very soft, fine dark grey fur)
Rib – fine gold wire
Thorax – as abdomen
Wing cases – grey herl (e.g. grey goose)
Legs – grey herl tips

~

Hare Stonefly Nymph

Hook – size 10-14 wet fly or nymph
Silk – brown
Underbody – lead wire
Tail – 2 dark brown goose biots
Abdomen – hare's fur
Rib – oval gold tinsel
Thorax – as abdomen
Wing cases – burnt wing cases, lacquered black
Legs – picked out hairs from thorax

~

Mouflon Stonefly Nymph

Hook – size 10-14 wet fly or nymph

Silk – black
Underbody – lead wire
Tails – 2 black goose biots
Abdomen – mouflon fur (or wool from a black sheep)
Rib – fine gold wire
Thorax – as abdomen
Wing cases – black herl
Legs – grouse or other dark soft hackle
Head – 2 turns bronze peacock herl
Antennae – 2 fibres bronze peacock herl, clipped

~

Brown Turkey Stonefly (Catskill Crawler)

Hook – size 10-14 nymph
Silk – brown
Tails – 2 peccary fibres or brown biots
Body – brown turkey herl
Rib – fine gold wire (optional)
Legs – tips of hen pheasant tail fibres
Wing cases – brown turkey feather slip
By tying similar patterns using black quill and light olive-brown quill for bodies and wing cases, the results are a black and yellow sally nymph respectively.

~

Yellow Sally Nymph

Silk – light brown
Tails – 2 light buff biots or moose body hairs
Body – light buff fur (fine synthetic or dyed rabbit etc.)
Rib – yellow thread
Legs – light ginger hen hackle
Wing cases – light mottled turkey quill slip

~

Large Stonefly Nymph 1

Hook – size 10-12 nymph or lure hook
Silk – brown
Underbody – lead wire
Tail – 2 brown goose biots
Abdomen – light-medium olive fur (e.g. rabbit)
Rib – very dark, blackish, peeled quill sheath from crow, grey goose etc.
Thorax – as abdomen
Wing cases – cock pheasant tail fibres
Legs – speckled brown partridge or upper wing covert of woodcock

Large Stonefly Nymph 2

Hook – size 8-12 nymph or lure hook
Silk – black
Underbody – lead wire
Tip – fluorescent orange floss silk
Tail – 2 dark brown goose biots
Body – light olive fur
Overbody – Flexibody/Swanundaze, lacquered black along back
Thorax – dark brown fur
Wing cases – dark brown herls
Legs – pheasant tail herls clipped to length
Antennae – 2 dark brown goose biots (optional)

PEACOCK STONEFLY NYMPH

RABBIT STONEFLY NYMPH 1

RABBIT STONEFLY NYMPH 2

BEAVER STONEFLY NYMPH

HARE STONEFLY NYMPH

MOUFLON STONEFLY NYMPH

BROWN TURKEY STONEFLY (CATSKILL CRAWLER)

YELLOW SALLY NYMPH

LARGE STONEFLY NYMPH 1

LARGE STONEFLY NYMPH 2

ADULT STONEFLIES

(Natural Stoneflies pp. 52-4)

Usually adult stoneflies occur on the water only during egg-laying, so the aim is to produce an imitation of the female fluttering or swimming across the water. Movement must either be built into the fly by using a bushy hackle (perhaps trimmed so the fly sits as low on the water as the natural insect) or by the angler twitching the fly across the water.

We begin with a basic adult stonefly recipe: by using this in conjunction with descriptions and/or living stoneflies, any European species can be imitated. This basic recipe is followed by specific stonefly imitations.

Basic Adult Stonefly

Hook – size 10-18 dry fly
Silk – as body colour
Body – tip of fluorescent lime or orange wool or floss silk to imitate egg sac (optional), then dubbed fine textured fur (natural or synthetic) or herl or (especially for small darker imitations) stripped peacock herl of appropriate colour
Body hackle – cock hackle palmered down body and trimmed close to body (optional, larger sizes 10-12 only)
Rib – (optional) fine gold or silver wire, or orange silk
Hackle – short fibred cock hackle, black or natural red for most species, golden-olive for Yellow Sallys.
Wings – quill slip tied low so that it lies flat over body, or bunch of hair, or a synthetic stonefly wing. For most species black or dark brown; for Yellow Sallys yellow

Examples are given below; also given are two modifications: a Spent Female Yellow Sally and a bushy well-hackled Adult February Red.

Dark Stonefly 1

Hook – size 12-16 dry fly
Silk – black
Tip – fluorescent lime floss
Abdomen – bronze peacock herl
Rib – fine copper wire
Body hackle – black cock, lower fibres clipped short
Thorax – bronze peacock herl
Wing – black quill slip, cut to length

Dark Stonefly 2 as Dark Stonefly 1 but with fluorescent red tip, 2 tails of bronze peacock herl (short), 2 antennae of black herl tips.

~

Brown Stonefly

Hook – size 12-16 dry fly
Silk – brown
Tip – fluorescent orange floss
Body – dark brown herl or fur
Rib – fine gold wire
Hackle – natural red cock
Wing – dark brown quill slip, cut to length

~

Quill Stonefly

Hook – size 12-16 dry fly
Silk – black
Body – stripped peacock quill
Hackle – black or dark brown cock hackle, palmered along body, clipped short top and bottom
Wing – black crow or very dark brown narrow quill slip, varnished and tied low over body

A good willow/needle fly/black stonefly pattern. It is worth tying some of these 'spent' to imitate dead and dying females after egg laying. The tying is precisely as above but instead of the quill slip wing, 2 pairs of black hackle points are tied in fully or semi-spent.

~

Yellow Sally

Hook – size 14-16 dry fly
Silk – yellow
Tip – fluorescent red floss
Body – yellow fur
Rib – fine gold wire
Hackle – golden-olive cock
Wing – yellow quill slip, cut to length

Spent Yellow Sally

Hook – size 14-16 dry fly
Silk – yellow
Body – yellow fur
Rib – fine gold wire
Wing – 2 lengths of yellow raffine, tied spent

Simplify and adapt other stonefly patterns to produce a range of spent stoneflies

~

Windswept February Red

Hook – size 12-14 dry fly
Silk – brown
Body – brown fur
Rib – fine gold wire
Body hackle – ginger cock, bushy
Hackle – ginger cock
Wing – 2 slips woodcock quill, tied semi-upright

Imitates a newly-hatched February Red blown onto the water and trying to take flight. Modify to produce similarly bushy well-hackled stonefly patterns.

~

Large Stonefly

Hook – size 10-12 lure hook
Silk – black
Tail – 2 black goose biots
Abdomen – dark brown fur
Rib – fine gold wire
Thorax – as abdomen, thicker
Wing – 2 dark brown quill slips
Head – dark brown deer fur, spun and clipped 'muddler-style'

This muddler-style pattern (p. 256) floats well and can be tweaked across the water to imitate an egg-laying female.
Note: CDC Category 3 patterns are also excellent adult stonefly imitations (p. 138) So too are several soft-hackled wet flies (pp. 128, 130, 134)

A basic Adult Stonefly

DARK STONEFLY 1

DARK STONEFLY 2

BROWN STONEFLY

QUILL STONEFLY

YELLOW SALLY

SPENT YELLOW SALLY

WINDSWEPT FEBRUARY RED

LARGE STONEFLY

DAMSELFLIES AND DRAGONFLIES

(Naturals p. 59)

Dragonfly nymphs tend to live in water that is too weedy for either trout or anglers, though in the USA several anglers have invented effective imitative Dragonfly Nymphs. One successful in weedy European lakes (shallow rainbow trout fisheries) is the:

Brown Dragon Nymph

Hook – size 8-12 longshank lure hook
Silk – brown
Underbody – lead wire wound to give a rounded abdomen and thorax
Tails – 3 tips cock pheasant tail fibres
Body – fine textured olive-brown fur (e.g. rabbit)
Legs – knotted cock pheasant tail fibres
Wing cases – bunch cock pheasant tail fibres tied over thorax, rear lying low over abdomen as wing buds
Fish this along lake margins slowly.

Damselfly patterns are more important than dragonfly imitations, because their nymphs swim more actively and adults are sometimes taken by fish. There are three stages to be imitated: the damselfly nymph swimming in the lake margin, the male damselfly in attendance on the female, the female laying her eggs underwater.

DAMSELFLY NYMPHS

Damselfly nymphs are very similar, with some colour variation (brown-olive to quite bright green).

Detached Body Damsel Nymph

Hook – A tandem mount of two size 10-12 wet fly hooks, the eye of the rear hook in line with the bend of the front hook. The bend, point and barb of the rear hook are cut away with wire cutters. This allows an 'extended body' to be tied, that folds away when a fish takes the fly, and allows a little 'wiggle' in the abdomen to simulate the action in the natural nymph.
Silk – black
Underbody – fine lead wire wound around front hook shank
Tails – three inch (0.7cm) lengths olive ostrich herl
Abdomen – medium olive fur (rabbit, hare, or soft fine synthetic) wound slim
Rib – fine gold wire or none
Wing cases – goose herl dyed olive
Thorax – fur dubbing as abdomen, a little thicker
Legs – bunch grey partridge hackle, dyed medium olive
Head – tying silk

Olive Damsel Nymph

Hook – size 8-12 longshank lure hook
Silk – black
Underbody – lead wire wound under thorax region
Tails – three inch (0.7cm) lengths olive ostrich herl
Abdomen – medium olive fur (rabbit, hare, or soft fine synthetic) wound slim
Rib – fine copper wire
Wing cases – olive goose herl
Thorax – olive ostrich herl
Head – tying silk

Ostrich Herl Damsel Nymph

Hook – size 10-12 longshank lure hook
Silk – olive or brown
Underbody – lead wire wound under thorax region
Tails – 3 tips olive or brown ostrich herls
Body – wound olive or brown ostrich herl from tails, thickening at give pronounced thorax at front
Rib – fine oval gold tinsel
Legs – long fibres partridge hackle dyed olive or brown
Wing cases – olive or brown dyed goose quill slips

Marabou Damsel Nymph as Ostrich Herl Nymph but with tail and body of olive or brown marabou.

These last two patterns (four flies in all, with brown and olive variants) exploit the mobile, living properties of ostrich and marabou. They are very effective, especially in the weedy margins of lakes.

Green Damsel Nymph

Hook – size 8-12 longshank lure hook
Silk – black
Underbody – lead wire wound under thorax region
Tails – 3 slips cut from green raffine
Abdomen – green Swanundaze or Flexibody wound over silver tinsel
Wing cases – green raffine
Thorax – seal fur dyed green

Light Brown Damsel Nymph

Hook – size 8-12 longshank lure hook
Silk – black
Underbody – lead wire wound under thorax region
Tails – bunch ginger cock hackle fibres
Abdomen – light brown seal fur
Rib – fine silver wire
Thorax – hare's ear
Hackle – brown speckled partridge
Head – tying silk

Dark Brown Damsel Nymph

Hook – size 8-12 longshank lure hook
Silk – black
Thorax – split shot fixed to hook behind eye, and painted dark brown (2 coats and allow to dry)
Tails – tips cock pheasant tail fibres
Abdomen – cock pheasant tail fibres
Rib – fine gold wire
Wing cases – cock pheasant tail fibres
Legs – bunch cock pheasant tail fibre tips

Cul de Canard Damsel Nymph

Hook – size 8-12 longshank lure hook
Silk – black
Tail – fibres olive CDC
Body – olive CDC, built up at the thorax
Rib – fine silver wire
Legs – fibres of olive CDC tied out at sides
Wing cases and Head – black CDC
Modify each for the full range of natural nymph colours. Fish along lake margins in a jerky manner.

Note: See also CDC Damselfly Nymph, p. 140, and Olive Rabbit Nymph p. 144.

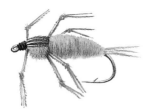

BROWN DRAGON NYMPH

DETACHED BODY DAMSEL NYMPH

OLIVE DAMSEL NYMPH

OSTRICH HERL DAMSEL NYMPH

MARABOU DAMSEL NYMPH

GREEN DAMSEL NYMPH

LIGHT BROWN DAMSEL NYMPH

DARK BROWN DAMSEL NYMPH

DANGLER DAMSEL

EGG-LAYING FEMALE DAMSELFLY

CUL DE CANARD DAMSEL NYMPH

ADULT DAMSELFLIES

These patterns are rarely essential: but it is worth having one tucked in the corner of the fly box just in case!

Dangler Damsel

Hook – size 10-12 longshank, bent with a pair of snipe-nosed pliers about halfway back from the eye to an internal angle of about 100-110°

Silk – finest black

Abdomen – stripped quill from the tip of a hen pheasant tail feather. This bare quill has a nice segmented pattern. The tip 25-35mm of quill is cut off and whipped along the top of the front of the hook shank as a detached body. Blobs of blue or red paint are then applied to imitate either blue or red damselfly males

Wings – two pairs of cock grizzle hackle points, tied out to either side. We are not imitating a resting damsel with wings held low over body, but a male that is in flight low over the water and has momentarily touched down on the water

Thorax – black crow quill herl

Hackle – black cock

Egg-laying Female Damselfly

Hook – size 8 longshank

Silk – black

Abdomen – well marked stripped peacock quill

Wings – two cock grizzle hackles, tied back over body

Thorax – three or four turns of fine lead wire with bronze peacock herl tied over

Legs – black henny-cock hackle, one turn

Head – two turns of bronze peacock herl in front of hackle

LAND-BUGS

(Natural Land-bugs p. 58)

It is pointless attempting to imitate all the species of land-bugs that appear on the water. With the exception of Aphids (see below), the number of potential species is vast. There is one style of artificial that imitates well the general shape of many land-bugs and lies flat in the water film like those naturals that have fallen onto the water, based on the Jassid pattern from the USA.

Jassid

Hook – size 14-22 dry fly
Silk – black
Body – tying silk
Hackle – black cock palmered along body, clipped. After palmering and tying in the hackle, trim all fibres sticking up above the hook shank and all fibres sticking down below the hook shank; this will leave only fibres sticking out at the side. Thus the fly will fish flat in the surface film in the same position as that in which land-bugs that have fallen onto the water usually find themselves.
Wing – one jungle cock (or substitute) 'nail' feather tied low

This can be one of the most useful dry flies; fish will take it when they are feeding on a wide variety of black land-bred insects including black gnats, land beetles, thrips and land-bugs. Highly commended.

~

Land-bug

Hook – size 14-22, dry fly
Silk – as body
Body – brown or green tying silk
Body hackle – cock hackle (natural red or dyed golden-olive), tied and trimmed as for Jassid (above)
Wing – strip of quill or herls (brown or green), lacquered for strength, and tied in low over body and clipped to shape and length.

One Green Land-Bug and one Brown Land-Bug, tied as above, will complement the Jassid by matching species of natural bugs such as the froghoppers and shield bugs. They will also catch fish that are feeding on other small insects in the surface film.

~

Basic Aphid (Greenfly)

Hook – size 22-28 dry fly
Silk – green
Body – light green floss, or goose herl dyed light green (2 turns) or lime-green fur (dyed natural or synthetic)
Hackle – white or pale blue dun cock or hen

Four examples are shown:
Aphid 1 has floss body, white hackle. **Aphid 2** has herl body, white hackle. **Aphid 3** has fur body and blue hackle. **Aphid 4** has herl body and white hackle
These are essential, especially in wooded country, during autumn. They are best fished in or just below the water surface film. See also Green Insect p. 130, CDC Category 3 p. 138.

WATER-BUGS

(Natural Water-bugs p. 56)

Water-bugs that live on the surface

Pond Skater

Hook – size 12-14 dry fly
Silk – brown
Body – waxed silk
Hackle – long-fibred soft brown hackle (e.g. grouse, brown partridge)

The important feature of this fly is that it should be fished on or in the surface quickly. Grease leader and oil fly to prevent it sinking.

Water-boatmen (including Corixa and Notonecta).

These artificial flies are essential in lakes, useful in rivers. See also CDC Water-boatman p. 141.

Basic Water-boatman

Hooks – size 12-14 wet fly
Underbody – lead foil or wire wound to give the shape of the natural insect – a flattened oval. This is essential, not only for shape, but so that the fly will sink deeply and can be fished jerkily off the bottom.
Silk – red (matches eyes of natural)
Back – black or dark brown herls (e.g. crow, peacock, dark turkey), or strip of synthetic wing sheet (e.g. raffine). This is tied in at the bend of the hook, the body is then wound over the underbody, and the back brought forward to cover the back of the fly and tied in at the head
Body – flat silver tinsel, or white, cream, pale buff or yellow floss silk
Legs – peacock or other dark herl (e.g. crow), 1 to either side, tied back
Head – red tying silk

~

Water-boatman 1

Back – crow herl
Body – silver tinsel
Legs – two strands peacock herl
Silk – green
Body – light green floss, or goose herl dyed light green (2 turns) or lime-green fur (dyed natural or synthetic)
Hackle – white or pale blue dun cock or hen

Water-boatman 2

Back – raffine
Body – white floss
Legs – crow herl

Water-boatman 3 as pattern 2, but with yellow floss body

Water-boatman 4

Silk – black.
Tip – flat silver tinsel
Back – brown synthetic plastic sheet
Body – pearl tinsel
Rib – silver wire
Legs – bunch furnace hen hackles

JASSID

Green

Brown

LAND-BUG

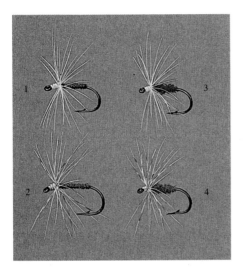

APHIDS

Basic aphid

POND SKATER

WATER-BOATMAN 1

WATER-BOATMAN 3

WATER-BOATMAN 2

WATER-BOATMAN 4

SEDGES (CADDIS-FLIES)

Two types of larvae may be imitated: cased and caseless.

CASED CADDIS LARVAE

(Natural Larvae p. 60)

Because cased caddis larvae occur on the river or lake bed it is essential that imitations are weighted so that they fish close to the bottom where they will be seen by fish that are grubbing about for the natural insect. This can be done in two ways:

(i) fine lead wire is wound around the hook shank in close turns as an underbody

(ii) strips of fine lead wire or foil are bound, lengthwise, along the top of the hook shank as an underbody.

The latter is preferable, because it also ballasts the fly so that it swims hook point uppermost, reducing the chance of the point snagging on the bottom (see p. 236).

Wind a thin covering of cream or palest olive floss silk (perhaps fluorescent) or wool over the lead; if there are small gaps in the body (case) then this wool or floss will show through as the juicy larval body.

Hooks for cased caddis imitations – size 8-14 longshank nymph or lure hooks
Silk for all cased caddis imitations – black.

Fur-bodied Caddis

Underbody – lead wire (see above)
Body – (Case) coarse brown or grey-brown fur dubbing (e.g. hare's mask) with spiky fibres picked out
Rib – fine copper or gold wire (optional)
Thorax – creamy-yellow fur tied at front of case
Legs – brown soft hackle (e.g. furnace hen), 2 turns
Head – tying silk

~

Feather-bodied Caddis

Underbody – lead wire (see above)
Body (case) – large, coarse hackles (mallard wing coverts, large grouse or partridge wing coverts) wound in a series palmered along the hook shank and then trimmed to produce a spiky body
Thorax – 2 turns of cream wool or any cream dubbed fur immediately in front of case
Legs – 2 turns of black hen (or waterhen or crow) hackle
Head – tying silk

~

Herl-bodied Caddis

Underbody – lead wire (see above)
Body (case) – brown (pheasant) or black (crow) herl
Rib – fine copper wire
Thorax – cream fur dubbing in front of case
Legs – black soft hackle (hen, moorhen, coot), 2 turns.

~

Lead Head Caddis Larva

Underbody – tie some with fine lead wire underbody – superheavies (the head only gives weight to the others)
Head – one split shot, attached with monofil (p. 222), and coated with black varnish
Body (case) – hare's ear, straggly
Thorax – tiny amount of white or cream fur dubbing at front of body to simulate the body of the larva peeping out of the case
Hackle – 1-2 turns of black hen

~

Black and Peacock Caddis

Underbody – fine lead wire (optional)
Body – bronze peacock herl
Thorax – tiny amount of white or cream fur dubbing at front of body to simulate the body of the larva peeping out of the case
Hackle – 2 turns of black hen
This is a modification of the Black and Peacock Spider: a great general wet fly, especially on lakes.

~

Latex Caddis Larva

Hook – size 10-12 wet fly or, better, curved grub/sedge
Silk – brown
Underbody – fine lead wire or foil, varnished and covered by fluorescent lime green floss
Overbody – latex strip
Thorax – dubbed hare's fur
Legs – picked out fibres of fur from thorax or hackle fibres from brown partridge hackle
Occasionally caddis larvae lose their case (e.g. during spates, or when anglers are wading clumsily) and are conspicuous and easy prey for trout. The Latex Caddis Larva matches these, and also (in smaller sizes) many species of caseless caddis.

CASELESS CADDIS LARVAE

These imitate Rhyacophila and Hydropsyche, two common caseless caddis larvae of rough, rocky rivers. For all imitations, tie a lead wire underbody (either whip lead wire along hook shank or wind around hook shank), so that the fly fishes close to the bottom (where the fish will encounter the natural).

Hook – size 10-14 wet fly hook or curved shank sedge or grub hook that will better mimic the curved body outline (a 'trigger' perhaps) of the natural.
Silk – brown, to give brown head colour of both Rhyacophila and Hydropsyche.

Rhyacophila 1

Underbody – fine lead wire (see above)
Abdomen – green dubbed fur (synthetic)
Rib – fluorescent lime-green floss silk
Thorax – hare's fur

FUR-BODIED CADDIS

HERL-BODIED CADDIS

BLACK & PEACOCK CADDIS

FEATHER-BODIED CADDIS

LEAD HEAD CADDIS LARVA

LATEX CADDIS LARVA

RHYACOPHILA 1

RHYACOPHILA 2

BODY GILLS RHYACOPHILA (MOSER)

HYDROPSYCHE 1

HYDROPSYCHE 2

Rhyacophila 2 as 1, but with a back of green raffine tied over abdomen and thorax, and held in place with ribbing; also legs of speckled brown partridge hackle.

Body Gills Rhyacophila (Moser)
Underbody – fine lead wire (see above)
Abdomen – light green Body Gills
Thorax – hare's fur

Note: For Cul de Canard Rhyacophila and Hydropsyche larvae, see p. 141.

Hydropsyche 1
Underbody – fine lead wire (see above)
Tail – tuft ginger cock hackle fibres, trimmed short
Abdomen – grey synthetic fur
Rib – fine copper wire
Thorax – hare's fur

Hydropsyche 2 as 1, but with a back of light brown raffine tied over abdomen and thorax, and held in place with ribbing of fluorescent white floss; also legs of speckled brown partridge hackle

SEDGE (CADDIS-FLY) PUPAE

(Natural Pupae p. 62)

The following patterns imitate the pupae (or pharate adults) in two positions in the water:

DEEP SEDGE PUPAE

These imitate pupae that have emerged from their pupal cocoon and are drifting close to the river or lake bed prior to swimming to the shore or surface, or that are slowly rising to the surface or swimming close to the bottom.

Sparkle Sedge Pupae

Hook – size 8-14 wet fly or nymph hooks
Silk – black
Underbody – close turns fine lead wire along hook shank
Abdomen – a sparkly, synthetic fur or a homemade mixture that includes chopped pearl and silver lurex*. Tie in grey, brown, pink-orange, green
Thorax – hare's fur

* The sparkle suggests the air bubble of the 'pharate sedge'. Tie the flies scruffily, with lots of bits of fur sticking out, to give a semblance of movement. These very simple yet effective patterns improve after a few fish have chewed them!

Variant Sparkle Sedge Pupae as above, but with a darker peacock herl thorax and two 'paddles' (swimming legs) of peacock herl.

~

Hare's Ear Goldhead Sedge

Hook – size 8-14 wet fly
Head – goldhead (see p. 222)
Silk – brown
Underbody – (optional) for fast deep water tie some with extra lead wire ballast (wound down hook shank after gold bead fixed in place)
Body – hare's ear fur, spiky (ideally dub with dubbing twirler)
Rib – fine gold wire

This is another very simple pattern that is also very effective when the fish are feeding deep in the water on sedge pupae. The flashy gold ball simulates the air bubble of the 'pharate sedge'. See also GRHE Goldhead, p. 124.

~

Deep Sedge Pupa

Hook – sizes 10-14 sedge or grub/shrimp
Silk – as body colour
Underbody – close turns of fine lead wire
Body – dubbed with a mixture (50:50) of coarse fur and Antron fibres
Overbody – Antron fibres (colour as underbody)
Hackle – a soft hackle (hen or game) to match underbody colour, tied with just a few fibres on each side of the body
Head – marabou fibres to match underbody colour

These very effective, but more complex tyings, are modified for European waters, from G. La Fontaine's book Caddisflies (USA). After tying in the lead wire ballast, a bunch of combed Antron fibres are tied in to the rear of the hook. The body fur/Antron mixture is then dubbed to the tying silk and wound to about a fraction of the hook eye. The free Antron fibres are brought forward and tied in to form a sheath over the underbody, with some fibres above, below and on either side of the underbody. There should be a narrow gap between underbody and Antron overbody. The hackle and ostrich herl head are tied in, and the fly completed.

Colours – the most useful colours appear to be:

Fur	Antron	Hackle	Ostrich
brown	russet	brown partridge	brown
bright green	olive	grouse	brown

~

Seal Fur Sedge Pupa

This series of imitative patterns relies on a very straggly body to imitate the pupal shuck surrounding the body of the pharate adult. The tying is:

Hook – generally size 10-14 (size 8 where the great red sedge is abundant) sedge or shrimp/grub
Silk – as thorax
Underbody – close turns of fine lead wire
Abdomen – coarse wiry fur. Seal's fur is the ideal medium (or a good synthetic substitute); dub the thread very loosely, so that the final abdomen has a chunky, shaggy outline.
Rib – flat gold tinsel
Thorax – ostrich herl; colour a little darker than abdomen
Hackle – one turn of long-fibred brown partridge, tied back
Head – tying silk
Colours – insect green, medium olive, cream and cinnamon are very effective.

~

Herl Pupa

Another series of sedge pupae, where movement and a fuzzy outline on the body is provided by herls.
Hook – size 10-16 sedge or shrimp/grub
Silk – colour as thorax
Underbody – close turns of fine lead wire or (shallow water) 0
Abdomen – dyed goose or swan herl
Rib – fine gold wire
Thorax – a natural fur (mix of underfur and guard hairs) dyed one shade darker than the abdomen
Hackle – long-fibred brown partridge, tied back
Head – tying silk
Colours – insect green, medium olive, cream and cinnamon are very effective.

Brown

Green

SPARKLE SEDGE PUPAE

VARIANT SPARKLE SEDGE PUPA

HARE'S EAR GOLDHEAD SEDGE

DEEP SEDGE PUPA

SEAL FUR SEDGE PUPA

HERL PUPA

EMERGENT SEDGE PUPAE

These patterns, fished just below or in the surface film, imitate the adult sedge as it struggles from the pupal shuck. They are the most effective of patterns during a hatch during a warm summer evening.

Emergent Sedge Pupae

The tying of these is as the Deep Sedge Pupa (see above), modified from the USA patterns of La Fontaine except that: **a**: there is no lead ballast, **b**: a few fibres of Antron are left trailing at the rear of the fly to imitate a stream of bubbles trailing from the emerging insect, **c**: a sparse wing of deer hair is tied in just behind the marabou head. This buoyant wing holds the surface film, as well as imitating the front of the adult emerging from its pupal shuck.

See also Emerger Sedge Pupa (CDC) on p. 140.

EMERGENT SEDGE PUPA

Suspender Sedge

Tying as the Deep Sedge Pupa (see above) except that: a) there is no lead ballast, b) a polystyrene bead, enclosed in nylon tights material, is tied in just behind the the thorax. This suspends the fly from the surface film. Some tyers colour the bead to match the general pupal colour: this is incorrect. Seen from below, the white bead appears only as a break or dimple in the surface film through which the adult sedge is struggling.

Emerging Sedge

Hook – size 8-16 dry fly hook or light wire
  curved-shank sedge or grub hook
Silk – same colour as abdomen
Abdomen – green, olive, buff, brown, cream dubbed
  fur or dyed swan or goose herl
Rib – fine gold or silver wire
Thorax – as abdomen; perhaps a shade darker
Wing Bud – one cul de canard feather, tied by butt
  before thorax is wound, and then brought forward
  and tied in again at front of thorax, leaving a gap
  between feather and thorax
Antennae – two long fibres of grey mallard, dark
  turkey, or other antennae-like filaments
Legs – fibres of herl tips (pheasant tail, dyed goose or
  swan)
Head – tying silk
The little 'bubble' of CDC veiling the thorax holds the fly just below the surface film in a very realistic way. This pattern represents the sedge pupa resting at the surface just before the adult emerges onto the surface and flies off.

~

Brown Emerger Sedge

Hook – size 10-12 sedge or wet fly
Silk – brown
Body – brown hare's mask
Back – strip of cinnamon goose herls
Rib – flat gold tinsel
Thorax – as body
Wing buds – slips of cinnamon goose herls
'Float' – loop of grey cul de canard feather, tips tied
  back
Antennae – 2 fibres grey mallard
A very effective pattern on both lakes and rivers during an evening hatch of adult sedges.

ADULT SEDGES (CADDIS-FLIES)

(Natural Sedges pp. 62-9)

Fly dressers have produced two different sorts of adult sedge patterns: the 'imitative' and the 'impressionistic'. Imitative sedge patterns resemble individual species (or groups of species with the same overall coloration); the impressionistic are designed so that they behave like real sedges without imitating a particular species. The latter are probably the most convenient to tie and use, because most sedges are active on the water in the evening and dark (when the fish cannot precisely see colour and fine detail). But there is great pleasure in dressing patterns that look more like real sedge species!

IMPRESSIONISTIC SEDGES

For use in poor light or rough water conditions.

Nocturnal Sedge

Hook – size 8-12 dry fly
Silk – brown
Abdomen – a mix of fur (chopped brown deer, olive
  seal, hare's ear/mask)
Wing – dark brown deer hair, tied low over abdomen
Thorax and Head – dark brown deer hair spun and
  trimmed in 'Muddler' fashion
There is no hackle in this pattern so that the body lies flat on the water, imitating a spent sedge in the surface film or, if tweaked across the surface, a newly-hatched or egg-laying female sedge. Effective at night. Very buoyant with lots of 'movement'.

~

Deerhair Sedge

Hook – size 8-12 dry fly
Silk – black
Body – scruffily dubbed brown deer hair
Wing – natural deer hair
Head – scruffily dubbed deer hair
The scruffy tying enhances movement in the fly, an important trigger when fishing sedge patterns after dark. A super, highly mobile pattern.

G & H Deerhair Sedge

Hook – size 8-12 dry fly
Silk – brown
Body – spun deer hair trimmed to give a sedge outline.
  Before adding the deer hair tying silk is tied in at the
  rear of the hook; after completing the trimmed deer
  hair body, coloured fur is spun on this silk, brought
  forward below the deer hair body and tied in at the head
  end to imitate the insect's abdomen.
Hackle – 2 natural red cock hackles
Antennae – stripped hackle stalks from 2 red cock
  hackles
Originally tied with natural (red) deer hair and a green seal's fur abdomen, colour can be varied by using dyed deer hair (brown, black etc.) and coloured fur for the abdomen. Because of the natural buoyancy of the deer hair, the G & H Deer Hair Sedges float well, even when tweaked across rough water to imitate a scuttling sedge.

~

Balloon Caddis

Hook – size 8-14 dry fly
Silk – brown
Body – dubbed fur (e.g. rabbit, dyed olive)
Wing – deer hair
Head – yellow Plastazote
In the light the Plastazote head looks incongruous, but in the dark it is hardly visible and helps the fly to float.

SUSPENDER SEDGE

EMERGING SEDGE

BROWN EMERGER SEDGE

NOCTURNAL SEDGE

DEERHAIR SEDGE

G & H DEERHAIR SEDGE

BALLOON CADDIS

DANCING CADDIS

RM SEDGE

Dancing Caddis

Hook – sizes 12-16 Swedish dry fly (upside down)

Silk – brown or olive

Body – fine dubbed fur, either synthetic or dyed natural (e.g. rabbit), in brown or olive

Hackle – sandy dun, natural red, cree or ginger cock

Wing – natural or dyed brown deer

This outstanding dry sedge floats high on the water and, on lakes it can be made to skate with the ripple and wind and on a river can be twitched across still pools without the chance of the fly sinking. This is partly because, being and upside-down fly, the hook point cannot pull down into the water.

RM Sedge

Hook – size 8-14 dry fly

Silk – brown

Body – dubbed brown deer hair

Wing – buff Poly-yarn or Antron

Head – dubbed brown deer hair

Another seemingly tatty pattern (by Austria's Roman Moser)that is so effective in the half-light or dark.

Note: The CDC Category 3 dry flies on p. 138 are also excellent impressionistic sedges.

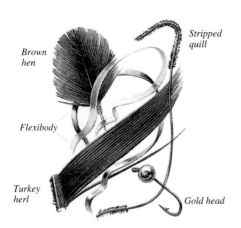

Brown hen

Stripped quill

Flexibody

Turkey herl

Gold head

IMITATIVE SEDGES

Vary size and colour by adapting this recipe:

Basic Sedge

Hook – size 8-16 dry fly
Silk – as body colour
Tip – a small tip of lime-green fluorescent floss may be wound bee the body to suggest the egg sac of egg-laying female sedges (optional)
Body – dubbed dyed or undyed fur (natural or synthetic), or goose herl dyed green, olive, grey, brown and black
Body hackle – natural red, ginger, blue dun, black or cree cock, palmered (optional)
Hackle – natural red, ginger, blue dun, black or cree cock
Wings – bunch of natural deer, elk or other hair, or slips of quill (e.g. woodcock, grouse, crow), or cock hackles tied 'wonderwing' or cut or burnt, or synthetic sedge (caddis) wings, tied low over the body, or small feathers glued to nylon tights material and cut to shape
Antennae – two long herls or stripped hackle stalks (as per antennae of natural) tied wards (optional)
Head – herl, fur, spun and clipped deer hair (optional)
Some very experienced fly dressers insist that there should not be a body hackle. A body hackle increases floatability, useful when twitching the fly across the water surface to imitate an egg-laying female sedge.

~

Great Red Sedge (Murrough)

Hook – size 8 dry fly
Silk – brown
Tip – fluorescent lime floss
Body – grey fur or wool
Body hackle – natural red cock, palmered
Rib – fine gold wire
Hackle – natural red cock
Wing – brown turkey slips
Antennae – 2 cock pheasant tail fibres

Imitates Great Red Sedge: essential on high lakes in summer. Tied in a range of sizes down to 14, this matches many other brown sedges.

~

Green Peter

Hook – size 10 dry fly
Silk – brown
Body – green fur or wool
Body hackle – ginger cock, palmered
Rib – fine gold wire
Hackle – ginger cock
Wing – hen pheasant wing slips
Imitates Green Peter; also cinnamon, caperer and sand-fly if tied in appropriate sizes.

~

Speckled Peter

Hook – size 10 dry fly
Silk – brown
Body – grey brown fur with fluorescent green wool at front
Body hackle – ginger cock, palmered
Rib – fine gold wire
Hackle – ginger cock
Wing – speckled turkey
Antennae – 2 fibres speckled turkey herl
Imitates Speckled Peter; also cinnamon, caperer and sand-fly if tied in appropriate sizes.

~

Peter

Hook – size 10 dry fly
Silk – brown
Body – green fur
Body hackle – natural red cock
Hackle – natural red cock
Wing – bunch deer hairs tied in by tips and clipped

~

Cinnamon Sedge

Hook – size 8-12 dry fly
Silk – brown
Tip – lime fluorescent floss
Body – olive-green fur
Rib – fine gold wire
Hackle – ginger cock
Wing – 2 slips duck quill dyed cinnamon
Imitates cinnamons, caperer and sand-fly

~

Chestnut-winged Sedge

Hook – size 12 dry fly
Silk – brown
Tip – fluorescent lime floss
Body – mid-brown fur
Body hackle – ginger cock, palmered
Rib – fine gold wire
Hackle – natural red cock
Wing – synthetic, cut-out
Antennae – 2 fibres cock pheasant tail

A basic dry sedge

GREAT RED SEDGE (MURROUGH)

GREEN PETER

SPECKLED PETER

PETER

CINNAMON SEDGE

CHESTNUT-WINGED SEDGE

Medium Sedge 1

Hook – size 12-14 dry fly
Silk – brown
Body – grey floss
Body hackle – ginger cock, palmered
Hackle – ginger cock
Wing – bunch blue dun hackle fibres

Medium Sedge 2

Hook – size 12-14 dry fly
Silk – brown
Body – beige-buff fur (e.g. opossum)
Hackle – ginger cock
Wing – synthetic, cut-out

Medium Sedge 3

Hook – size 12-14 dry fly
Silk – brown
Body – grey goose herl
Wing – synthetic, cut-out
Head – natural deer hair spun and clipped, muddler style
A hackleless pattern that relies on deer hair for flotation.

Medium Sedge 4

Hook – size 12-14 dry fly
Silk – brown
Body – cream fur
Rib – black thread
Hackle – ginger cock
Wing – bunch brown squirrel tail hairs

Medium Sedge 5

Hook – size 12-14 dry fly
Silk – brown
Body – hare's ear
Hackle – sandy-dun cock
Wing – bunch deer hair

Elk Hair Caddis or Medium Sedge 6

Hook – size 12-14 dry fly
Silk – brown
Body – brown or olive-brown fur
Body hackle – natural red cock (This pattern is often
  more effective without a hackle)
Rib – fine gold wire
Wing – elk hair
An American pattern; tie in all sizes from 8-16 as a
general pattern and in sizes given as Medium Sedge.

~

Brown Sedge 1

Hook – size 10-14 dry fly
Silk – brown
Body – red (brown) squirrel (or similar) fur
Body hackle – natural red cock
Wing – red (brown) squirrel hairs

Brown Sedge 2

Hook – size 10-14 dry fly
Silk – brown
Body – dubbed olive-brown fur
Hackle – natural red cock
Wing – synthetic, cut-out
Trailing Legs – a few deer hairs, tied back
Antennae – 2 bronze mallard fibres

Brown Sedge 3

Hook – size 10-14 dry fly
Silk – brown
Body – dubbed brown fur or brown herl
Body hackle – natural red cock
Hackle – natural red cock
Wing – woodcock upper wing covert, on nylon tights

Brown Sedge 4

Hook – size 10-14 dry fly
Silk – brown
Body – dubbed dyed brown deerhair
Wing – synthetic, cut-out
Head – as body
A hackleless pattern relying on deer hair for flotation.
Note: Patterns 3 and 4 are useful Alder imitations, p. 197.

~

Grey Sedge 1 (Grey Flag)

Hook – size 10-14 dry fly
Silk – black
Tip – fluorescent magenta floss
Body – grey herl (goose)
Wing – fine grey deer hairs
Head – fine grey deer hairs, spun and clipped
A hackleless pattern relying on deer hair for flotation

Grey Sedge 2

Hook – size 10-14 dry fly
Silk – black
Body – blue-grey fur (natural or synthetic)
Hackle – blue dun cock
Wing – bunch deer hairs
Antennae – 2 fine grey-brown herls

~

Black Sedge 1

Hook – size 12-16 dry fly
Silk – black
Abdomen – black herl (crow)
Rib – fine flat gold tinsel
Thorax – grey herl
Hind Legs – 2 furnace hackle tips tied back
Hackle – black cock
Wing – under grey, upper black, cock hackles tied
  'wonderwing'

Black Sedge 2

Hook – size 12-16 dry fly
Silk – black
Body – black horsehair
Hackle – black cock
Wing – 2 black cock hackles tied back, cut to length

Black Sedge 3

Hook – size 12-16 dry fly
Silk – black
Body – black fur
Rib – fine copper wire
Hackle – black cock
Wing – black cock hackle tied 'wonderwing'
Antennae – 2 grey mallard fibres
Artificial Black Sedges match black silverhorns as well
as natural black sedges.

MEDIUM SEDGE 1

MEDIUM SEDGE 2

MEDIUM SEDGE 3

MEDIUM SEDGE 4

MEDIUM SEDGE 5

MEDIUM SEDGE 6 or ELK HAIR CADDIS

BROWN SEDGE 1

BROWN SEDGE 2

BROWN SEDGE 3

BROWN SEDGE 4

GREY SEDGE 1 (GREY FLAG)

GREY SEDGE 2

BLACK SEDGE 1

BLACK SEDGE 2

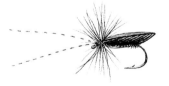

BLACK SEDGE 3

Be-Ge Sedge

Hook – size 10-16 dry fly
Silk – as per body
Body – cul de canard
Wing – synthetic sedge wing
Thorax – chamois fur

Tied in a range of sizes and shades of body (grey, dark brown and olive) Henning von Monteton's Be-Ge Sedges will deceive trout not only in their German home rivers, but throughout Europe.

~

Big Caddis

Hook – size 8-10 longshank
Thread – brown
Body – brown and black thread woven
Wing – fine deerhair
Legs – 4, black rubber band
Head – fine deerhair

After completing the body, a bunch of very fine deerhairs is tied in facing wards, then brought back when it is again tied down to create the head and wing. This is one of Norwegian Torill Kolbu's woven-bodied flies; excellent on very fast streams or on lakes at night when tweaked across the surface.

~

Fantastic Caddis

Hook – size 12-16 dry fly
Thread – as body colour
Body – fine synthetic fur
Hind legs – 2 herls (turkey, pheasant, crow) tied back
Wing – sparse bunch fine hair (e.g. squirrel) dyed, with cut synthetic wing over
Hackle – mixed brown and black cock
Antennae – 2 brown or black microfibbets

Another Norwegian pattern that can be tied in a range of shades to match all natural caddis flies.

~

Fluttering Sedge

Hook – size 10-16 dry fly
Silk – as per body (black in example)
Body – herl (black)
Rib – fine wire (green-coated)
Rear Legs – 2 herls tied back (black)
Hackle – long-fibred cock (black)
Wing – 4 cut strips of white raffine, tied flared
Antennae – 2 herls (black)

Excellent on very rough, turbulent water; tie also in brown and grey.

~

Spent Sedge

Hook – size 10-16 dry fly
Silk – as per body (brown in example)
Abdomen – herl or fur (brown fur in example)
Rib – fine copper wire
Rear Wings – white raffine, tied spent
ewings – wide hackle points (cinnamon in example)
Thorax – coarse fur with strands pulled out for legs (brown in example)

Often effective at dawn; tie also in black and grey.

Microcaddis

Hook – size 16-20 dry fly
Silk – as per body (brown in example)
Body – fine fur (brown)
Hackle – small cock (natural red cock)
Wing – hackle tied 'wonderwing' (brown)

Tie also in black and grey; but it is uncommon to have fish selecting natural microcaddis.

DIVING SEDGES

Many sedges oviposit by crawling or diving beneath the water surface. This behaviour is worth exploiting in imitative flies. Traditional wet patterns may be useful, but far better is a weighted pattern that sinks quickly and that can be brought through the water jerkily rather like a swimming sedge.

Any sedge pattern can be modified by the addition of lead wire beneath the body, and a small heavy gold or silver ball at the head. The flash caused by this metallic sphere, as the artificial dives, mimics the air bubbles carried down with the natural fly.

Example:

Diving Goldhead Sedge

Hook – size 8-12 wet fly
Head – gold or silver bead
Silk – brown
Body – hare's ear or other brown fur
Wing – 2 strips white raffine,
Hackle – brown long fibred soft hackle (partridge or grouse), 3 turns

~

Swimming Female Caddis

Hook – size 10-14 wet fly
Silk – black
Underbody – fine lead wire
Body – fine textured fur, synthetic or dyed natural (e.g. rabbit), olive or brown
Wings – rear cream, front brown: fine slips of raffine
Legs – long fibres brown partridge or similar soft hackle, tied back

In the evening or at night this is a most effective pattern. Few anglers exploit the underwater, swimming, female caddisflies.

~

Diving Caddis

Hook – 10-14 wet fly
Thread – brown
Underbody – lead or copper wire, lightly weighted
Body – fine synthetic fur
Underwing – 3-4 strands of fine brown Crystal Hair
Overwing – cut synthetic sedge wing
Legs – few brown partridge fibres tied back
Head – as body

Torill Kolbu's imitation of a diving, egg-laying caddis, this is a very effective pattern to use in the late evening. Fish it slowly... and be prepared for a violent take!

The Bustards (p. 136) are also good imitations of swimming caddisflies. Also the Sedge patterns of soft-hackled wet flies (p. 132).

BE-GE SEDGE

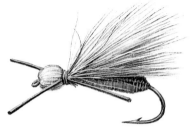

BIG CADDIS

FANTASTIC CADDIS

FLUTTERING SEDGE

SPENT SEDGE

actual size

MICROCADDIS

DIVING GOLDHEAD SEDGE

SWIMMING FEMALE CADDIS

DIVING CADDIS

TWO-WINGED FLIES

(Natural Flies p. 70-6)

REED-SMUT

The most profitable stage to imitate is the adult rising from the pupal case on the riverbed to the surface. During a hatch there will be fish feeding close to the surface, but nothing appears to be hatching (the adults leave the water so quickly that during a big hatch it may appear to be raining on the water where the adults are plopping out).

Silverhead Smut

Hook – size 16 wet fly
Silk – black
Head – a 3mm silver-plated ball is slipped over the hook point and shank to the eye bee the fly is tied
Body – fine black herl (crow) herl
Rib – fine silver wire
Hackle – black or dark grey soft hackle, 1-2 turns
The silver ball gives the illusion of the bubble of air in which the natural insect rises to the surface.

~

Emerger Smut

Hook – size 20-22 dry fly
Silk – black
Body – fine black herl (e.g. crow)
Legs – black or dark grey soft hackle, 1-2 turns
Wing – cul de canard feather, tied low over body and trimmed short
Alternative: very small Suspender Black Midge (p. 190). The fly is not oiled, but fished so that the body and legs lie in or slightly below the surface film, held there by the wing holding the fly at the surface.

~

Dry Smut

Hook – size 22-26 dry fly
Silk – black
Abdomen – stripped peacock herl, 2-3 turns
Thorax – unstripped peacock herl, 2 turns
Hackle – tiny black cock, 2-3 turns
Wing – 2 tiny white hackle points, or transparent synthetic wing
Less effective than the first two patterns because, during a hatch of reed-smuts, the adults leave the water surface very quickly and the fish find it easier to take them below the surface.

   Alternatives, any of the black adult midge imitations given on p. 192, or MP65 p. 138, or La Petite Merde p. 194, or black soft-hackled wet flies pp. 127-35, tied in small sizes (22-26).

PHANTOM FLY

Larvae, pupae and adults are eaten by fish in lakes.

Phantom Fly Larva

Hook – size 14-16 dry fly
Silk – orange
Underbody – flat silver tinsel with 2 turns of fluorescent orange floss in middle
Body – clear strip from polythene bag, wound slender
Thorax – orange fur

Phantom Fly Pupa

Hook – size 14-16 dry fly
Silk – white
Underbody – flat silver tinsel
Body – clear strip from polythene bag, wound slender
Thorax – peacock herl
Hackle – 2 turns white hen hackle (optional)
Fished just beneath the surface, these will take lake trout that are filtering plankton from the water. For Phantom Fly adult, see Adult Midges below.

MIDGES OR BUZZERS

Three stages may be imitated:
a) the larvae close to the lake or river bed;
b) the pupae, (i) close to the river or lake bed, (ii) rising through the water to hatch, (iii) hanging from the surface film prior to hatch;
c) the adult, (i) that has just hatched and is sitting on the water, (ii) the dead spent female lying in the surface film after she has laid her eggs. Fish may feed selectively on any of these.

By far the most important triggers are size, shape – general outline and position in the water; other possible triggers such as colour and appendages seem to be of no importance or of secondary importance as far as the fish are concerned, with some exceptions (e.g. wings in adult midges). This must be borne in mind when it comes to imitating all natural flies: we are trying to deceive the fish and not ourselves!

Midge Larvae

The most effective imitations are of those larvae that have haemoglobin and a red body, 'bloodworms':

Bloodworm 1

Hook – size 14-16 wet fly
Silk – red
Body – one piece of red nylon floss silk (about 2.5 cm), with end singed in flame or knotted, tied to hook with tying silk
Rib – fine black silk

Bloodworm 2

Hook – size 14-16 longshank sedge
Silk – red
Body – one piece of red nylon floss silk (about 2.5 cm), with end singed in flame or knotted, with several turns at the head and a tuft sticking up over the eye
Rib – finest copper wire
The red floss moves in the water to imitate the writhing of some species of bloodworms.

SILVERHEAD SMUT

EMERGER SMUT

DRY SMUT

PHANTOM FLY LARVA

PHANTOM FLY PUPA

BLOODWORM 1

BLOODWORM 2

BLOODWORM 3

BLOODWORM 4

Bloodworm 3
Hook – size 14-16 longshank sedge
Silk – red
Underbody – orange-red floss silk
Body – one layer of strip cut from polythene bag
Rib – fine silver wire
Head – peacock herl

Bloodworm 4
Hook – size 14-16 longshank sedge
Silk – black
Body – translucent synthetic red strip (e.g.
  Swanundaze)
Head – peacock herl

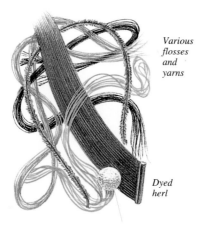

Various flosses and yarns

Dyed herl

Polystyrene bead

Other midge larvae are grey, green or olive and can be imitated by modifying the above patterns, e.g:

Green Midge Larva

Hook – size 16-18 wet fly
Silk – black
Body – short length (about 2cm) lime-green nylon floss silk singed in flame or knotted at end, whipped to hook shank
Rib – fine black silk

Olive Midge Larva

Hook – size 16-18 longshank caddis
Silk – olive
Underbody – olive floss silk
Overbody – one layer of silk cut from polythene bag
Rib – fine silver wire
Head – peacock herl

Midge Pupae

There is no doubt, from autopsies, that fish devour huge numbers of midge pupae. Recent years have seen an explosion in the numbers of published imitations (more, perhaps, than any other insect group). Use the basic recipe below to select materials for a good range of artificials:

Basic Midge Pupa

Hook – size 12-18 wet fly or, preferably, curved shank sedge or grub
Silk – brown
Abdomen – swan or goose herl, dyed olive, orange and brown, grey heron (goose as substitute) herl, black crow herl or cock pheasant tail dyed black, or finest fur dubbing (natural or synthetic) of same range of shades
Rib – fine gold or silver tinsel or wire, or silk
Thorax – peacock herl, or a herl or fur that is a shade darker than abdomen

Some tyers add a tuft of clipped white feather fibres or wool or Poly-yarn at the tip of the abdomen and head to simulate the respiratory gills of the natural. However there is no evidence that this is a trigger used by trout.

Examples:

Olive Buzzer: olive herl abdomen, fine oval gold tinsel rib, peacock herl thorax

Black Buzzer: black herl abdomen, fine oval silver tinsel rib, peacock herl thorax

Orange Buzzer: orange herl abdomen, fine oval gold tinsel rib, brown fur thorax

Grey Buzzer: grey herl abdomen, fine silver wire rib, peacock herl thorax

Some anglers have argued that the resting pupa, just below the surface film, is better imitated by a fly tied 'the wrong way round' (i.e. with thorax at the hook bend). The two examples illustrate this:

Reverse Olive Buzzer: olive herl abdomen, oval silver tinsel rib, peacock herl thorax, and with tufts of white Poly-yarn at head and tail to simulate gills

Reverse Black Buzzer: black floss silk abdomen, oval silver tinsel rib, peacock herl thorax

By carrying a wide range of sizes and shades based on the Basic Buzzer recipe, all natural buzzers are adequately matched. Anglers wishing to imitate buzzer pupae (and these must be imitated, for they are very important in both lakes and rivers) should not neglect thorax soft-hackled spider wet flies (see pp. 128-34; also Spider Greenwell's Glory p. 124). Tests have shown that flies such as the Black Magic are sometimes superior to more precise imitations, perhaps because the sparse hackle provides essential 'life' or 'movement' (see note on p. 127)

~

Basic midge pupae patterns will fish below the surface film, but it is difficult to keep them hanging from the surface film (to imitate a pupa that is resting just prior to hatching). The basic pattern can be modified to meet this situations as follows:

Emerger Midge Pupae

Suspender Buzzer

Use a small polystyrene bead enclosed in nylon tights material or a carved piece of Plastazote tied in at the head of the basic pupal patterns.

Examples:

Olive Suspender Buzzer, Black Suspender Buzzer (sizes 12, 20 and 24 to show size range). These imitate those pupae that are resting, hanging from the surface film. The size 24 imitation is excellent on rivers during a hatch of reed smuts (see p. 188).

GREEN MIDGE LARVA

OLIVE MIDGE LARVA

BASIC MIDGE PUPA

OLIVE BUZZER

BLACK BUZZER

ORANGE BUZZER

GREY BUZZER

REVERSE OLIVE BUZZER

REVERSE BLACK BUZZER

SUSPENDER BUZZER

The full range of Emerger Midge Pupae needed to imitate the range of sizes of the natural pupae.

Emerger Midge

Take the basic pupa pattern, but tie the polystyrene bead or Plastazote ball a little way back; tie in a cock hackle and parachute it around the base of the bead.

Examples:

Orange Emerger

Tail – white Poly-yarn fibres (optional)
Body – orange herl (or fur), thickened at thorax
Rib – fine silver tinsel
Float – polystyrene bead
Hackle – natural red cock
Head filaments white Poly-yarn fibres (optional)

Black Emerger as the Orange Emerger, but with black herl and a grizzle cock hackle

Olive Emerger as Orange Emerger, but with olive herl and a blue dun cock hackle. These imitate those midges that are in the process of hatching from the pupal shuck.

An alternative emerger pattern is

Para-emerger Midge

Hook – size 14-18 curved-body grub or sedge
Silk – as abdomen (black in example)
Abdomen – herl (black in example)
Thorax – peacock herl
Wing – bunch of Poly-yarn or Antron, tied in bee the thorax, upright
Hackle – black (in example), natural red, blue dun or olive cock
Again, tie these in a range of sizes and shades; when fishing them oil the wing and hackle only.

~

Adult Midge

Like midge pupae, the main differences between the various species of adult midges are size and colour; thus from a basic recipe can easily be adapted to include all natural midges:

Basic Adult Midge

Hook – size 14-28 dry fly
Silk – either the colour of the body material or of a neutral (grey, buff) colour
Head – tying silk
Abdomen – one or two strands of heron (goose as substitute) herl (grey midges), crow herl (black midge), or goose or swan dyed olive, buff, brown, orange, red and green. Stripped peacock herl produces a superb dark midge abdomen. Fine synthetic dubbings are very efficient especially for buff, green, olive and red midges. For the smallest sizes (24-28) an effective abdomen can be produced by using an appropriate colour of tying silk, perhaps overwound with clear polythene.

Thorax – build up with several turns of tying silk or extra turns of body material. In dark midge patterns unstripped peacock herl (larger sizes) or herls from cock pheasant tail dyed black are very effective.
Wing – a pair of blue dun, cream or white cock hackle points; or a sparse bunch of white, cream or pale grey Poly-yarn; or Antron yarn; or a white or blue dun hackle tied 'wonderwing'; or a wing cut to the appropriate shape from one of the synthetic sheets sold for this purpose (e.g. Wasp Wing). The wings should lie flat over the body; they should extend back not quite to the tip of the abdomen.
Hackle – blue dun cock hackle on most, with the exceptions of natural red on orange and red midges, olive or golden-olive on olive midges and dark blue dun (iron blue) or natural black on black and grey midges.

Dark olive, grey or black adult midge patterns will also match the hatches of Phantom Fly adults, Biting Midges, Mosquitoes, Torrent Midges and Meniscus Midges (pp. 70, 72-3), provided hook shank length is matched to natural insect body length.

Examples:

Black Midge 1

Abdomen – floss silk
Rib – fine silver wire
Thorax – peacock herl
Hackle – blue dun cock
Wings – 2 cream cock hackle points, tied back
Also shown, a similar **Olive Midge**, where the abdomen and thorax are olive herl and the rib is gold wire.

Black Midge 2

Abdomen – stripped peacock herl
Thorax – unstripped peacock herl
Wing – white raffine
Hackle – none – optional on such a small size (28); a black hackle on large sizes

Black Midge 3 as 2, but with Wasp-Wing wing, and black hackle.

Black Midge 4 as 2, but with white hackle point wings, and a blue dun hackle.

Black Midge 5 as 3, but with a black herl abdomen, and a wing of white Antron.

Black Midge 6 as 3, but with a tiny red herl tip (to imitate egg sac of female) and a black quill slip wing.

Black Midge 7 as 4, but with a black hackle wonderwing.

ORANGE EMERGER

BLACK EMERGER

OLIVE EMERGER

PARA-EMERGER MIDGE

Basic Adult Midge

Black   BLACK MIDGE 1   *Olive*

BLACK MIDGE 2

BLACK MIDGE 3

BLACK MIDGE 4

BLACK MIDGE 5

BLACK MIDGE 6

BLACK MIDGE 7

Grey Midge as Black Midge 6, but with a grey body, cream hackle and cream wing.

Red Midge 1 as Grey Midge, but with a red herl body, natural red hackle and grey wings.

Orange Midge as Red Midge, but with an orange herl body and a blue dun hackle.

Olive Midge as Orange Midge, but with an olive herl body.

The illustrations show examples tied in hook sizes 24-26: when fish are eating natural midges, it is usually essential that the artificial matches the size of the natural and small must be matched by small. Most anglers fear that such tiny hooks will not hook the fish or that the hookhold will give way but these tiny hooks work, and the hold is usually excellent. The same patterns, however, can be tied on the whole range of hook sizes recommended for artificial midges in the basic recipe.

~

Herl Midge

Hook – size 24-28 dry fly
Silk – finest black
Body – black ostrich herl

A very easy tie, and a very effective pattern for all tiny dark midges and also reed-smuts.

~

Red Quill Midge

Hook – size 22-28 dry fly
Silk – finest black
Tail – few fibres natural red cock hackle
Body – stripped peacock quill
Hackle – natural red cock

Vincent Marinaro discovered that the general dry fly, Red Quill, when tied in tiny sizes, is very effective when trout are eating tiny midges.

~

Legged Midge 1

Hook – size 14-16 dry fly
Silk – finest black
Abdomen – fine grey herl
Rib – fine flat gold tinsel
Hackle – black cock
Wing – sandy dun hackle wonderwing
Legs – 4-6 herls, spread

Legged Midge 2

Hook – size 14-16 dry fly
Silk – finest black
Abdomen – natural red cock quill, stripped
Thorax – brown fur dub
Hackle – natural red cock
Wing – 2, sandy dun hackle wonderwing
Legs – 4-6 strands black horsehair, kinked and spread

Long-legged Midge 3

Hook – size 14-18 dry fly
Silk – finest black
Abdomen – pearl tinsel
Thorax – brown fur dub

Hackle – black
Wing – dark (iron) blue hackle wonderwing
Legs – 4-6 strands black horsehair, spread

These three patterns were devised to add a possible trigger to midge imitations that other midge imitations lack: feet (at the end of long legs) on the water surface. In the most difficult of flat calms, on lakes, they have been very effective.

Note: CDC Category 3 Dry Flies (p. 138) are excellent midge imitations.

BLACK GNATS, HAWTHORN FLY AND HEATHER FLY

Land-bred flies; only the adults are of importance when they fall onto the water.

La Petite Merde

This is perhaps one of the most effective tiny dry flies to use when trout are feeding on 'little dark things': midges, smuts, tiny land-bred insects, e.g. thrips. And it works equally well on rivers and lakes.

Hook – size 18-28 short shank dry fly
Silk – brown or black
Abdomen – brown cul de canard
Wing – white or brown cul de canard
Thorax – brown cul de canard

The thorax is tied in front of the wing to hold the wing low. In dull light or dark water the white wing shows better than the brown, and vice versa. This is currently my first choice when trout are feeding on tiny smuts or midges. A Swiss-French pattern (by Petitjean) that is very similar to the older F-Fly of M. Fratnik and can be tied with olive, black and yellow-olive body, and in larger sizes (to 16) to match larger midges.

~

Black Gnat

Hook – size 12-14 dry fly for Hawthorn Fly and Heather Fly, 12-20 for Black Gnat species
Silk – black
Abdomen – black floss silk, herl or quill, carried slightly around the hook bend to simulate the often curved abdomen of the natural fly
Rib – fine silver wire or none (in quill body)
Thorax – pronounced, black peacock or ostrich herl, or dubbed black fur
Wings – white or pale blue dun hackle points, or bunch of hackle fibres or synthetic material (e.g. Antron), tied back.
Hackle – black cock (if imitating Heatherfly a dark red or furnace cock hackle may be used)
Rear Legs – optional, when tying Hawthorn fly. 2 fibres of peacock herl or black horse hair, knotted and cut to length.

Sometimes the fish will select only those naturals that have sunk into the surface film and refuse a high-floating dry fly. Simply modify the dry fly by trimming away the hackle below the body, and do not oil the fly. It will then sit in the surface film.

GREY MIDGE

RED MIDGE

ORANGE MIDGE

OLIVE MIDGE

HERL MIDGE

RED QUILL MIDGE

LEGGED MIDGE 1

LEGGED MIDGE 2

LONG-LEGGED MIDGE 3

LA PETITE MERDE

HAWTHORN FLY, *legged*

BLACK GNAT, *unlegged*

Cul de Canard Hawthorn

Hook – size 14 dry fly
Silk – black
Body – grey-black CDC feather, thickened at thorax
Hind Legs – 2, knotted CDC feather stalks, knotted
Wing – broad 2 hackle points, white

Many other black flies (e.g. spider wet flies p. 127, Jassid p. 174, black adult midges p. 192) will also take fish that are selecting black gnats, hawthorns and heather flies.

CDC HAWTHORN

CRANE-FLY OR DADDY-LONG-LEGS

A landbred fly; only the adults are eaten by fish when they fall onto the water.

Hook – A fine wire size 8-12 fairly longshank dry fly. Tie some smaller ones especially for upland or northern waters (peaty uplands produce smaller species than fertile lowlands)

Silk – brown

Body – see patterns below

Legs – knotted cock pheasant tail fibres

Knotting: it is much easier to hold tips of pheasant tail fibres and knot from the 'thicker' stiffer end than the other way round. 2-3 knots per leg. Using 2 tail fibres per leg makes the legs far more durable.

Legs are the major trigger. Natural daddy-long-legs have 6 legs but trout cannot count so use 8 if the legs are made from single pheasant tail fibres, arranged either in a bunch or splayed out to either side.

Wing – 1 or 2 pairs cock hackle points: ginger or natural red

Natural daddy-long-legs have 2 wings, but some tyers add 2 pairs of wings. Many tyers insist that the wings be set in a 'spent' position, at right angles to the body; some insist that the wings should be tied back, over or alongside the body. After a few casts the mer style comes to look like the latter and still catches fish.

Hackle – natural red, blue dun or ginger cock

Daddy-long-legs 1

Body – brown or buff herl (e.g. hen or cock pheasant tail fibres)

Silk, legs, hackle and wings – as above

Daddy-long-legs 2

Body – cork trimmed to shape and bound onto hook shank

Silk, legs, hackle and wings – as above

Daddy-long-legs 3

Body – deerhair, extended, ribbed black thread

Thorax – fine brown fur

Silk, legs, hackle and wings – as above

~

Dung Fly (Wickham)

Hook – size 12-16 dry fly

Silk – light brown

Body – flat gold tinsel

Rib – fine gold wire

Hackle – red (natural brown) cock, palmered

Wings – teal quill slips

A very old pattern that is outstanding as a dungfly imitation.

~

Bluebottle

Hook – size 12-16 dry fly

Silk – black

Body – black floss

Rib – peacock herl

Wing – transparent, polythene or other synthetic sheet

Hackle – black cock

This matches all black 'chunky-bodied' dipterans, including bluebottles and houseflies.

~

Gravel Bed

Hook – size 12 dry fly

Silk – white

Body – grey heron or goose quill

Rib – fine silver wire

Legs – 4 or 6 (2-3 pairs) stripped blue-dun hackle stalks

Wings – two blue dun hackles, tied as 'wonderwings'

The fly sits in, not on, the surface film. Also a good imitation of small Daddy-long-legs.

~

Green Lacewing

Hook – size 14 dry fly

Silk – white

Body – light green Antron

Wing – light green Niche wing

Hackle – white cock, short fibred

A great pattern in summer, especially under trees.

BEETLES

(Natural Beetles p. 76)

Adult Beetles

The patterns suggested for Land-bugs (p. 174) are recommended for landbred beetles that fall onto the water. A useful alternative (especially for stillwaters):

Poly Beetle

Hook – size 12-16 dry fly

Silk – black

Body – strip of black or white Ethafoam or Plastazote, tied to rear of hook shank and brought ward and tied in at front or 2-3 polystyrene balls enclosed in nylon tights material

Legs – sparse hackle or 6 short strands of knotted horsehair or peacock herl

This can be fished on the surface or, by using a sinking line perhaps with a split shot on the leader, beneath the surface to imitate an aquatic beetle.

Black Ethafoam/Plastazote makes an excellent **Black Beetle**; colour white beetles as you wish (as in the two Ladybirds) but note that most landbred beetles are black underneath and will appear black to the fish!

Deer Hair Beetle

Hook – size 12-16 dry fly

Silk – black

Body – peacock herl or black fur; tied fat

Wing cases and Legs – bunch deerhair tied in at back of body and then at front. Legs 2-3 fibres of wing case cut at each side.

For an aquatic beetle, add an underbody of lead wire.

~

Beetle Larvae: see Alder Larva (opposite)

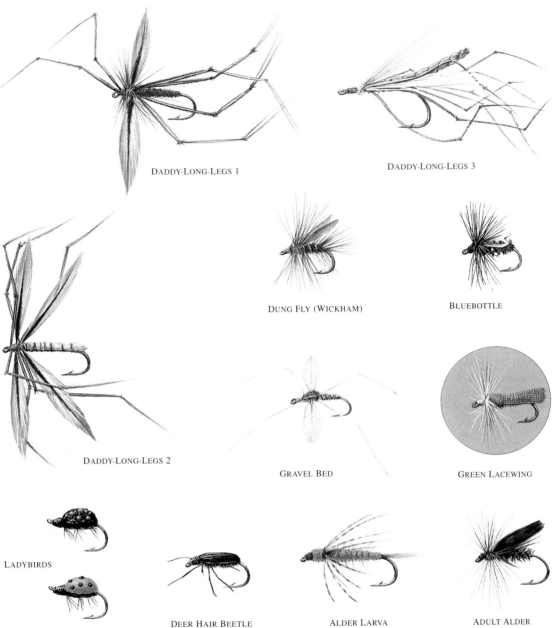

DADDY-LONG-LEGS 1

DADDY-LONG-LEGS 3

DUNG FLY (WICKHAM)

BLUEBOTTLE

DADDY-LONG-LEGS 2

GRAVEL BED

GREEN LACEWING

LADYBIRDS

DEER HAIR BEETLE

ALDER LARVA

ADULT ALDER

ALDERS   *(Natural Alders p. 76)*

Despite the fact that adult alderflies do not normally occur on the water (and are thus rarely eaten by fish), imitations of adult alders are perhaps better known than imitations of the larvae (that do live in water and are eaten by fish). Alder larvae are very similar to many aquatic beetle larvae, so the fish could take imitations as either beetle or alder.

Alder Larva

Hook – size 12-14 longshank nymph
Silk – brown
Tails – bunch of buff or olive hackle fibres
Underbody – fine lead wire or foil tied along hook shank tapering from front of shank to rear

Body hackle – buff or olive cock hackle, palmered over body, all fibres on top, underside trimmed away
Body – buff or olive fur (natural or synthetic)
Legs – short fibred soft hackle (e.g. partridge), 1-2 turns
Head – 2 turns of buff or olive herl
Effective fished in margins late April to June, this pattern also resembles many aquatic beetle larvae.

Adult Alder

Hook – size 12-14 dry fly
Silk – black
Body – bronze peacock herl
Wing – speckled brown hen quill slips tied back
Hackle – black cock
As alternative, use small brown sedge pattern, p. 184.

MOTHS

(*Natural Moths p. 79*)

Use sedge patterns (p. 180) or Bustards (p. 136) of appropriate size and colour for adults.

Caterpillar

Hook – size 10-14 curved shank sedge or grub
Silk – brown or green
Body hackle – white, palmered along body and
  trimmed short
Body – fine textured fur – green or olive-brown mix
Head – 2 turns of olive or brown herl
Especially useful under trees from which caterpillars may descend or fall onto the water

GRASSHOPPER

(*Natural Grasshopper p. 78*)

A useful pattern for late summer and autumn, that will bring dour fish to the surface, is:

Quill Hopper

Hook – size 10-12 dry fly
Silk – brown or green
Body – length of cut quill dyed brown or green with
  holes sealed with cork
Hind Legs – brown or green dyed and knotted horse
  hair, thick herl or thick monofilament (10+ kg test),
  tied back to either side of body
Antennae – two herl tips of pieces of fine
  monofilament dyed brown or green
This will float all day: cast on surface and twitch occasionally.

~

Two other Grasshopper imitations to try on big rivers or lakes from July to the end of the trout season are:

Troth's Hopper

Hook – size 8-14 dry fly
Silk – olive or brown
Body – elk hair dyed olive or brown
Wing – green or brown quill slip
Legs & Head – olive or brown deer hair, spun
  muddler style then clipped to give a large head, with
  some fibres trailing for legs.

Gartside's Hopper

Hook – size 8-12 dry fly
Silk – olive
Tail – a few fibres of dark moose body
Body – olive Antron
Body hackle – furnace cock, palmered, with all fibres
  clipped short on top and underneath to about gape width
Underwing – 8-12 olive deer hairs
Wing – back feather from cock pheasant, cut to shape
Legs – 4-6 brown deer hairs at each side of body
Head – olive deer hair, spun muddler style and
  clipped to shape
The trout do take these, but whether for a grasshopper or for a big sedge I do not know.

ANTS

(*Natural Ants p. 78*)

Always carry a couple of ant imitations, especially in summer:

Red Ant and Black Ant

Hook – size 12-16 dry fly
Silk – as body
Body – red or black tying silk, built up to produce an
  ant-like shape; varnish bee completing fly
Hackle – natural red (red ants) or black (black ants) or
  blue dun (both) cock hackle
Wings – white or pale blue dun cock hackle points,
  tied back (optional)

Fur-bodied Ant

Hook – size 12-16 dry fly
Silk – brown or black
Body – two small balls of fine synthetic fur dubbing;
  red-brown (red ant) or black (black ant)
Hackle – natural red or black, tied and would at waist
  between the two fur balls
Wing – 2 pale blue dun hackle points (optional)

CRUSTACEANS

(*Natural Crustaceans p. 80*)

Three patterns are suggested here, the Opossum Shrimp (useful in northern waters), the Water Hog-louse and the Freshwater Shrimp (one of the most useful of weighted flies in the anglers' armoury, in small sizes this also matches the mud-shrimp). Fish will sometimes feed selectively on these; when feeding on other large crustaceans they tend not to be selective and the Freshwater Shrimp or other weighted pattern will score. Most planktonic freshwater crustaceans are too small to imitate on a fly hook.

Opossum Shrimp

Hook – size 10-14 longshank nymph
Silk – white or pale grey
Underbody – strips of fine lead wire bound to top of
  hook shank
Tails – 3-4 tips of white marabou strands
Body – wound white marabou from tails
Rib – fine flat silver tinsel
Hackle – palest grey or white soft hackle, sparse
Eyes – heavy monofilament burnt at either end to
  produce small round, black eyes
Head – wound white marabou
A very useful pattern for grayling, trout and arctic charr in arctic and subarctic lakes

Freshwater Shrimp

Hook – size 10-16 wet fly or curved body grub or sedge
Underbody – lengths of fine lead wire or foil, whipped
  to hook shank to give shrimp-like humped back

~

Grey Shrimp 1

Silk – brown
Body – grey synthetic fur
Shellback – narrow strip from polythene bag (this is
  tied in at rear of body, brought over completed body
  and tied in at head bee ribbing is added.
Rib – silver wire

CATERPILLAR

RED ANT

BLACK ANT

FUR-BODIED ANT

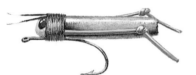

QUILL HOPPER

TROTH'S HOPPER

GARTSIDE'S HOPPER

RED SHRIMP 1

RED SHRIMP 2

RED SHRIMP 3

GREY SHRIMP 1

GREY SHRIMP 2

OPOSSUM SHRIMP

GREY SHRIMP 3

GREY SHRIMP 4

Grey Shrimp 2

Silk – orange
Tail – grey partridge hackle fibres
Body – hare's mask
Shellback and Rib – as Grey Shrimp 1

Grey Shrimp 3

Silk – orange
Body – hare's ear
Legs – a grey partridge hackle
Shellback and Rib – as Grey Shrimp 1

Grey Shrimp 4

Silk – black
Body – grey cul de canard feather
Rib – copper wire

Red Shrimp 1

Silk – red
Body – mix hare's ear, and yellow and red seal's fur
  (sub.) proportions 1:1:2
Shellback and Rib – as Grey Shrimp 1

Red Shrimp 2

Silk – red
Tail – bronze mallard fibres
Body – hot orange seal's fur (sub.)
Shellback and Rib – as Grey Shrimp 1
Antennae – bronze mallard fibres

Red Shrimp 3

Silk – black
Body – deep orange-red cul de canard feather
Rib – copper wire

Water Hog-louse 1

Hook – size 14-16 wet fly

Silk – green

Underbody – fine lead wire wound round hook and then flattened on top and bottom

Tail – a few fibres speckled brown partridge hackle

Body – hare's ear

Back – grey-brown herls (e.g. goose), lacquered

Rib – fine gold wire

Antennae – a few fibres speckled brown partridge hackles

Water Hog-louse 2 as pattern 1, but with a brown fur body and legs of speckled brown partridge hackle

~

Freshwater Prawn

Hook – saltwater size 2-4

Silk – white

Antennae and claws – pair red cock hackle points and bunch tan bucktail hair

Eyes – lead eyes painted black

Body – tan bucktail, ribbed orange Crystal Hair

Overbody – clear epoxy-glue

Tail – brown partridge hackle

Tied in several sizes this is effective in waters where fish feed on crayfish and prawns. In brackish water use stainless steel hooks.

~

Brackish Water Shrimp

Hook – bait hook size 2/0-4

Silk – white or transparent

Eyes – lead eyes or burnt mono

Body – Lureflash Fritz, pearl

Legs – heron substitute

Antennae – fibres herl substitute plus pearl Crystal Hair

Back – flexible drinking straw, coloured brown

An alternative to the Freshwater Prawn. A super pattern by G. Coxon for brackish water where sea trout and bass are feeding.

~

Crayfish

Hook – size 1/0-4 stainless steel

Silk – buff

Eyes – lead eyes painted black

Underbody – fine lead wire

Body – hare's ear

Tail and back – Niche wing, fine sandy

Rib – fine silver wire to give segmentation

Claws – Niche wing, knotted and cut to shape

Antennae – two sandy cock hackle stalks

Fish on a dead drift as for a nymph. Also an excellent estuary fly for bass and sea trout.

~

Crab

Hook – size 2-6 stainless steel

Silk – buff

Eyes – lead eyes painted black

Underbody – fine lead wire

Body – olive-brown deerhair, spun and clipped to shape

Carapace – fine sandy Niche wing

Claws – Niche wing, knotted and cut to shape

A fine estuary crab imitation for sea trout, bass and freshwater fish feeding in the estuary channel at low water.

MOLLUSCS   *(Natural Molluscs p. 82)*

The fly fisher will find just one useful imitation, for lakes in summer when snails are migrating along the underside of the surface film:

Floating Snail

Hook – size 10-12 dry fly

Silk – black

Body – piece of cork carved to snail shape and whipped to the hook shank

Antennae – 2 short pieces of monofilament

When complete, coat the whole 'fly' with black varnish. Useful in summer when fish are seen feeding at the surface with no food in evidence. When fish are feeding on tiny snails, a slowly-fished black spider wet fly (p. 128) is also very effective.

AMPHIBIAN TADPOLES

(Natural Tadpoles p. 84)

These can be important foods, especially in the margins of weedy lakes and river bays.

Tadpole 1

Hook – size 12-14 wet fly

Silk – black

Tail – a short bunch of black marabou

Underbody – a ball wound from fine lead wire

Overbody – black herl (e.g. peacock, pheasant tail)

Tadpole 2 as pattern 1, but with a tail of 2 cock hackle points

FISH IMITATIONS

(Natural Fish p. 84)

An increasing number of anglers are appreciating the importance of lesser fish in the diet of trout, especially big trout. In rivers where the average weight of trout may be only 250g (from fishing with insect imitations), a large fish-imitating fly will often reveal the presence of numbers of much larger fish (weighing 2kg or more). These big fish want big foods. The same applies in many lakes. In artificially stocked rainbow trout reservoirs, the bigger trout hunt smaller fish (even recently stocked rainbows) and will rarely fall for any fly that does not imitate their preferred food. Also, in summer and early autumn many lake trout hunt fry in the margins, then you need a good fry imitation.

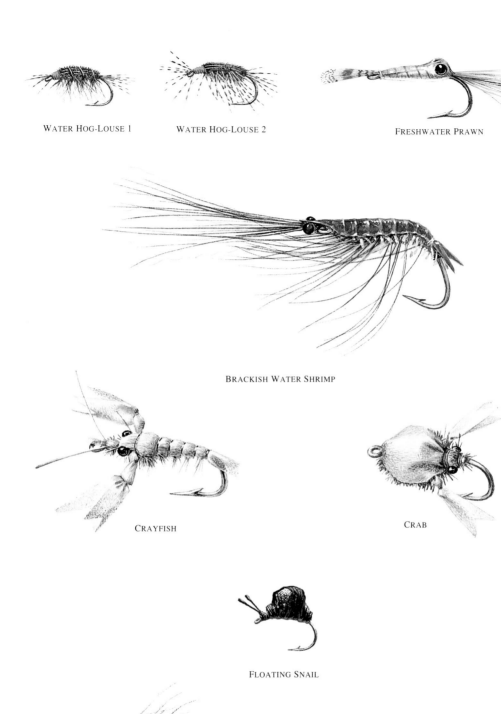

WATER HOG-LOUSE 1   WATER HOG-LOUSE 2   FRESHWATER PRAWN

BRACKISH WATER SHRIMP

CRAYFISH   CRAB

FLOATING SNAIL

TADPOLE 1

TADPOLE 2

Many fancy wet flies (such as Peter Ross) and streamers (such as the Marabou Streamers) might reasonably be considered fish imitations, but the following selection has proved to be more realistic and successful. The trout like them!

MUDDLER MINNOWS

The original Muddler Minnow was designed to imitate a small fish called the darter or muddler minnow in the Nipigon River in the USA. The major feature of this lure is a head and ruff made from deer hair: this results in a broad buoyant floating lure which creates a distinct wake as it swings across the river or is pulled through the lake surface. Although initially designed for fishing at the surface, muddler-style lures are also very effective deep lures. Several layers of touching turns of lead wire may be added as an underbody. Ideally this should be just enough to take the minnow to the bottom, but not so much that the fly will hang-up on every cast. On this point: minnows that are to be fished in rivers need more lead than similar sized minnows for lake fishing, because the lead must overcome both buoyancy of the deerhair head and the flow of the river.

Muddler Minnow

Hook – size 2-12 longshank bucktail/streamer
Silk – black
Tail – 2 matched slips of oak turkey
Body – flat gold tinsel
Rib – fine gold wire
Wing – sparse bunch grey squirrel tail with 2 matched slips of oak turkey outside
Muddler Head and Collar – natural deer hair spun and clipped muddler-style

~

Sculpin Muddler 1

Hook – size 2-12 longshank bucktail/streamer
Silk – black
Tail – 2 cree hackle points
Body – creamy-buff seal's fur (substitute)
Rib – oval gold tinsel
Wing – 2 pairs cree hackles tied in matuka style
Muddler Head & Collar – mottled with mixed white, brown, olive and natural deer hair spun and clipped to simulate the square flattened head of the miller's thumb (sculpin)
Pectoral Fins – 2 speckled brown partridge hackles tied in at side just behind head (optional)

Sculpin Muddler 2

Hook – size 2-10 longshank bucktail/streamer
Silk – black, olive or brown
Body – cream or white seal's fur (or substitute) or Antron, with a narrow band of fluorescent orange or red at front, behind head and fins, to simulate gills
Rib – oval gold tinsel
Wing – 2 olive or brown speckled marabou plumes, tied matuka style. These extend back beyond end of hook to also produce the tail

Muddler Head & Collar – mottled and barred by spinning and stacking black, brown, olive, rust and white deer hair; cut to the flattened, square head of the muddler minnow (sculpin)
Pectoral Fins – 2 speckled brown partridge hackles tied in at side just behind head (optional)

~

Black Bullhead Muddler

Hook – size 2-12 longshank bucktail/streamer
Silk – black
Tail – black marabou plume at top, white plume below
Body – (as tail) a black marabou plume on top of hook shank, white below (this also provides the 'wing')
Muddler Head & Collar – mottled and barred by mixing and spinning natural and black deer hair; cut to the flattened, square head of the muddler minnow (sculpin).
An excellent pattern for night fishing.

DEEP MINNOWS

A series of fairly simple-to-tie patterns, invented by Bob Clouser, that simulate tiny bait fish. Highly commended! They will deceive trout, perch, pike, chub – any fish looking to eat lesser fish.

Lead Eyes

One of the features of these lures is the way they sink to great depth quickly. This is because of the lead eyes tied in at the front of the hook. Take a Twin Lead Eyes (p. 222): size 2 (0.9 g) for hook sizes 2-4, size 1 (0.45g) for hook sizes 6-8. Lash firmly to the top of the hook shank, 2-4mm behind the hook eye; superglue for extra security. If not already with painted eyes, paint the eyes yellow or white with black or red pupil. Prepare several hooks in one tying session and complete in the next session when the eyes are dry.

With the lead eyes so positioned, the lure will fish point-up, so the back of the lure is on the same side as the hook point. This also means that the fly is tied 'upside-down': the bunch of hair ming the 'belly' is tied in first, on top of the hook shank, the hook is reversed and the middle wing and 'back' are then tied on the underside of the hook shank.

Deep Minnow Silver Shiner

Hook – size 2-8 wide gape, standard shank length, ged wet fly
Silk – white
Lower wing (Belly) – white bucktail
Middle wing (Lateral Line) – rainbow Crystal Hair
Upper wing (Back) – pale grey bucktail
Head – painted twin lead eyes

Deep Minnow Golden Shiner

Hook – size 2-8 wide gape, standard shank length, ged wet fly
Silk – white
Lower wing (Belly) – white bucktail
Middle wing (Lateral Line) – gold Crystal Hair
Upper wing (Back) – brown bucktail
Head – painted twin lead eyes

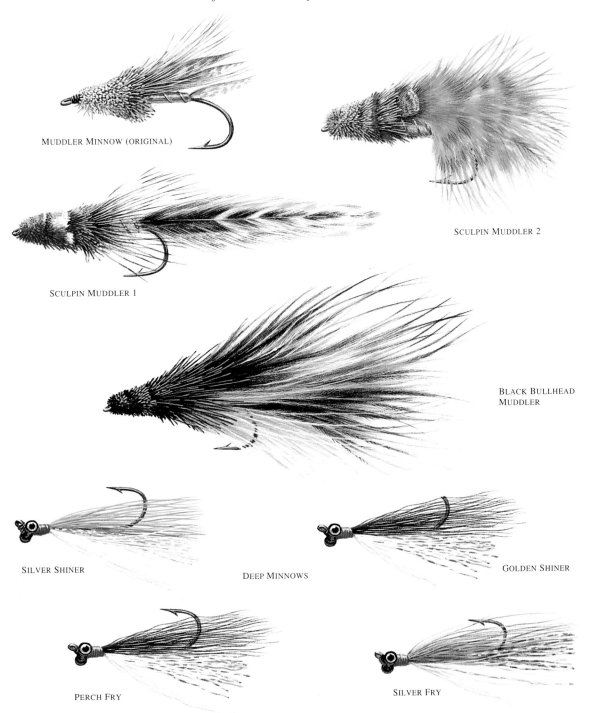

MUDDLER MINNOW (ORIGINAL)

SCULPIN MUDDLER 2

SCULPIN MUDDLER 1

BLACK BULLHEAD MUDDLER

SILVER SHINER

DEEP MINNOWS

GOLDEN SHINER

PERCH FRY

SILVER FRY

Deep Minnow Perch Fry

Hook – size 2-8 wide gape, standard shank length, ged wet fly
Silk – olive
Lower wing (Belly) – light green bucktail
Middle wing (Lateral Line) – green or peacock Crystal Hair
Upper wing (Back) – dark olive bucktail
Head – painted twin lead eyes

Deep Minnow Silver Fry

Hook – size 2-8 wide gape, standard shank length, ged wet fly
Silk – white
Lower wing (Belly) – white bucktail
Middle wing (Lateral Line) – silver Crystal Hair
Upper wing (Back) – olive bucktail
Head – painted twin lead eyes

THUNDER CREEK LURES

A superb series of fish-fry imitations, based on bucktail, devised in the USA by Keith Fulsher. Though they are more difficult to tie than traditional hair-winged patterns, the time and eft is worthwhile, especially for anglers seeking sea, lake and river trout that include smaller fish in their diet. They are also good for perch and small pike.

The 'Wing' of some Thunder Creek lures has three different colours of bucktail: a 'lateral line' consisting of one sparse bunch of bucktail, a 'back' of another bunch of bucktail, and a 'belly' of another bunch of bucktail. Others have just two bunches of bucktail, with no lateral line. If the pattern has a lateral line, this is tied in conventionally on top of the hook shank behind the eye bee the back and belly hairs. The back and belly hairs are tied ward (back on top of the hook, belly under the hook – reverse the hook in the vice) and then pulled backwards bee tying down in their final position. This creates a long head which is then thoroughly soaked in cement or epoxy-resin. Finally the eyes are painted in.

Thunder Creek Black-nosed Dace

Hook – size 2-10 of the longest shanked hooks procurable (Partridge make a special Thunder Creek hook)
Silk – white
Body – embossed silver tinsel
Rib – fine oval silver tinsel
Back – brown bucktail
Lateral Line – black bucktail
Belly – white bucktail
Eyes – painted white with black pupil

~

Thunder Creek Golden Shiner

Hook – size 2-10 of the longest shanked hooks procurable (Partridge make a special Thunder Creek hook)
Silk – white
Body – yellow tinsel
Rib – fine oval gold tinsel
Back – brown bucktail that has been dyed green
Lateral Line – yellow bucktail
Belly – white bucktail
Eyes – painted cream with black pupil

Thunder Creek Silver Shiner

Hook – size 2-10 of the longest shanked hooks procurable (Partridge make a special Thunder Creek hook)
Silk – white
Body – embossed silver tinsel
Rib – fine oval silver tinsel
Back – brown bucktail
Lateral Line – 0
Belly – white bucktail
Eyes – painted cream with black pupil

~

Thunder Creek Charr

Hook – size 2-10 of the longest shanked hooks procurable (Partridge make a special Thunder Creek hook)
Silk – white
Body – flat silver tinsel
Rib – fluorescent orange floss silk
Back – brown bucktail
Lateral Line – orange bucktail
Belly – white bucktail
Eyes – red with black pupil

~

Thunder Creek Minnow

Hook – size 2-10 of the longest shanked hooks procurable (Partridge make a special Thunder Creek hook)
Silk – white
Body – flat silver tinsel
Rib – fluorescent red floss silk
Back – olive bucktail
Lateral Line – grey bucktail
Belly – white bucktail
Eyes – painted white with black pupils

~

Thunder Creek Perch Fry

Hook – size 2-10 of the longest shanked hooks procurable (Partridge make a special Thunder Creek hook)
Silk – white
Body – flat silver tinsel
Rib – fluorescent pink floss silk
Back – olive bucktail
Lateral Line – dark green bucktail
Belly – light green bucktail; make 3 narrow vertical bars with black marker pen down body after completing
Eyes – painted yellow with black pupils

~

Epoxy-fry

Hook – size 2-12, longshank bucktail/streamer
Silk – white
Tail – silver, blue and green Crystal Hair, mixed
Underbody – flat silver tinsel, with silver, blue and green Crystal Hair (from tail) tied over
Body – Devcon clear epoxy-resin, built up to shape
Head – as overbody
Eyes – premed, stuck in place with epoxy-resin
When does a 'fly' become a plug or spinner? Glue a diving vane on this and you have a plug. Why not use a plug? That is not fly fishing. These are questions that a 'fly-fisher' who builds (rather than ties) flies from epoxy-resin, cork and Plastazote/Ethafoam might like to answer. Especially when going to fish a fly-only water.

~

THUNDER CREEK BLACK-NOSED DACE

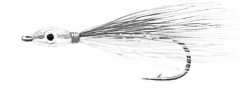

THUNDER CREEK GOLDEN SHINER

THUNDER CREEK SILVER SHINER

THUNDER CREEK CHARR

THUNDER CREEK MINNOW

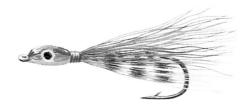

THUNDER CREEK PERCH FRY

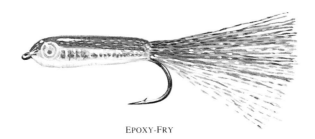

EPOXY-FRY

Mylar Tube Fry

Hook – size 2-12, longshank bucktail/streamer
Silk – black
Tail – olive or brown raffine
Underbody – white floss silk
Body – Mylar tube
Back – olive or brown raffine (from tail)
Hackle – few fibres of scarlet or blue dun hackle
Head – black cement
Eyes – painted in black and white or premed and
  glued in position

One of my basic fry patterns; slender underbody and
fine Mylar for roach, rudd, whitefish; thicker for bream
and perch; red hackle for roach, rudd and perch, grey
for bream and whitefish.

~

Mylar Minnow

Hook – size 2-12, longshank bucktail/streamer
Silk – black
Tail – bronze peacock herl
Underbody – fluorescent red floss silk or wool
Body – silver or pearl Mylar tube
Back – bronze peacock herl
Head – black cement
Eyes – painted, black and white

Very easy to tie, and especially effective in rivers (it
will also catch sea trout). Also effective with olive or
brown marabou for back and tail.

~

Polystickle

Hook – size 2-12, longshank bucktail/streamer
Silk – black
Tail – brown or dark olive raffine cut to shape
Underbody – black silk ribbed narrow flat silver
  tinsel, with fluorescent red or magenta floss at front
Body – narrow strip of clear polythene, built up to
  give fish shape
Back – brown or dark olive raffine
Hackle – hot orange hackle fibres, as beard
Head – black cement
Eyes – painted black and white

A superb pattern. Back and tail from the same piece of
raffine.

~

Floating Fry

Hook – size 2-12, longshank bucktail/streamer
Silk – black, red or white
Tail – white Ethafoam or Plastazote, cut to shape
Body – white Ethafoam or Plastazote (from tail) cut to
  shape
Head – tying thread

John Wadham's pattern to imitate a dead roach, rudd or
bream fry; a very effective late summer lake pattern for
lake trout.

~

Floating Sculpin (Rasputin)

Hook – size 2-12, longshank bucktail/streamer
Silk – black
Tail – slip of brown speckled turkey quill
Body – fish-shaped piece Plastazote, slit to
  accommodate hook and firmly fixed on shank with
  waterproof glue
Back – speckled brown turkey (from tail)
Pectoral Fins – two bunches cock pheasant tail fibres,
  clipped to shape
Head – black cement
Eyes – painted, black and white

Trout will eat dead fish; often they savagely attack
shoals of lesser fish and then turn back to collect the
dead and dying. This imitates a drifting dead fish.

~

Sinfoil's Fry

Hook – size 2-12, longshank bucktail/streamer
Silk – black
Underbody – flat silver tinsel on front $\frac{3}{4}$ shank
Body – 3 mm wide clear polythene strip wound to
  produce fry-shaped body; at front narrow collar of
  bright scarlet floss
Back – strip bronze mallard tied as low wing
Head – black cement
Eyes – painted black and white

~

Whitefish

Hook – size 2-12, longshank bucktail/streamer
Silk – white
Tail – white marabou
Underbody – flat silver tinsel or painted shank
Body – pearl Mylar tube
Back – silver mallard flank feather, tied as low wing
Head – white cement
Eyes – painted black and white

Russian and Fenno-Scandinavian rivers and lakes
where whitefish abound.

~

Woolly Bugger Fry

Hook – size 2-12, longshank bucktail/streamer
Silk – black
Tail – white marabou
Body – white chenille
Rib – fine oval silver tinsel
Hackle – long-fibred white cock, palmered
Head – black cement
Eyes – painted black and white

A simple, impressionistic fry imitation, or so the trout
think – even if it looks little like a fish to us!

~

MYLAR TUBE FRY

MYLAR MINNOW

POLYSTICKLE

FLOATING FRY

FLOATING SCULPIN (RASPUTIN)

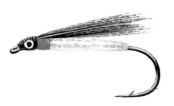

SINFOIL'S FRY

WHITEFISH

WOOLLY BUGGER FRY

FISH EGG IMITATIONS *(Natural Eggs p. 85)*

Trout often eat the eggs of other fish, such as grayling eggs in late spring. The two patterns that I have found successful in European waters when trout are feeding on eggs are tied on size 12 wet fly hooks; tie a spherical lead wire underbody first and soak this with clear cement. Allow to dry bee continuing.

Chenille Egg

Silk – orange
Body – hot orange chenille, wound as ball

Fire Ball Egg

Silk – pink or orange
Body – Fire Ball Fluff, wound and trimmed to size (5-7 mm diameter)

CHENILLE EGG   FIRE BALL EGG

SWIMMING MICE AND FROGS

(Natural Mice and Frogs p. 84)

Fish are often opportunistic feeders and will often take a small frog, mouse, vole, lemming etc. that is swimming across the water: especially big fish! One that is very effective is my own **Night Muddler**, it has taken fish in rivers and lakes throughout Europe, especially at night.

Night Muddler

Hook – a tandem mount, with size 4-8 Low Water Salmon hook in front of a size 10-12 treble hook, the eye of the treble should be approximately in line with the band of the front hook (see illustration)
Silk – black
Body – deer hair spun, muddler fashion, the entire length of the shank of the front hook; the body is then trimmed to shape, leaving several strands trailing

The aim is to create a wake on the water: in lakes retrieve jerkily, on rivers cast across and let the 'fly' drag across the current.

Alternatively, why not use **deer hair,** spun on the hook and trimmed, to make more realistic swimming frogs and mice. They certainly will catch fish!

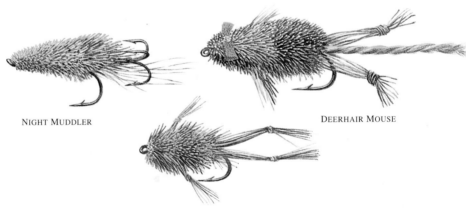

NIGHT MUDDLER   DEERHAIR MOUSE

DEERHAIR FROG

TOOLS AND MATERIALS

The following is a check-list of tools and materials, some essential and some optional, which you will need to tie imitative flies. Use the list in conjunction with suppliers' catalogues or when visiting fishing tackle shops. You may like to keep a note alongside this check-list of materials of those you have in stock and of those you need or would like to acquire. Many items will appear on the list that you might not easily be able to obtain: don't worry, use another from the list. You may see something that is not on the list: use it instead of the materials listed (I have a small piece of lion skin, the fur of which makes splendid adult sedge bodies!).

No fish ever rejected a fly simply because good substitutes were used instead of the so-called correct materials. In order to escape from the straitjacket of "You must use this particular item to tie this fly", I often suggest a range of materials that will do the job equally well.

TOOLS

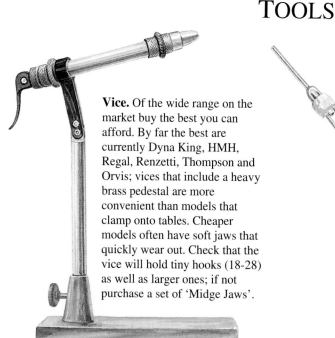

Vice. Of the wide range on the market buy the best you can afford. By far the best are currently Dyna King, HMH, Regal, Renzetti, Thompson and Orvis; vices that include a heavy brass pedestal are more convenient than models that clamp onto tables. Cheaper models often have soft jaws that quickly wear out. Check that the vice will hold tiny hooks (18-28) as well as larger ones; if not purchase a set of 'Midge Jaws'.

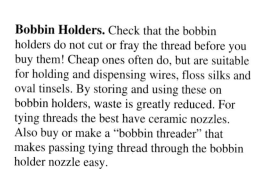

Bobbin Holders. Check that the bobbin holders do not cut or fray the thread before you buy them! Cheap ones often do, but are suitable for holding and dispensing wires, floss silks and oval tinsels. By storing and using these on bobbin holders, waste is greatly reduced. For tying threads the best have ceramic nozzles. Also buy or make a "bobbin threader" that makes passing tying thread through the bobbin holder nozzle easy.

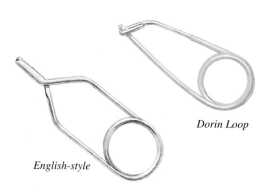

Dorin Loop

English-style

Hackle Pliers. Check English-style hackle pliers before purchase – sometimes the jaws do not hold hackles securely or are so sharp that they will cut through the hackle. Obtain at least two pairs: one large for big hackles, and one small (Dorin Looped-Wire are simple but the best) for dry fly hackles.

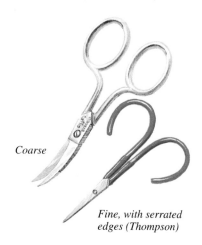

Coarse

Fine, with serrated edges (Thompson)

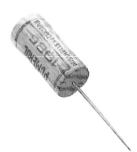

Dubbing Needles. Used with every completed fly to add a drop of varnish to the head; also in straggly fur-bodied flies to tease strands of fur from the dubbed body. By inserting the eye of a sewing needle into a cork you can make one which is finer than most commercially available.

Scissors. Have one pair for cutting wires, tinsels and coarse materials, and one pair with fine points and serrated cutting edges (that prevent fibres sliding rather than being cut) for fine work with soft materials. Before purchasing the fine scissors, check that they cut to the ends of the blades, as many do not. If you are going to tie many flies using deer hair, a pair of hair scissors is a great advantage.

Velcro Dubbing Teaser.
Stick a piece of velcro to a
stick and use it to tease fibres
from dubbed fur bodies.

Hair Stacker. Used to align
the tips of a bunch of hairs for
hair-wings etc.

Dubbing Twister. Used for
making fur hackles, fur heads,
fur chenille etc.

*Mayfly wing
burner*

Stonefly wing burner

Wing Cutters. Used for cutting
out shaped wings from feathers or
synthetic sheet winging material.

Wing Burners. An alternative to wing cutters
where the winging material is held in the burner
and excess burnt (rather than cut) away.

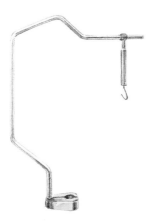

Half-hitch Tool. Excellent for
those who prefer to finish off
their flies with 3-4 half-hitch
knots. It is possible to make a
3- or 4-turn whip-finish with
this tool (see p. 235)

Gallows Tool. Useful for tying
parachute hackles on dry flies.

Whip-finish Tool. Essential for
those who cannot whip-finish a
fly by hand.

MATERIALS

Make your own

Fly dressing materials are expensive, especially when it comes to buying several items dyed in a wide range of colours. Instead find your own and dye your own!

In late May-July collect moulted quills from farmyard geese and swans on the local lake. During the hunting season ask shooting friends to let you have the pluckings and skins from their bag. Collect road casualties, take them home and trim off the fur or pluck out the feathers that you require. Brush the dog and cat regularly: their underfur makes excellent dubbed bodies on nymphs, dry flies etc.

Obtain a wide range of special fly-dressers' dyes. They are inexpensive, simple to use, and very effective, and they allow you to produce shades and dyed materials that are not otherwise available. Full instructions are given: follow them precisely. For imitative fly dressing the following are most useful: black, blue dun, dark claret, hot orange, purple, bright yellow, insect green, green olive, medium olive, olive dun, brown olive, dark brown, cinnamon, ginger.

Small patches of material can also be dyed with permanent felt-tip pens (but make sure the solvent does not damage the material).

Few natural fish foods are uniformly one colour. When you have a range of coloured furs try blending them together to produce a more effective dubbed body for dry flies and wet flies. Put a small amount of each fur in a jar of water, shake so that the furs are mixed, strain and allow to dry before using the mix. Alternatively, use a kitchen blender. Permutations are endless. Try this one for the body of a Freshwater Shrimp imitation: 2 parts medium olive rabbit fur, 2 parts natural hare's ear, 2 parts natural (wild) rabbit fur, 1 part seal's fur, mohair or finely chopped sheep's wool dyed red. It looks good and fish feeding on Freshwater Shrimps love it! It is also often more effective to produce a particular, subtle shade of fur by mixing several colours than by dying the fur in one solid colour.

Fluorescent colours are very popular among fly dressers, but it must be stressed that only tiny areas of natural foods carry fluorescent pigments and that accordingly fluorescent materials should be added only sparsely to artificial flies. A tiny amount in a blend of several furs, or a fine fluorescent rib, or a small fluorescent tip to the abdomen or patch at the base of wings etc. Do not over-use fluorescents or their impact will be lost, certainly in imitative flies.

Varnish (= cement)

There is nothing more tiresome than the silk head of a fly unravelling. Add a drop of fine varnish to cement the whipped silk head. For most imitative flies a clear varnish is used. But when a distinctly black head is needed, then a black varnish is better. For fry patterns, where the head and eye are painted with varnish, you will need black and white (or yellow) varnish. Obtain also some Thinners (varnishes thicken quickly as the solvent evaporates).

HOOKS

The hooks that we use to tie imitative flies should serve five functions:

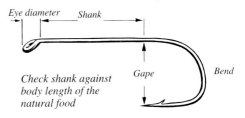

Check shank against body length of the natural food

1. The hook is the skeleton on which we tie the body of the fly, and onto and around which we arrange the tail, hackle, legs, wings and so on. We choose different hooks (i.e. skeletons) for different styles of flies.

2. The hook, to some extent, dictates the size of fly that we are tying. Clearly we need to choose a hook that will allow us to tie a fly that is of the same size as the natural insect that the fish is eating.

3. The hook can be used to help in constructing the shape of the fly: we can choose a curved hook to mimic the curved abdomen of many nymphs, larvae and pupae, or we can choose very long shanked hooks to dress slender fish imitations.

4. The hook attaches the fish to our line, after the fish has taken our fly and we have tightened into it to set the hook. The most efficient form of hook for this purpose has a round bend, a very short point, and will either be barbless or have a very tiny barb. I would advise all anglers to fish with barbless hooks: simply press down the barb with fine snipe-nosed pliers or with artery forceps. The barbless hook penetrates the jaw of a fish far better than a barbed hook, it holds the fish as well as a barbed hook (despite the fears of many anglers that fish escape more easily on barbless hooks, they do not!), and it is easier to remove a barbless hook from the fish's jaw than a barbed hook. Note also that in some parts of Europe it is illegal to use barbed hooks.

Debarbing a hook

5. The hook should hold onto the fish while we are playing it. Strong wire, perfect hardening and tempering, and the use, wherever possible, of forged hooks (where the hook wire is flattened at the bend of the hook) are essential. When fishing dry fly it is necessary to choose a hook that is light enough to prevent the fly from sinking, yet is strong enough not to break or open out when the fish is hooked and being played out.

You can test the strength of a hook quite easily. Fix one in the fly vice by the bend, and give the eye of the hook a firm tweak so that it goes 'twang'. If the hook breaks or does not return to its normal shape then it is too weak. It is unlikely that any of the hook patterns recommended below will suffer from this problem. But occasionally a bad batch will escape onto the market. If you do happen to buy a packet of weak hooks, the manufacturers will always replace them if you send them the bad packet.

~

The number of different hook patterns on the market can be quite bewildering to someone who has just taken up fly fishing and fly tying. This section suggests the hooks to buy for different jobs, for there is more to hook selection than simply buying, say, some trout fly hooks in size 12 or 14. There are different hooks for different jobs.

Europe has three main hook manufacturers: **Partridge** of Redditch is an English company and one of the oldest hook manufacturers in the world. **Mustad** is a Norwegian company, and produces more hooks than any other in the world. **Viellard, Migeon et Cie** (**VMC**) is a French manufacturer making a small range of fine hooks. These three give each style of hook a code number, sometimes also a name, so that, having found a hook that you like or one that has been recommended, you can order that hook simply by its code number and manufacturer. Furthermore, if you read the catalogues produced by the manufacturers, other details of the hook are given.

Hooks for different jobs

I have chosen six basic hook types, out of the scores available. Each is shown here in the complete range of sizes, life size. If you take a hook of unknown size and place it over the illustrations, you should be able to get a good idea of what size of hook yours is. These six patterns, in the full range of size, are enough for dressing any of the flies in this book.

DRY FLY HOOKS

Partridge L3A or GRS3A – Mustad 94840 – VMC 9288 or 9289

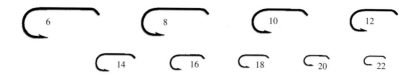

These hooks are ideal for all dry flies, and also for 'emerger patterns' that will float just under or in the surface film.

MIDGE HOOKS

Partridge K1A – Mustad 94859 or 94840 (small sizes) – VMC 9288 and 9289 (both in small sizes)
Note that the Partridge K1A and Mustad 94859 are made specially as midge hooks, the others being plain dry fly hooks made in tiny sizes.

These tiny hooks are essential for imitating minute insects – midges, thunderflies, small ants, micro-caddis and so on.

WET FLY HOOKS

Partridge L2A – Mustad 94845 – VMC 8526

These are slightly heavier in the wire than the equivalent dry fly hooks, so they are stronger. They can be used for all wet flies; also for nymph, larval and pupal imitations. However there are hooks specially made for these purposes.

NYMPH HOOKS

Partridge H1A – VMC 8527 – Mustad 94833 (this latter has a slightly longer hook shank length than the Partridge and VMC)

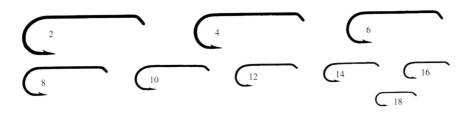

These nymph hooks are longer in the shank than the equivalent sizes of wet fly hooks. This is to allow the fly tyer to create the long slender abdomen and thorax characteristic of most nymphs. In the smaller sizes (10-18) they are also ideal for bigger dry flies such as sedges, grasshoppers, daddy-long-legs and the large mayflies.

CURVED BODY GRUB/EMERGER/SHRIMP HOOKS

Partridge K4A and K2B – Mustad 37160 – VMC does not produce these

Many larvae and pupae, and also the freshwater shrimp, have curved bodies. Straight shanked hooks can be used to imitate these, but a curved hook gives a much more realistic shape. An increasing number of curved hooks are being sold.

STREAMER/LURE/FISH IMITATION HOOKS

Partridge D7A, D3ST, D4A – Mustad 79580, 9672, 9674 – VMC 9283

These very long shanked hooks are designed for tying fish imitations. There is a wide range of styles available, some having longer shanks than others, some having a down eye and others a straight eye. The one illustrated is the Finnish Streamer Hook (D7A) and has been devised especially for fishing with big streamer patterns and fish imitations for very large fish-eating trout in the rivers of Finland and Russia.

THREADS OR SILKS

With a few exceptions, all flies are tied using silks, either natural or synthetic though often they are all referred to as 'threads'.

Tying threads are gauged according to their diameter as follows: 2/0, 3/0, 4/0, 5/0 and so on, the larger the number the finer the thread.

For the majority of imitative flies, tied on hooks to sizes 16, choose threads that are pre-waxed and size 8/0 or finer in black, brown, grey, olive, orange, red, white. Remember that it is easier and makes for a neater fly to use fine silks, even when tying fish imitations on very large hooks.

For hooks smaller than size 16 choose pre-waxed threads size 12/0 or finer (the finest currently available are 18/0-20/0 and only white – if necessary colour this with a permanent felt-tip pen). If you are going to tie flies with bodies made of tying thread, choose round, real silk thread (e.g. Pearsalls), for none other produces the same body effect. Obtain these in as wide a range as possible, but

Tying threads come in a wide range of bobbin sizes

including primrose, yellow, orange, black, purple, crimson. Before tying with this silk, wax by pulling the thread quickly three times across a piece of clear wax (fly-tying wax can be obtained from materials suppliers).

Floss silks: obtain these in a range of colours for they produce fine bodies, especially for slender nymphs, larvae and pupae. Also obtain some fluorescent flosses: pieces can be chopped up and added to fur mixtures (see above); or one or two turns can be added as a tip to the body or at the base of wings; or a very fine strand can be used as a body ribbing. Do not over-use fluorescent materials.

WIRES AND TINSELS

Wires. The best copper, silver and gold wires are used for ribbing bodies of flies to enhance the segmented effect. They also make flies more durable. Copper wire is used instead of silk in tying of some upwinged fly nymphs (p. 142).

Flat tinsel (or mylar or lurex), copper, silver and gold. Use these in the finest sizes as ribbing; also in wider sizes as underbody or body of fish/fry imitations. A pinch of chopped fine silver or gold mylar can be added to a fur mixture (see above) to add sparkle: this is especially useful in imitating aquatic insects such as sedge pupae.

Obtain a wide range of tinsels and wires of different colours and diameters

Oval tinsel. Fine or very fine oval silver and gold tinsels are ideal for ribbing bodies of many flies, especially larger ones (such as large stonefly nymphs).

Mylar tubing. Silver mylar tubing of various diameters is ideal for the body of fish imitations.
Fine lead wire or foil: essential for underbodies of flies that are fished deeply in the water, e.g. deep nymphs, larvae, pupae, water boatmen.

Monofilament fishing line and thick 'button thread' also serve as useful ribbing material.

Natural Furs

Beaver (natural and dyed): dry fly and nymph body dubbing.

Brown Hare mask/ears (natural and dyed): dubbed bodies of shrimps, nymphs, dry flies etc; hairs picked out to simulate legs.

Calf Tail (natural colours and dyed): dry fly tails and wings, but avoid curly hairs at end of tail.

Cat (natural and dyed): underfur from brushings of pet cats makes excellent body dubbing.

Deer, Red (natural or dyed): sedge wings, mayfly tails, also spun for Muddler Minnows and sedge heads.

Deer, Roe (natural and/or dyed): sedge wings.

Deer, White-tailed: sedge wings, upwinged fly tails.

Dog (natural and dyed): underfur from brushings of pet dogs makes excellent body dubbing.

Elk: caddis and upwinged fly wings and tails; dyed olive, Mayfly Dun bodies.

Horse tail (natural colours and dyed): small dry fly bodies, ribbing larger flies.

Mohair (dyed): a whole range of bodies.

Mole (natural and dyed black and olive): dubbed bodies in spider wet flies and nymphs.

Mouse (also vole, shrew and lemming): makes excellent dubbed bodies for small nymphs – the household cat usually provides a good supply.

Muskrat: dubbed nymph and dry fly bodies; longer guard hairs used for upwinged fly tails.

Opossum: dubbed nymph and dry fly bodies.

Rabbit (natural or dyed): dubbed bodies of nymphs, dry flies (perhaps the most useful of all furs).

Sheep's Wool (remnants of knitting wool): dubbed bodies of nymphs, pupae etc. One ingredient in the body fur mix for Tup's Indispensable is cream-coloured fur taken from the scrotal sacs of rams!

Seal (natural or dyed): dubbed nymph, pupa, shrimp etc bodies. Over much of Europe seal's fur is becoming difficult to obtain, for its import into some countries is now prohibited. There are many good synthetic substitutes.

Squirrel, Fox, Red and **Grey** body fur: dubbed nymph and dry fly bodies (note, not squirrel tails – their use is primarily for streamer, sea trout and salmon flies).

Water Vole (Water Rat): excellent dubbing for nymph, pupa and wet fly bodies.

Beaver

Hare's mask or ear provides a range of shades and textures

Red deer

Dyed

Mole fur

Natural

An easy-to-dub, fine fur, rabbit is one the best natural furs.

Fox Squirrel

Seal. A traditional fur, outstanding for fly bodies

FEATHERS

Dry fly hackles: choose the best quality cock hackles, ideally of a genetic strain raised for the fly-dressing market (Hebert, Hoffman, Keough, Metz and Spencer are recommended), or Grade A Indian capes. They are expensive, but they produce the perfect dry fly. Obtain black, dark blue (iron) dun, blue dun, natural red, light ginger, cream, white, grizzle, furnace, badger, cree, sandy dun. Dye white or grizzle hackles to produce olives etc. Note: the only problem with some genetic hackles is that the stalk is very thick. Before tying the hackle in, cut off the base of the stalk and squeeze it between forefinger and thumb nail to reduce this thickness. Fibres from the larger hackles make the best dry fly tails.

Indian cock hackle

Spencer cock hackle

Hen hackle (used in wet flies and nymphs)

Indian Grade A cock hackle

Hoffman cock hackle

The advantage of using genetic hackles is that the feathers are much longer than the equivalent non-genetic; and that there is an abundance of short, stiff hackle fibres. It would take two or three Indian cock hackles to equal one Hoffman.

Wet fly/nymph/shrimp etc., hackles and legs: obtain soft hen hackles in a range of shades (including dyed), but better are soft hackles from species such as the woodcock (upper and under wing coverts), moorhen/waterhen (underwing coverts), snipe (upper and lower wing coverts), partridge (brown hackles from back, grey hackles from neck and breast which can be dyed), golden plover (upper wing coverts), capercaillie (neck feathers), grouse/ptarmigan (wing coverts and neck feathers), crow and jackdaw (neck), and starling neck and underwing coverts. Besides being wound as a hackle or having feather fibres tied into the fly to simulate legs, also useful as tails in subsurface flies.

All hackles can be used as wings in dry flies, as either whole feathers (e.g. in large Mayflies), or as hackle tips (e.g. spent upwinged fly spinners), or as wings cut or burnt from pairs of hackle feathers see pp. 249, 252.

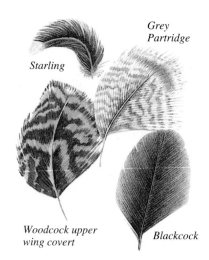

Grey Partridge

Starling

Woodcock upper wing covert

Blackcock

Soft game hackles, ideal for spider wet flies and nymph and shrimp legs

Coq de Leon

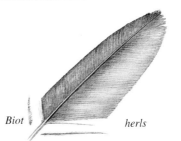

Biot

herls

Coq de Leon (Pardo) hackles, from a special strain of fowl raised in Spain, are excellent for dry fly tails.

Herls. Herls are the long fibres of primary and secondary wing feathers and tail feathers, and are usually taken from large birds (giving longer herls). When 3-5 herls are tied in and then wound along the hook shank they produce a very realistic, translucent body. Obtain crow, goose (dyed), heron (natural or dyed olive), ostrich (natural or dyed), peacock (natural or dyed black); cock pheasant tail (natural or dyed black), swan (dyed). Ideal for dry fly, nymph, pupa, bodies.

Biots. The outer fibres in goose primary wing feathers are short, stiff and known as biots. When dyed appropriately they make excellent tails for stonefly nymphs.

Hackle stalks. White, cream or badger cock or hen hackles, stripped and dyed, make excellent segmented bodies for dry flies.

Peacock quill. Peacock herl, with the flue removed, makes an excellent segmented dry fly body. Quills are also useful for ribbing imitative flies to exaggerate body segmentation.

Marabou. This soft feather comes from the thighs of the turkey. Obtain a supply at Christmas from a local turkey farm and dye it a whole range of shades for bodies and tails of nymphs, pupae and other subsurface flies.

Winging quill slips. Many dry flies are winged with slips of feather cut from pairs of primary or secondary quill feathers (see p. 255). For small dry upwinged flies starling is traditional but very difficult to use: try teal, wigeon, pintail or mallard instead. For darker wings use coot or white duck quills dyed dark blue dun or black. For sedges, alders, stoneflies use dyed duck quills, or quills from wings or tails of grey partridge, peacock, pheasant (hen and cock), grouse, turkey, (natural speckled brown or white and dyed), woodcock, crow, magpie and jay.

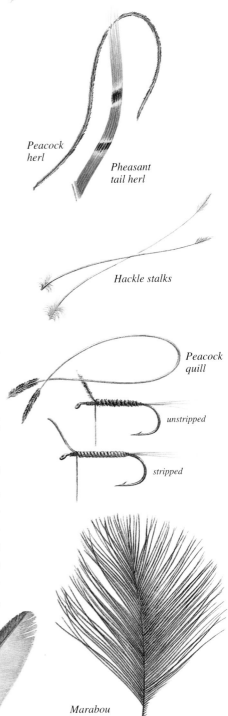

Peacock herl

Pheasant tail herl

Hackle stalks

Peacock quill

unstripped

stripped

Winging quill slips

Marabou

Cul de Canard. These feathers are found around the preen gland of ducks; they are short, plumy feathers with a structure and natural oiliness that repels water; they make superb wings for dry flies and emergers. Obtain them undyed in white, beige, grey and blackish, and dyed in olive, pink, blue-grey.

Cul de canard

Drake Mallard, Teal, Pintail and Wigeon flank feather. The barred black-and-white feathers make superb fish/fry imitations.

Jungle cock. The enamel eye feathers, though mostly used in salmon flies, have uses in imitative trout flies. If the real thing cannot be obtained, paint eyes on starling neck feathers with white enamel paint for a good substitute.

Mallard flank

Some species of mammal (e.g. seals) and of birds (heron, swan) are protected by law in most European countries. There are excellent substitutes: synthetic furs for seal, grey goose for heron, farmyard goose for swan. Sometimes, however, you find a dead mammal or bird: these provide the real thing. Moulted heron feathers and swan quills may often be found by the waterside: collect them.

Jungle cock eye

SYNTHETIC MATERIALS

An increasing number of synthetic materials are now being used in fly-dressing as substitutes for natural furs and feathers. Usually these are excellent, and essential when a particular natural material is difficult or impossible to obtain (for example, over an increasing part of Europe, seal's fur and jungle cock feathers). The major problem with synthetics is that, should a manufacturer cease production of a certain material then it will no longer be available. And do not forget that the majority of synthetics are not made for fly-dressing, which is a minor outlet for manufacturers. This problem has already occurred several times and it is worth giving an example. In the early 1920s J.W. Dunne experimented with a material called Cellulite Floss and published his observations and a completely new set of imitative flies based on Cellulite Floss in a book *Sunshine and the Dry Fly*. In the 1950s the manufacture of this came to an abrupt halt. Dunne's flies could no longer be tied; his book became obsolete.

There is also the problem of availability. One synthetic material may be popular today, but forgotten tomorrow. Or, one brand or type of synthetic material may be available in certain shops, or in some regions, but not in the majority.

It is important therefore that fly dressers ought to be encouraged to experiment with modern synthetics but also that published fly patterns should not recommend one particular brand or sort of synthetic material. Like Dunne's, such fly patterns may be worthless in ten years time. Or, if a reader cannot obtain the recommended synthetic material then the pattern is also worthless for that reader. For this reason I have tried to avoid naming brands of synthetic materials; there are one or two exceptions. I have also tried to include fly patterns that have readily available, common materials. Materials that will still be on the fly dressers' work benches at the end of the 22nd century.

Synthetic furs (range of dyed colours): dubbed bodies of all types. Choose brands with fine, soft texture. Many brands are now available and most offer an enormous range of colour and shade; some are recommended for dry flies because of their water repellence, others are recommended for wet flies and nymphs etc because they tend to absorb water quickly. Some are a mix of several shades and textures; some mixes include chopped pieces of fine silver or gold mylar to add sparkle (you can include this in your own mixes).

One brand of synthetic fur. A good substitute for natural fibres not easily obtainable

Synthetic bodies. A wide range of synthetic body materials includes chenilles (for larger flies), various sorts of plastic or polythene fibres (or sheets from which the tyer cuts thin strips) that are wound around the hook shank to produce a translucent segmented body, and raffine (artificial raffia) used in Mayfly bodies.

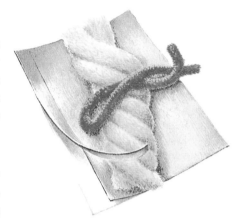

Synthetic tails. Several types of artificial tails, especially useful for tying upwinged fly duns and spinners are available. Many sold to fly dressers are simple stiff nylon fibres from artists' brushes, scrubbing brushes etc.

Synthetic body material: chenille and Flexibody

Nylon bristles make good tails

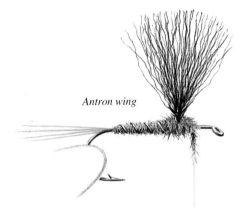

Antron wing

Synthetic wings. Some manufacturers produce very realistic (to our eyes) wings with veins printed on them to imitate sedges, stoneflies and upwinged flies. They come in sheets or strips and you simply cut around the printed wing and tie it in place. Also available are translucent sheets from which wings of any shape can be cut to imitate the veined, but transparent, wings of adult midges, hawthorn flies and other two-winged flies.

Various yarns are also sold in a wide range of shades for synthetic hair wings (e.g. Antron, Poly-yarn)

A printed, synthetic sedge wing

Suspender Balls. Polystyrene balls, as used in pet beds, make super floats for nymphs and pupae hanging from the surface film. They are tied in at the head of the fly, enclosed in a small piece of nylon tights material (see p. 149).

water line

Suspender balls, position in water

Goldheads and silverheads. Drilled gold-plated and silver-plated brass balls provide weight and 'flash' (imitating the flash of an air bubble) to the head of deep nymphs and pupae. Obtain them in 3mm and 4mm diameter.

Goldheads and silverheads

Leadheads and Lead Eyes. Of course, European anglers no longer use lead shot but a non-toxic substitute; the name Lead-head comes from days before leadshot ceased to be used. Like Goldheads these add weight to the front of the fly. Many anglers pinch the split shot around the shank of the hook but often it falls off when being cast. Instead use this method: fix shot firmly onto fine monofilament and tie in the 2 ends of monofilament so that shot is tight to the hook shank just above the hook eye. Also made recently available are Lead Eyes that can be tied directly to the hook immediately behind the eye of the hook. These can be painted to match the eyes of fish fry (e.g. p. 202).

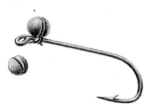

Split shot and method of attachment

   Do not neglect common everyday synthetic materials. Strips cut from balloon rubber or latex surgical gloves make super pupa and nymph bodies. Strips cut from polybags can be used to make a translucent overbody in dry and wet flies, fish fry imitations and 'shellbacks' in Freshwater Shrimp imitations. A very realistic nymph body can be built using a brown rubber band. The supply is almost endless.

FLY-TYING

I t is impractical to cover all techniques and materials as developed over the last three or four centuries. Fly-tying can rapidly become so delightful and absorbing a craft, given few and simple tools, that for many people it becomes almost an end in itself. All over the world, there are books, magazines, clubs and more informal gatherings, for whom the invention and perfection of patterns goes far beyond the practical aim of attracting and catching fish – the main preoccupation of this book. The passion for fly-dressing is easily understandable: and it is not to decry it if we have to stress certain caveats where angling is concerned.

The section on techniques is for the beginner to the art of imitative fly-dressing; yet at the same time it will provide tips that a more experienced fly-dresser may find useful in terms of tying materials in a less conventional way to produce a slightly better result (e.g. tying 'out-rigger tails', or 'cul de canard nymph wing-case loops').

It is, of course, impossible to give a complete guide to fly-dressing in just a few pages. Fly-dressing demands a book in its own right, and there are several excellent volumes on the market, produced by and for European tyers or written by leading American tyers and imported into Europe. The advice given earlier in this book is thus repeated: 1 read and have available for reference one or two books on the subject; 2 take out a subscription to a fly-dressing journal; 3 join a fly-dressing class and a fly-dressing club.

IMITATION

Trout use simple triggers to identify their food (see p. 15) and an effective artificial fly will have those triggers. However many very able fly dressers ignore triggers. Instead they painstakingly copy every feature of a particular insect on a hook : a perfect replica. The number of legs is correct but also the size, shape and colour of each leg joint. The head bears antennae of precise shape and size; the eyes are there, and so is the mouth. There are the correct number of body segments, each of which is perfect in size, shape and colour. An entomologist might look at such an ultra-imitation and be able to identify it to species (and perhaps age and sex). Such ultra-imitation is not necessary for angling. It might be a disadvantage and even a sign of failure, signifying the tyer's inability to work out the simple triggers used by a feeding trout!

Ultra-imitation stonefly nymph: stiff materials lacking movement are the major ingredients.

The topic of ultra-imitation was considered by E. Leiser and R.H. Boyle in their book *Stoneflies for the Angler*. They noted that: 'There is just something about a stonefly nymph that prompts many fly tyers to go all out. Ted Niemeyer, Poul Jorgensen, and Yaz Yamashito have concocted incredibly realistic imita-

*Imitation Stonefly nymph: soft ingredients are the major ingredients. They **move** in the water.*

tions; Yaz even goes so far as to put two claws in each leg. Considering that some of these nymphs can take up to 10 hours to tie, it's no wonder that most are framed rather than fished.'

'Ultra-realistic imitations are marvellous to look at, and Niemeyer found that the trout agreed – they *looked* more often than they hit. "The nymphs were too realistic," Niemeyer says. "They were too stiff. Realism is motion as well as design." Or, as Leiser and Boyle put it, shape and colour are important "but motion – action – is critical."'

If you are an angler and fly tyer, aim to tie simple triggers on the hook. One of those triggers must be motion.

Neatness

Trout foods, especially those found underwater, flicker with life. One way to simulate this 'life' or to impart 'motion' or 'action' is to incorporate into the fly loose, trailing or straggly fibres that move in the water. We can do this with fur bodies, by teasing out fur fibres after the body is completed or by not winding the dubbing too tightly. We can use hair for wings rather than stiff materials. One current vogue, to prevent feather slip wings splitting is to use a glue to stiffen them : this looks good to us, but it loses points when it comes to simulating motion. We can use soft materials, such as soft hackle fibres, to simulate moving legs, and gills, and tails. Such may sometimes make the fly look a bit scruffy out of the water, but it imparts life to the fly in the water.

Today many fly tyers decry the traditional hackle, but it moves in and on the water and imparts motion.

Unfortunately there is a tendency to overlook motion, action, life in the fly. In the many fly-dressing competitions (local, regional, national and international) the neatest, tightest and most 'perfect' (to our eyes) flies will always win. This encourages those tyers who do not win to become neater, tighter and more 'perfect'. Fair enough for competition flies, or for flies that will be framed as pieces of artwork. But when a fly is cast into a river or lake the trout is sole judge of what is or is not a good fly. And the trout will always choose a fly with motion and action, one that flickers with life.

The 'to-tie-this-fly-it-is-essential-to-use-a-particular-material' fallacy

In the past, though happily less so today, fly dressers were extremely niggly and precise about what fur or feather to use when tying a particular fly. For instance, when tying a Waterhen Bloa (see p. 128) the hackle had to be taken from a certain row of underwing coverts of the waterhen, not just any old underwing covert. To tie some of the Olive Duns, the body had to be mole fur or heron herl dyed in picric acid : white rabbit fur or goose herl dyed olive would not do! Now it just so happens that few fish can read. And of those that can, none read fly-tying textbooks. Thus we have never come across a trout that has said, when a fly has sailed over its nose, 'Ah! That is a ginger hackle and it should be honey dun. Or that is not heron herl – it looks more like goose to me!'

This syndrome is usually linked with the practice of giving artificial imitative flies names that bear no relationship with what they are imitating, and having a precise recipe of materials under that name. Greenwell's Glory, Tup's Indispensable, Lunn's Particular, Kite's Imperial, Wickham's Fancy. Sturdy's Fancy, Grey Wulff. Names of world famous flies, with precise tyings that must never be strayed from except by an infidel. But does a trout check that Kite's Imperial is tied properly with purple silk before it grabs hold? Never! Tie some with olive, brown and black silk and ask the trout!

I agree that, from the perspective of fly tying history, these precise tyings should be preserved. Some such tyings are included here. But we should remove some of the straitjacket of 'this material must be used and this material only'. For this reason many alternative materials have been suggested for you to choose from in many of the recipes that were given in the last section. Use whichever you have available. For they have all been tested on the trout, and the trout do not mind. It is time that we should drop the game of giving imitative trout flies fancy names : artificial flies should be named by either the dominant materials in their dressing, or the natural flies they are meant to represent. Perhaps too, in certain instances, the special region where or time of the year when the natural fly is dominant in the diet of trout.

National and regional variations in artificial flies

Any angler who travels widely through Europe, or even his or her own country, will notice regional differences in the way similar flies are tied. Or that, in one country or region, quite differenT styles of artificial flies are tied to imitate the same natural fly. This is because, until very recently, fly dressers worked in isolation, and solved the problems of imitating natural foods in quite different ways. For instance, an angler in northern Britain may use a Waterhen Bloa when olive duns are hatching : a very simple, sparsely dressed wet fly. A chalkstream angler in southern Britain or Normandy may choose a delicately dressed Olive Quill. An angler from southeastern France or Switzerland might choose a Cul de Canard dry fly. One from Austria or southern Germany may pick out a Deerhair Emerger. And an angler from Norway or

Sweden may well select a fur-bodied dun pattern. Occasionally an angler from one region will tell a visitor from another region, after looking into the visitor's fly box, 'They won't work here! Try my flies, they are much better!'

In the majority of cases such statements are just not true. I have been lucky to have fished for trout and grayling in almost every country of Europe, as well as many far beyond. Over the last eight years, whilst researching this and other books, I have collected and used fly patterns from all of them both in their 'local' lakes or rivers and far from their native home. And I have found that, provided the artificial fly has the triggers that the trout use when identifying the corresponding natural fly, they work everywhere. Used correctly they catch fish (just as when used wrongly, they will not).

SLOVENIAN   GERMAN   AUSTRIAN

BRITISH   AMERICAN   SCANDINAVIAN

The patterns chosen for this book are taken from throughout Europe; some are from North America and Australasia. They have been chosen because they effectively match, from the trout's point-of-view, species or groups of species of natural trout foods.

Confidence in your flies

If you have no confidence in a particular fly pattern, do not use it. Many anglers, looking through this book, may doubt the effectiveness of Oliver Kite's Bare Hook Nymph or Ed Zern's Pheasantless Pheasant Tail Nymph (p. 142). 'How can such a simple thing deceive a trout?' But they do, if you have the confidence to use them properly. The first time I used the Bare Hook Nymph I cast badly and the fly landed upstream of, and about one metre to the side of the trout I was aiming for. As the hook, with a few turns of wire wound round the shank, drifted downstream, the trout swam that metre to take the fly boldly! Yet I have many friends, good anglers who know this tale and who have seen the Bare Hook Nymph in action, who would never tie a Bare Hook Nymph on their leaders. They are right, for they would be stupid to use a fly that they had no confidence in. And often they use certain flies, effectively, that I am not confident of using.

Some flies are invented and then the recipe published before the fly has seen a trout! Never accept anybody's word for the efficiency of a new pattern. Test it yourself first.

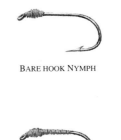

BARE HOOK NYMPH

The Holy Grail of fly dressing is the artificial fly that will catch, at the appropriate time, every fish that it is cast over. There is currently no such fly, and it is to be hoped that there never will be. Otherwise the fascination of inventing and testing new patterns will be gone for ever. Nevertheless there have been some anglers who, over the years, have described how whenever or wherever they cast their special flies they invariably caught the trout they were seeking. Such anglers deceived themselves by exaggerating successes and forgetting the failures! Remember that no matter how good an artificial fly, it will not catch every fish that it passes over.

PHEASANTLESS PHEASANT TAIL NYMPH

All one can advise is : try as many as you like and, based on your experience and careful observation of the natural foods of fish, make your personal choice of one or as many patterns as you like for each set of circumstances. Artificial flies are a part of the beauty of fly-fishing, and the freedom to make one's own selections and have favourites is high among its pleasures.

PARTS AND PROPORTIONS OF IMITATIVE FLIES

Wherever possible, match proportions with those of the natural insect. Time spent at the waterside with the natural insect and a notebook is never wasted but it is so easy to concentrate on colour and overlook the far more important triggers of shape, size and proportions. Of course, proportions do vary from one insect to another, so one cannot ever say categorically that, for instance, all dry flies should have a tail length equal to body length: in upwinged fly duns they may be shorter, in spinners much longer.

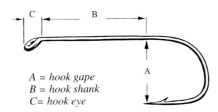

A = hook gape
B = hook shank
C = hook eye

At the same time many experienced fly-dressers adopt their own preferred proportions that may differ from those adopted by other similarly experienced fly-dressers. For instance, one may tie wings that are a little longer than most would tie them; some tie bodies that extend back level with the point of the hook while others, tying the same fly, tie the body back to the extreme end of the hook shank, and others would be somewhere in between. Who is correct? Let the fish be the judge! And since we are talking of experienced anglers as well as fly-dressers, then it is certain that the fish have happily confirmed that all are correct – at least, some or most of the time.

Nevertheless, there are some basic rules of parts and proportions that the novice would be recommended to obey and perhaps experiment with and modify in the light of experience.

Dry Flies

Tip: very short, e.g. 1-2 turns floss silk; imitates egg-sac in females or paler or darker tip to abdomen; optional and not tied on most flies.

Tail: length equals body length or 2× hook gape; in dun imitations it may be a little shorter and in spinners a little longer.

Body: length from just behind head to halfway between barb and point of the hook (minimum), or from just behind head to end of hook shank (maximum). There are exceptions (e.g. Black Gnats p. 194) where the body may be tied partway around bend of hook to mimic curved abdomen of natural. Try to taper the body, making it progressively wider to the front. Often it is worth trying to tie a slimmer abdomen and a thicker thorax, the thorax occupying about 40% at the front of the body.

Rib: wind in open turns with either a constant distance between turns or with turns gradually becoming further apart to the front, imitating the slightly wider segments at the front of the natural fly.

Note: Besides imitating the segmentation of a fly, the rib also reinforces the body. It is good practice to wind the ribbing material in the opposite direction to that in which the body was wound, so that the windings bind the body material. If wound in the same direction, then the turns of rib will tend to sink into the body material (especially fur and herl).

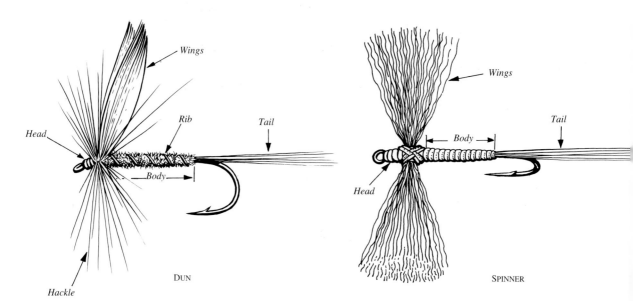

DUN   SPINNER

Body hackle: in sedges; hackle fibre length about 1× hook gape.

Hackle (or head or shoulder hackle): hackle fibre length about $1\frac{1}{2}$× hook gape.

Wings: upright in duns, spent in spinners, 'tied back' in sedges. In duns and spinners, maximum length 2× hook gape and width about equal to hook gape. In sedges maximum length of wings is a fraction greater than body length (so that they extend to or just beyond hook bend).

Head: equal in length to the diameter of the hook eye.

Antennae: in sedges, length about 1× body length or shorter.

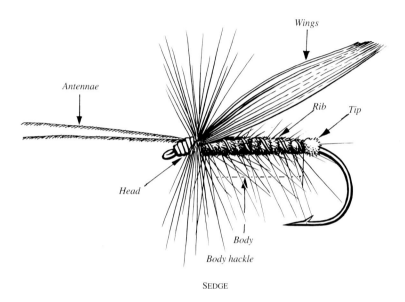

SEDGE

Soft-hackled Wet Flies

Tails: length about 1× body length or extending back to level with the tip of the wings.

Body: extends from just behind the head along the shank to opposite a point midway between barb and point of the hook.

Rib: regular open turns (usually 4-5 depending on hook size), see p. 241.

Hackle: fibre length either equal to body length (in winged patterns and some wingless patterns, depending on hackle material and to some extent personal preference), or extending to about the back of the hook bend (wingless patterns).

Wing: length 1-$1\frac{1}{2}$× hook length (varies with tradition and opinion and feeling of the dresser).

Head: length equal to hook eye diameter.

Nymphs

Tails: length generally equal to length of abdomen or about 50% hook shank length.

Abdomen: length $\frac{1}{2}$× shank length or, in some (e.g. Damselfly Nymphs) $\frac{2}{3}$× shank length; shape to match the general shape of the natural insect.

Rib: number of turns of ribbing material (usually at least 4) depend on size of nymph and the diameter of the ribbing material.

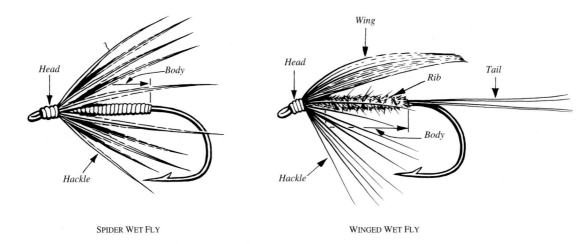

SPIDER WET FLY   WINGED WET FLY

Thorax: in length this is usually about $\frac{1}{2}\times$ hook shank length minus head length (or about $\frac{1}{3}\times$ shank length) but varies depending on natural nymph size and proportion; shape usually thicker than abdomen.

Wing cases (or wing buds): these imitate the buds of the developing wings; tied over back of thorax.

Legs: variable, but generally length equal to thorax length.

Head: length equal to hook eye diameter.

Pupae

Tails: (optional), length about $\frac{1}{3}\times$ length of abdomen.

Abdomen: about 60% of shank length (note, to imitate curved outline of natural abdomen the artificial abdomen is often tied slightly round the bend when straight shank hooks are being used; alternatively curved shank hooks are used). Slender.

Rib: usually 4-6 turns depending on size of hook and width of ribbing.

Thorax: about 40% of shank length; pronounced.

Head: length equal to hook eye diameter.

Head filaments: (optional), length about $\frac{1}{3}\times$ of abdomen.

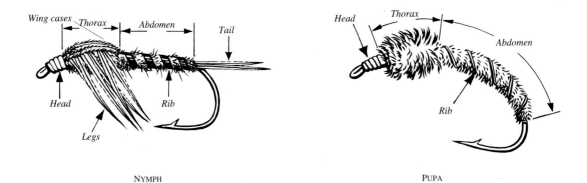

NYMPH   PUPA

PUTTING THE HOOK IN THE VICE

Some tyers put the hook deeply in the vice, completely hiding the point of the hook, others clamp the hook by just the bend so that point of hook is well exposed. The latter is correct: always fix the hook by just the extreme rear of the bend.

There are several reasons why this is the correct method, the chief ones being:

1. Many hooks have an offset or kirbed point (the point is set off sideways in relation to the rest of the hook to increase hooking power); to clamp hard over these points will lead to damage to the hook.

2. By having the minimum of the hook masked by the jaws, it is easier to see that the fly is being tied proportionally correctly.

3. By clamping the tip of the vice jaws to the bend of the hook the hook is held more securely (it tends to pivot when the bend is held at the back of the jaws).

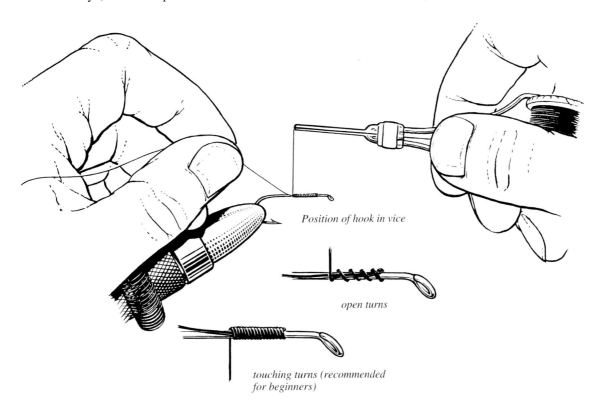

Position of hook in vice

open turns

touching turns (recommended for beginners)

Alternative methods of tying first bed of silk wraps on hook shank

SILK

With very few exceptions it is the tying silk (or, more often today, synthetic thread) that is used to bind all the parts of an artificial fly together. The hall-mark of a competent fly-dresser is the ability to manipulate thread; to make just the right number of wraps at each stage in the tying; to use the thread so that it binds in and holds perfectly each item in the fly; to exert the correct amount of pressure with the thread while tying; to complete the fly so that the thread does not undo while the fly is being fished. Choose the finest and strongest thread available.

Starting off

Beginning just behind the eye*, make turns of silk down the hook shank to the point where you will start tying in materials (tails etc.): where the body is a simple silk one, leave no gaps, nor accidentally lay one turn over a previous turn. Most tyers wrap thread by bringing the thread upwards on their side of the hookshank, over the top and then down on the opposite side. The loose end of thread, trapped by the turns of thread on the hookshank, is cut off 1-2 turns before the end of the body.

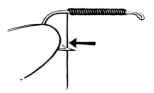

Thread wound down hookshank to midway between point and barb of hook. Note space left behind hook eye.

* One of the biggest mistakes made by beginners is to leave insufficient room at the front of the fly to tie a neat head. Leave one eye diameter clear of thread, body, rib, hackle and wing for the final tying of the head.

Pinch-and-loop

This is the method to use when some material is to be tied in so that it is bound firmly to the top of the hook shank (e.g. wings, tail fibres).

a. Hold material in position over hook using thumb and forefinger of right-hand (if you are right-handed). Check that length is correct.

b. Next grasp material between balls of thumb and middle finger of left hand (most books recommend forefinger and thumb – middle finger gives better alignment), with hook shank immediately below. Do not hold too tightly: just enough pressure to keep the material in position.

c. Holding bobbin-holder in right hand, bring thread up and over the material in a big loop, trapping the top of the loop between thumb and middle finger just above the material. We have now got the material that is to be tied in surrounded, but the loop does not touch nor bring pressure to bear on the material.

d. Bring the thread down and round, under the hookskank immediately below the materials that are to be tied in.

e. Now pull upwards, smoothly and firmly. As the loop tightens it will pull the materials onto the hookshank into the position that they were aligned by the finger-and-thumb 'pinch'.

f. Repeat to make the tie down more secure, and then make 1-2 more wraps.

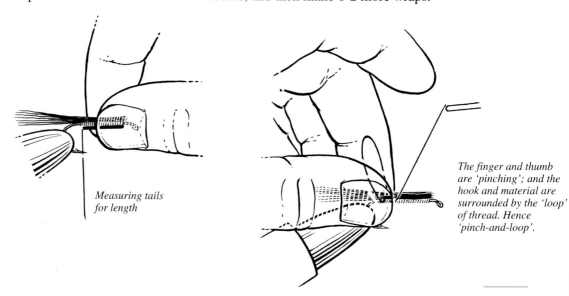

Measuring tails for length

The finger and thumb are 'pinching'; and the hook and material are surrounded by the 'loop' of thread. Hence 'pinch-and-loop'.

Soft Wraps and Hard Wraps

One of the most frustrating things for the novice is the way that materials slide around the hook when the silk is being wrapped over them or the end of a piece of material flicks away, pushed by the silk, when it is being tied in. Equally frustrating, for the novice who is wary of breaking the tying silk, is the finished fly that is not tied tightly enough and the entire dressing revolves around the hook or begins to unravel just after the fly is completed. These problems disappear when the tyer comes to appreciate and uses soft wraps and hard wraps.

Hard Wrap is where the thread is wrapped around the hook at the start of tying the fly, or to secure materials firmly, or to finish the fly. It is a wrap where the tension on the thread is great, but not so great that the silk breaks. We all suffer from breakages until we learn exactly how much force can be used in making hard wraps without breaking the silk.

It is also a problem faced by the beginner who has threads of several types, for each will have a different strength. I recommend all beginners to use just one type of thread (e.g. 8/0) made by the same manufacturer.

Soft Wrap is where the thread is wrapped around the hook and materials with very little tension: softly, but not too softly. Again, the learner must learn how soft to make good soft wraps. The soft wrap is the perfect wrap to use when tying in materials such as wire and tinsel ribbings, quill and herl bodies, synthetic wings, some sorts of tails (e.g. Micro-fibbets and goose biots), polythene shellbacks for shrimps etc. In fact, anything that does not demand a pinch-and-loop (see above), such as hair and feather wings, hair and feather fibre tails.

Exercise: Put a hook in the vice, wrap silk from head to end of shank with hard wraps: the silk wraps should not revolve when you pull down, firmly, on the end of the silk. Take hold of a piece of monofilament line. Hold it against and along the back of the hookshank and tie it in with two hard wraps – it will probably flick out of the way and you will have failed to tie it in!

Now try again, this time with very little tension on the silk. The monofilament stays in place and is trapped by the two soft wraps. But they are not tight enough to hold it firmly in place. Make two hard wraps and the monofilament is securely tied in. Repeat the exercise to learn just how tight you can make a hard wrap, and the limits of tension of the soft wrap.

Then, take a piece of monofilament, hold it along the top of the hookshank with the end just behind the hook eye, and tie it in and then secure it with touching wraps along the top of the hookshank. This is not as easy as it sounds! But it is a useful way of learning how to manipulate thread and make perfect soft wraps and hard wraps.

Number of wraps for tying in materials: Keep these to a minimum. Usually 2 are sufficient; perhaps 3.

At the rear end of the fly: you need to tie in tails, ribbing and body material. How? Put the hook in the vice and make hard wraps from just behind the eye down the shank to the point at which these materials must be tied in.

A basic rule of fly dressing is to tie tail, rib and body material onto the hook in the reverse order that they will later be used. Thus tie in tails first – 1-2 pinch-and-loops or 1-2 soft wraps. Next the rib, with 1 soft wrap (this soft wrap also adds another wrap over the tail base). Finally the body material (e.g. bunch of herls) with 1-2 soft wraps and 1 hard wrap. All these 'tying in' wraps progress slightly backwards so that you are not building wrap-on-wrap and a lump at the end of the body. Now wind the silk forwards with alternating soft wraps and hard wraps over all previous wraps, continuing to the point that will be the front of the body. Cut waste tail butts, rib and body material at the front.

If these 'wastes' are cut too short (so that they do not underlie all the body) then there will be a step or uneven lump in the body. Wind the body material forwards in close (touching), but not overlapping. turns: tie it in at the front with 2 hard wraps and trim away excess. Wind the rib in the opposite direction to the body: tie it in with 2 hard wraps and trim away excess.

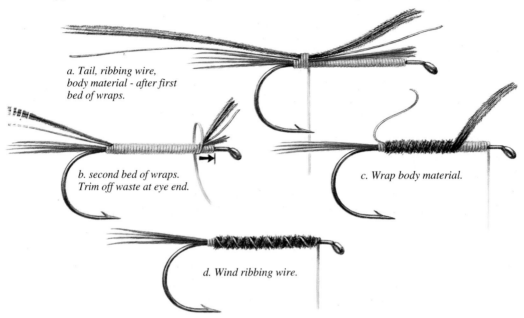

a. Tail, ribbing wire, body material - after first bed of wraps.

b. second bed of wraps. Trim off waste at eye end.

c. Wrap body material.

d. Wind ribbing wire.

Figure-of-eight

This is a useful way of separating a bunch of material fibres into two or three (for example, separating a bunch of tail fibres to give two or three distinct tails; separating a bunch of hairs or feather fibres to produce two distinct wings).

Tie in the material with 1-2 soft wraps and 1-3 hard wraps. Now separate into 2 bundles. Bring the thread forwards between the 2 bundles and back to the other side of the shank. Bring the thread back under the shank and then pass it back through the wings, crossing the original separating thread. Thus the two wings (or tails) are separated by a figure-of-eight thread. Provided very fine thread (8/0 or thinner) is being used, repeat the figure-of-eight process to firm-up the separation.

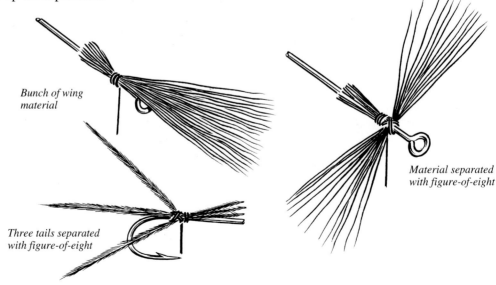

Bunch of wing material

Material separated with figure-of-eight

Three tails separated with figure-of-eight

Finishing off the fly: silk heads.

The fly is almost complete, but we need to tie off the silk at the head so that it will not undo. Make wraps of silk just behind the eye, building up a neat head. You can now tie-off in one of two ways:

a. Half-hitch. The traditional way (pre-dating the whip-finish). Make 2-4 separate half-hitches; tighten the last, cut off and give the head a good coat of varnish to seal the knots.

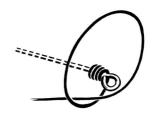

b. Whip-finish. The most secure way. This can be done by hand or by gadget; most tyers today use a whip-finish tool. Newcomers to fly-dressing are urged to purchase a good (Matarelli or Thompson are available throughout Europe) whip-finish tool. Full instructions are provided.

Also available is the half-hitch tool: buy one of these (or several with different sizes of holes at the front to fit over different sizes of hook eye. A good alternative is a range of ball-point pen cases with the inner ball-point tube removed. This can be used both to make half-hitches and 3-4 turn whip finishes.

To make half-hitches – hold the silk taut between fly head and bobbin holder (in left hand); hold half-hitch tool under and at right angles to thread; twist half-hitch tool down and round the thread trapping a single loop; slide hole at front of half-hitch tool over eye of hook; pull on silk and allow the loop to slide down the tapering front of the tool and over the eye of the hook; remove tool and pull half-hitch tight.

To make simple whip-finish – as for half-hitch but make 3-4 turns with the tool around the thread, trapping 3-4 loops around the tool. Slide these to the head of the fly and then tighten up, the result is a 3-4 turn whip-finish.

A useful tip: keep the turns round the tool fairly slack and, when sliding the loops from tool to the head of the fly, keep the tool almost vertical over the hook eye. The loops will slide easily, aided by gravity.

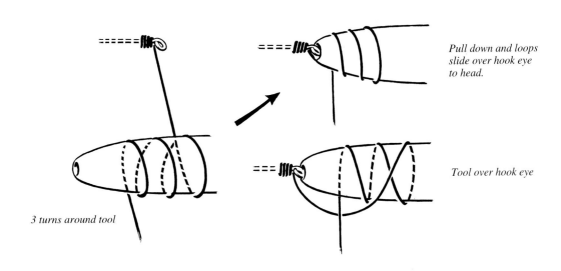

Pull down and loops slide over hook eye to head.

Tool over hook eye

3 turns around tool

WEIGHTED UNDERBODIES

It is essential that many larval, pupal and nymphal imitations are weighted so that they sink quickly. The main way of achieving this is with an underbody of lead wire or foil (note that while the use of lead split shot has been banned in certain European countries because of the harm it may cause to waterfowl, lead wire has no such effects and is not prohibited).

Wound wire underbodies

Whip the end of a piece of lead wire along the top of the hook shank, with the end of the wire just in front of where the end of the body will be (but keep the space clear behind the eye for the head of the fly). Then wind the lead wire in close turns round the hookshank. Bind these turns down with silk, before completing the fly.

In some wind just a lead wire 'under-thorax': this will help produce a pronounced thorax and also result in flies that are about midway in weight between a full-leaded body and an un-leaded body. These middle-weights can be used in slower or shallower water where the fully-leaded ones might snag the bottom.

Strip wire bodies

In these the wire (or foil) is whipped in straight lengths along the hook shank. It is possible to:

1. have various weights, by tying underbodies with 0, 1, 2, 3 and more lead wire or foil strips.

2. to pre-shape the body of the finished fly with the lead wire or foil underbody. For instance, build up a humped underbody for Freshwater Shrimp imitations; or to make a tapering underbody for upwinged fly nymph imitations; or to combine a wire strip under-abdomen with a wound wire under-thorax to produce an effective stonefly nymph underbody. It is often useful to spend a tying session just whipping lead wire underbodies to hooks, completing the tyings during a later session. The underbodies can then be given a coat of thin cement, with plenty of time to dry. It is always good practice to cement thoroughly over lead underbodies. This inhibits the metal lead oxidising (to lead oxide) and discolouring the body.

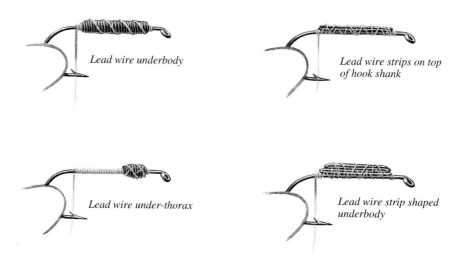

Lead wire underbody

Lead wire strips on top of hook shank

Lead wire under-thorax

Lead wire strip shaped underbody

TAILS

Hackle fibre tails are the most traditional (both cock hackle fibres for dry flies, and hen or soft hackle – e.g. partridge – for wet flies and nymphs). Tie these in by pinch-and-loop or with soft and then hard wraps at the end of the hook before tying in the body (and ribbing). Often these fibres will bed down in one tight clump; splay them after making the first 2 wraps by pressing down on them with the thumb nail.

Microfibbet tails are a synthetic alternative to the cock hackle fibre tails in dry flies. Tie in 3 or 6, 2 or 4; separate them using the tying silk 'figure-of-eight' to make three or two tails (each with 1 or 2 fibres)

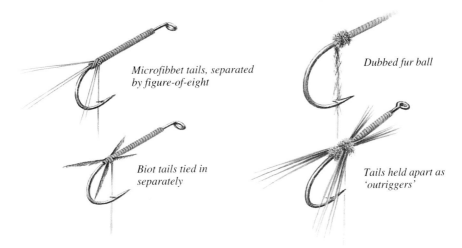

Microfibbet tails, separated by figure-of-eight

Dubbed fur ball

Biot tails tied in separately

Tails held apart as 'outriggers'

Biot/Monofil Nymph tails are tied in separately at the side of the end of the abdomen. Usually 2 tails, tie one in on each side using a soft wrap followed by a hard wrap.

Outriggers are excellent dry fly tails; the body must be made of fur. Take a tiny wisp of fur dubbing, dub on the silk, and wind a tiny ball to represent the end of the abdomen. Now take one tail – a sparse bunch of cock hackle fibres, 1-2 microfibbets – and tie in at one side immediately behind the tiny fur ball. Tie in another bunch to the other side. Check the arrangement is correct before completing the body of dubbed fur: the two tails should stick out at an acute angle from the body in about the same plane as the hook shank.

Separated hackle tails are an alternative form of outrigger where the dry fly body is not fur. Tie in a piece of floss silk (colour as body colour) at the end of, and extending in line with, the hookshank. Tie in a bunch of cock hackle fibres (the tail) on top of the floss silk. Separate this bunch of hackle fibres by pulling the floss silk through the split bunch and binding it down tightly. Complete the fly. In very small dry flies tying thread can be used instead of the thick floss.

Floss silk and bunch of tails tied in

Floss silk brought forward to split tails

Floss silk tied down before body is dressed

BODIES

Think constantly of the thickness and shape of the body of the insect you are trying to imitate when you tie bodies; it is easy to tie bodies that are over-thick. Also remember that most insects have a slender abdomen and thicker thorax, a feature that might be a 'trigger' for the fish.

Silk bodies

2 layers of silk, the first being the initial wrap from behind the hook eye to the end of the hook shank (see proportions); the second wrap is back over this first layer (perhaps after tying in tails and rib at the end of the body).

Floss silk bodies

These produce slender flat bodies; rib them with fine wire, tinsel etc. Take a length of floss silk and untwist it before tying in at the end of the hook shank and winding forwards. Many floss silks will produce a lumpy body if they are not unwound first.

Herl bodies

A super body material. Tie in herls (heron, goose dyed or undyed, crow, pheasant tail, unstripped peacock etc) by their tips, wind silk back to the front of the body, and wind the herls forwards in close, but not overlapping, turns. Number of herls: for most bodies, 5-6 for size 10-12 hook, 3-4 for size 14-16 hook; where herls are short, increase number used by 1-2. For durability always rib (e.g. with fine wire) remembering to wind the rib in the opposite direction to that in which the herls were wound. Although most fly tying recipes do not stipulate it, make two extra turns of herl, over each other, at the front of the body to represent the thorax.

Dubbed fur bodies

Also superb, though neglected by some who do not know how to dub fur correctly. After winding silk to end of hook shank, take a pinch of fur and spin it onto the thread between finger and thumb of right hand (right-handed tyers); hold fur over the silk between thumb and middle (or forefinger) of right hand and spin by moving thumb on top to the left, finger underneath to right; repeat until the fur is nicely moulded around the silk.

Beginners find this difficult: the dubbing movement is a rolling of fur, between finger and thumb, around the thread. It is easier to achieve with tiny amounts of fur than big chunks. If a thick body is needed, dub the fur in several tiny amounts rather than all at once.

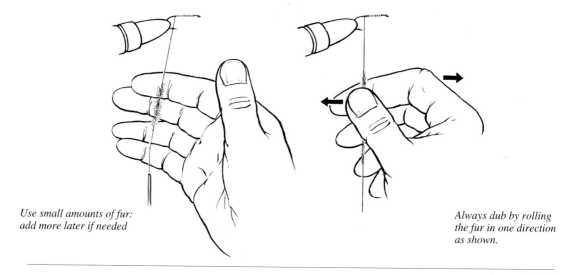

Use small amounts of fur: add more later if needed

Always dub by rolling the fur in one direction as shown.

Wind that dubbed silk around the hook to make the body; add extra dubbing, a little at a time until the body is completed. Beginners should always start dubbing with soft fine furs with long hairs (e.g. rabbit) before trying coarser furs with short hairs (e.g. hare's ear, seal).

As with herls, try to produce a narrow abdomen and slightly thicker thorax: dub the fur a little more thickly at the front of the body.

Note that in nymph, pupa and emerger imitations there is an advantage in having a dubbed body on the scruffy side: bits of fur sticking out add life to the fly; perhaps they simulate gills. Some tyers deliberately pull out hairs to increase the straggliness of the fly: this is done with the Gold Ribbed Hare's Ear to simulate legs (p. 124).

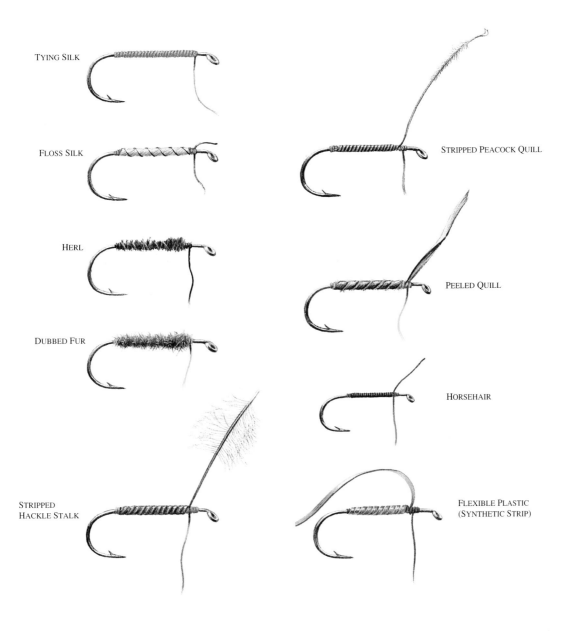

TYING SILK

FLOSS SILK

HERL

DUBBED FUR

STRIPPED
HACKLE STALK

STRIPPED PEACOCK QUILL

PEELED QUILL

HORSEHAIR

FLEXIBLE PLASTIC
(SYNTHETIC STRIP)

Stripped hackle stalk bodies

Look excellent in dry flies. Take some cock or hen hackles of the appropriate shade (or white ones and dye them after stripping). Strip away all fibres; tie in at the end of the shank by the tip and wind forwards with touching wraps; tie off with 3 hard wraps.

Stripped peacock quill bodies

Take some herls from a peacock eye; hold by the tips in left hand and, using thumb and fore-finger of right hand, rub down the herl removing of all the short fibres. (Note that some people use an eraser to rub off these fibres.) When fully stripped the quill can be dyed or used as natural. Tie a stripped quill in by the tip and wind over the silk wraps along the hook shank; for extra durability, give the hook shank a thin coat of varnish before winding on the quill.

Peeled quill bodies

(These are also often used for abdomen rib in stonefly nymph imitations, p. 167). Soak some large quills (goose, crow, pheasant) in warm water to soften the outer sheath. Take a sharp knife and make a nick in the quill; grasp this nick and pull, peeling the quill outer sheath away. From one quill you may obtain 2-4 peeled strips. Put the peeled strip glossy (outer) side down on a hard surface and scrape away any pith. If necessary, dye to appropriate colour. Trim sides parallel with each other; point the tip. Tie in by pointed tip and wind forwards: these produce a superbly segmented body and a splendid rib over a dubbed fur body for nymphs.

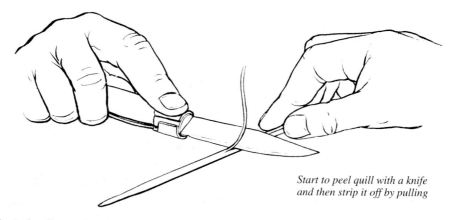

Start to peel quill with a knife and then strip it off by pulling

Horsehair bodies

Excellent for smaller dry flies and nymphs. Obtain hairs from horse tails: black, brown, white (white ones can be dyed). Tie in hair at end of hook shank and wind in touching turns. For a particularly super segmented body wind two hairs of different colour (e.g. black and light brown).

Synthetic strip bodies

These include materials that must be cut from a large piece (e.g. 'flexibody', latex, plastazote, polythene from a clear or coloured poly-bag) or that come already in a strip (e.g. Swanundaze). Used mostly for nymphs and pupae, often with an underbody (e.g. dubbed fur, silk). Take silk to end of hook shank; tie in tails; tie in a thin strip (2-3cm) of cream latex (from medical glove); dub thread with fine-textured light olive fur and wind to the front of the fly, making this underbody thicker at the front; wind latex over in slightly over-lapping turns (to give segmentation). This can be the basis for many nymphs (e.g. Latex Mayfly p. 162, Stonefly p. 167).

Detached bodies

For dry flies, also some 'wiggle' nymphs; these can be purchased; making your own is quite straightforward. Take a sparse bunch of deerhair, hold along a slender needle, and bind down with thread. Then run thread down body to give segmentation, and tie off the other end. Cement thread and slide body from needle. Tie in different shades of deerhair to imitate mayflies, p. 164, damsel nymphs, p. 172, daddy-long-legs p. 197.

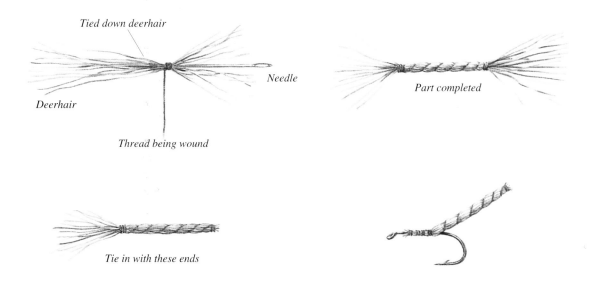

Tied down deerhair

Needle

Deerhair

Part completed

Thread being wound

Tie in with these ends

Tying detached bodies

Ribbing

Ribbing simulates segmentation and, when the rib is of wire or oval tinsel, adds durability to the fly. Some have argued that the use of copper, gold or silver wire or tinsel adds 'flash', but this is not always the case for the wire and tinsel simply reflect the colour of light surrounding them and thus tend to take on the reflection of water colour.

Tie in the tip of a length of ribbing material, after the tails have been tied in, before the body material; form the body and then wind the rib in open turns forwards around and along the body. It is standard practice to wind the rib **in the opposite direction to the direction that the body was wound**: this tends to bind down on the body rather than sink into the body material.

Segmentation, being such a conspicuous feature of the bodies of all insects and crustaceans, may be an important trigger and is something well worth incorporating into any imitation.

An evenly ribbed dubbed fur body

Body Divisions

Often the body is tied, not as a single unit, but as 'abdomen', 'thorax', and sometimes also 'head'. Many examples are given in the section on imitative flies. It is always worth trying to incorporate these into imitative flies because by doing so a more realistic shape of artificial fly will be produced; and remember that shape can be an important 'trigger'.

The basic technique is to tie in an abdomen of herl, silk, dubbed fur etc. at the end of the hook shank and wind around the rear 50% of the hook shank. Rib this abdomen. Next tie in the thorax material (of the same or a different material) and use this as the next 40% of the body. The head, of silk, or sometimes herl or dubbed fur, is wound on the front 10% of the body. For dry flies, try stripped quill abdomen, fur or herl thorax, silk head; silk abdomen and head with herl or fur thorax; horsehair abdomen, fur or herl thorax, silk head. For stonefly nymph, try herl abdomen, and fur thorax and head.

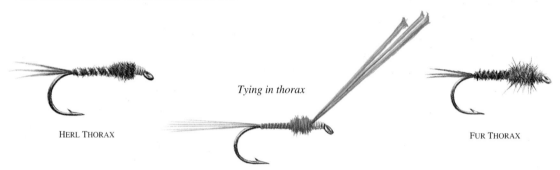

Tying in thorax

HERL THORAX

FUR THORAX

Some imitative flies have backs: e.g. Grey Shrimp 2 (p. 199). The basic technique is: after completing lead underbody (p. 236), at rear tie in first a bunch of grey partridge hackle fibres for the tail, second a length of silver wire for the rib and last a thin strip of polythene. Now dub the silk with fur from a hare's mask and wind this forwards over the underbody to form the body. Secure with 2 turns of silk behind the eye. Bring the polythene strip forwards over the back of the body and tie down with 2 turns of silk. Now wind the wire forwards in wide turns, to form the rib, suggest segmentation and also tie down the back; make 2 turns of silk to tie down the wire, then cut away surplus wire. Make several wraps of silk at the head and tie off with half-hitches or whip-finish.

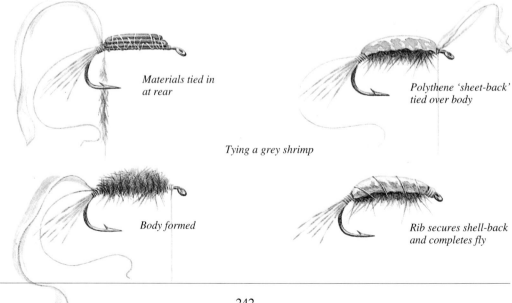

Materials tied in at rear

Polythene 'sheet-back' tied over body

Tying a grey shrimp

Body formed

Rib secures shell-back and completes fly

HACKLES

Hackles suggest legs; they are also used to aid flotation in dry flies.

Dry Fly Hackles

Usually top quality cock hackles with, in recent years, specially bred, 'genetic' strains (e.g. Hebert, Keough, Metz, Hoffman, Spencer) dominating. The three main hackling styles are:

Hackles = Head Hackles = Shoulder Hackles

These are wound at the front of the body, behind the head. The basic technique is: complete the fly up to the hackle; take a cock hackle with the correct fibre length (see p. 229). Strip away the down and softer fibres at the base of the hackle. Hold the hackle with stalk extending to rear and feather to front, the stalk lying alongside the body; have concave (inner) side of feather facing you. Now make three wraps of silk that fix hackle in position, making wraps backwards from just behind eye (leave room for head). Now fix hackle pliers to tip of hackle and wind hackle around the hook in close touching turns, making the turns backwards towards the tail; the concave inner side of the feather fibres should face forwards. When the hackle has been wound, bring the silk forwards in open turns through the wound hackle so that it is firmly bound down. Make several turns in front of the hackle to create the head; tie off the silk. Finally snip away the surplus hackle feather tip and stalk.

Some dry flies may have 2-3 different hackles: these might be separate (one in front of the other) or mixed (one wound through the other or both wound simultaneously).

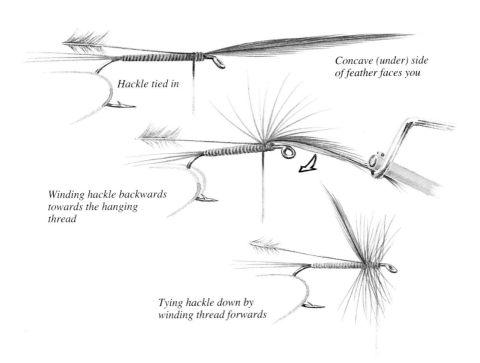

Hackle tied in

Concave (under) side of feather faces you

Winding hackle backwards towards the hanging thread

Tying hackle down by winding thread forwards

Palmered Hackle = Body Hackle

This is a cock hackle wound round and along the entire body of the fly from tail to just behind the head; commonly used in Sedge imitations (p. 182). Technique: complete the fly body but leave the ribbing material trailing at the rear. Take a cock hackle and strip away down and soft fibres at base. Hold feather, at the front of the body, at right angles to the hook shank with stalk down and feather up, concave inner side of feather facing forwards; make 2-3 tight wraps around base of hackle and hook to hold hackle firmly in place. Now fix tip of hackle in hackle pliers and wind hackle in open turns down body; keep hold of hackle pliers and wind rib in the opposite direction through the hackle, and up the body in open turns. Make 2-3 turns of silk around rib material close to the head; snip away surplus rib and the hackle stalk.

In dry sedge imitations, another conventional hackle is often tied in front of the palmered hackle to increase flotation.

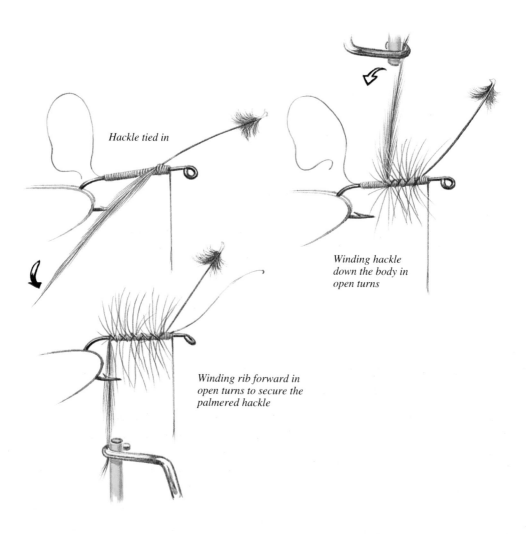

Hackle tied in

Winding hackle down the body in open turns

Winding rib forward in open turns to secure the palmered hackle

Parachute Hackle

In conventional hackle and palmered hackles the hackle is wound around the hook; in parachute hackle the hackle is wound around some support that stands vertically up from the hook shank (e.g. base of wings). Technique (as for Olive Dun 5, p. 154): complete the fly with tails, body and wing, the wing being tied vertically (see Wings, below). Make 3 turns of silk around the wing base. Take a cock hackle and strip away down and soft fibres from base; tie this in at base of wing, with concave side of feather downwards. Take tip of feather in hackle pliers and wind hackle around base of wing, making successive turns beneath earlier turns. Move forward facing fibres back and make 2 turns of silk over tip of feather and hook shank just behind eye. Complete head and finish fly. Clip away hackle stalk and tip. Stroke front hackle fibres forwards.

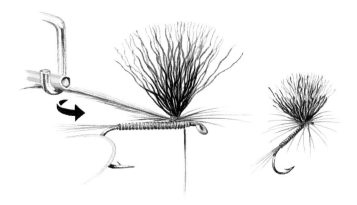

The hackle has been tied in at wing base and is being wound around the wing base. Note that, with the hackle tied concave side down, the hackle fibres tend to curve downwards. Whip finish with the half-hitch tool (p. 235); this prevents forward pointing hackle fibres being trapped.

Wet Fly/Nymph Hackles

These are generally soft hackles (e.g. hen, partridge, grouse) that will 'work' in the water. There are two main ways of tying them:

1. Hackles with fine stalks (hen, starling): complete the fly up to the hackle. Take the hackle and strip away base down. Tie in with 2-3 turns of silk, stalk pointing backwards and feather forwards with convex (top) of feather pointing towards you, the tyer. Fix tip of hackle in hackle pliers and wind the hackle round the hook, 2-3 turns at most, each turn being made behind the previous one. Wind silk forwards through the hackle, pull fibres backwards, make turns of silk at head and tie-off. Snip out hackle stalk and surplus tip.

2. Hackles with thick stalks (partridge, grouse, woodcock, snipe): as above except that the hackle is tied in by its tip. Take the hackle tip in the hackle pliers and stroke back all the fibres. Take the hackle from the hackle pliers and tie in as above, but this time by the tip. Fix hackle pliers onto the stalk for winding hackle around hook; 2 turns. Tie in hackle, tie off fly, and snip away hackle stalk and tip.

Hackles with thin stalks

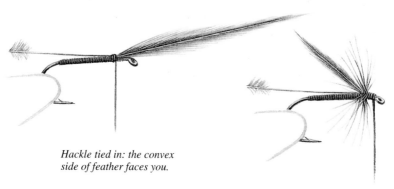

Hackle tied in: the convex side of feather faces you.

The hackle has been wound, 3 times, backwards. The silk is then wound forwards in 2-3 turns through the hackle to bind it down.

Hackles with thick stalks

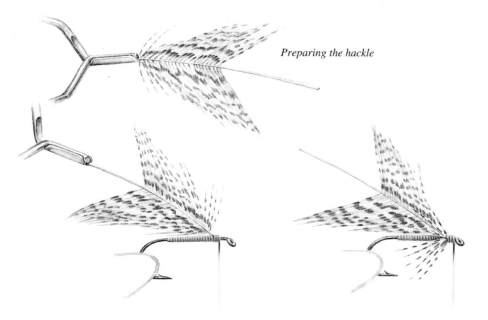

Preparing the hackle

The hackle has been tied in by its tip and the first turn is being made around the hook shank in front of the thread.

Two turns of hackle have been made and the thread wound forward through the hackle in 2-3 turns.

LEGS

Instead of a hackle, some flies have legs tied in a different way:

False Hackle

A bunch of hackle fibres (or herl tips) is taken and tied in either as a single bunch under the hook at the front of the body, or as two bunches, one to either side at the front of the body.

Technique: in each case, take a bunch of fibres in the right hand, hold in position and check for length. Transfer to left hand, hold them in position, and make 1-2 soft wraps and then 1-2 hard wraps to tie them in. Snip away the bases of the fibres.

One bunch of herl tips tied at one side of the hook

A second bunch is tied in on the other side

The herl bases are clipped away to leave the two bunches of legs

Hackle Legs

A whole feather is taken and used to produce the legs.

Technique: Take a suitable hackle (e.g. brown partridge); hold tip in hackle pliers and stroke other fibres backwards. Tie this feather in by its tip, feather stalk pointing backwards and concave (underside) of the feather pointing upwards, on the back of the fly either at the end of the abdomen (as in Freshwater Shrimp and Hog-louse imitations, pp. 198-200) or base of the thorax (nymphs). After completing the body/thorax, bring that feather forwards over the back of the body/thorax and tie in at the head with 2 hard wraps; snip off surplus. The concave side will now point down, and the fibres of the feather that are sticking out from the side will tend to point out-and-down like real insect legs along abdomen/thorax. The addition of the back (see above) or wing cases (see below) will further tend to push the legs downwards.

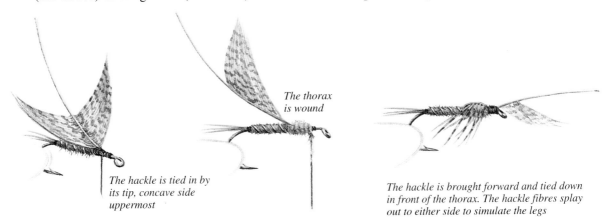

The thorax is wound

The hackle is tied in by its tip, concave side uppermost

The hackle is brought forward and tied down in front of the thorax. The hackle fibres splay out to either side to simulate the legs

Herls and Hackle Stalks

These can be tied in and cut to length to simulate legs. Tie in individual legs with 1-2 soft wraps, then 1-2 hard wraps. See Corixa (p. 174), adult Legged Midges (p. 194) and Hawthorn Fly (p. 195). In Daddy-long-legs imitations, pheasant tail herls are knotted twice before tying in (p. 196).

WING CASES

Wing cases are found covering the back of the natural nymph thorax; as the nymphs grow so the wing cases enlarge and become a conspicuous feature, perhaps an important trigger. There are two general ways of imitating wing cases:

Wrapped Wing Cases

Complete the abdomen but, before tying in the legs and thorax, tie in the wing case material at the front of the abdomen on the upper (back side) of the nymph. Technique: take the bunch of herls, strip of raffine, slip of feather fibres from a quill, or bunch of hairs for the wing cases and tie them in (with 2 soft and 1 hard wraps) so that they point backwards (herl or hair, tie in by the tips). Now tie in the thorax and legs; complete those stages. Bring the wing case material forwards over the back of the thorax and tie it down firmly at the front. Note: if the pattern has legs make sure that there is enough wing case material to extend partly down the sides of the nymph to force the legs slightly downwards.

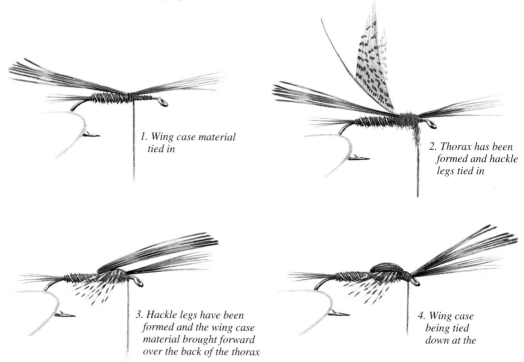

1. Wing case material tied in

2. Thorax has been formed and hackle legs tied in

3. Hackle legs have been formed and the wing case material brought forward over the back of the thorax

4. Wing case being tied down at the

Cul de canard wing buds

These are tied in exactly as above, in unweighted nymphs – use 1-2 CDC feathers as wing bud; but where the wing case is cul de canard the aim is to mimic the nymph at the water surface in the process of hatching. So leave a tiny gap between back of thorax and cul de canard; this gap will hold air and support the fly in the surface film.

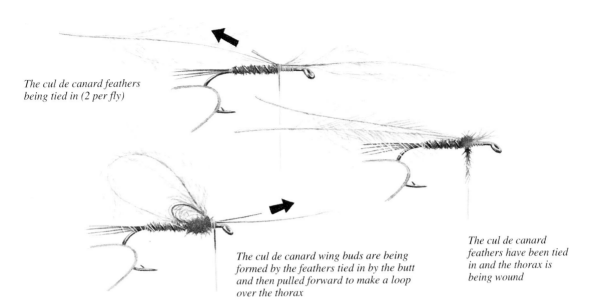

The cul de canard feathers being tied in (2 per fly)

The cul de canard wing buds are being formed by the feathers tied in by the butt and then pulled forward to make a loop over the thorax

The cul de canard feathers have been tied in and the thorax is being wound

Tied-back Wing Cases

In these the fly is completed up to the end of tying in thorax and legs; the wing cases are then tied in before the head is tied. Technique: using either wing burners (nymph wing case) or by cutting, produce a wing case from a latex sheet, raffine or a lacquered section of quill slip. Tie in firmly so that the wing case extends back over the top of the thorax and base of the abdomen.

Some tyers add two wing cases: they tie one in when the rear half of the thorax has been constructed, and the other when the thorax has been completed. Colour either before or after tying in with suitable lacquer or permanent felt tip pen.

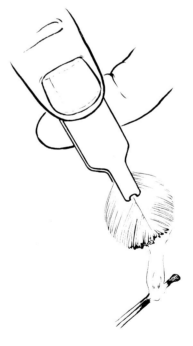

A tied-back wing case: this lies over the back of the thorax

The wing burner is ideal for making tied-back wing cases. After centering the feather in the tool, all the feather is burnt away leaving the intact wing case. Burners come in different styles and sizes to create the complete range of insect wings. This one is to simulate stonefly wings.

WINGS

For many new fly dressers, tying in wings (especially feather and hair wings) is the most difficult stage in tying dry flies. Before attempting to wing any fly, the beginner is urged to practise
winging a plain hook shank with just a single layer of wound tying silk. When this shank can
be 'winged' correctly, then move on to winging entire flies.

   Here we will start with the simpler forms of winging and advance to the more complicated.

Synthetic cut wings

These come printed on sheets and it is simply a matter of
cutting out the wings and tying them onto the fly. Many of
these printed sheets print the wings in rows, and give the
ideal hook size for the wings in each row. These are most
popular for stonefly and sedge imitations, where the wing
is tied at the front of the thorax so that it lies back low over
the body (as in adult stoneflies and sedges).

Wing cut out *Wing before
cutting out*

Synthetic hair wings:

Example, Antron, poly-yarn. These are very easy to handle compared with natural furs; because the individual fibres are fine and not tapering they tend not to splay out like many natural furs. These are tied in three main ways:

Upright wing

As in upwinged fly imitations: when starting the fly, take a length of poly-yarn and tie in about
3 eye diameters back from the hook eye on top of the hook shank, with the part that will eventually be the wing pointing forwards over the hook eye. Continue to wind silk down the hook
shank over the butt of the winging material. Now tie tails, abdomen and ribbing. Then take
material for thorax (herls, dubbed fur etc, which may be the same as for the abdomen) and
wind forwards to behind the wing and then round and in front of the wing: this thorax material
should force the wing into an upright position. Tie in and wind the hackle (if the fly is hackled); note that this sort of wing lends itself to a parachute hackle (see p. 245). After completing
the fly, trim the wing to length.

Wing tied in and body being formed   *Turns of body material in front of the wing
                                             raises the wing into the upright position*

Sloping back wing

As in stoneflies, sedges and two-winged flies: tie the fly to completion of the abdomen. Now take a length of poly-yarn and tie it in just in front of the abdomen by the tip, the wing pointing backwards over the abdomen. Now take the thorax material and wind over the root of the wing. Complete the fly and cut the wing to length.

If you want to have the wing standing slightly upwards as well as sloping back over the body, make one turn of body material behind the tied-in wing (this will lift the wing a little) before making turns in front of the wing (this semi-back style can be used for upwinged fly dun imitations).

Wing tied back with thorax material in front

Spent wings

As in spent mayfly spinners: tie the fly to completion of the abdomen. Now take a length of poly-yarn and tie it across the top of the hook shank in front of the abdomen, so that you form two wings, one to either side, at right angles to the hook shank. To do this, after making 1-2 soft wraps and 1-2 hard wraps, make figure-of-eight turns around both wings and hook shank (see p. 234). Now take the thorax material: this may be herls tied in by their tips in front of the wings or fur dubbed onto the silk. Wind this material around the bases of both wings in a similar figure-of-eight; the pronounced thorax thus formed will also support and hold the wings in position. Complete the fly. Finally take hold of both wings, hold them up together directly above the body, and cut to length (this guarantees that they are the same length).

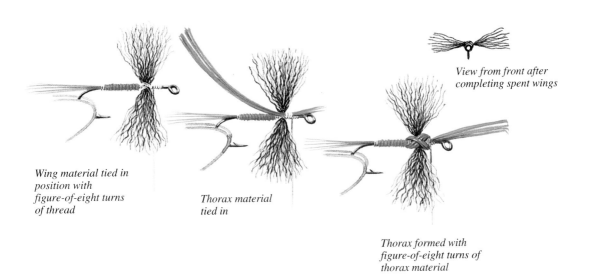

View from front after completing spent wings

Wing material tied in position with figure-of-eight turns of thread

Thorax material tied in

Thorax formed with figure-of-eight turns of thorax material

Feather bunch wings

Can be used in all dry flies with wing upright (as for upwinged flies), tied back (as for stone-flies, sedges and two-winged flies) or in a spent position (dead flies lying on the water). Feather bunch wings may use either **a bunch of feather fibres stripped from a quill**, (hackle fibres, herl fibres) or **whole feathers**, (cul de canard, dyed teal or mallard breast or flank). They are tied in and manipulated in exactly the same way as synthetic hair wings, but are more tricky to use (partly because you start off with a much shorter bunch of material).

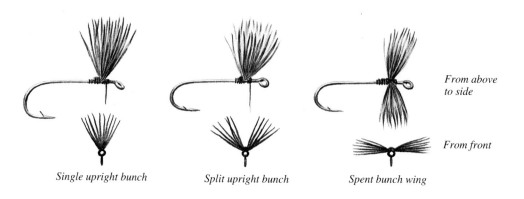

*From above
to side*

From front

Single upright bunch   *Split upright bunch*   *Spent bunch wing*

Hackle Point Wings, Burnt Wings, Cut Wings

Because of their similarity as far as tying is concerned I treat these together. The difference comes in selection and preparation of the wing: hackle point – the tip (or point) of a hackle or other feather is used for the wing; burnt wing – a feather selected to make the wing is held in a specially shaped pair of forceps ('wing burner'), and surplus feather burnt away leaving an un-burnt shaped wing in the forceps; cut wing – the wing is cut, using a special wing cutter, from a feather selected (it works rather like a pastry cutter).

In all cases the wing is tied in by the shaft or quill of the feather that has been stripped of its fibres just below the part of the feather that will be the wing of the fly. Do not peel these fibres away, trim them with scissors leaving a toothed quill: this will increase purchase when the wing is tied in.

These wings are tied in, one to either side of the body, using 1- 2 soft and then 1-2 hard wraps. The two wings can then be manipulated into their final position (upright or spent) using figure-of-eight turns with the tying silk (and thorax material).

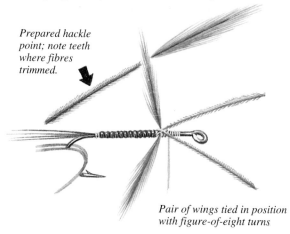

*Prepared hackle
point; note teeth
where fibres
trimmed.*

*Pair of wings tied in position
with figure-of-eight turns*

Hair wings

Hair makes superb wings. Begin with fine furs (e.g. squirrel) before progressing to deer, elk, moose which tend to splay round the hook shank when they are tied in. It is essential to practise these on a bare hook before trying to tie them into a fly.

Preparation of wing: cut a bunch of hairs, hold by the tips and stroke away any down or shorter hairs at the base. Make sure that the hair tips are all in line; if necessary use a hair stacker, p. 211.

Hair Stacker: after removing fluff and short hairs from the base of the bunch, put tips downward into stacker. Tap, hard. The tips will be aligned

Hair wing tied back, flat over body

Flat wing

The easiest hair wing is one that is tied back over the body (for a sedge or stonefly imitation). Hold the bunch of hairs in the right hand and check for length. Transfer to left hand, holding in thumb and middle finger low over hook. Tie in pinch-and-loop style (p. 232), making first 1-2 loops as soft wraps, then 1-2 loops as hard wraps, each turn being in front of the previous turn. Trim away surplus butts. Now soak base of hairs with cement. hold wing firmly in place and make 2-3 more hard wraps over wet base of wing.

Split hair wing

Take the bunch of hairs, check the wing length required, and tie down with hair (wing) tips pointing forwards over eye of hook: tie in pinch-and-loop style (p. 232), making first 1-2 loops as soft wraps, then 1-2 loops as hard wraps, each turn being behind the previous turn. Trim away surplus butts. Now soak base of hairs with cement. Hold wing firmly in place and make 2-3 more hard wraps over wet base of wing.

Now decide which of the three winging styles is required:

For upright single – pull the wing into an upright position, make 2-3 turns of silk round the hook shank in front of the wing, then make 3-5 turns of silk around the base of the wing to bind

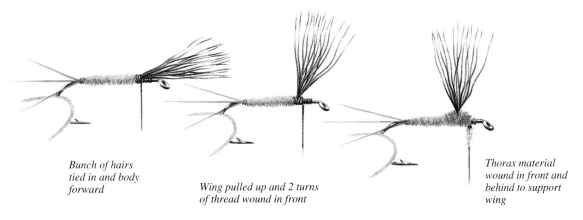

Bunch of hairs tied in and body forward

Wing pulled up and 2 turns of thread wound in front

Thorax material wound in front and behind to support wing

the wing fibres together. Then take the thorax material (e.g. dubbed fur) and wind around the hook shank, with at least 2 turns in front of the wing to keep the wing in a vertical position. As in synthetic hair wings (above), ideally a parachute hackle can be wound around the base of the wing.

For upright split wings – pull the wing into an upright position, make 2-3 turns of silk around the hook shank in front of the wing. Now divide the wing into two, and separate the bunches with 2 figure-of-eights; then make 2-4 turns of silk around each wing base to bind the hairs more tightly together.

For spent split wings – divide the wing into two bunches and pull each bunch backwards, so that it points out flat at right angles to the hook shank; tie the wings firmly in position with figure-of-eight turns of the silk and then make 2-4 turns of silk around the base of each wing to bind the hairs more tightly together.

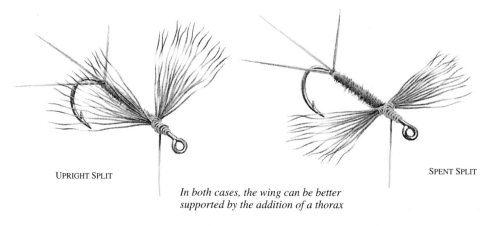

UPRIGHT SPLIT

SPENT SPLIT

In both cases, the wing can be better supported by the addition of a thorax

Wonderwing

This is a very effective winging style for sedge and two-winged fly adult imitations (e.g. pp. 184, 192). It is the style that also is used in 'One-feather flies' (p. 159).

Take a long-fibred hackle feather or a grey mallard breast feather. Hold it by the extreme tip between thumb and forefinger of the left hand; now stroke feather fibres backwards using thumb and forefinger of right hand, stopping when you have formed an elongated oval shape with hackle fibres. Hold tight with right hand, release left, snip away tip of feather (that is not part of the oval) and you have a wonderwing. To tie one into the fly: complete the fly up to winging; take the winging feather and prepare as above (without cutting out the tip); tie stalk with stroked backward-pointing fibres down with 1-2 soft and 1-2 hard wraps so that wing lies back over body. If some feather fibre tips have flicked out of the wing during tying, pull on the tip of the feather to produced the desired length and shape of the wing. Now snip off the tip of the feather to leave the completed wonderwing.

Forming the 'oval' between feather tip and feather base

WONDERWING

Wonderwing tied: the tip has been removed

Back-sloping quill-slip wings

These are often used in adult sedge imitations (p. 182) also winged soft-hackled patterns (p. 130). Complete fly up to winging. Take a pair of quills for winging (one from left wing of bird and one from right). Measure width of wing and cut out slips from each feather. Hold slips side by side (longer side of slips uppermost) over back of body to measure correct wing length; tie down with 2 pinch-and-loops (p. 232) and then 1-2 hard wraps. Snip away surplus material at butts and complete fly.

Upright split quill-slip wings

One of the most traditional ways of winging a dry fly. Most references recommend starling primary or secondary quills as winging medium: ignore them and use either mallard or teal primary quill instead (much easier to use, the fibres do not fall apart as readily). As with most parts of an artificial fly, there is more than one way to produce the right end effect. In this case the easiest is:

A matched pair of feathers (one from each wing); the wing slips must be taken from precisely the same position on each feather.

Complete tail, body and rib of the fly. Take a matched pair of mallard or teal quills (the same feather from left and right wing); remove lower shorter fibres; then, with a dubbing needle, separate out one wing from each feather making sure that they are the same width. Firmly grasp the slip from one feather and tear it off the quill in a downwards direction; do the same with the other feather. Arrange the two slips together, side by side, so that the natural curve is to the outside (when tied in the wings will tend to separate from each other), with longer edge to the front and shorter convex edge to the rear. Check for length and then grasp both wings together in forefinger and thumb of left hand, tips pointing backwards, butts forwards, and tie on top of hook shank just in front of body with 2 pinch-and-loops (p. 232). Snip away surplus and make 1-2 hard wraps at front. Now lift wings and make 1-2 turns behind (to help hold wing upright); then separate wings and make 1 figure-of-eight through them. Now tie in hackle (see p. 243) and wind hackle backwards with turns in front of wings (over wing butt) and behind wings. Bring silk forwards through hackle, form silk head and tie off.

Many experienced fly-dressers tie in the wing first, before tails, body, etc. This does give a neater fly. However, the beginner may often find that he will damage these fragile wings as the other stages are carried out.

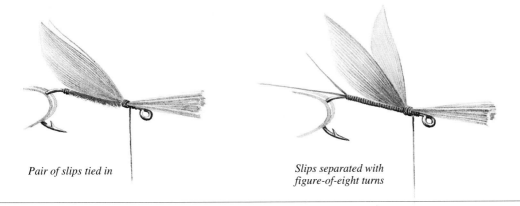

Pair of slips tied in

Slips separated with figure-of-eight turns

HEADS

Usually the head is simply several turns of silk just behind the hook eye, whip-finished or half-hitch finished, and varnished with tying cement. Alternatives:

Dubbed fur: a little fur is dubbed onto the silk and wound as a head, with the silk tied off immediately in front of, or behind, this head.

Herl: 1-2 strands of herl are tied in by their tips and wound 1-2 times just behind the hook eye to form head, with silk tied off immediately in front of this head.

Spun and trimmed deer hair (= Muddler style): take a small bunch of deer hair, hold it across the hook shank just in front of the body/wing etc, bring the silk over the hair and round the hook shank twice, to give two soft wraps and then pull on the silk. The deer hair will spin around the hook shank. Push this spun deer hair back tightly with finger nails and repeat 1-2 times until head is full to eye of hook. Tie off silk at front, ideally using the half-hitch tool method (p. 235). Now trim back the deer hair to produce a neat head. Extremely useful in dry sedges (p. 180).

DUBBED FUR HEAD

HERL HEAD

Bunch of deer hair loosely tied across shank with 2 turns of thread

Pull down on thread. The bunch of deer hair flares or opens round hook shank

Build up a large head with many small bunches of hair, each being spun before the next is tied in

Trim the head to shape

Antennae

As found in some sedge imitations (p. 182) and stonefly nymphs (p. 167). Tie these in just before completing the head.

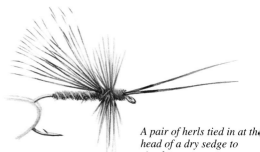

A pair of herls tied in at the head of a dry sedge to simulate antennae

PRESENTATION OF THE FLY

There may be readers of this book who have never fly fished for trout and grayling but who would now like to take up the sport. Or there may be readers who have only recently taken up fly fishing. This short section is for them. Here we will consider the basics of tackle and technique of casting a fly to the fish.

TACKLE

As in so much else, when it comes to buying fishing tackle you get what you pay for. The best is expensive; but is less likely to let you down and gives pleasure to use. The cheapest may let you down and can be frustrating to use. So buy the best you can afford.

Fly Lines

Most people would think that the first item of tackle to be considered is the fly rod and reel. This is quite wrong. In fly fishing the line is the weight that is used to flex the rod and enable the fly to be cast. it is the most important element. The line's weight varies along its length as the line tapers (see below): at the tip there is a 60cm (2 feet) section of fine, untapered, level line and behind this short section the line thickness and weight increases into the belly of the line. It is this thicker and heavier portion of the line that we use to load the rod during casting. Fly lines are graded by weight in an international system known as the AFTM (Association of Fishing Tackle Manufacturers) rating. This is based on the weight (using the old Imperial measure *grains*, 1 grain = 0.065 grammes) of the first 9.1m (30 feet) of the fly line excluding the 60cm (2 feet) tip section: AFTM 1 is the lightest, AFTM 12 the heaviest used for freshwater fishing (for salmon on big rivers) in Europe:

AFTM Rating	#1	#2	#3	#4	#5	#6	#7	#8	#9	#10	#11	#12
Weight in Grains	60	80	100	120	140	160	185	210	240	280	330	380

Line Profiles

The way that the weight in the fly line is distributed along the fly line is known as the 'line profile'. Today there are three basic profiles:

Double Taper: this is abbreviated to DT. In these lines there is a fine 60cm (2 foot) level section at each end. Behind these are the tapers that build up the the broad belly of the line. Though popular, they are perhaps not the best lines to learn to cast with.

Shooting Head Taper: abbreviated to SH. This is not the line for a novice: to cast a shooting head well you must already be a good caster.

Weight Forward Taper: this is abbreviated to WF. In these lines there is one 60cm (2 foot) level tip behind which is a taper that builds up to a short line belly. Again the 9.1 metre (30 foot) length immediately behind the fine level tip will match the AFTM standard. Behind the belly is a very short taper to the rest of the line which is a fine, level 'running' line. All the weight is thus concentrated at one end of the line and this makes the weight forward line easier to cast for longer distances: the weight is cast and the fine running line pulled out, when the angler shoots line on the forward cast, by the fast moving weight. WF lines can be used only one way round, with the running line being attached to the backing. Make sure a WF line is attached the correct way round: the running line is usually tagged saying 'This End', meaning 'Tie this end to the backing on the reel'.

Start your fly fishing with WF lines.

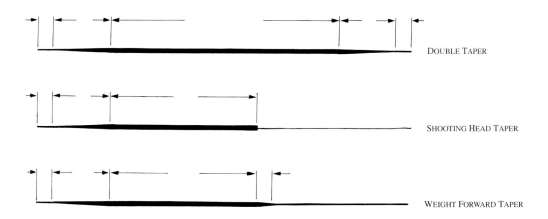

DOUBLE TAPER

SHOOTING HEAD TAPER

WEIGHT FORWARD TAPER

Line Density

Fly lines can be floating or sinking. A floating fly line floats on the surface: this is the line to use:

a. for most river trout fishing situations (the exception is when fishing fish imitations close to the river bed or in very fast water)

b. for fishing dry flies, unweighted wet flies, nymphs and fish imitations close to the surface, and weighted flies in shallow water, in lakes

c. for learning to cast.

There is a wide range of densities of sinking lines: 'Intermediate' (this is such a slow sinker that it penetrates just below the surface film, though if left for some considerable time in a lake it will eventually sink to the bottom), 'Sink Tip' (the majority of the line floats with just the tip sinking), 'Slow Sink', 'Medium Sink', 'Fast Sink', 'Ultra Fast Sink' and so on, depending upon the descriptions used by the manufacturer. An experienced angler will have all these lines on reels so that the one most appropriate to a particular fishing situation can be chosen quickly. In a deep lake an ultra-fast sinker may be chosen to fish the fly close to the bottom; if the fish are feeding in midwater a medium sink may be better; and so on.

Start off your fly fishing with a WF Floating line. Later buy sinkers as the need arises.

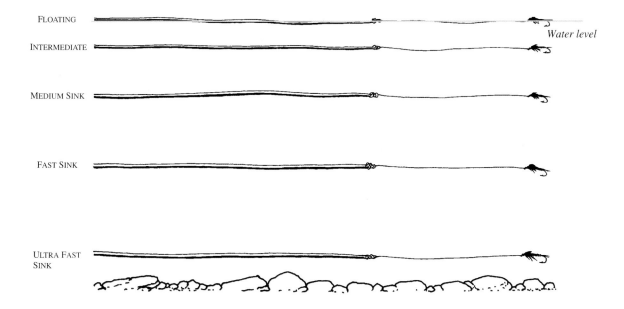

FLOATING

INTERMEDIATE

MEDIUM SINK

FAST SINK

ULTRA FAST SINK

Water level

Fly Line and Reel

Fly reels are usually the simplest of reels: buy a reel that will hold your chosen fly line plus about 100 metres of 'backing' (reel boxes will give you this capacity information).

Backing is strong braided or monofilament line attached securely to the back-end of the fly line. If a big fish takes the fly and zooms off, it may take all the relatively short fly line (most fly lines are only 25 metres long) from the reel and then some backing before it stops. Backing is thus essential insurance for the day when you catch that monster trout.

Buy reel, backing and fly line together: most reputable tackle dealers will put the correct amount of backing and the fly line on the reel for you, making sure that the connections between backing and reel, and backing and fly line are secure.

Fly Line and Rod

All good fly fishing rods have the recommended AFTM line number marked on them, so that the rod can be matched to the optimum weight of line that it can cast.

Rods are available in several materials, from traditional built cane to space age carbon (also called graphite) and boron fibre. The best material for all fly fishing is carbon, and the beginner should not consider any other.

For most European trout fishing situations choose fly line and then rod as follows:

1. small river trout and grayling with small flies: AFTM 3-5. The ideal rod will be 8 feet (2.4 m) – 10 feet (3.0 m) carbon.

2. big river trout and grayling with small flies: AFTM 4-6. The ideal rod will be 9 feet (2.7 m) – 11 feet (3.3 m) carbon.

3. big river trout and grayling with very large heavy flies: AFTM 6-7. The ideal rod will be 9 feet (2.7 m) – 11 feet (3.3 m) carbon.

4. lake fishing with small light flies for trout: AFTM 5-7. The ideal rod will be 9 feet (2.7 m) – 10 feet (3.0 m) carbon.

5. lake fishing with big heavy flies and with very fast sinking lines: AFTM 7-10. The ideal rod will be $9\frac{1}{2}$ feet (2.85 m) – $10\frac{1}{2}$ feet (3.15 m) carbon.

Most experienced anglers, who fish a wide variety of rivers and lakes, will have several sets of tackle. However most beginners would be recommended to start off with an AFTM 6 WF line matched to a $9 – 9\frac{1}{2}$ feet (2.7-2.85 m) carbon rod. This will serve well in most river and lake situations: later other sets of tackle can be purchased as the need arises.

Leaders

We now have a well balanced outfit comprising rod, reel, fly line and backing which are in harmony through their AFTM rating. We need now to fit a 'leader' on the end of the fly line. Later the fly will be tied to the fine tip of the leader (known as a leader tippet or leader point).

There are several sorts of leader:

Braided Tapered Leaders

These commercially produced leaders are gaining in popularity. They are attached to the end of the fly line via a loop that is fixed permanently to the end of the fly line. A short tippet of fine monofilament is tied to the end of the braided leader; the fly is attached to this.

Both major European manufacturers of braided tapered leaders (Air-Flo of Wales and Roman Moser of Austria) provide a series of leaders that cover all trout and grayling requirements. They also offer sets of leaders, that can be changed according to water conditions, and whether the fly should be presented high in or on the water, or deep close to the bottom in fast water: floating leaders, intermediate leaders, sink tip leaders, slow sink leaders and very heavy fast-sinking leaders. The Roman Moser leader set also includes a 'Strike Indicator' for use with the heavier leaders: this is a float attached to the base of the leader; when a fish takes the deep fly the strike indicator bobs under telling you to strike.

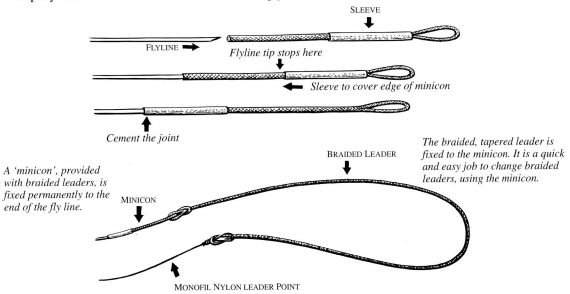

SLEEVE

FLYLINE ➡

Flyline tip stops here

⬅ *Sleeve to cover edge of minicon*

Cement the joint

BRAIDED LEADER

The braided, tapered leader is fixed to the minicon. It is a quick and easy job to change braided leaders, using the minicon.

A 'minicon', provided with braided leaders, is fixed permanently to the end of the fly line.

MINICON

MONOFIL NYLON LEADER POINT

Tapered Monofilament Leaders

Commercial Leaders: these are available tapering but knotless. They come in a range of lengths and tippet strengths. For practical purposes it is best to carry small spools of leader tippet monofilament so that new tippets can be tied to the end of the tapered leader when required (for example, when the leader has become shortened following many changes of fly, or when a lighter tippet is required).

Homemade Knotted Leaders: many anglers still make their own monofilament leaders by knotting together (using Water Knot p. 274) lengths of line as follows:

kg test	lbs test	2.7m leader	9ft leader	3.6m leader	12ft leader
13.6	30	0	0	120cm	48"
11.8	26	120cm	48"	60cm	24"
8.6	19	38cm	15"	30cm	12"
6.4	14	23cm	9"	30cm	12"
4.5	10	23cm	9"	30cm	12"
3.6	8	23cm	9"	30cm	12"
2.7	6	46cm	18"	60cm	24"

If a lighter tippet (point) is required, reduce the length of the fine tippets given in the bottom line of the table to 23 or 30cm and knot on a 46-60cm lighter point. If a leader of a different length is needed, simply increase or decrease all the lengths given in the table proportionally.

Droppers

Sometimes more than one fly is tied to a leader. One is tied to the tip of the leader (point fly) and other(s) to 'droppers'. Droppers should be about 10cm long, and be spaced 60-75cm apart. They are tied using the Water Knot (p. 274).

For most river trout and grayling situations a leader of about 2.7m (9') is usually adequate, on lakes 3.6m (12'). But increase these in deep fast water when the fish are lying deep, or in calm clear conditions when the splash of the fly line may disturb the fish: in rivers to 3.6m (12') and lakes to 4.5m (15').

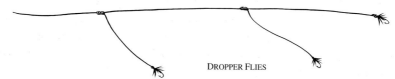

DROPPER FLIES

Monofilament line strength is measured in three ways:

1. by the ancient X grade, a survivor of the days of drawn silkworm gut.
2. by the diameter of the line (in mm).
3. by the breaking strain or 'test' of the line in pounds or kilogrammes/grammes.

The last, breaking strain or test, is by far the best because it gives an accurate assessment of what force is required to break the line.

Most monofilament on the market is plain, straight line. There are, however, others called 'pre-stretched' or 'extra-fine'. These lines have a much finer diameter for their breaking strain than ordinary monofilament but their knot strength is very weak unless the knot is perfectly tied. For this reason, the beginner is advised to use plain monofilament line and to avoid super-fine, pre-stretched lines.

Choice of monofilament line

Always choose the strongest line possible for a particular fishing situation – there is no merit fishing with such fine lines that there is a risk of breakage should a large fish take hold.

However it is essential, when using very small flies, to use very fine lines because the stiffness of thicker lines would not enable these flies to be fished properly. At the same time, especially on some heavily fished waters, fish are occasionally 'line-shy', particularly if they have been caught several times and in such circumstances it may be necessary to use a lighter, thinner line than one would normally use.

Suggested test breaking strains of leader tippets for different sizes of hooks/flies are as follows:

- Tiny dry flies (hooks size 24-28): about 0.5 kg (1-$1\frac{1}{2}$ lb)
- Small dry flies, wet flies and nymphs (hooks size 16-22): about 1 kg (2-$2\frac{1}{2}$ lb)
- Medium sized dry flies, wet flies and nymphs (hooks size 12-14): about $1\frac{1}{2}$ kg (3 lb)
- Larger dry flies, wet flies and nymphs *in the day* (hooks size 8-10): about 2 kg (5 lb)
- Larger dry flies, wet flies and nymphs *at night* (hooks size 8-10): about 2 -3 kg (5 -7 lb)
- Large fish fry imitations (hooks longshank sizes 2-8): about 4 -7 kg (9-15 lb)

Care of Monofilament Lines

Monofilament deteriorates in light and heat, and can be badly frayed after a day's fishing. So:

1. store in the dark in a cool place.
2. replace fly leader tippets before starting to fish.
3. at the first sign of fraying, cut away the affected portion.

4. replace all lines at least once each year.

5. purchase line from big retailers and not small tackle shops. Turn over in a big store is so rapid that you can be confident that what you buy is fresh.

Flotants and Sinkants

When nymphing it is essential that the tip of the floating fly line floats, for this is a major indicator that a fish has taken the fly. Carry a small tub of grease (e.g. Mucelin) and if the tip of the fly line shows signs of sinking, coat it liberally.

Dry flies should float on the surface. To reduce the chances of them sinking, treat all dry flies (other than those dressed with cul de canard feathers) with flotant. Some flotants are liquid: for instance Cul de Canard Oil. They are fine for most types of dry fly. However where the fly includes many synthetic materials in its dressing (for instance, Antron and Poly-yarn, a stiffer flotant such as Gink or Dilly-wax is more effective).

When fishing dry fly on smooth calm water the leader extending from the fly across the water surface, rather like a large antenna, is a major cause of trout rejecting the fly. One problem with nylon is that it tends to float. Floating Leader Syndrome (FLS) is a major problem. Always, at the start of a day's dry fly fishing and later at the first sign of the leader floating, treat the leader with sinkant.

FLS: a problem especially in calm, flat water

Similarly, when nymph or wet fly fishing with monofilament leaders, hasten the sinking rate of the fly (by preventing FLS holding the fly close to the surface) by treating the leader with sinkant. There are several commercial ones on the market: equally good (often better) is a homemade sinkant:

Mix Fuller's Earth powder with washing-up liquid to produce a smooth paste. A convenient way of carrying this, so that it is readily to hand: cut the rear end of an empty toothpaste tube, open the tube and spoon in the sinkant. Re-seal the tube with two large staples and 'superglue'. Fix the tube by a zinger to the fishing waistcoat/vest/jacket.

THE SIMPLE CAST

People who take up golf usually go to a professional for lessons. Like golf, fly casting involves precise timing, positioning of feet and body, use of hands, and controlled power. For this reason, anyone contemplating taking up fly fishing ought to consult a qualified professional casting instructor.

The following notes and illustrations will enable someone to make a basic overhead fly cast. We will assume the angler to be right handed (left handed anglers, read left for right and vice versa). This simple lesson is best carried out on short grass, making sure before you start that you have about 20 metres all round with no obstacles, including other people. Set up the tackle, but instead of a fly, tie a piece of brightly coloured wool to the end of the leader. Pull about 5 metres of fly line through the tip rod ring and lay it and the leader out in a straight line on the grass. Take up a comfortable stance, with feet slightly apart and with right foot slightly forwards and pointing in the direction of the line on the grass. Hold rod handle in right hand with thumb on top and the palm and fingers wrapped around the handle. (There are other ways of holding the rod, but this is the most effective.) For this simple cast you are going to use only the right hand, wrist, forearm, elbow and upper arm. You must not move the shoulder or back at all! This is a most important point: when you go fishing, you will be tempted to 'roll the shoulder' and 'arch the back' in an attempt to cast for that far-off trout. But these are flaws in casting, and they will result in shorter, bad casts!

There are six parts or components of the simple cast. Whilst each component is described separately, in the actual cast they merge together to produce a smooth-flowing action.

1. *The get ready.* Point rod tip low, and pull in any slack between rod tip and line on the grass with the left hand. This is a most important point: when you go fishing, try always (just before you make a cast) to start with the rod tip low, and to pull in slack line so that the tip will begin to work immediately on straight, tight line on or in the water.

2. *The lift off.* Keep the hand and forearm in line with a stiff wrist, and raise the rod smoothly to the 10 o'clock position, using the elbow joint and upper arm.

3. *The back-cast power stroke.* Accelerate with an up-and-back flick of the rod from the 10 o'clock to 1 o'clock positions, using the breaking of the wrist and the elbow to provide the power. This important and sudden addition of power after the slow, smooth lift off (2), must be timed perfectly and whilst the rod tip is moving in the 10-1 o'clock arc. Beginners tend to put too much power in early (through the lift off stage) and to continue past the 1 o'clock position so that the line flies over their heads and collapses on the ground. The aim of this component is to throw the line back and high with the rod; and to use just enough muscle to flex the rod so that it carries out this task.

4. *The stop.* As soon as the back-cast power stroke is completed (with rod at 1 o'clock) you must make an abrupt 'Stop'. The line now travels back in a loop that gradually straightens. If the back-cast (stages 1-4) has been perfectly executed then, if you look over your shoulder at rod tip and line, you will see the line straighten and, as it straightens, pull back on the stationary rod tip (in the 1 o'clock position).

5. *The forward-cast power stroke.* As soon as – not a split second before or after – the line has straightened on the backcast and is pulling on the rod tip (you can often feel that pull on the rod) the rod is flicked forward, with a hammer blow, from the 1 o'clock to 10 o'clock position,

1. The Get Ready: rod low; slack line pulled in.

The right hand holds the rod. The line can be trapped under forefinger when pulling line from the reel, or slack line on the water, with the left hand.

2. The Lift Off

4. During the Stop the line extends back and, when fully extended, the Forward Power Stroke is made.

3. The Power Stroke followed by the Stop at 1 o'clock.

5. The Forward Power Stroke is stopped at about 10 o'clock, so that the line shoots out high above the water.

6. The rod is lowered in the Follow Through.

Release line held by left hand in the Power Stroke and this line will be 'shot' or pulled through the rod rings by the extending line.

using mainly the wrist with a little subsidiary elbow movement. This well-timed power stroke propels the line forward in a loop that will straighten out in the air and before the line falls on the water. Most beginners feel that they should be aiming to cast at the water: not so. Aim for a target 2-3 metres above the water and the line will extend in the air and fall gently in a straight line on the water. Aim for the water, by making the power stroke continue to the 9 o'clock position and the cast will be a splashy coiled heap.

6. *The follow through*: As the line begins to extend immediately the forward-cast power stroke has been made, follow through by lowering the rod tip to the 9 o'clock position. But note that there is no power at all in this movement.

In this simple cast the six stages – the get ready, the lift off, the back-cast power stroke, the stop, the forward-cast power stroke, the follow through – merge in one continuous, fluid motion. Memorize these and, as you practise, say out loud the stage as you make it.

So far in this simple cast you have picked the line from the grass (or water), cast it back and then forward so that it lands again on the grass (or water) in a straight line. Make sure that you can do this perfectly before continuing further. The next step is one of false casting and lengthening line.

False Casting

Start as before, with about 5 metres of line laid out on the grass. But this time, when you reach stage 5 (The forward-cast power stroke) do not go into stage 6 (The follow through). Instead, after the forward power stroke, have another 'Stop' but with the 'stop' made to the front with the rod held firmly at the 11 o'clock position. The line will straighten to the front and then, as soon as it does, flick the rod tip backwards in another stage 3 (The back-cast power stroke) movement. You have now made one false cast (that is used in dry fly fishing to dry the fly in the air between casts onto the water).

Practice false casting until you can cast the line forwards and backwards in the air perfectly for five continuous false casts. All forward-cast power strokes except the last will be false casts because they do not result in the line and fly landing on the grass (water).

False casting is essential for dry fly fishing as it flicks water from the fly, drying it between casts and ensuring that it will float on the next cast to a fish.

Lengthening Line

In the simple cast, line is lengthened during forward-cast power strokes. Pull a length of line (about 50cm) from the reel with the left hand and keep hold of it. Then, as you make the forward power stroke of a false cast and as the line shoots forward, release this loop of line from the left hand. The line being shot forward will pull out this extra line.

Practice false casting until you can cast the line forwards and backwards in the air perfectly for five continuous false casts. But this time, as each forward cast is made, shoot another 50cm of line. And shoot another 50cm on the final delivery cast that throws the line out and onto the grass (water). You started with 5 metres of line: there should be about 8 out at the end.

Practise, practise, practise. Within, say, 20 hours of practice, you should be able to make the simple cast perfectly each time, and be able to false cast and lengthen the line so that you can cast up to 20 metres. Now you are ready to go fishing.

PRESENTING THE FLY IN RIVERS

The aim of imitative fly fishing is to fool the fish into believing that our artificial fly is a real one. And correct presentation is as important as the selection of artificial fly because with good presentation the artificial behaves like the real one.

Direction of cast

We choose a fly that suitably matches what our trout is eating. We must now cast the fly. But rivers flow from uphill to downhill. So there are several positions that we could take up, before casting, so that we might cast our fly:

1. directly upstream to the trout
2. up-and-across the stream to the trout
3. directly across the stream to the trout
4. down-and-across the stream to the trout
5. directly downstream to the trout

Which one do we choose? Consider the following points:

Firstly, the trout lie in rivers facing upstream. If they are approached from upstream, with a downstream cast, they are more likely to see you, the angler, waggling your rod and line, and be scared: a frightened trout is unlikely to take the fly, and one that has fled will certainly not!

We might not be able to see the fish, but the fish might be able to see us. Especially if we are standing upstream, or very close, waving the rod over it. A disturbed trout will not take a fly.

Secondly, there is the increased chance of hooking the fish to an upstream cast (diagram overleaf, **1** and **2**) or an across stream cast (**3**). When the fish takes to the upstream cast, a strike pulls the hook point back into the mouth of the fish. When the fish takes to an across stream cast, a sideways tightening of the line pulls the hook point into the jaw or scissors of the fish. In

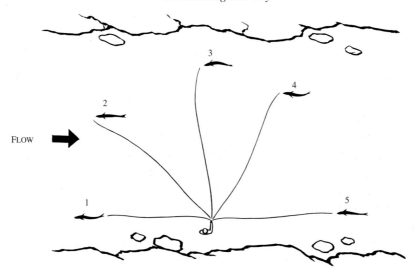

contrast, if the fish takes downstream of the angler, after a downstream cast (**4** or **5**), tightening will tend to pull the hook from the mouth of the fish.

Thirdly, it is easier to float a fly naturally, like so many of the creatures that the trout eat, down the flow by casting up, or up-and-across, or across the stream. You are fishing your flies on the same current that is carrying the natural flies. The fly is cast upstream of the fish and, as it drifts down, slack line is drawn in. There is still a problem of drag, especially in complex river currents, but these are usually quite easy to overcome (see below). The drag problem is nothing compared with the drag resulting from a long, tight line that has been cast down and across the river. When fish, especially older and more fastidious large wild trout, are feeding on surface foods, they demand that the artificial drifts down like the real insect. Get it right and the biggest fish will take confidently. Get it wrong and the fish will be cowering in cover!

Fly and fish are downstream: a strike will tend to pull fly away from the fish. The fish may not be hooked.

Fly and fish are upstream: a strike will tend to pull the fly into the fish and improve chances of hooking.

Fourthly, because casts 1-3 result in a more natural presentation, these casts tend to take bigger fish than the downstream casts 4 and 5.

There is a fifth reason for casting up, up-and-across or across the flow, when fishing a leaded fly that you want trundling along the bottom. Cast up-and-across and it will sink deeper (and is more likely to reach the deep-lying trout or grayling) than if cast down-and-across.

In general, casts 1, 2 and 3 are the best line of attack. Sometimes you may have no other option but to cast in directions 4 and 5, for example if a fish is lying immediately downstream of you and the only way to catch it is by casting directly downstream. Or a fish is lying under tree branches and the only way to get your fly to it is by casting (with a down-and-across cast) just upstream of the tree and letting the fly and line drift downstream under the branches. However, you must prevent the line from causing the fly to drag across the surface in these situations.

Drag

Perhaps the greatest problem facing a river trout angler (and one that often perplexes the still-water angler the first time he visits a river) is drag. It is a problem that is most apparent when fishing the dry fly, for in extreme cases it may result in the fly performing quite a remarkable skating display across the water surface in directions and at speeds that bear no relation to the direction and speed of river flow. However drag can equally occur when fishing wet fly, un-weighted nymph and weighted nymph – although, because the fly cannot been seen, most anglers never consider drag as the reason why they fail to catch when fishing the subsurface fly. Drag can completely ruin fly presentation. Even the slightest degree of drag, where the fly drifts downstream just a fraction quicker than the natural insect, or at a slightly different angle to the flow, will usually result in the fly being ignored by the trout.

Why does drag occur? The easiest way to answer this is to go down to the river during a hatch of fly and find a pool where there is a strong flow down the middle with slower flow close to either bank. Watch. Flies hatching in the central band of fast water are carried quickly downstream, those hatching in the slower bands drift more slowly. In the fast water the trout look to flies that are being carried quickly downstream, in the slower water they expect the flies to be drifting more slowly. Because trout expect flies to be moving along the conveyor belt of the river at the speed of the flow over their particular lie, then if our imitative fly moves at a different speed it ceases to imitate the natural fly (no matter how perfect the tying) and the trout will ignore it.

Now tie on a well-oiled dry fly, stand on one side of the river and cast a straight line squarely across the fast water so that the fly lands on the slow water beyond. Look carefully at what happens to the fly line and fly. The floating line that lies across the fast water is carried down-stream more quickly than the fly line, leader and fly lying in the far band of slow water. A downstream belly forms in the fast water, and this pulls the dry fly quickly down and across the slow flow. The fly skates or 'drags' from A to B to C. It moves faster than the natural flies that are drifting downstream in the slow flow. It moves *across* the flow, instead of directly downstream *with* the flow. At best a feeding trout will ignore the fly, at worst (especially in heavily fished waters) it will turn the fish off from feeding or, to use the old expression, 'put the fish down'.

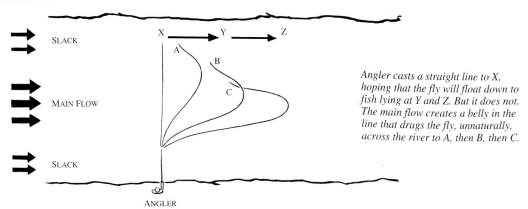

Angler casts a straight line to X, hoping that the fly will float down to fish lying at Y and Z. But it does not. The main flow creates a belly in the line that drags the fly, unnaturally, across the river to A, then B, then C.

There are two major ways of avoiding drag or, at least, postponing drag so that it does not affect the fly until it has drifted naturally over the feeding trout: working out and then taking up the best position before casting, or modifying casting technique.

In simple situations (as in the above example) one of the following will overcome the problem. In more complicated situations you will have to use more than one trick to avoid drag. After reading the water and deciding to cast to a certain lie or fish, ask yourself: 'If I put the fly there from here, will it drag?' and 'Where is the best place to stand or kneel?'

Often drag can be eliminated by casting directly upstream or almost so. By wading below the fish so that you stand and cast in the band of flow in which the fish is lying. Then you have no bands of different flow speed between you and the fish.

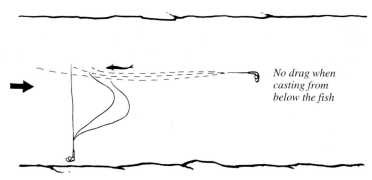

No drag when casting from below the fish

Drag occurs when casting from here

Sometimes it is impossible to wade directly below the fish: it may be too deep, there may be bushes in the way, the fishery rules may prohibit wading, or there may be other fish that you do not wish to disturb. So you will be looking to cast up-and-across or across the stream, or even, if obstacles prevent one of these, down-and-across (remember that it is more difficult to hook fish on a downstream cast and that the fish is more likely to see you). Other casting techniques are invaluable here, such as a 'slack line cast'.

Slack Line Cast

This is easy to master. If you make a forward cast and, as the line is extending out over the water, wiggle the rod tip from side to side, the line lands in a snake like way on the water. Before the current can form a belly in the fly line and cause the fly to drag, it must first of all take up all these wiggles. And until all these wiggles have been taken up, the fly will drift downstream naturally. Of course, if a fish lies ten metres away, you will be casting not just ten metres of line, but ten metres plus the extra length taken up by the wiggles you will put into the slack line cast. Again, judging this is a matter of practice and experience. The easiest way to judge the correct distance is to make a short slack line cast so that the fly lands short of the fish, and then estimate how much extra line you will have to shoot on the next cast to cover the fish.

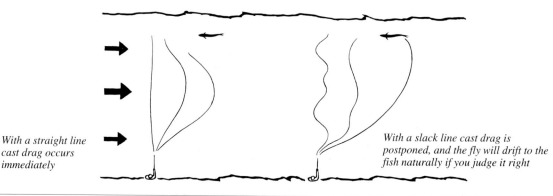

With a straight line cast drag occurs immediately

With a slack line cast drag is postponed, and the fly will drift to the fish naturally if you judge it right

PRESENTING THE FLY IN LAKES

In many lakes, most of the fish will be cruising along the margins, in water up to 3 metres deep, where most food is concentrated. A properly presented fly in the margins is thus more likely to be successful than one cast beyond the margin. For this reason, from the shore do not make every cast straight out at right angles to the shore: cast in all directions to fish the entire margin; from a boat, concentrate in the shallow margins rather than deeper water in the middle.

The Importance of Depth

When you look out over any lake you usually have no idea of depth. The lake bed might plummet straight down to 50 metres or more in a distance of only ten metres, for all you know by looking at the surface. It often does, especially in corrie tarns that may provide excellent bank fishing for trout and charr in mountain areas. On the other hand, the shore may extend far out into the lake as a shelf covered by less than one metre of water (and be too shallow to hold trout other than at night). It fish are feeding at the surface then the problem is irrelevant, for you will be presenting your flies close to the surface (see below), but if they are lying deep, perhaps on the bottom, you need to know *how deep*. But then, once you know the depth, it is of no use unless you can present your flies at that particular depth. A tape measure is of no use!

The way to consider depth when fishing in deep water is by using a sinking fly line and counting so that sinking time is a function of depth. So, to assess how deep the water is, cast out and leave fly and line to sink for 10 seconds. Retrieve the fly slowly by pulling in line. Does the fly snag bottom? Are there tell-tale pieces of weed or leaf debris on the hook? No! Then the fly did not reach the bottom. Repeat the process with 20, 30, 40 or more second sinking times until you know how deep. For instance, the answer might be 80 seconds of sinking time.

You can now present your flies at specific depths, based on counting seconds of sinking time before you begin to retrieve the flies. So, suppose that you catch a fish close to the bottom (depth measured at 80 seconds, fish caught at 70 seconds), then by the timing method you can present the fly consistently at the same depth of 70 seconds. There is now no guesswork.

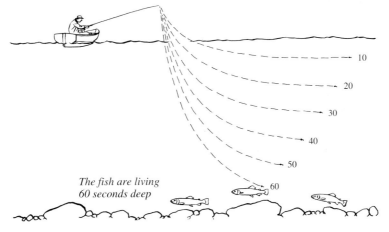

When fishing close to the bottom in shallower water (for instance, close to weedbeds or in the shallow margins) a floating fly line with a long monofilament leader (or intermediate braided leader with monofilament point) is far more effective. A weighted general or imitative pattern (such as a Hares Ear Goldhead or Mayfly Nymph or Caddis) is fished on the point and one or two unweighted patterns fished on droppers. After casting allow the flies to sink. Then slowly and deliberately raise the rod tip by about 50cm: this will pull line in and make the flies rise vertically through the water. Lower the rod and at the same time gather in the slack; as you do this the flies will sink once more. Repeat until the cast has been fished out.

So much for presenting the fly deep in lakes. When trout are feeding at or close to the surface the two main problems are choosing the correct fly that matches what the trout are eating (look for or collect these and choose appropriate patterns) and, especially important, presenting the fly in the correct position in relation to the surface film. For instance, when trout are feeding on a hatch of buzzers they may select pupae just below the surface, pupae resting and attached to the underside of the surface film, emergers where the pupa is attached to the surface film and the adult is hatching onto the surface, or occasionally adult midges that have just hatched and are standing on the water.

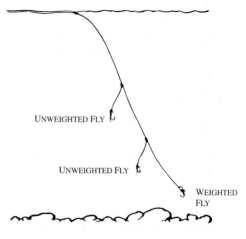

We can offer the fish different stages of one life cycle by using droppers. During an evening sedge hatch they may take pupae just below the surface film.

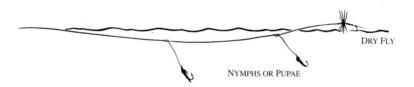

In this arrangement the point fly is a dry fly (it imitates the hatched insect) and the two nymphs or pupae, on droppers, imitate the stage close to the surface before hatching.

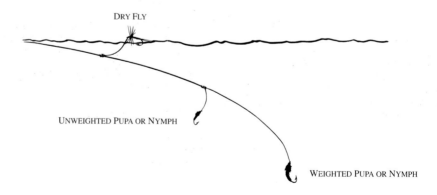

In this arrangement the dry fly is on the top dropper. A weighted nymph or pupa fishes deep on the leader point and an unweighted nymph or pupa fishes just below the surface. We thus offer the fish a choice of three depths and stages of the life cycle.

In both cases we know if a fish takes the pupae or nymphs: the dry fly will disappear suddenly. Strike immediately!

KNOTS

Knots are essential but are weak links in the fly fishing rig. More fish are hooked and then lost because a knot fails than, perhaps, for any other reason. Good anglers tie good knots; poor anglers tie poor knots and then protest at the quality of the fishing line! Never rush when tying a knot; make sure that every one is tied correctly, that every turn and tuck is perfect.

One great problem is that most of the knots we tie involve nylon monofilament. This is very slippery stuff. Also, when a knot is tied incorrectly it may be stretched (the monofilament just behind the knot may look frayed or curly) and weakened. Whichever knot is being tied, *always*:

1. Wet the knot thoroughly with saliva or water before pulling it tight.

2. Pull the knot tight very slowly so that the line slides into position smoothly.

Practise knots that you have never tied before at home; never tie a knot for the first time when you are fishing.

The following knots are all easy to tie and very effective.

Knots that connect lines

Loop Knot

This knot is tied to the end of two lines that will be joined by a loop-to-loop connection (see below) – as in joining leader point to braided butt.

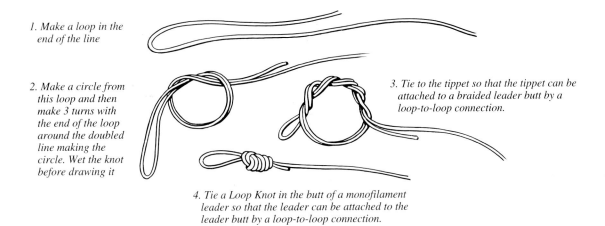

1. Make a loop in the end of the line

2. Make a circle from this loop and then make 3 turns with the end of the loop around the doubled line making the circle. Wet the knot before drawing it

3. Tie to the tippet so that the tippet can be attached to a braided leader butt by a loop-to-loop connection.

4. Tie a Loop Knot in the butt of a monofilament leader so that the leader can be attached to the leader butt by a loop-to-loop connection.

Loop-to-Loop Connections

Used to join leader to flyline or leader butt, or joining backing line to fly line.

Insert one loop (loop A) through the other (loop B), and then pass the end of the line A through its own loop A.

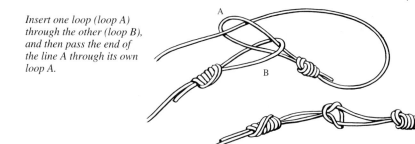

Pull tight slowly, making sure that neither length of line is snagged on the loop knots.

Water Knot

Use this knot to join lengths of monofilament (as when making knotted leaders, or for tying a fine tippet to a thicker one when changing from large to small flies).

The Water Knot is also ideal for tying droppers to the leader; one of the loose ends can be left as a dropper. But note, despite what has often been written, the end that is pointing away from the rod and towards the end of the leader should be used as the dropper; to use the other end will result in many breakages.

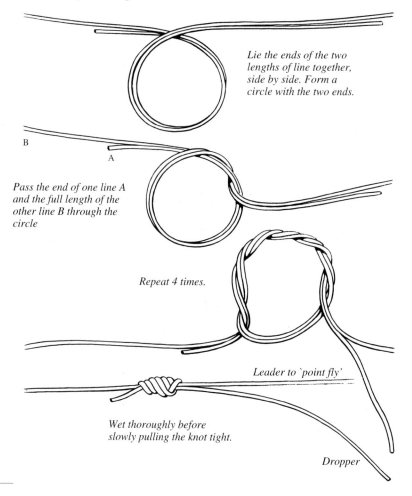

Lie the ends of the two lengths of line together, side by side. Form a circle with the two ends.

Pass the end of one line A and the full length of the other line B through the circle

Repeat 4 times.

Leader to `point fly'

Wet thoroughly before slowly pulling the knot tight.

Dropper

Needle Knot

This is the best knot to attach fly line to monofilament backing, and monofilament leaders to fly line (see also minicons p. 261).

For leaders: a butt of 10-12 kg test monofilament can be needle knotted in place, and the rest of the leader attached by a loop-to-loop connection (see above). The butt can thus be kept permanently in place (change after one year or if frayed) and leaders changed as and when required.

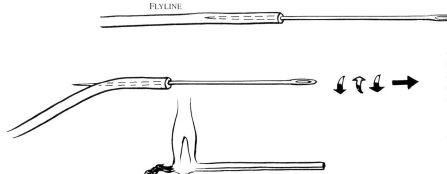

Insert a needle that is a little thicker than the monofilament into the centre of the core at the end of the fly line; push into the fly line for about 1cm and then push the needle so that it emerges through the side of the line.

Take a lighted match and heat the needle until the fly line just begins to bend. Hold the hot needle with a pair of pliers and rotate the fly line on the needle as the needle cools. Remove the needle.

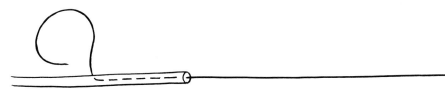

Cut the end of the monofilament backing or leader butt to a sharp point and insert through the hole formed in the fly line so that about 15cm protrudes from the exit hole

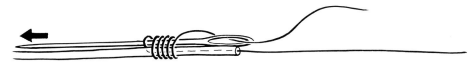

Take a large-eyed darning needle and lay it along the fly line, with the eye just beyond the tip of the line. Wind monofilament forwards over needle and tip of fly line for 5 close turns; then thread and of monofilament through the eye of the needle.

Pull tip of needle so that the end of the monofilament slides through the turns. Remove needle, and pull on both ends of monofilament to tighten the knot.

To make a smooth connection between fly line and monofilament, use thread (fly-tying, sewing); whip finish and give 3 coats of varnish (allow to dry between coats).

Knots for attaching fly to leader

Basic Blood Knot

This very simple knot ties fly to leader point.

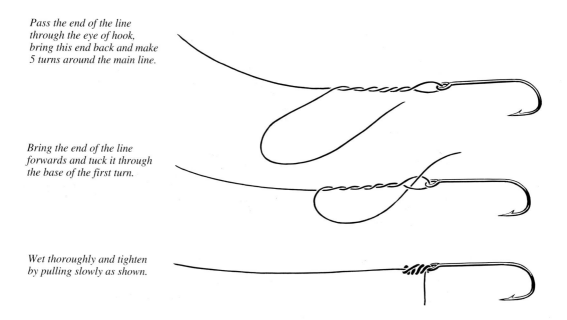

Pass the end of the line through the eye of hook, bring this end back and make 5 turns around the main line.

Bring the end of the line forwards and tuck it through the base of the first turn.

Wet thoroughly and tighten by pulling slowly as shown.

Note: this is as most anglers tie this knot, and when tied properly it will rarely fail. For extra insurance the following modification is worth considering:

Tucked Blood Knot

As the basic, but only 4 turns needed. But after bringing the end of the line forwards and tucking it through the base of the first turn, take it back and tuck through the loop of the last turn.

Use this knot (preferably tucked modification) only for larger flies, size 14 or bigger.

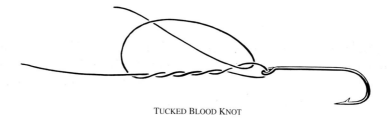

TUCKED BLOOD KNOT

Turle Knot

An alternative to the blood knot for tying fly to leader point. This is the better knot for tiny flies (smaller than, say, size 16). Note: this knot grips the hook behind the eye and is particularly useful in dry fly fishing with small flies.

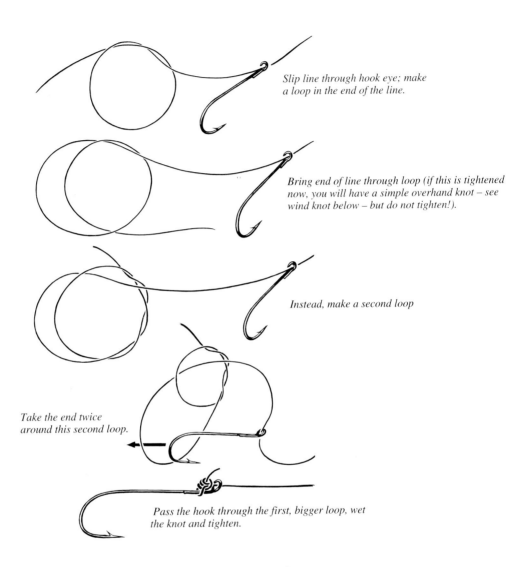

Slip line through hook eye; make a loop in the end of the line.

Bring end of line through loop (if this is tightened now, you will have a simple overhand knot – see wind knot below – but do not tighten!).

Instead, make a second loop

Take the end twice around this second loop.

Pass the hook through the first, bigger loop, wet the knot and tighten.

Wind Knots

Overhand knots often appear, as if by magic, in lines during fishing. They are usually caused by faults in technique, particularly casting; but we anglers blame the wind instead of ourselves! They greatly weaken the line. Examine your leader at regular intervals and if a wind knot appears, discard that leader and tie on a new one.

If you see this knot in your leader, replace the leader!

BIBLIOGRAPHY

The literature, in many languages, is extensive. The following is a selection of titles that the reader may find helpful.

FISH FOODS

Brauer, A. ed. *Die Süsswasserfauna Deutschlands*. Gustav Fischer, Jena, 1909.

Chinery, Michael. *Collins Guide to the Insects of Britain & Europe*. HarperCollins, London. 1986.

Clegg, John. *Freshwater Life of the British Isles*. Frederick Warne, London. 1952.

Despax, R. Plectoptères. Fauna de France. Paris. 1951.

Eaton, A.E. A revisional monograph of recent Ephemeridae or mayflies. *Trans. Linn. Soc. Lond.* 3:1-352.

Gaidy, Charles. Ephemeras Mayflies. Edicom, New York. 1986.

Goddard, John. *Trout Fly Recognition*. A. & C. Black, London. 1966

Grandy, M. *Ephemeroidea*. Fauna d'Italia. Caderini Edizioni. Bologna. 1960.

Harris, J.R. *An Angler's Entomology*. Collins, London. 1952.

Hicken, Norman E. *Caddis Larvae*. Hutchinson, London. 1967.

Lumini, Piero. *Imitazione di Effimere*. Editorial Olimpia. nd.

Lumini, Piero. *Imitazione di Tricotteri*. Editorial Olimpia. nd.

Mosely, M.E. *The British Caddis Flies*. George Routledge, London. 1939.

Perou, Ulf & Gustavsson, Thommy. *Flugfiskarens Insekter*. Fiskeboken, Stockholm. 1990

Puthz, V. *Limnofauna Europea*. Stuttgart. 1978.

Schrodt, J. *Insektenkunde für Fliegenfischer*. Parey Verlag, Hamburg & Berlin. 1984.

Those books offer a great deal of information on trout foods, but for advanced study the indispensable works are the keys produced by the Freshwater Biological Association, and for southern and alpine species the Société Entomologique Suisse.

Keys of the Freshwater Biological Association:

No 13 *Gastropods*. T.T. Macan, 4ed 1977

No 16 *Water Bugs*. T.T. Macan, 2ed 1965

No 17 *Stoneflies*. H.B.N. Hynes, 3ed 1977

No 28 *Adult Caddisflies*. T.T. Macan, 1973

No 31 *Dixidae*. R.H.L. Disney, 1970

No 35 *Megaloptera & Neuroptera*. J.M. Elliott, 1977

No 37 *Chironomidae*. L.C.V. Pinder, 1978

No 43 *Caseless Caddis Larvae*. J.M. Edington & A.G. Hildrew, 1981

No 47 *Adult Ephemeroptera*. J.M. Elliott & U.H. Humpesch, 1983

No 48 *Larval [Nymphs] Ephemeroptera*. J.M. Elliott, U.H. Humpesch and T.T. Macan, 1988

No 50 *Water Bugs*. A.A. Savage, 1989

No 51 *Cased Caddis Larvae*. I.D. Wallace, B. Wallace & G.N. Philipson, 1990

Keys of the Société Entomologique Suisse in the series Insecta Helvetica:

No 1 *Plectoptera*. J. Aubert, 1959
No 9 *Ephemeroptera*. D. Studemann et al., 1992

IMITATIVE FLY DRESSING AND FISHING

Anders, W.A. *Nass und Trocken*. Parey Verlag, Hamburg & Berlin. 1967. A good summary of wet and dry trout flies.

Boisset, Louis de. *La Truite de Grand Sport*. Librairie des Champs Elysées, Paris. 2nd ed. 1948.

Boisset, Louis de. *Les Mouches du Pêcheur de Truites*. Librairie des Champs Elysées, Paris. 3rd ed. 1971.

Boisset, Louis de. *L'Ombre Poisson de Sport*. Librairie des Champs Elysées, Paris. 2nd ed. 1958. Three great works on fly fishing.

Caucci, A. & Nastasi, B. *Hatches II*, Piscataway, New Jersey. 1975. A classic work linking natural fly hatches and imitative flies.

Edwards, Oliver. *Flytyers' Masterclass*. Merlin Unwin, Ludlow. 1994. A superb book on imitative flies

Eipeltaur, N. *Fliegenbinden für Anfänger*. Parey Verlag, Hamburg & Berlin. 1975.

Eipeltaur, N. *Fliegenbinden für Fortgeschrittene*. Parey Verlag, Hamburg & Berlin. 1979.

Greenhalgh, Malcolm. *Trout Fishing in Rivers*. Witherby, London. 1987.

La Fontaine, Gary. *Caddisflies*. Nick Lyons, New York. 1981. The standard work.

Leiser, Eric & Boyle, Robert H. *Stoneflies for the Angler*. Stackpole, Harrisburgh. 1982.

Marinaro, V.C. *A Modern Dry-Fly Code*. Nick Lyons, New York. 1950. Still one of the best books.

Martin, Darrel. *Fly-Tying Methods*. David & Charles, Newton Abbot. 1987. Highly recommended.

Pequegnot, J-P. *Répertoire des Mouches Artificielles Françaises*. Besancon. 1975. Contains several excellent imitative flies.

Pequegnot, J-P. *L'Art de la Pêche à la Mouche Sèche*. Flammarion, Paris. 1969. A textbook of imitative dry fly fishing.

Porte, F. de la. *Nymphenfischen*. Parey Verlag, Hamburg & Berlin. 1983.

Poso, Rafael del. *Moscas Para la Pesca*. Editorial Everest. Madrid. 1987.

Proper, Datus. *What the Trout Said*. Nick Lyons, New York. 2ed 1989. A thoughtful look at imitative fly design from the point of view of the fish.

Rocher, Raymond. *Confidences d'un Pêcheur à la Mouche*. Sedetec, Paris. 2ed 1980. A classic work on trout fishing.

Sawyer, Frank. *Nymphs and the Trout*. A. & C. Black, London. 1958. Essential reading on the development and fishing of modern nymphs.

Steinfort, H. *Fliegenfischen für Anfänger*. Parey Verlag, Hamburg & Berlin. 1973.

Steinfort, H. *Fliegenfischen für Fortgeschrittene*. Parey Verlag, Hamburg & Berlin. 1980.

Steinfort, H. *Meisterhaftes Fliegenfischen*. Parey Verlag, Hamburg & Berlin. 1983. These three books provide an excellent course in fly fishing techniques.

Swisher, D. & Richards, C. *Selective Trout*. Nick Lyons, New York. 1971. Although this book deals with North American insects, the tying techniques in it are easily applicable in Europe.

THE TROUT

Greenhalgh, Malcolm & Sutterby, Rod. *The Wild Trout*. George Phillip, London, 1989.

Schweibert, Ernest. *The Trout*. Dutton, New York. 1978

CASTING

Jaworowski, Ed. *The Cast*. Stackpole, Harrisburgh. 1992 (English edition 1994). The best book available on the subject.

INDEX OF FLIES